TRUTH AND PROGRESS
Philosophical Papers, Volume 3

This volume complements two highly successful volumes of Richard Rorty's philosophical papers: *Objectivity, Relativism, and Truth* and *Essays on Heidegger and Others.*

The underlying theme of the collection is Rorty's view that we should think of inquiry, in science or any other area of culture, as solving problems rather than as aiming at truth. Only the discredited correspondence theory of truth makes it plausible to think of truth as the name of a goal. Once that notion is given up, we can give up the idea of inquiry converging to a predestined point and consider the horizons of inquiry as constantly expanding as we encounter new problems.

The essays in the volume engage the work of many of today's most innovative thinkers, including Robert Brandom, Donald Davidson, Daniel Dennett, Jacques Derrida, Jürgen Habermas, John McDowell, Hilary Putnam, John Searle, and Charles Taylor. The collection also touches on problems in contemporary feminism raised by Annette Baier, Marilyn Frye, and Catharine MacKinnon, and considers issues connected with human rights and cultural differences.

Anyone with a serious interest in contemporary philosophy and what it can do for us in the modern world will enjoy this invaluable collection.

TRUTH AND PROGRESS

Philosophical Papers, Volume 3

RICHARD RORTY

CAMBRIDGE
UNIVERSITY PRESS

PUBLISHED BY THE PRESS SYNDICATE OF THE UNIVERSITY OF CAMBRIDGE
The Pitt Building, Trumpington Street, Cambridge CB2 1RP, United Kingdom

CAMBRIDGE UNIVERSITY PRESS
The Edinburgh Building, Cambridge CB2 2RU, UK   http://www.cup.cam.ac.uk
40 West 20th Street, New York, NY 10011-4211, USA   http://www.cup.org
10 Stamford Road, Oakleigh, Melbourne 3166, Australia

First published 1998

Printed in the United States of America

Typeset in Baskerville 10/13, in QuarkXPress™ [AG]

Library of Congress Cataloging in Publication Data
Rorty, Richard.
Truth and progress / Richard Rorty.
p.   cm. – (Philosophical papers ; v. 3)
Includes index.
ISBN 0-521-55347-4 (hardbound) – ISBN 0-521-556864 (pbk)
1. Truth.   2. Progress.   3. Ethics.   I. Title.   II. Series:
Rorty, Richard.   Philosophical papers ; v. 3.
B945.R52T78   1998
191 – dc21   97-37616
                                                        CIP

A catalog record for this book is available from the British Library.

ISBN 0 521 55347 4 hardback
ISBN 0 521 55686 4 paperback

TO MARY

after twenty-five years

CONTENTS

INTRODUCTION

"There is no truth." What could that mean? Why should anybody say it?

Actually, almost nobody (except Wallace Stevens) does say it.[1] But philosophers like me are often said to say it. One can see why. For we have learned (from Nietzsche and James, among others) to be suspicious of the appearance–reality distinction. We think that there are many ways to talk about what is going on, and that none of them gets closer to the way things are in themselves than any other. We have no idea what "in itself" is supposed to mean in the phrase "reality as it is in itself." So we suggest that the appearance–reality distinction be dropped in favor of a distinction between less useful and more useful ways of talking. But since most people think that truth is correspondence to the way reality "really is," they think of us as denying the existence of truth.

Our critics – the philosophers who agree that that is indeed what truth is – do not think that the useful–useless distinction can take the place of the old appearance–reality distinction. They believe that less useful ways of talking are descriptions of what only appears to be going on, whereas more useful ones are descriptions of what is really going on. For example: primitive scientists, or conformist members of a slaveholding society, describe what misleadingly appears to be going on. Modern physicists, like believers in universal human rights, know what is really going on. Our critics need the reality–appearance distinction to prevent the notion of "corresponding to reality" from being trivialized. For every belief, no matter how primitive or

---

1 "It was when I said, / 'There is no such thing as the truth,' / That the grapes seemed fatter, / The fox ran out of his hole" (Wallace Stevens, "On the Road Home," in *The Collected Poems* [New York: Vintage, 1990], 203).

vicious, corresponds to some "world" – the "world" that contains the objects mentioned by the belief (Ptolemy's crystalline spheres or the subhuman nature of the slaves). So those who want to hang on to the notion of "correspondence" have to take the idea of how things *really* are seriously.

The essays in this volume argue that philosophy will get along better without the notions of "the intrinsic nature of reality" and "correspondence to reality" than with them. For those who find these notions indispensable, but only for them, this will look like an argument that there is no truth. When I protest that my pragmatist views still allow me to call some statements "true" and others "false," and to argue for so calling them, my critics tell me that that is not good enough. For, they explain, I have drained all the meaning out of the terms "true" and "false." I have left us without "substantive," and with merely "aesthetic" or "relativist," senses of these terms. This charge of "relativism" is hard to shake off.

Truth is, to be sure, an absolute notion, in the following sense: "true for me but not for you" and "true in my culture but not in yours" are weird, pointless locutions. So is "true then, but not now." Whereas we often say "good for this purpose, but not for that" and "right in this situation, but not in that," it seems pointlessly paradoxical to relativize truth to purposes or situations. On the other hand, "justified for me but not for you" (or "justified in my culture but not in yours") makes perfect sense. So when James said that "the true is the good in the way of belief," he was accused of confusing justification with truth, the relative with the absolute.

James would, indeed, have done better to say that phrases like "the good in the way of belief" and "what it is better for us to believe" are interchangeable with "justified" rather than with "true." But he could have gone on to say that we have no criterion of truth other than justification, and that justification and betterness-to-believe will always be as relative to audiences (and to ranges of truth candidates) as is goodness to purposes and rightness to situations. Granted that "true" is an absolute term, its conditions of application will always be relative. For there is no such thing as belief being justified *sans phrase* – justified once and for all – for the same reason that there is no such thing as a belief that can be known, once and for all, to be indubitable. There are plenty of beliefs (e.g., "Two and two are four"; "The Holocaust took place") about which nobody with whom we bother to argue has any doubt. But there are no beliefs that can be known to be immune to all possible doubt.

This last claim sums up the antifoundationalism that has now become the conventional wisdom of analytic philosophers. But antifoundationalism in epistemology is not enough to rid us of the metaphysical distinction between appearance and reality. For it does not diminish the appeal of the following argument: since truth is an absolute notion and consists in correspondence, there must be an absolute, non-description-relative, intrinsic nature of reality to be corresponded to. Granted that the *criterion* of truth is justification, and that justification is relative, the *nature* of truth is not.

To get around this argument, we followers of James and Nietzsche deny one of its premises: namely, that truth is correspondence to reality. But then we are told that we have a duty to offer an alternative theory of truth, one that tells us what the nature of truth *really* is. When, like James and Nietzsche before us, we fail to produce such a theory, we are told that "the pragmatist attack on correspondence has failed."

The greatest of my many intellectual debts to Donald Davidson is my realization that nobody should even try to specify the nature of truth. A fortiori, pragmatists should not. Whether or not one agrees with Davidson that it is important to be able to give a definition of "true-in-*L*" for a given natural language (by means of a Tarski-type "truth theory" for that language), one can profit from his arguments that there is no possibility of giving a definition of "true" that works for all such languages. Davidson has helped us realize that *the very absoluteness of truth is a good reason for thinking "true" indefinable and for thinking that no theory of the nature of truth is possible.* It is only the relative about which there is anything to say. (This is why the God of orthodox monotheists, for example, remains so tiresomely ineffable.)

Davidson's nonrepresentationalist way of looking at truth arises from his conviction that Tarski is the only philosopher to have said anything useful about truth and that Tarski's discovery was that we have no understanding of truth that is distinct from our understanding of translation.[2] The latter doctrine is puzzling to philosophers who regard our understanding of truth as an understanding of a word–world relation such as "fitting" or "correspondence" or "accurate representation," but it sums up the upshot of Davidson's attack on representationalist views of language.

If pragmatists cannot offer a theory of truth, what can they do? They can point out, I argue in the first essay of this volume, that truth is not a goal of inquiry. If "truth" is the name of such a goal then, indeed, there is no truth. For the absoluteness of truth makes it unserviceable as such a goal. A goal is something you can know that you are getting closer to, or farther away from. But there is no way to know our distance from truth, nor even whether

2 See Donald Davidson, "On the Very Idea of a Conceptual Scheme," in *Truth and Interpretation: Perspectives on the Philosophy of Donald Davidson,* ed. Ernest LePore (Oxford: Blackwell, 1986), 194.

we are closer to it than our ancestors were. For, once again, the only criterion we have for applying the word "true" is justification, and justification is always relative to an audience. So it is also relative to that audience's lights – the purposes that such an audience wants served and the situation in which it finds itself. This means that the question "Do our practices of justification lead to truth?" is as unanswerable as it is unpragmatic. It is unanswerable because there is no way to privilege our current purposes and interests. It is unpragmatic because the answer to it would make no difference whatever to our practice.

But surely, it will be objected, we know that we *are* closer to truth. Surely we have been making both intellectual and moral progress.

Certainly we have been making progress, by our lights. That is to say, we are much better able to serve the purposes we wish to serve, and to cope with the situations we believe we face, than our ancestors would have been. But when we hypostatize the adjective "true" into "Truth" and ask about our relation to it, we have absolutely nothing to say.

We can, if we like, use this hypostatization in the same way that admirers of Plato have always used other hypostatizations – Beauty, Goodness, and Rightness. That is, we can tell a story about how recent developments in the arts or science or morals or politics have gotten us closer to these stately reifications. But the point of telling such stories is unclear. For nominalizing such adjectives does nothing to help us answer skeptical questions – for example: How do we know that greater predictive power and greater control of the environment (including a greater ability to cure diseases, build bombs, explore space, etc.) gets us closer to truth, conceived of as an accurate representation of how things are in themselves, apart from human needs and interests? How do we know that increased health, security, equality of opportunity, longevity, freedom from humiliation, and similar indices of greater human flourishing are indices of moral or political progress?

A lot of people still want philosophers to produce interesting answers to these questions. Such people will get nothing out of Nietzsche, James, Davidson, or the essays in this volume. Kant's prognosis remains as sound as ever: as long as we try to project from the relative and conditioned to the absolute and unconditioned, we shall keep the pendulum swinging between dogmatism and skepticism. The only way to stop this increasingly tiresome pendulum swing is to change our conception of what philosophy is good for. But that is not something which will be accomplished by a few neat arguments. It will be accomplished, if it ever is, by a long, slow process of cultural change – that is to say, of change in common sense, changes in the intuitions available for being pumped up by philosophical arguments.

Once one gives up the appearance–reality distinction, and the attempt to relate such things as predictive success and diminished cruelty to the intrinsic nature of reality, one has to give separate accounts of progress in science and in morals. We call something a science insofar as it enables us to predict what will happen, and therefore to influence what will happen. There are, of course, many criteria for good scientific theories other than successful prediction, and many motives for becoming a natural scientist other than the urge to help bring nature under control. But prediction is nevertheless a necessary condition for being put in the box labeled "science." We hesitate to put economics, sociology, history, or literary criticism in that box, because none of those disciplines seems capable of answering questions of the form "If we do this, what will happen?"

Once one sees that "Science can predict insofar as it gets reality right" is an incantation rather than an explanation (because we have no test for the explanans distinct from our test for the explanandum), it seems enough *good* simply to define scientific progress as an increased ability to make predictions. Once one gives up on the idea that we have become less cruel and treat each other better because we have more fully grasped the true nature of human beings or of human rights or of human obligations (more pseudo-explanations), it seems enough to define moral progress as becoming like ourselves at our best (people who are not racist, not aggressive, not intolerant, etc., etc.). But what of philosophical progress? How does that relate to scientific and moral progress?

As I see it, philosophical progress occurs to the extent that we find a way of integrating the worldviews and the moral intuitions we inherited from our ancestors with new scientific theories or new sociopolitical institutions and theories or other novelties. I have often cited Dewey's doctrine that "the distinctive office, problems and subject-matter of philosophy grow out of stresses and strains in the community life in which a given form of philosophy arises."[3] The stresses and strains Dewey has in mind are those that arise from attempts to pour bubbly and expansive new liquids into old bottles. I have also frequently cited Dewey's dictum that "philosophy can proffer nothing but hypotheses, and . . . those hypotheses are of value only as they render men's minds more sensitive to the life about them."[4]

That may seem an odd way to describe the activity in which men like Plato, Descartes, Kant, Hegel, and Dewey himself engaged. But it becomes more plausible when one notes that one way of becoming more sensitive to

3 John Dewey, *Reconstruction in Philosophy* (Boston: Beacon Press, 1948), v.
4 Ibid., 22.

the achievements and the promise of one's own time is to stop asking questions that were formulated in earlier times. The great Western philosophers should be read as therapeutic rather than as constructive: as having told us what problems *not* to discuss: scholastic problems in the case of Descartes, Cartesian problems in the case of Kant, Kantian problems in the case of Hegel, and metaphysical problems (including those raised by Hegel's attempt to prove that reality is intrinsically spiritual in character) in the cases of Nietzsche, James, and Dewey.

It would be an oversimplification to say that the task of philosophy is to stop people from thinking of things in obsolete terms inherited from great dead philosophers – to persuade them to throw away the indispensable ladders up which our culture has climbed in the past. But that is certainly a large part of their job. If you try to impose Aristotelian terminology on Galileo, or Cartesian terminology on Darwin, or the terminology of Kantian moral philosophy on debates about abortion, you will be making needless trouble for yourself. To sluff off an obsolete terminology makes us more sensitive to the life about us, for it helps us to stop trying to cut new, recalcitrant material to fit old patterns.

I end various essays in this volume (in particular the first and third) by urging that a culture in which we no longer took the skeptic's question about whether we are getting nearer to truth would be better than the one in which we ask the philosophy professors to assure us that we are indeed doing so. For in such a culture we would be more sensitive to the marvelous diversity of human languages, and of the social practices associated with those languages, because we shall have ceased asking whether they "correspond to" some nonhuman, eternal entity. Instead of asking, "Are there truths out there that we shall never discover?" we would ask, "Are there ways of talking and acting that we have not yet explored?" Instead of asking whether the intrinsic nature of reality is yet in sight (the secular counterpart of asking whether things are *dis aliter visum),* we should ask whether each of the various descriptions of reality employed in our various cultural activities is the best we can imagine – the best means to the ends served by those activities.

Such a change in our intellectual habits would have at least two more specific advantages. First, it would help us stop assigning one of these activities (religion, for example, or natural science) priority over others. Second, it would help us stop worrying about objectivity by letting us be satisfied with intersubjectivity. It would help us stop asking idle questions like "Are there objective facts about right and wrong in the same sense that there are objective facts about electrons and protons?"

Dewey anticipated Habermas by claiming that there is nothing to the notion of objectivity save that of intersubjective agreement – agreement reached by free and open discussion of all available hypotheses and policies. He hoped that the widespread adoption of this view would render us more sensitive to the life about us. It would put an end to attempts to set up a pecking order among cultural activities and among parts of our lives. By getting rid of the Kantian distinction between the cognitive, the moral, and the aesthetic, for example, it would stop the "hard" sciences from looking down on the soft, stop both from looking down on the arts, and end attempts to put philosophy on the secure path of a science. It would stop people from worrying about the "scientific" or "cognitive" status of a discipline or of a social practice. It would stop philosophers trying to cordon off a special area for themselves and would sweep away distinctions like that between the transcendental and the empirical (Kant) or the conceptual and the factual (Ryle) or the ontological and the ontic (Heidegger).

If one wants to carry through on these Deweyan suggestions, it helps to think of progress in the way in which Thomas Kuhn urged us to think of it: as the ability to solve not only the problems our ancestors solved, but also some new problems. On this account, Newton made progress over Aristotle, and Einstein over Newton, but neither came closer to the truth, or to the intrinsic character of reality, than any of the others. Hume made progress over Leibniz and Hegel over Hume, but the later figures were no closer than the earlier to the Correct Solution to the Problems of Philosophy. Analogously, the Athenian polis made moral and political progress over the Persian monarchy, the slavehood-abolishing nation-states of nineteenth-century Europe over the Athenian polis, and the social democracies of modern times progress over their proletariat-immiserating nineteenth-century predecessors. But none of these societies was closer to the Demand of Morality.

If one says that later societies made progress in recognizing the existence of human rights, I argue in the ninth essay in this volume, one should only mean that they conformed more closely to the way we wealthy, secure, educated inhabitants of the First World think people should treat one another. We are quite justified in thinking as we do, but we cannot check our view of the matter against the intrinsic nature of moral reality. We will not get anywhere by asking our philosophy professors to make sure that there really are such things as human rights and that they are as we describe them. Nor will we get anywhere by telling those who think differently that they are out of touch with moral reality or that they are behaving irrationally.

The question of whether there really *are* human rights is, from the point of view I am proposing, as pointless as the question of whether there really *are* quarks. Human rights are no more or less "objective" than quarks, but

① i.e. part of our theory of elementary particles. Rorty wrongly buys the Quinean attack on language/theory

this is just to say that reference to human rights is as indispensable to debates in the UN Security Council as is reference to quarks in debates in the Royal Society. The causal independence of quarks from human discourse is not a mark of reality as opposed to appearance; it is simply an unquestioned part of our talk about quarks. Anybody who doesn't know this fact about quarks is as unlikely to grasp what they are as is somebody who thinks that human rights were there before humans. We can say, with Foucault, that both human rights and homosexuality are recent social constructions, but only if we say, with Bruno Latour, that quarks are too. There is no point to saying that the former are "just" social constructions, for all the reasons that could be used to back up this claim are reasons that would apply to quarks as well.

One of the benefits of getting rid of the notion of the intrinsic nature of reality is that you get rid of the notion that quarks and human rights differ in "ontological status." This, in turn, helps you reject the suggestion that natural science should serve as a paradigm for the rest of culture, and in particular that philosophical progress consists in philosophers' getting more scientific. These latter bad ideas played a part in the genesis of the intellectual tradition now known as "analytic philosophy." But that tradition has, since Kuhn, been in a position to throw away those particular ladders.

It is often thought that an attack on the correspondence theory of truth, on "realism," is an attack on analytic philosophy itself. But this is a mistake. The intellectual tradition begun by Frege and Russell led to Sellars and Davidson (analytic philosophers by anybody's account), just as the intellectual tradition established by Galileo and Newton led to Einstein. Nobody thinks that Einstein stabbed modern physics in the back by denying some central Newtonian doctrines, and nobody should think that Davidson stabbed analytic philosophy in the back by refusing to take the distinction between realism and antirealism seriously, or that Sellars did so by refusing to take seriously the distinction between knowledge by acquaintance and knowledge by description.

On the view of philosophical progress offered in this volume, philosophy makes progress not by becoming more rigorous but by becoming more imaginative. Progress in this field, as in most others, is made by a few people in each generation glimpsing a possibility that had not previously been grasped. Frege and Mill, Russell and Heidegger, Dewey and Habermas, Davidson and Derrida are people of this sort. The rest of us – the underlaborers to whom it is left to clean up and dispose of what these imaginative pioneers have seen to be rubbish – perform a useful social function. We do the dirty work. (But this is, of course, not our only function. We also do a lot of pedagogic, drum-beating, and popularizing work.) To say that we perform our work "rigorously" or "professionally" is just to say that we perform it in ways acceptable to, and adapted to, the community of philosophy professors to which we belong.

There are, of course, many such communities. Comparing them with one another is a matter of comparing the legacies of original thinkers with one another. Each legacy has obvious advantages and obvious disadvantages. To argue that Continental philosophy ought to become analytic, or conversely, or that we should revive natural theology or Husserlian phenomenology or Aristotelian essentialism, is to argue that the balance of advantages and disadvantages dictates a certain decision.

I have no such argument to offer, or any views about what form philosophy ought to take. I see no point in saying that philosophy *as such* ought to be done historically or ahistorically, or in saying that one or another area of philosophy is "first philosophy." There is no more point in discussing "philosophy" in a sense broad enough to include Parmenides, Averroes, Kierkegaard, and Quine than in discussing "art" in a sense broad enough to include Sophocles, Cimabue, Zola, and Nijinsky. The attempt to gain neutrality by rising to that level of abstraction produces only banal platitudes or polemical slogans. The attempt to state the nature or the task or the mission of philosophy is usually just an attempt to build one's philosophical preferences into a definition of "philosophy."

The so-called analytic–Continental split is the location of many such building projects, and of many attempts to excommunicate philosophers one does not wish to read by defining "philosophy" in such a way as to exclude their work. As I see it, this split is, first and foremost, a split between two disciplinary matrices – and in particular between two ways of training would-be philosophy professors. These two matrices have emerged and solidified in the past hundred years, are very different indeed, and are very unlikely to blend with each other. If you get an "analytic" training, you will be encouraged to concentrate on the "frontline" problems, those discussed in current journal articles by important analytic philosophers. You may well treat your courses in the history of philosophy, and perhaps also your courses in formal logic, as distractions from this training – good for the soul, maybe, but not for the career. If you get a "Continental" training, you will be expected to learn quite a lot about the history of philosophy and to make an informed choice among various differing narratives that connect events in that history (those offered by, for example, Hegel, Heidegger, and Blumenberg). You may never have read any "analytic" philosopher, except perhaps Wittgenstein.

The training you get influences the books you are likely to read and the sort of philosophers you are best able to admire. Of the three philosophers discussed most extensively in this volume, Davidson will be more highly appreciated for his originality by those raised "analytically" than will either Habermas or Derrida. In the case of those raised "Continentally," the converse will be true. But such differences in background are, of course, overcome all the time.

I have sometimes been mistakenly commended for originality, simply because I often put apparently dissimilar figures – for example, Nietzsche and James, Davidson and Derrida – in the same box. But there is a difference between being original and being eclectic. The latter is just a result of getting easily bored and looking around for something new. I get restless, look for new heroes while remaining reasonably loyal to old ones, and so have wound up a syncretist.[5] But even the most successful syncretism cannot hope to imitate the truly heroic philosophical achievements: the ones that let us see everything from a new angle, that induce a Gestalt-switch.

Inducing such a switch is the most difficult, and the rarest, of philosophical achievements. There is no more reason to expect such a heroic achievement to arise out of the analytic tradition in philosophy than out of the Continental tradition, or conversely. Genius always takes us by surprise. It can blossom in any climate, under any sun. When Goethe was asked whether he or Schiller was the greater poet, he replied, "Just be glad you have both of us." That seems to me the appropriate attitude for philosophers on both sides of the analytic–Continental divide.

Philosophy will continue to make progress as long as geniuses keep on emerging. The rubbish-disposal projects of nongeniuses help clear, and prepare, the ground for such emergence. Or, to vary the metaphor, they fill the compost heaps out of which something unexpected may, with luck, emerge. This unexpected growth cannot be encouraged by sedulously following a "method" (for example, detecting nonsense or bracketing experiences or analyzing concepts or deconstructing concepts or assuming the transcendental standpoint or speaking ontologically). So-called methods are simply descriptions of the activities engaged in by enthusiastic imitators of one or another original mind – what Kuhn would call the "research programs" to which their works gave rise.

---

5 Back in the sixties, when I was a thrusting young analytic philosopher, I heard an admired senior colleague, Stuart Hampshire, describe a star-studded international conference on some vast and pretentious topic – a conference from which he had just returned and the results of which he had been asked to sum up at the final session. "No trick at all," Hampshire explained, "for an old syncretist hack like me." At that moment I realized what I wanted to be when I grew up.

We should remember that it is the initial Gestalt-switch, not the ensuing triumphalistic and professionalized busyness, that matters. The history of philosophy is the history of Gestalt-switches, not of the painstaking carrying-out of research programs. Such programs always trickle out into the sands eventually, but the Gestalt-switches may remain and make possible new such switches in the future. To give up on the idea that philosophy gets nearer to truth, and to interpret it as Dewey did, is to concede primacy to the imagination over the argumentative intellect, and to genius over professionalism.

The first section of this volume ("Truth and Some Philosophers") takes up various things that contemporary philosophers have been saying about truth. None of the eight essays in this section presents a theory of truth or a definition of "true." Instead, they argue against the theory that true beliefs or statements correspond to the intrinsic nature of reality, and also against the view that we now need a new theory of truth to replace this correspondence theory. They are not constructive in tone, but dismissive: they dismiss various questions and controversies as leading nowhere. They do not propose a philosophical research program, but instead criticize various research programs as misconceived. They take up what some philosophers have said about truth in the hope of discouraging further attention to this rather unfruitful topic.

These essays may be thought of as footnotes to Davidson's claim that "[we] should not say that truth is correspondence, coherence, warranted assertibility, ideally justified assertability, what is accepted in the conversation of the right people, what science will end up maintaining, what explains the convergence on single theories in science, or the success of our ordinary beliefs."[6] Whether "pragmatism" is a suitable name for the philosophical outlook that results from accepting Davidson's advice is one of the few issues on which Davidson and I still differ.

The second section ("Moral Progress: Toward More Inclusive Communities") contains four essays on moral progress. Here I argue that this sort of progress should not be conceived of as the convergence of human opinion to Moral Truth or as the onset of greater rationality, but rather as an increase in our ability to see more and more differences among people as morally irrelevant. This ability – to see the difference between people's religions, nations, genders, races, economic status, and so on as irrelevant to the possibility of cooperating with them for mutual benefit and as irrelevant to the

6 "The Structure and Content of Truth," *Journal of Philosophy* 87 (June 1990), 309.

need to alleviate their suffering – has increased considerably since the Enlightenment. It has created human communities that are more inclusive than had previously been thought possible. Our Western liberal picture of a global democratic utopia is that of a planet on which all members of the species are concerned about the fates of all the other members.

I argue in some of these essays that an increase in the ability to sympathize with those different from ourselves is not usefully seen as an index of better use of a truth-seeking faculty called Reason. I argue in others (those about feminism and about cultural difference) that it is imagination, rather than a clearer grasp of our moral obligations, that does most for the creation and stability of such communities. This latter claim is of a piece with my view, expressed in earlier writings, that novels rather than moral treatises are the most useful vehicles of moral education.

These first two sections are fairly unified, in that the same line of thought is reiterated in each of the essays included in one or the other section. But the third section ("The Role of Philosophy in Human Progress") is more miscellaneous. Its five essays are metaphilosophical. They try to say something about what philosophers – defined as people who read Plato, Kant, and the rest of the Western philosophical canon and think about the issues raised in those texts – can do for human progress.

The first two essays in this section are about the historiography of philosophy and argue that what counts as "philosophy" is a matter of who is deciding, for what purposes, which historical figures count as "philosophers" (rather than, for example, as scientists, theologians, political scientists, or litterateurs).

The final three essays attempt to tell a story about recent philosophy that gives due importance to the contributions of John Dewey, Jürgen Habermas, and Jacques Derrida. I see Habermas's theory of "communicative reason" as a giant step toward completing the task Dewey began – reformulating traditional philosophical conceptions in ways that will make them more useful for the self-description of a democratic society. The only point on which I differ from Habermas – the utility of the notion of "universal validity" – is unimportant, when compared with the overlap between our views.[7]

Derrida is as different from both Dewey and Habermas as the latter are similar to each other. I find myself returning to his work over and over again,

---

7 I discuss the question of universal validity at length in "Sind Aussagen universelle Geltungsansprüche?" *Deutsche Zeitschrift für Philosophie* 42, no. 6 (1994), 975–88. I have not reprinted this essay in this volume, because a revised version of it will appear as a chapter in a monograph that I hope to publish a few years from now.

always unable to get a clear synoptic view of his intent, but always fascinated. I think of him as our century's analogue of Nietzsche. My hunch is that the next century's assimilation of his work will be as long, and as vexed, as our own century's assimilation of Nietzsche's.

With two exceptions, noted later, these essays were written in the course of the 1990s. All but four will have appeared in print elsewhere by the time this volume is published. The versions offered here are only slightly different (an occasional change of phrase, an omitted paragraph, a few additional footnotes) from the previously published versions. Their antecedents are as follows.

1. "Is Truth a Goal of Inquiry? Donald Davidson versus Crispin Wright" started out as a review of Crispin Wright's *Truth and Objectivity*, but swelled beyond the compass of a review. The editors of the *Philosophical Quarterly* kindly printed it nonetheless, in vol. 45 (July 1995), 281–300, and have granted permission for it to be reprinted here.

2. "Hilary Putnam and the Relativist Menace" was published as "Putnam and the Relativist Menace" in the *Journal of Philosophy*, vol. 90 (September 1993), 443–461. I thank the journal's editors for permission to reprint it.

3. "John Searle on Realism and Relativism" was a response to Louis Menand's invitation to give one of a series of lectures on academic freedom for the American Association of University Professors. I used the invitation as an occasion to respond to Searle's view about the importance of the correspondence theory of truth for cultural politics. My paper was published under the title "Does Academic Freedom Have Philosophical Presuppositions?" first in *Academe,* the journal of the AAUP (vol. 80 [November–December 1994], 52–63), and later in *Academic Freedom,* ed. Louis Menand (Chicago: University of Chicago Press, 1996). I thank both the AAUP and the Press for permission to reprint it.

4. "Charles Taylor on Truth" was a contribution to *Philosophy in an Age of Pluralism: The Philosophy of Charles Taylor in Question,* ed. James Tully (Cambridge University Press, 1994). A response to my essay by Taylor is included in that volume.

5. "Daniel Dennett on Intrinsicality" was originally published as "Holism, Intentionality and the Ambition of Transcendence" in *Dennett and His Critics: Demystifying Mind,* ed. Bo Dahlbom (Oxford: Blackwell, 1993), reprinted by permission. A response by Dennett to my essay is included in that volume.

6 and 7. These two essays, on the work of Robert Brandom and John McDowell respectively, have not been published previously. They were among ten lectures I gave in Catalonia, as José Ferrater Mora Visiting Professor at

Girona, in June 1996. I am grateful to Professor Josep-Maria Terrecabrias, the directer of the Ferrater Mora Chair, for this opportunity and for inviting Brandom and McDowell to Girona to offer their reactions to my views about their work.

8. "Antiskeptical Weapons: Michael Williams versus Donald Davidson" was read at a symposium on Michael Williams's *Unnatural Doubts: Epistemological Realism and the Basis of Scepticism* held at the annual meeting of the Central Division of the American Philosophical Association in April 1995. It has not been published previously.

9. "Human Rights, Rationality, and Sentimentality" was delivered as an Oxford Amnesty Lecture in the spring of 1993 and was published in *On Human Rights: The 1993 Oxford Amnesty Lectures,* ed. Susan Hurley and Stephen Shute (New York: Basic Books, 1993). I am grateful to Basic Books for permission to reprint it.

10. "Rationality and Cultural Difference" was given at a conference on that topic organized by the Indian Institute of Philosophy and held at Mount Abu in the winter of 1991. It was published as "A Pragmatist View of Rationality and Cultural Differences" in *Philosophy East and West,* vol. 42 (October 1992), 581–96, and is reprinted by courtesy of the University of Hawaii Press.

11. "Feminism and Pragmatism" was delivered as a Tanner Lecture at the University of Michigan in the spring of 1991 and was published in *The Tanner Lectures on Human Values,* vol. 13 (Salt Lake City: University of Utah Press, 1994). It is reprinted here by the kind permission of the Tanner Trustees.

12. "The End of Leninism, Havel, and Social Hope" was written for a conference entitled "The End of History" held in 1991 at Michigan State University, and centered around the ideas of Francis Fukuyama. A shortened, revised version appeared as "The Intellectuals at the End of Socialism," *Yale Review,* vol. 80, nos. 1 and 2 (1992), 1–16. The full version appeared in *History and the Idea of Progress,* ed. Arthur M. Melzer et al. (Ithaca, N.Y.: Cornell University Press, 1995), 211–26. I am grateful to Professor Meltzer and his colleagues for the initial stimulus and to the Press for permission to reprint this version.

13. "The Historiography of Philosophy: Four Genres" is reprinted from *Philosophy in History* (Cambridge University Press, 1984), a volume of essays on the historiography of philosophy that I coedited with J. B. Schneewind and Quentin Skinner.

14. "The Contingency of Philosophical Problems: Michael Ayers on Locke" was written for a conference held at Göttingen in honor of Lorenz

Krüger. It will appear in a conference volume to be edited by Wolfgang Carl and Lorraine Daston.

15. "Dewey Between Hegel and Darwin" was written for a conference organized by Dorothy Ross and Olivier Zunz, and held at Bellagio in 1991. It was published first in French translation in *Rue Descartes*, nos. 5 and 6 (1992), 53–71, and subsequently in *Modernist Impulses in the Human Sciences*, ed. Dorothy Ross (Baltimore: Johns Hopkins University Press, 1994). It also appeared in *Rorty and Pragmatism*, ed. Herman Saatkamp (Nashville, Tenn.: Vanderbilt University Press, 1995). It is reprinted here by courtesy of the Johns Hopkins University Press.

16. "Habermas, Derrida, and the Functions of Philosophy" appeared in *Revue Internationale de Philosophie*, no. 4 (1995), 437–60, and is reprinted here by permission of the editors of that journal.

17. "Derrida and the Philosophical Tradition" is a slightly revised version of a review article on *Jacques Derrida*, by Geoffrey Bennington and Jacques Derrida, published in *Contemporary Literature*, vol. 36 (Spring 1995), 173–200, under the title "Is Derrida a *Quasi-*Transcendental Philosopher?" It is reprinted here by permission of the editors of that journal.

The task of putting these papers together into a single manuscript was made easy by the help given by Andrew Moser and Mary Racine.

I

TRUTH AND SOME PHILOSOPHERS

1

IS TRUTH A GOAL OF INQUIRY?
DONALD DAVIDSON VERSUS CRISPIN WRIGHT

Pragmatists think that if something makes no difference to practice, it should make no difference to philosophy. This conviction makes them suspicious of the distinction between justification and truth, for that difference makes no difference to my decisions about what to do. If I have concrete, specific doubts about whether one of my beliefs is true, I can resolve those doubts only by asking whether it is adequately justified – by finding and assessing additional reasons pro and con. I cannot bypass justification and confine my attention to truth: assessment of truth and assessment of justification are, when the question is about what I should believe now, the same activity.[1] If, on the other hand, my doubts are as unspecific and abstract as Descartes's – are such that I can do nothing to resolve them – they should be dismissed, with Peirce, as "make-believe." Philosophy should ignore them.

This line of thought suggests to pragmatists that, although there is obviously a lot to be said about justification of various sorts of beliefs, there may be little to say about truth.[2] The sort of thing philosophers typically have said – that truth is some sort of correspondence to, or accurate representation of,

---

1 Of course, when the question is not about deciding what to believe now, but about explaining what has happened, the distinction between justification and truth is useful: we often explain our failures by saying, "I was quite justified in believing that, but unfortunately it was not true." But though useful, it is not essential. We can explain our failure equally well by saying "What I thought would happen did not," and in many other ways.
2 However, what there is to be said about justification is local rather than global: quite different, unconnected things have to be said about justification in, for example, mathematics, jurisprudence, and astrology. So philosophers are hardly the people to say it. This point chimes with Michael Williams's argument (in his *Unnatural Doubts: Epistemological Realism and the Basis of Scepticism* [Oxford: Blackwell, 1991]) that "knowledge" is neither the name of a natural

reality – seemed empty and pointless to many[3] nineteenth-century idealists, and also to Dewey. The early pragmatists agreed with their idealist opponents that doubts about correspondence to reality can be settled only by assessing the coherence of the dubious belief with other beliefs. To both, the difference between true beliefs considered as useful nonrepresentational mental states, and as accurate (and *therefore* useful) representations of reality, seemed a difference that could make no difference to practice. No one profits from insisting on the distinction, both concluded, except for those who enjoy entertaining make-believe doubts.

Since the pragmatists, unlike the idealists, took Darwin and biology seriously, they had an additional reason for distrusting the idea that true beliefs are accurate representations. For representation, as opposed to increasingly complex adaptive behavior, is hard to integrate into an evolutionary story. Within such a story, it is easy to think of beliefs, with Bain and Peirce, as habits of action, patterns of complex behavior. But it is hard to imagine that, at a certain point in the evolutionary process, somewhere between the squids and the apes, these patterns began to be determined by inner representations, having previously been determined by mere neurological configurations. Even if one chooses to treat sufficiently complex neurological configurations *as* representations, the question of their accuracy seems to collapse immediately into that of their utility. So, once again, we seem to have a difference that makes no practical difference.[4]

kind nor the topic of useful global theorizing. I am indebted to Williams for the realization that the Cartesian notion of a natural, ahistorical, and transcultural "order of reasons" is essential to Descartes's "dreaming" argument, and more generally to both epistemological skepticism and the feasibility of epistemology as a discipline.

3 Not all. Some idealists argued that all truths are true by virtue of their correspondence to a single object (the Absolute), thereby eviscerating the idea of correspondence.

4 Of course, a host of contemporary philosophers (notably Ruth Millikan, David Papineau, and Fred Dretske) have retained the notion of "inner representation" and interpreted it biologistically, as a matter of the evolutionarily designed ability of an organism to respond differentially to different stimuli. In contrast, followers of Wilfrid Sellars (such as George Pitcher, David Armstrong, Daniel Dennett, and myself) lump the neurological arrangements that make possible such differential responses to differential stimuli together with the internal states of (for example) thermostats. We treat perceptions as dispositions to acquire beliefs and desires rather than as "experiences" or "raw feels," and hence we disagree with Thomas Nagel that there is "something it is like" to have a perception. I see the Sellarsian strategy we employ as an example of the pragmatist habit of refusing to recognize the existence of trouble-making entities. This habit strikes nonpragmatists like Nagel as a refusal to face up to the facts.

As I suggest at the end of this essay, we pragmatists too want to be faithful to Darwin. But we think that the Millikan–Papineau–Dretske revivification of the notion of "representation" is an insufficiently radical way of appropriating Darwin's insight. These philosophers want to reconcile Darwin with Descartes's and Locke's "way of ideas." In contrast, we want to follow up on Dewey's suggestion that Darwin has made Descartes and Locke obsolete.

William James said, "'The true' . . . is only the expedient in the way of our thinking, just as 'the right' is only the expedient in the way of our behaving."[5] Elsewhere he said, "The true is the name of whatever proves itself to be good in the way of belief, and good, too, for definite, assignable reasons."[6] His point in analogizing truth to rightness and to goodness was that once you understand all about the justification of actions, including the justification of assertions, you understand all there *is* to understand about goodness, rightness, and truth.[7]

Philosophers who, like myself, find this Jamesian suggestion persuasive, swing back and forth between trying to reduce truth to justification and propounding some form of minimalism about truth. In reductionist moods we have offered such definitions of truth as "warranted assertibility," "ideal assertibility," and "assertibility at the end of inquiry." But such definitions always fall victim, sooner or later, to what Putnam has called the "naturalistic fallacy" argument – the argument that a given belief might meet any such conditions but still not be true. Faced with this argument, we pragmatists have often fallen back on minimalism and have suggested that Tarski's breezy disquotationalism may exhaust the topic of truth.[8]

In an article on Donald Davidson published in 1986, I suggested that we interpret Davidson both as a sort of pragmatist and as a sort of minimalist – as someone who, like James, thought that there was less to say about truth than philosophers had usually believed.[9] More specifically, I interpreted Davidson as saying that the word "true" had no explanatory use, but merely

5 *Pragmatism and The Meaning of Truth* (Cambridge, Mass.: Harvard University Press, 1975), 106.

6 Ibid., 42. James also, unfortunately, said a lot of other, conflicting things about truth – such as that it consists in some kind of agreement between ideas and reality. Later in this volume, in "Dewey Between Hegel and Darwin," I argue that Dewey was wise to avoid saying the latter sort of thing and to eschew analyses or definitions of "truth" or of "true."

7 Two recent books show how this suggestion can be worked out in detail: Barry Allen's *Truth in Philosophy* (Cambridge, Mass.: Harvard University Press, 1993) and Robert Brandom's *Making It Explicit* (Cambridge, Mass.: Harvard University Press, 1994).

8 For an account of this strategy, see Hilary Putnam's "Does the Disquotational Theory Solve All Problems?" in his *Words and Life* (Cambridge, Mass.: Harvard University Press, 1994), 264–78. Putnam there criticizes two philosophers whom he construes as disquotationalists – Paul Horwich and Michael Williams – for remaining in the grip of a "positivistic picture" and for being closet reductionists. This is a criticism he has often made of me (see, e.g., "The Question of Realism," 295–312, in the same volume). On Putnam's view, all three of us ignore the need to admit the existence of genuine "directedness" and "intentionality." I am not sure whether Putnam would make the same criticism of Davidson.

9 Richard Rorty, "Pragmatism, Davidson and Truth," in *Truth and Interpretation: Perspectives on the Philosophy of Donald Davidson*, ed. Ernest LePore (Oxford: Blackwell, 1986), 333–68. This article is reprinted in my *Objectivity, Relativism, and Truth* (Cambridge University Press, 1991).

a disquotational use, a commending use, and what I called a "cautionary" use. The latter is its use in such expressions as "fully justified, but perhaps not true." The reason there is less to be said about truth than one might think, I suggested, is that terms used to commend or caution – terms such as "good!" "right!" "true!" "false!" "way to go!" and "watch it!" – do not need much philosophical definition or explication.

My underlying idea in that 1986 article was that the entire force of the cautionary use of "true" is to point out that justification is relative to an audience and that we can never exclude the possibility that some better audience might exist, or come to exist, to whom a belief that is justifiable to us would not be justifiable. But, as Putnam's "naturalistic fallacy" argument shows, there can be no such thing as an "ideal audience" before which justification would be sufficient to ensure truth, any more than there can be a largest integer. For any audience, one can imagine a better-informed audience and also a more imaginative one – an audience that has thought up hitherto-undreamt-of alternatives to the proposed belief. The limits of justification would be the limits of language, but language (like imagination) has no limits.

In an article of 1990, Davidson partially repudiated my interpretation.[10] He said that he should be considered neither a deflationist nor a disquotationalist. He defined "deflationism" as the view that "Tarski's work embraces all of truth's essential features" and said that I was mistaken in attributing this view to him on the basis of his eschewal of attempts to define "true" for variable L as opposed to defining "true-in-L" for particular values of L.[11] He went on to say that

> Tarski's definitions [of the term "true-in-L" for various values of L] give us no idea of how to apply the concept [of truth] to a new case. . . . [T]hey depend on giving the extension or references of the basic predicates or names by enumerating cases; a definition given in this way can provide no clue for the next or general case.[12]

Davidson concluded that "[t]he concept of truth has essential connections with the concepts of belief and meaning, but these connections are untouched by Tarski's work."[13] He summed up by saying:

> What Tarski has done for us is to show in detail how to describe the kind of pattern truth must make. What we need to do now is to say how to identify the presence of such a pattern or structure in the behavior of people.[14]

10 Donald Davidson, "The Structure and Content of Truth," *Journal of Philosophy* 87, no. 6 (1990), 279–328. This article comprises Davidson's Dewey Lectures.
11 Ibid., 287.   12 Ibid.   13 Ibid., 295.   14 Ibid.

The way we identify this pattern, Davidson tells us, is to gather information "about what episodes and situations in the world cause an agent to prefer that one rather than another sentence be true."[15] This information can be gleaned without knowing what the agent's sentences mean. But once we have enough such evidence we can, Davidson says, "make the crucial step from the nonpropositional to the propositional,"[16] from the nonintensional to the intensional. For the use of intensional terms to describe human behavior marks the emergence of the pattern that truth makes – the pattern that links those episodes and situations in the world with the noises and marks made by the agent. They are linked into the behavior we call "using a language." Detection of that pattern is what makes the adoption of what Dennett calls "the intentional stance" both possible and useful in our dealings with the agent. There is, Davidson says, "a fundamentally rational pattern that must, in general outline, be shared by all rational creatures."[17] This pattern that rationality makes is the same pattern truth makes, and the same pattern meaning makes. You cannot have language without rationality, or either without truth.[18]

It is important to realize that what Davidson adds to Tarski, when he displays the connections between the concept of truth and those of meaning and belief, has nothing whatever to do with the question of whether, or how, we can tell when a belief is true. Although Davidson describes himself as, in his Dewey Lectures, filling in the missing "content" of the "concept" of truth, all this filling-in amounts to is instructions for constructing an empirical theory for explaining and predicting behavior – a theory of truth for one or more speakers. "A theory of truth," as he says, "is an empirical theory about the truth conditions of every sentence in some corpus of sentences."[19]

---

15 Ibid., 322.   16 Ibid., 323.   17 Ibid., 320.

18 A good statement of the view that you *can* separate these is Wright's description of metaphysical realism, as asserting the possibility that "despite the apparent cognitive richness of our lives, we are somehow so situated as not to be enabled to arrive at the concepts which fundamentally depict the character of the real world and the nature of our interaction with it" ("Putnam's Proof That We Are Not Brains in a Vat," in *Reading Putnam*, ed. Peter Clark and Bob Hale [Oxford: Blackwell, 1994], 238). Assuming that "fundamentally depict the character of . . ." means "are required to tell the truth about," then Davidson is committed to saying that this situation cannot arise: there can never be what Wright calls "a thought whose truth would make a mockery of humankind and its place in nature" (ibid., 240). The worst that can happen is that people whose language we are quite capable of learning (the Galactics, say) might offer us some astonishingly impressive substitutes for our present beliefs about selected special topics (e.g., the microstructure of matter or how to achieve world peace).

19 Davidson, "Structure," 309. Some commentators on Davidson have taken a truth condition to be a nonlinguistic state of affairs, a fact rather than a sentence in the truth theorist's language – despite Davidson's polemic against the notion of "fact" in "True to the Facts," in *Inquiries into Truth and Interpretation* (Oxford: Clarendon Press, 1984), 36–54.

Philosophers who discuss truth have often hoped to underwrite our assumption that, the more justification we offer of a belief, the likelier it is that
that belief is true. The most familiar attempt at such ratification begins by
saying that, at least in some areas of culture, and at the very least when we
are concerned with observable physical objects, our predictions succeed insofar as our beliefs fit reality. It then goes on to say that each successive substitution of a better-justified for a worse-justified belief is an improvement in
degree of fit. Such talk of "fit" interprets an increase in the coherence of
nonobservational sentences with observation sentences as a sign of closer fit
between the former sentences and the things observed.

Davidson, however, has no sympathy for this line of thought. His criticisms of the notion of "fitting reality," in "On the Very Idea of a Conceptual
Scheme," parallel James's and Dewey's. In his Dewey Lectures he says:

> I have argued that certain familiar attempts to characterize truth which go be-
> yond giving empirical content to a structure of the sort Tarski taught us how
> to describe are empty, false, or confused. We should not say that truth is cor-
> respondence, coherence, warranted assertibility, ideally justified assertability,
> what is accepted in the conversation of the right people, what science will end
> up maintaining, what explains the convergence on single theories in science,
> or the success of our ordinary beliefs. To the extent that realism or antireal-
> ism depend [sic] on one or another of these views of truth we should refuse
> to endorse either.[20]

Passages such as this suggest that Davidson would categorically repudiate
the suggestion that philosophers need to explain why an increase in justification leads to an increased likelihood of truth, as opposed to acceptability
to more and more audiences. For Davidson seems to think that philosophers
have done *all* they need to do with the concept of truth once they have
shown how to detect a certain pattern of behavior – the pattern exhibited
in the truth theory for a language. It is hard to see how such detection could
help to underwrite or improve our practices of justification, and Davidson
gives no reason to think that it could or should.[21] This is, presumably, why
he calls truth a "nonepistemic" concept.

---

20 Davidson, "Structure," 309.
21 Michael Williams in *Unnatural Doubts* suggests that an inability to "account for the truth-
    conduciveness of justfication" will lead to skepticism (231). My view, and the one I am at-
    tributing to Davidson, is that what leads to skepticism is the initial assumption of truth-
    conduciveness rather than the failure of attempts to back up this assumption. So I deny
    Williams's claim that "it is surely an essential feature of epistemic justification that justify-
    ing a belief makes it more likely to be true" (229). I enlarge on this denial in "Sind Aus-
    sagen universelle Geltungsansprüche?" (*Deutsche Zeitschrift für Philosophie* 42, no. 6 [1994],
    975–88), a criticism of Habermas's and Apel's views on truth.

① this is just DD's version of the claim that to believe P is to believe that P is true.

I suspect that the only epistemological comfort that Davidson has to offer is his notorious thesis that most of our beliefs – most of *anybody's* beliefs – must be true. This thesis is, however, both less bracing and less provocative than it may seem at first. For when we remember that Davidson will have no truck with the idea that truth consists in correspondence to, or accurate representation of,[22] reality, we realize that he is not saying that our minds are, thanks to God's or Evolution's contrivance, well suited to the task of getting reality right. He can perfectly well agree with Goodman, Putnam, and Kuhn that there is no such task, because there is no Way the World Is. He is, rather, saying that most of anybody's beliefs must coincide with most of *our* beliefs (because to ascribe beliefs in the first place one must invoke the Principle of Charity) and that to reject that mass of shared beliefs (as perhaps not corresponding to reality) is to bring back a tangle of uncashable and useless metaphors – those used to state the scheme–content distinction. To say, as Davidson does, that "belief is in its nature veridical" is not to celebrate the happy congruence of subject and object but rather to say that the pattern truth makes is the pattern that *justification to us* makes.[23]

22 For his repudiation of the notion of "representation," see Davidson's "The Myth of the Subjective," in *Relativism: Interpretation and Confrontation*, ed. Michael Krausz (Notre Dame, Ind.: Notre Dame University Press, 1989), 165–6.

23 But I may be missing something here, and my blind spot may conceal a real and important disagreement between Davidson's views and my version of pragmatism. For in "Structure," Davidson says that "[s]ince the concept of truth is central to the theory [i.e., to an empirical theory that entails T-sentences], we are justified in saying that truth is a crucially important explanatory concept" (313). It does not look particularly central to me. As I see it, what Davidson calls a "theory of truth" could equally well be called "a theory of complex behavior" or "a theory of justificatory behavior." Granted that the production of the sort of biconditionals Tarski called "T-sentences" is the whole point of the theory, I am not sure why the production of these sentences illustrates the centrality, or the crucial importance, of the concept of truth.

I am quite willing to withdraw my 1986 claim that "true" has no explanatory use, which was a misleading way of putting the point that "It's true!" is not a helpful explanation of why science works or of why you should share one of my beliefs. But although the sort of theory to which Davidson thinks "the concept of truth" central is indeed explanatory, it seems to me somewhat awkward and unnecessary to pick out a given concept that is explicated by reference to such theories and say that *it* has a crucial explanatory role. Avoiding such favoritism would be more congruent with Davidson's fundamental point that a theory of truth is automatically a theory of meaning and of rationality – as well as with his doctrine that every intensional concept is intertwined with every other such concept.

Another way of locating the point at which Davidson and I may differ is that he thinks it significant that we use the same word to designate what is preserved by valid inference as we use to caution people that beliefs justified to us may not be justified to other, better audiences. As far as I can see, there is no deep reason why "true" is used to do both of these jobs, why one of the words that we use to describe the pattern of behavior necessarily exhibited by language users (logical inference) should also be one of the words we use to caution people that they may be believing something that better-advised people would not believe. So I see no reason to look behind both uses for some feature of the *meaning* of

Without charity, we cannot detect the pattern truth makes. But charity entails seeing most of what the natives say as justified. If there is no justification of the sort that strikes us as reasonable, there will be no coherent set of inferential relationships to be detected between the various strings of marks and noises produced by speakers, and therefore no rationality – no pattern of the requisite sort. This seems to me the *sole* force of Davidson's claim that the guiding principles used in detecting this pattern "derive from normative considerations"[24] and of his reference to "the norms that govern our theories of intensional attribution."[25] The need to justify our beliefs and desires to ourselves and to our fellow agents subjects us to norms, and obedience to these norms produces a behavioral pattern that we must detect in others before confidently attributing beliefs to them. But there seems no occasion to look for obedience to an *additional* norm – the commandment to seek the truth. For – to return to the pragmatist doubt with which I began – obedience to that commandment will produce no behavior not produced by the need to offer justification.

So far I have been sketching the sort of minimalism about truth that I would still wish to attribute to Davidson, even after accepting his repudiation of deflationism. But this minimalism is very different from certain other philosophical accounts of truth that have been called by that name. To highlight these differences, I turn now from Davidson to Crispin Wright.

Wright cares deeply about the topics of realism and antirealism, and sees insouciance about such issues as undesirable "quietism," defined as the view that "significant metaphysical debate is impossible."[26] James's and Dewey's pragmatism was, among other things, an attempt to shut off such debate – not by showing it to be impossible or senseless, but by showing it to be pointless. So Wright's *Truth and Objectivity* is a good example of contemporary opposition to pragmatism. If the argument of that book is on the right track, then pragmatism is merely an unhappy attempt to evade questions that are absolutely central to philosophical reflection.

Like Davidson, Wright distrusts deflationism. But his reasons are very different. For Davidson, Tarski failed to show us how to detect in nature the pattern his truth theories for specific languages exhibit. But for Wright what

---

"true" which makes that word suitable for both assignments. If I could see such a reason, I might be in a better position to appreciate what Davidson means by the "centrality" of the concept and to see why he speaks of himself as "filling in the content" of this concept.

24 Davidson, "Structure," 319.   25 Ibid., 325.

26 Crispin Wright, *Truth and Objectivity* (Cambridge, Mass.: Harvard University Press, 1992), 202.

Tarski failed to give us is a *norm*. Wright thinks our statement-making practices are regulated by two distinct norms: warranted assertibility and truth. These two are, Wright says, "distinct in the precise sense that although aiming at one is, necessarily, aiming at the other, success in the one aim need not be success in the other."[27] From Wright's point of view, the trouble with deflationism is not that it does not tell you how to work up a truth theory for a given natural language, but that it does not even mention your duty to attain the truth. It leaves you thinking that you have done enough if you have done all the justifying you can.

That, of course, is just what pragmatists want you to think. Here, it seems to me, Davidson can happily concur with the pragmatists. For, as I have already suggested, I see no way to fit the idea of truth as a goal of inquiry into Davidson's account of what we need to say about truth. So in order to widen still further the gulf that yawns between Davidson's quietism and the metaphysical activism urged by Wright, I shall stress the entanglement of Wright's claim that truth is a distinct norm with his unpragmatic and anti-Davidsonian attempt to keep the notions of "correspondence" and "representation" alive.

Wright says that "deflationism . . . is committed to the idea that warranted assertibility is the *only* norm operating over assertoric discourse."[28] But, he says, even the deflationist has to admit that "while 'is T' and 'is warrantedly assertible' are normatively coincident, satisfaction of the one norm need not entail satisfaction of the other."[29] So, Wright concludes, "deflationism reinflates." But this argument seems insufficient. The fact that beliefs can be justified without being true does not entail that two norms are being invoked. Analogously, the fact that an action can be fully justified to a given audience and still not be the right thing to do does not show that we have two duties – one to justify our actions to each other and another to do the right thing. It merely shows that what can be justified to some audiences cannot be justified to others.

Wright, however, has a more detailed argument for his claim that "deflationism is an inherently unstable view."[30] He takes the deflationist to say that the content of the truth predicate is "wholly fixed" by what he calls the Disquotationalist Schema:

"*P*" is true if and only if *P*.

Then he says that there is an "explanatory biconditional link effected by the Disquotational Schema between the claim that a sentence is T and its proper assertoric use."[31] He defines a predicate as "(positively) descriptively

27 Ibid., 19.   28 Ibid., 21.   29 Ibid., 23.   30 Ibid., 34.   31 Ibid., 17.

② False – no such link !

normative" just in case "participants' selection, endorsement, and so on of a move is as a matter of fact guided by whether or not they judge that move is F."[32] This enables him to conclude that

> 'T' is descriptively normative in the sense that the practices of those for whom warranted assertibility is a descriptive norm are exactly as they would be if they consciously selected the assertoric moves which they were prepared to make or allow in the light of whether or not the sentences involved were T.

False

False

He sums up by saying that "any actual assertoric practice will be just as it would be if T were a self-conscious goal."[33] Although the behavior of those selecting for warranted assertibility will be the same as that of those selecting for truth, Wright thinks that we can distinguish two selections by asking whether they are "as a matter of fact guided" by one consideration rather than another.

But is it enough for there to be a fact of such guidance that the agent thinks there is such a fact?[34] Consider an analogy: I am trying to decide whether to prosecute my father for impiety. In the course of doing so I sometimes describe myself as trying to do what I am justified in thinking pious and sometimes as trying to obey the will of the gods. Socrates has pointed out to me that although the two criteria are normatively coincident, satisfaction of the first criterion does not entail satisfaction of the second – for my community, the one that has given me my sense of what counts as satisfactory justification, may be out of touch with the gods. Still, my hope of satisfying both criteria persists.

An atheist, however, may tell me that I am "as a matter of fact" guided by only one norm and have only one self-conscious goal – that only one process of conscious selection is at work in my decision making. Since there are no gods, he says, there is no such thing as their will, and I cannot, even if I want to, obey the norm of conformity to that will. But I, of course, shall rejoin that this line of thought is reductionist and that my belief in the gods is enough to enable me to attempt to obey this norm. What norms one obeys, after all, is a matter of what norms one thinks one is obeying.[35]

---

32 Ibid., 16.   33 Ibid., 17.

34 Wright identifies the claim that to possess truth is "to meet a normative constraint distinct from assertoric warrant" with the claim that "truth is a genuine property" (ibid., 35). I avoid the issue of whether truth is a property – an issue that seems to me to boil down eventually, just as Wright says, to the question "one norm or two?" I agree with what Davidson says about this issue ("Structure," 285).

35 This line of argument is often employed against, for example, a Hobbesian reductionist who says that the actions I think are motivated by my desire to be a good citizen are really motivated by my fear of sanctions. Hobbes's and Thrasymachus's strong point is that a causal explanation of my action that does not refer to good citizenship may be as useful as one that does. Their opponent's strong point is that the need for causal explanation is not our only motive for attributing motives.

I do not think that Wright should be happy with this line of defense against the atheist. For the force of his term "as a matter of fact guided by" disappears once one grants that a belief in guidance is proof of guidance. An imaginative agent who proliferates goals, and thus lights by which to perform the self-conscious selection of moves, will soon have more guidance systems going than we can shake a stick at. He will, for example, be trying to hit every bull's-eye he aims at, to win all the archery competitions, to become known as a superb archer, to become world archery champion, to please the goddess Diana, and to find a sympathetic defender in the councils of the gods. He will see all of these as prescriptively coincident – they all lead him to perform exactly the same actions – while acknowledging that achievement of the last two goals may not be extensionally coincident with achievement of the first four. For he has heard rumors that Diana has long since lost interest in archery and is now into karate.

Wright must either concede that a goal is "descriptively normative" for an action if the agent thinks it is, or else give us a further criterion for detecting *real* descriptive normativity. I am not sure what such a criterion could look like. But if he cannot specify one, he may have to admit that, just as "deflationism reinflates," so atheism retheologizes.

My own view is that attaining divine favor was indeed a goal distinct from hitting the target for religious archers and that attaining truth as distinct from making justified statements *is* a goal for metaphysically active inquirers. We metaphysical quietists deplore the fact that most people in our culture can be incited to this sort of activity. They still, alas, take seriously such bad, unpragmatic questions as "subjective or objective?" "made or found?" "*ad nos* or *in se?*" "socially constructed or for real?" But just as religious archers can be (and to some extent have been) replaced by atheist archers, so we pragmatists hope our culture will eventually replace itself with the culture that James and Dewey foresaw. In that culture, the question "Are you trying to attain truth as well as to form justified beliefs?" would be greeted with the same puzzlement with which "Are you seeking divine favor?" is greeted by atheist archers.[36]

I shall return to the topic of cultural change at the end of this essay, but first I want to direct attention to Wright's motive for emphasizing the difference between deflationism, which does not recognize that truth is a distinct

36 These last six paragraphs are heavily indebted to Bjorn Ramberg and Barry Smith. They replace a section of an earlier version of this essay, a version read and discussed by Smith and Ramberg. Ramberg kindly conveyed Smith's (well-taken) criticisms of that version to me and suggested ways to avoid these criticisms – suggestions I have gratefully adopted.

norm, and his own brand of minimalism, which does. Wright has two aims
in his book. The first is to give deflationism its due by admitting that "truth
is not intrinsically a metaphysically heavyweight notion."[37] This puts Wright
in a position to rebuff "error-theorists" like John Mackie, who think it a mistake to apply the word "true" to moral judgments. For, as Wright rightly says,
"the minimalist proposal is conservative of our ordinary style of thought and
talk about the comic, the revolting and the delightful, the good, and the
valuable, which finds no solecism in the description of contents concerning
such matters as 'true.'"[38] Defeating philosophers like Mackie is Wright's first
aim, and Davidson and Dewey would both applaud this project.

His second aim, however, is to make clear that "we do not, in going min-
imalist about assertoric content and truth, set ourselves on a fast track to quietism about traditional philosophical controversy concerning realism and
objectivity."[39] Wright thinks that

> talk of 'representation of the facts' is not just admissible phrasing, a harmless
> gloss on talk of truth, but incorporates a philosophically correct – as we might
> say, *seriously dyadic* – perspective on the truth predicate (at least for discourses
> where realism is appropriate).

His deflationist opponent, he goes on to say, will insist that such talk "is additional metaphysical theory, foisted onto phrases which, while characteristic of the idea of truth, can be saved by a deflationary account and merit no
such metaphysical interpretation."[40]

Dewey or Davidson could hardly have expressed his quietistic antipathy
to the notions of correspondence and representation with better words than
those that Wright here puts in the deflationist's mouth. James's and Dewey's
post-Darwinian attempt to naturalize our self-image by dissolving the traditional oppositions between mind and nature and between subject and object, as well as Davidson's later assault on the scheme–content distinction,
are both nicely epitomized in the claim that our perspective on the truth
predicate should *not* be "seriously dyadic."

One of the great merits of Wright's very dense and argument-packed
book is that he sees the need to say more than Dummett does about the pragmatic cash value of the ideas of "realism," "representation," and "correspondence." He sees that the logical terminology made current by Dummett – in his explications of "realism" with the aid of notions like bivalence
and failure of excluded middle – does not adequately capture the motives
for traditional debates. He notes that David Wiggins attempted to remedy

---

37 Wright, *Truth and Objectivity*, 72.   38 Ibid., 75.   39 Ibid., 86.   40 Ibid., 83.

this defect by suggesting that a tendency toward convergence is a sufficient criterion for the applicability of such notions. But Wright criticizes Wiggins's suggestion on the ground that the presence of such a tendency would, for example, make judgments about the comic representational if, for some accidental sociohistorical reason, there was steady convergence toward consensus on the comic.

Wright is surely right that the idea of representationality, and thus of realism, needs to be explicated with the help of a notion that is neither merely logical nor merely sociological. But his choice of a candidate for such an intermediate notion is very revealing. He says that what lies behind the intuitive association of representationality with convergence is "the Convergence/ Representation Platitude," namely:

> If two devices each function to produce representations, then if conditions are suitable, and they function properly, they will produce divergent output if and only if presented with divergent input.[41]

This so-called platitude is supposed to flesh out the intuitive difference between the cognitive and the noncognitive, and thus between discourses (e.g., physics) for which realism is appropriate and others (e.g., argument about what's funny) for which it is not. Wright says that in the latter example "the base – the sense of humor – may blamelessly vary from person to person." But when it comes to reporting on the colors and shapes of middle-sized pieces of dry goods, or to astronomical theory, we can blame people for not getting them right, not representing accurately, not living up to their cognitive responsibilities, not corresponding to reality.

One might think, however, that blamability itself might blamelessly vary for contingent sociohistorical reasons. Wright sees this point and grasps the nettle. Metaphysical questions, such as those about the cognitive status of a discourse, can, he says, be settled only a priori. He boldly offers the following definition:

> A discourse exhibits Cognitive Command if and only if it is a priori that differences of opinion arising within it can be satisfactorily explained only in terms of 'divergent input'; that is, the disputant's working on the basis of different information (and hence guilty of ignorance or error, depending on the status of that information) or 'unsuitable conditions' (resulting in inattention or distraction and so in inferential error, or oversight of data and so on) or 'malfunction' (for example, prejudicial assessment of data, upwards or downwards, or dogma, or failing in other categories already listed).[42]

41 Ibid., 91.   42 Ibid., 93.

One might paraphrase this definition by saying that you are under Cognitive Command if you are functioning as a well-oiled representation machine. The picture Wright is using is the one used by all epistemologists who think of "prejudice" and "superstition" as sand in the wheels, the sort of foreign ingredient that causes malfunctions. Such philosophers share a picture of human beings as machines constructed (by God or Evolution) to, among other things, get things right. Pragmatists want our culture to get rid of that self-image and to replace it with a picture of machines that continually adjust to each other's behavior, and to their environment, by developing novel kinds of behavior. These machines have no fixed program or function; they continually reprogram themselves so as to serve hitherto undreamt-of functions.

Wright's so-called platitude suggests that pragmatists should do to him what he did to Wiggins. We should say that representation drops out for the same reasons convergence did. When we drop both notions, what we are left with is their common cash value: the claim that it is a demarcating mark of the appropriateness of realism for a given discourse that a certain picture be applicable to that discourse: the picture of truth as the output of a well-functioning machine that incarnates an a priori knowable input–output function. Notice that it is not enough for Wright's purposes if we merely know a priori that some input–output function or other is at work and that failure of the machine to operate in accord with this function is a malfunction. That requirement will be uninterestingly satisfied by indefinitely many functions, and equally uninterestingly unsatisfied by equally many others. What Wright requires is that we should know a priori which of these functions is the *right* one – that our knowledge of the *content* of the output (for example, the comic, the geometric, the valuable) should pick out a particular function.[43]

I shall return to this last point later, when I take up Wright's response to McDowell's argument for quietism. For the time being, however, I simply note that pragmatists, particularly after reading Kuhn, discard the terms "prejudice" and "dogma," as well as the idea that before the New Science came along, with its prejudice-detecting rationality and superstition-dissolving rigor, our cognitive machinery malfunctioned.[44] Pragmatists doubt that cog-

---

43 I cannot figure out how somebody who invokes a priori knowledge as blithely as Wright does can say, equally blithely, that "apriority generally is an artifact of description" (ibid., 129).

44 Wright has read Kuhn too, of course, and discusses "theory-ladenness" in some detail. But the upshot of his discussion is rather disappointing: "[T]he hope must be either that we can yet win through to some purified notion of an observation statement, one that does not involve 'theory-ladenness' of the sort which is giving the trouble, or – more likely – that the Cognitive Command constraint can and must be refined in some way while remaining faith-

nitivity amounts to more than historically contingent consensus about what shall count as proper justification for a belief. They see such consensus as what distinguishes what Kuhn calls "normal science" from what he calls "revolutionary science." Whereas Wright thinks that philosophers can look at the "content" of a discourse[45] and decide the a priori question of whether it is apt for Cognitive Command, pragmatists see the aptness or inaptness of Wright's "representation machine" terminology as up for historicosociological grabs – as much up for such grabs as the aptness or inaptness of religious language for describing the human situation.

Pragmatists think that Wright's "Consensus/Representation Platitude" can be made plausible only if one specifies that the two devices in question were machines for representing something *according to the same conventions*. For wildly different outputs can count as representations of the same input, depending on the purpose that the representational machinery serves. A videotape, an audiotape, and a typed transcript represent the same press conference. Anything, indeed, can count as a representation of anything, if there is enough antecedent agreement that it will count as such. More generally, representationality, and thus cognitivity, is something we can create, if not exactly at will, at least by agreement.

Content, pragmatists say on the basis of this argument, counts for vanishingly little in determining cognitivity, and de facto agreement on conventions for everything. That is why pragmatists think cognitivity a purely empirical, historicosociological notion. But if conventions of representation

---

ful to its motivation in the idea of representational function. I have no easy solution to suggest" (167–8).

    This passage is typical of Wright's hope to smooth over the anomalies that arise from attempts to make explicit the presuppositions of traditional, intuitive distinctions. Pragmatists rejoice in no longer needing to invoke those distinctions or to have those intuitions. So what looks like undesirable quietism to Wright looks like vigorous philosophical progress to them. This is the same sort of dialectical standoff that obtained between Leibniz and Newton. Newton shrugged off, quietistically, many traditional Aristotelian problems. Leibniz insisted that such shrugs were symptoms of intellectual irresponsibility and that metaphysical, as well as physical, explanations were required.

45 "If our interest is in the question whether comic discourse, *by virtue of its very content*, is fitted to express the products of a seriously representational mode of function, then any constraint designed to capture that idea must, it seems, be so formulated that satisfying it requires the possibility of a priori knowledge that the relevant conditions are met" (ibid., 94). In Wright's usage, it seems to me, the concepts "content of a discourse" and "a priori knowledge about that discourse" are mutually definable. For the only way one would know whether one had zeroed in on the content of a discourse, as opposed to the mechanisms of its production, would be to figure out what could be known about that discourse a priori. For Quinean holists like Davidson, of course, these mutually definable concepts are equally dubious.

can vary as blamelessly as sense of humor – or, more to the point, if the only relevant sort of blame is the sort that attaches to those who are insufficiently cooperative in achieving shared practical goals – then representationality, like convergence, is a broken reed. It is of no help in pinning down the nature of cognitivity or in offering a seriously dyadic account of truth.

How destructive to his overall program is this objection to Wright's putative platitude? I think the best way to find out is to turn to the only place in his book where Wright explicitly argues against quietism – his final chapter. For there he discusses a notion, "meaning," which is close kin to that of "convention of representation." The only argument in favor of quietism that he discusses is Wittgenstein's "rule-following argument."

Wright agrees with Gareth Evans that this argument is a "metaphysical wet blanket," to be tossed off if at all possible. For Wright, the *only* concession to the quietist that need be made is the one made in his first chapter: that truth and falsity can be had even where realism is out of the question (as it certainly is in the case of comedy and may be in the case of morals).[46] He considers two brands of wet Wittgensteinian blanket: McDowell's and Kripke's. For McDowell, Wright says, the moral noncognivitist is "driven by a misbegotten construal of *ethical* fact and objectivity"; like her Platonist, moral realist opponent, she labors

> under the misapprehension that anything worth regarding as moral cogni-
> tivism has to make out how the relevant subject matter is *there*, so to speak, for
> any enquiring agent, independently of an evaluative 'point of view'. Since, as
> Wittgenstein teaches us, no subject matter is ever 'there' in that kind of way,
> no disadvantageous comparison remains to be made. The appreciation of
> moral fact requires, to be sure, a moral point of view. But then, the apprecia-
> tion of *any* fact requires a point of view.[47]

Wright rejects this attempt to undermine "realist/anti-realist debate in general."[48] He thinks that one great advantage of his notion of Cognitive Command is that it involves no "hyper-objectified conception of fact" of the sort Wittgenstein and McDowell criticize. For "the question whether it is a priori that differences of opinion formulable within a particular discourse will, prescinding from vagueness, always involve something worth regarding as a

---

46 ". . . quietism makes at least one important contribution, viz., the insight that it is a meta-
    physical hypostasis of notions like truth and assertion to write their applicability within a
    discourse into the substance of a realist view about its subject matter" (ibid., 204).
47 Ibid., 207.   48 Ibid., 208.

cognitive shortcoming" is to be settled "by reference to what we conceive as the range of possible sources of such differences."[49]

This, however, is not a sufficient reply to McDowell. For to have a conception of the range of possible sources of such differences, we first need to specify an input–output function; without that, we will not be able to distinguish the smooth functioning of a representation machine from its malfunction. But many input–output functions will describe the machine, and not all these functions will range over the same inputs. There are many ways to classify the flux of causal interactions in which the statement maker is involved, and each will offer a new candidate for "input." The problem of whether Wittgenstein has in fact shown that the relevant subject matter is never "there" in the relevant sense is the problem of whether there is a way to isolate input without reference to what Wright calls "an evaluative point of view." This is the sixty-four-dollar question: whether we can (as Dewey and Davidson insist we cannot) separate out "the world's" contribution to the judgment-forming process from our own.

Wright has no doubts about the existence of isolable truth makers. At one point, for example, he says that

> the world's making such statements [those that are what he calls "superassertible"] likely is something conceptually quite independent of our standards of appraisal – something, as it were, which is wholly between the statement and its truth maker, and on which we impinge only in an (at most) detective role.[50]

But how are we suppposed to separate out these truth makers from the flux of causal interactions in which the statement maker is involved? One of Davidson's reasons for having no truck with the idea of "truth makers"[51] is his hunch that only completely artificial objects called "facts" – what Strawson sneeringly called "sentence-shaped objects" – can meet Wright's needs.

---

49 Ibid., 208.
50 Ibid., 77. Elsewhere Wright speaks of "the kind of state of affairs conferring truth on P" (117). The homiletic tone of "between the statement and its truth-maker" recurs when Wright says that "where we deal in a purely cognitive way with objective matters, the opinions which we form are in no sense optional or variable as a function of permissible idiosyncrasy, but are *commanded* of us" (146). Contrast the *libertinisme erudit* implicit in the concluding words of Davidson's "Structure": ". . . truth thus rests in the end on belief and, even more ultimately, on the affective attitudes" (326).
51 See Davidson, *Inquiries into Truth*, 194, for his rejection of the idea of "truth makers." See also, in the same volume, his 1969 essay "True to the Facts," which contrasts the Tarskian notion of a sentence being satisfied by objects that can be individuated without the use of the sentence with that of "a sentence being made true by a fact." Since writing that essay, however, Davidson has dropped the claim that the former notion gives us any sort of correspondence account of truth.

The problem is not with funny, Platonic, "hyper-objectivized" facts, but with *any* sentence-shaped nonsentence, any putatively (in McDowell's words) "nonconceptualized configurations of things in themselves." Insofar as they are nonconceptualized, they are not isolable as input. But insofar as they are conceptualized, they have been tailored to the needs of a *particular* input–output function, a *particular* convention of representation.[52]

That any causal transaction can exemplify many different input–output functions was, of course, Wittgenstein's point when he remarked that all my previous additions could be seen as satisfying indefinitely many different rules for the use of "plus." But it is only when Wright turns from McDowell's Wittgenstein to Kripke's that he takes up this sort of difficulty explicitly. In discussing Kripke's, he considers the possibility that "the thesis that there are no 'facts of the matter' as far as rules and meanings are concerned . . . must necessarily inflate . . . into a *global* irrealism: the thesis that there are no facts of the matter anywhere." For

> if there are no substantial facts about what sentences say, there are no substantial facts about whether or not they are true. Thus, irrealism about meaning must enjoin an irrealism about truth, wherever the notion is applied. And irrealism about truth, wherever the notion is applied, is irrealism about all assertoric discourse.[53]

---

52 Wright seems to be speaking to this issue when, in a pregnant, compressed, and baffling footnote, he says that "it seems just plain obvious that the reaction-dependence of rules, the ceaseless involvement of our sub-cognitive natures in our step-by-step appreciation of the requirements of rules which Wittgenstein emphasizes, cannot be at ease with the mythology of the epistemically transparent yet fully substantial propositional object" (226). He suggests that the moral to be drawn from Wittgenstein may be that "something irreducibly *human and subcognitive* actively contributes to our engagement with any issue at all – a contribution . . . presumed shared among thinkers who engage the issue in question" (227). If that is what Wittgenstein told us, he chose a remarkably roundabout way of saying that we can presume that our interlocutors' bodies respond to the environment pretty much as ours do. One difference between Wright and Davidson is that Davidson would, I think, see no point in distinguishing between a cognitive nature or level and a noncognitive nature or level, for the same reasons he sees none in distinguishing between scheme and content, or between subject and object, or between "knowing a language and knowing our way around the world generally" ("A Nice Derangement of Epitaphs," in *Truth and Interpretation*, ed. LePore, 445–6). From his point of view, such distinctions hypostatize two descriptions, one in propositional and one in nonpropositional terms, of the same events.

I confess, however, that Davidson's attachment to the doctrine of the indeterminacy of translation, and his related insistence that there is a philosophically interesting difference between the intentional and the nonintentional, suggests that he qualifies the thoroughgoing antidualism I am attributing to him here. I discuss this attachment in "Davidson's Mental–Physical Distinction," forthcoming in *The Philosophy of Donald Davidson*, ed. Lewis Hahn, The Library of Living Philosophers (La Salle, Ill.: Open Court).

53 Wright, *Truth and Objectivity*, 211.

On this account of what Wittgenstein was up to, the problem is not, as with McDowell's Wittgenstein, that the indefinite plurality of rules (or conventions of representations, or input–output functions) makes it impossible to draw an interesting representational–nonrepresentational line between discourses, but that we have (by some criterion of nonrepresentationality that remains obscure) discovered that there is no such thing as getting meanings right, no such thing as representing meanings accurately.

Wright has an answer to this suggestion, one that I found very hard to follow and will not try to summarize.[54] But it seems clear that this suggestion is not the interesting one. For the interesting question about quietism, the one to which Wright's final chapter is devoted, is whether the whole terminology of "getting right" and "representing accurately" is a useful way of separating off discourses from one another. This question, raised by McDowell's Wittgenstein, is begged by Kripke's.

Wright seems to recognize this point, for in the penultimate paragraph of his book, he grants that there is a "residual concern" to which he has not spoken. The following is his final formulation of this concern:

> [W]hether, even if the key distinctions [between representational, cognitive, substantive truth, and the other, merely minimalist sort of truth] can be formulated in ways that allow the status of a discourse to be determined independently of the rule-following dialectic, their serviceability as vehicles for the expression of realist intuition may not be so severely compromised by a proper understanding of that dialectic that there is no longer any *point* to the taxonomy which they might enable us to construct?[55]

Raising this doubt – a doubt about whether there was a point to the book we have just finished reading – on the book's last page seems to me a very honest, and rather brave, thing to do.

Wright's response to this doubt, in his final paragraph, is that though there may be a case to be made for the view that there is no point, his book has helped set the terms for debating any such case by giving us "a more pluralistic and fine-grained conception of the realist/anti-realist debates than has been commonplace."[56] It has indeed given us such a conception, but the increased fineness of grain may not serve the purpose Wright suggests. For what looks like desirable fineness of grain to Wright looks like the pointless addition of further epicycles to his pragmatist opponents.

Wright's suggestion – which, though I have scanted it for my purposes in this essay, is at the heart of his book – is that there are different truth

54 See ibid., 227.   55 Ibid., 229–30.   56 Ibid., 230.

predicates for different discourses. He argues that we should use a min-imalist, thin truth predicate in discourse about the comic, and various thicker alternatives (such as Cognitive Command), correlated with various a priori determinable relations between other discourses and the rest of the world, for other discourses.[57] But of course for pragmatists, what Wright thinks of as permanent a priori determinable relations are just local and transitory historicosociological differences between patterns of justification and blame. These differences – subpatterns within the single overall pattern justification makes – should not, pragmatists think, be imported into the concept of truth. To do so is to do what Davidson calls "humanizing truth by making it basically epistemic."[58]

Much of what I have said can be summed up in the claim that the central is-sue between Wright's metaphysical activism and Davidson's quietism con-cerns the point of inquiry. For Wright truth, considered as a desirable non-causal relation between language and nonlanguage, is a goal of such inquiry (if only in those areas of culture, such as physical science, for which "real-ism" is thought appropriate). For Davidsonians, on the other hand, the most consistent position is to hold that

(a) the arguments from the indefinite plurality of ways of going on/input–output functions/conventions of representations leave no room for any such desirable noncausal relation,
(b) so there is no reason to think that even an infinite amount of justifica-tion would get us closer to such a relation,
(c) so there is nothing that can plausibly be described as a *goal* of inquiry, although the desire for further justification, of course, serves as a *motive* of inquiry.

If Dewey and Davidson were asked, "What is the goal of inquiry?" the best either could say would be that it has many different goals, none of which have any metaphysical presuppositions – for example, getting what we want, the improvement of man's estate, convincing as many audiences as possible,

---

57 "There are a *variety* of features that may be possessed by minimally truth-apt discourses, any of which may contribute in some measure towards clarifying and substantiating realist preconceptions about it. . . . A basic realism about a discourse (of course, the epithets "re-alism" and "anti-realism" come to seem less and less happy from a pluralistic perspective) would be the view that it is qualified by *no* interesting feature serving to give point to an in-tuitive realism about it – that it deploys minimally truth-apt contents, and that's the whole of the matter" (ibid., 141–2).
58 Davidson, "Structure," 298.

solving as many problems as possible. *Only* if we concede to Wright that "truth" is the name of a distinct norm will metaphysical activism seem desirable. For Dewey and Davidson, that is an excellent reason not to view it as such a norm.

Some Davidsonians might see no reason why they too should not say, ringingly, robustly, and commonsensically, that the goal of inquiry is *truth*. But they cannot say this without misleading the public. For when they go on to add that they are, of course, not saying that the goal of inquiry is correspondence to the intrinsic nature of things, the common sense of the vulgar will feel betrayed.[59] For "truth" sounds like the name of a goal only if it is thought to name a *fixed* goal – that is, if progress toward truth is explicated by reference to a metaphysical picture, that of getting closer to what Bernard Williams calls "what is there *anyway*." Without that picture, to say that truth is our goal is merely to say something like: we hope to justify our belief to as many and as large audiences as possible. But to say that is to offer only an ever-retreating goal, one that fades forever and forever when we move. It is not what common sense would call a goal. For it is neither something we might realize we had reached, nor something to which we might get closer.

We pragmatists think that philosophers who view the defense of "our realistic intuitions" as an important cultural or moral imperative are held captive by the picture of getting closer to a fixed goal. As an initial step in breaking free of this picture, we suggest following Davidson in abandoning what he calls "standard ideas of language mastery." Then one will think of such mastery as involving "no learnable common core of consistent behavior, no shared grammar or rules, no portable interpreting machine set to grind out the meaning of an arbitrary utterance.[60] Dropping these standard ideas makes it very difficult to take seriously the idea of human beings

---

59 For a good example of the outrage that results from such betrayal see John Searle, "Rationality and Realism: What Is at Stake?" *Daedalus* 122, no. 4 (1993), 55–83. Searle believes that there are ways of getting around the traditional problems with the notion that truth is accuracy of representation (65–6) and that those of us (he mentions Kuhn and Derrida, as well as myself) who think these problems insoluble are, by departing from what he calls the "Western Rationalistic Tradition," endangering the universities. I reply to Searle's article later in this volume in "John Searle on Realism and Relativism."

60 Davidson, "A Nice Derangement," 445. Dropping these ideas also makes it very difficult to get excited about Wittgenstein's rule-following argument. For freedom from these ideas permits one to see it as simply a version (adapted to the needs of those who still take the notion of "rules of language" seriously) of a generic argument against the existence of any relation that is both natural (i.e., not simply a product of contingent human practices) and noncausal. That is the sort of relation which representationalists are constantly invoking: For the Sellarsian version of this argument, see Brandom, *Making It Explicit*, and my "Robert Brandom on Social Practices and Representations," in this volume.

as portable representing machines that incorporate a priori knowable in-put–output functions.

The idea of such a machine lies behind both Wright's notion of Cogni-tive Command and his Kripkean suggestion that language, meaning, truth, and knowledge might all collapse together if, *horribile dictu,* it should turn out that there is no fact of the matter about what we have been meaning by "addition." But the skepticism described by Kripke's Wittgenstein holds no terrors for those who follow Davidson in abandoning the whole idea of "rules of language." Analogously, skepticism about an a priori recognizable attribute of discourses called cognitivity or representationality, and about the utility of the notions of cognitivity and representationality, holds no ter-rors for those who, like Bacon, Dewey, and Kuhn, see artisans and natural scientists as doing the same kind of thing: employing whatever propositional or nonpropositional tools they think may help with the problems currently before them.[61]

If, as good Darwinians, we want to introduce as few discontinuities as pos-sible into the story of how we got from the apes to the Enlightenment, we shall reject the idea that Nature has settled on a single input–output func-tion that, incarnated in each member of our species, enables us to represent our environment accurately. For that idea requires that Nature herself has divided up the causal swirl surrounding these organisms into discrete inputs and has adopted a particular input–output function as distinctively hers – a function whose detection enables us to offer justification according to Na-ture's own criteria (or, as Wright would say, Commands) rather than to those of transitory and local audiences. So, for Darwinians, there is an obvious ad-vantage in *not* dividing the activities of these organisms into the cognitive, representational ones and the others. This means that there is an obvious advantage in dropping the idea of a distinct goal or norm called "truth" – the goal of scientific inquiry, but not, for example, of carpentry. On a

---

61 Kuhn summed up his claim that science should be thought of as problem solving by saying, "[W]hether or not individual practitioners are aware of it, they are trained to and rewarded for solving intricate puzzles – be they instrumental, theoretical, logical or mathematical – at the interface between their phenomenal world and their community's beliefs about it" ("Afterwords," in *World Changes: Thomas Kuhn and the Nature of Science,* ed. Paul Horwich (Cambridge, Mass.: MIT Press, 1993), 338). Like Dewey, Kuhn thought that a historico-sociological account of the origin of these interfaces and these puzzles can replace a meta-physical account of the nature of representation. "I aim," he says, "to deny all meaning to claims that successive scientific beliefs become more and more probable or better and bet-ter approximations to the truth and simultaneously to suggest that the subject of truth claims cannot be a relation between beliefs and a putatively mind-independent or 'exter-nal' world" (ibid., 330).

Deweyan view, the difference between the carpenter and the scientist is simply the difference between a workman who justifies his actions mainly by reference to the movements of matter and one who justifies his mainly by reference to the behavior of his colleagues.

In previous essays – in particular one called "Science as Solidarity"[62] – I have urged that the romance and the idealistic hopes that have traditionally been elaborated in a rhetoric of "the pursuit of objective truth" can be equally well elaborated in a rhetoric of social solidarity – a rhetoric that romanticizes the pursuit of intersubjective, unforced agreement among larger and larger groups of interlocutors. But I agree with those who insist that the former rhetoric is that of contemporary common sense. So I think that pragmatism should not claim to be a commonsensical philosophy. Nor should it appeal, as David Lewis suggests metaphysics must appeal, to intuition as final arbiter.

If contemporary intuitions are to decide the matter, "realism" and representationalism will always win, and the pragmatists' quietism will seem intellectually irresponsible. So pragmatists should not submit to their judgment. Instead, they should see themselves as working at the interface between the common sense of their community, a common sense much influenced by Greek metaphysics and by monotheism, and the startlingly counterintuitive self-image sketched by Darwin, and partially filled in by Dewey. They should see themselves as involved in a long-term attempt to change the rhetoric, the common sense, and the self-image of their community.

The pragmatist who says, "The difference between justification and truth makes no difference, except for the reminder that justification to one audience is not justification to another" – the claim I put in her mouth at the beginning of this essay – has not yet said enough. For there is another difference: justification does not call for metaphysical activism but truth, as understood by contemporary, representationalist common sense, does. The pragmatist regrets the prevalence of this representationalist picture and of the "realist" intuitions that go with it, but she cannot get rid of these unfortunate cultural facts by more refined analyses of contemporary common sense. She cannot appeal to neutral premises or to widely shared beliefs.

She is in the same situation as are atheists in overwhelmingly religious cultures. Such people can only hope to trace the outlines of what Shelley calls "the gigantic shadows which futurity casts upon the present." They foresee a time when the notions of Divine Will and of Cognitive Command will, for

---

62 Included in my *Objectivity, Relativism, and Truth.*

similar reasons, have been replaced by that of a Free Consensus of Inquirers. But, in the meantime, the pragmatist who urges our culture to abandon
metaphysical activism cannot argue that such activism is inconsistent with a
mass of our other beliefs, any more than ancient Greek atheists could say
that sacrificing to the Olympians was inconsistent with a mass of other Greek
beliefs. All the pragmatist can do is the sort of thing they did: she can point
to the seeming futility of metaphysical activity, as they pointed to the seeming futility of religious activity.

In the end, we pragmatists have no real arguments against the intuitions
to which books like Wright's *Truth and Objectivity* appeal. All we have are
rhetorical questions like: Are all those epicycles really worth the trouble?
What good do the intuitions you painstakingly salvage do us? What practical difference do they make?[63] But such rhetorical questions have been instruments of sociocultural change in the past, and may be again.

---

63 Putnam thinks we have more, namely demonstrations of the incoherence of nonpragmatic
positions. In *Words and Life* (Cambridge, Mass.: Harvard University Press, 1994) he explains
"incoherence" as the fact that "attempts at a clear formulation of the [metaphysical realist]
position never succeed – because there is no real content there to be captured" (303). I
think that clarity is a matter of familiarity rather than a property whose presence or absence
can be demonstrated, and that Wright, Bernard Williams, and others find clear as the noon-
day sun what Putnam finds irremediably unclear. So I prefer to talk of lack of convenience
rather than lack of clarity. James Conant discusses the metaphilosophical issue between Putnam and myself in his introduction to *Words and Life* (xxx–xxxi).

2

HILARY PUTNAM AND
THE RELATIVIST MENACE

In his *Realism with a Human Face,* Hilary Putnam says that he is "often asked just where I disagree with Rorty."[1] I am often asked the converse question. People ask us these questions because Putnam and I agree on a number of points that a lot of other philosophers do not accept.

For example, I wholeheartedly agree with what Putnam says in the following passages:

(I) ". . . elements of what we call 'language' or 'mind' *penetrate so deeply into what we call 'reality' that the very project of representing ourselves as being 'mappers' of something 'language-independent' is fatally compromised from the start.* Like Relativism, but in a different way, Realism is an impossible attempt to view the world from Nowhere."[2]

(II) "[We should] accept the position we are fated to occupy in any case, the position of beings who cannot have a view of the world that does not reflect our interests and values, but who are, for all that, committed to regarding some views of the world – and, for that matter, some interests and values – as better than others."[3]

(III) "What Quine called 'the indeterminacy of translation' should rather be viewed as the *'interest relativity of translation.'* . . . '[I]nterest relativity' contrasts with *absoluteness,* not with objectivity. It can be objective that an interpretation or an explanation is the correct one, *given* the interests which are relevant in the context."[4]

(IV) "The heart of pragmatism, it seems to me – of James' and Dewey's

1 Hilary Putnam, *Realism with a Human Face* (Cambridge, Mass.: Harvard University Press, 1990), 20.
2 Ibid., 28. 3 Ibid., 178. 4 Ibid., 210.

pragmatism, if not of Peirce's – was the insistence on the supremacy of the agent point of view. If we find that we must take a certain point of view, use a certain 'conceptual system', when we are engaged in practical activity, in the widest sense of 'practical activity', then we must not simultaneously advance the claim that it is not really 'the way things are in themselves'."[5]

(V) "To say, as [Bernard] Williams sometimes does, that convergence to one big picture is required by the very concept of knowledge is sheer dogmatism. . . . It is, indeed, the case that ethical knowledge cannot claim absoluteness; but that is because the notion of absoluteness is incoherent."[6]

Since we agree on all this, I have long been puzzled about what keeps us apart – and in particular about why Putnam thinks of me as a "cultural relativist."[7] I am grateful to Putnam for taking up this question explicitly in the pages of *Realism with a Human Face*. He begins as follows:

> For Rorty, as for the French thinkers whom he admires, two ideas seem gripping. (1) The failure of our philosophical 'foundations' is a failure of the whole culture, and accepting that we were wrong in wanting or thinking that we could have a foundation requires us to be *philosophical revisionists*. By this I mean that, for Rorty or Foucault or Derrida, the failure of foundationalism makes a difference to how we are allowed to talk in ordinary life – a difference as to whether and when we are allowed to use words like 'know', 'objective', 'fact', and 'reason'. The picture is that philosophy was not a reflection *on* the culture, a reflection some of whose ambitious projects failed, but a *basis*, a sort of pedestal, on which the culture rested, and which has been abruptly yanked out. Under the pretense that philosophy is no longer 'serious' there lies hidden a gigantic seriousness. If I am right, Rorty hopes to be a doctor to the modern soul.[8]

I do not think that I have ever written anything suggesting that I wish to alter ordinary ways of using "know," "objective," "fact," and "reason." Like Berkeley, James, Putnam, and most other paradox-mongering philosophers (except maybe Korzybski),[9] I have urged that we continue to speak with the vulgar while offering a philosophical gloss on this speech which is different from that offered by the Realist tradition.[10] I have written at tedious

---

5 Hilary Putnam, *The Many Faces of Realism* (La Salle, Ill.: Open Court, 1987), 83.

6 Putnam, *Realism with a Human Face*, 171.

7 For Putnam's use of this term, see his "Why Reason Can't Be Naturalized," reprinted in his *Realism and Reason* (Cambridge University Press, 1983), 229–47.

8 Ibid., 19–20.   9 On Korzybski, see ibid., 120.

10 This suggestion does not conflict with (IV) above. The distinction between the vulgar and the philosophical ways of speaking is not an appearance–reality distinction, but a distinction between contexts in which a word is used. Contexts are individuated by the questions regarded as relevant in regard to statements made using the word. Some questions about the sun's motion are asked by astrophysicists but not by people admiring dawns or sunsets; some questions about truth are asked in philosophy but are not asked in the marketplace.

length *against* the idea that philosophy has been a pedestal on which our culture rests. In particular, I have complained over and over again about Heidegger's and Derrida's overestimation of the cultural importance of philosophy.[11] So on this first point I think Putnam is just wrong about what I say.

It seems to me that my writings evince no more and no less a desire to be a doctor to the modern soul than do Putnam's own. Both of us think that getting rid of the idea of "the view from Nowhere" – the idea of a sort of knowing that has nothing to do with agency, values, or interests – might have considerable cultural importance. It would probably not change our day-to-day ways of speaking, but it might well, in the long run, make some practical differences. For changes of opinion among philosophical professors sometimes do, after a time, make a difference to the hopes and fears of non-philosophers.

The second idea that Putnam says I find gripping, one that reveals what he calls my "analytic past," is evinced by the fact that

> when he [Rorty] rejects a philosophical controversy, as for example, he rejects the "realism/antirealism" controversy, or the "emotive/cognitive" controversy, his rejection is expressed in a Carnapian tone of voice – he *scorns* the controversy.[12]

Here I think Putnam has a good point. There *is* a tone of Carnapian scorn in some of my writings (particularly in the overly fervent physicalism of *Philosophy and the Mirror of Nature*),[13] and there should not be. I should not speak, as I sometimes have, of "pseudo-problems," but rather of problematics and vocabularies which might have proven to be of value but in fact did not. I should not have spoken of "unreal" or "confused" philosophical distinctions, but rather of distinctions whose employment has proved to lead nowhere, proved to be more trouble than they were worth. For pragmatists, the question should always be "What use is it?" rather than "Is it real?" Criticism of other philosophers' distinctions and problematics should charge relative inutility rather than "meaninglessness" or "illusion" or "incoherence."

On the other hand, I think that Putnam goes too far when he follows

---

11 See, especially, the closing pages of "Philosophy as Science, as Metaphor and as Politics," a lecture given in 1985, and of "Deconstruction and Circumvention," published in *Critical Inquiry* in 1984. Both are reprinted in my *Essays on Heidegger and Others* (Cambridge University Press, 1991); see esp. 21–6, 104–6.

12 Putnam, *Realism with a Human Face*, 20.

13 Richard Rorty, *Philosophy and the Mirror of Nature* (Princeton, N.J.: Princeton University Press, 1980).

Stanley Cavell in saying that "the illusions that philosophy spins are illusions that belong to the nature of human life itself."[14] This notion, common to Cavell and Derrida, appears prominently in James Conant's long, helpful introduction to *Realism with a Human Face*. Conant says, for example:

> [U]nless one carefully examines the character of a given philosophical position's seductiveness to those who are attracted to it, as well as the character of the disappointment it provokes in those who reject it – what allows for it to appear initially so innocent and yet the implications of its failure so precipitous – one's gesture of rejecting the picture will inevitably represent a further form of participation in it and victimization by it.[15]

I do not see how Putnam, Cavell, or Conant could tell whether, for example, the distinction between "our experience" and "the external world," or what Davidson calls the "scheme–content distinction," is among "the illusions that belong to the nature of human life itself" or is as ephemeral as the distinction between the superlunary quintessence and the four sublunary elements has proved to be (or as I hope the distinction between the divine and the human may prove to be). The *nature* of human life? Everywhere and always? For all the ages to come? Surely not. Talk about *the* nature of human life does not fit in well with the pragmatism sketched in (I)–(V) above, or with Putnam's view (cited later) that "our norms and standards of warranted assertibility . . . evolve in time." As these norms and standards evolve, so does our notion of what constitutes a live philosophical option, as well our sense of the difference between such options and futile, "scholastic" quibbles.

When Conant speaks of the "inevitability" of participation and victimization, he draws on an analogy between philosophical therapy and psychoanalysis – an analogy that turns on the notion of "the return of the repressed" and that both Cavell and Derrida have developed in detail. The idea is that it is terribly difficult, and probably impossible, to avoid "complicity" with phallogocentrism (Derrida) or skepticism (Cavell) or some other theme of the philosophical tradition. These are supposed to be as hard to wriggle out from as are one's childhood myths about one's parents.

This analogy strikes me as a symptom of professional deformation – of the same urge to exalt the importance of the topics listed in the Philosophy 101 syllabus as is evinced by the suggestion that philosophy has been the

14 Putnam, *Realism with a Human Face*, 20.
15 Ibid., lv.

pedestal on which culture rests.[16] Cavell and Derrida of course, *might* be right: maybe these philosophical themes *will* always creep back in disguise, maybe they *are* ineradicable kinks, maybe they *will* always hunt us down the arches of the years. But we shall never find out whether he is right unless we do our level best to escape them, to forget them actively by getting involved with new themes, and by talking in ways that make it hard for those old themes to come up.[17] Questions of whether we are unconsciously participating in, and being victimized by, the old, or instead have succeeded in making it new, should, I think, be referred to future intellectual historians.[18] There is not much point in speculating about these questions now.

So much for my doubts that Putnam, in his description of these two ideas, gets at the underlying difference between us. But before leaving those ideas, let me offer a preliminary suggestion about what this underlying difference is. This suggestion has to do with the fervent physicalism that he and I once shared and of which, as he rightly says, I still retain a trace.

What I retain is the conviction that Darwinism provides a useful vocabulary in which to formulate the pragmatist position Putnam and I share, the position summarized in (I)–(V) above. By "Darwinism" I mean a story about

16 There is a difference between hoping for the end of Philosophy 101 and hoping for the end of philosophy. I am still thought of (as by Putnam, ibid., 19) as recommending "the end of philosophy," despite my explicit rejection of this label on the last page of *Philosophy and the Mirror of Nature* and my attempts in subsequent writings to scrape it off. Perhaps it may clarify matters if I say that I hope that people will never stop reading, e.g., Plato, Aristotle, Kant, and Hegel, but also hope that they will, sooner or later, stop trying to sucker freshmen into taking an interest in the Problem of the External World and the Problem of Other Minds.

17 Conant, in his gloss on Putnam's remarks about my Carnapian scorn, says that my "overwhelming emotion, when faced with the traditional problems of philosophy, is one of impatience – a desire to get on to something more fruitful" (li) and that "Rorty's recommendation appears to be that one should leave the fly in the fly-bottle and get on with something more interesting." Conant here gets me exactly right. Despite my regret for my tone of Carnapian scorn, I have no apology to make for my impatience. For some examples of this impatience, see my remarks in the introduction to *Objectivity, Relativism, and Truth* (Cambridge University Press, 1991), 2, 12, about the cultural lag evidenced by British and U.S. philosophers' continued attention to issues about realism and antirealism. I am impatient to see what culture will look like when these issues come to seem as obsolete as do controversies about the nature of the elements of the Eucharist. One thing I like about contemporary "Continental" philosophy is that our colleagues beyond the Channel seem to be glimpsing such a culture.

18 For an example of the sort of debate among intellectual historians I have in mind, see Hans Blumenberg's criticisms of Karl Löwith's claim that the problems of contemporary secular culture are simply the return of repressed theological problems (in Blumenberg's *The Legitimacy of the Modern Age*, trans. Robert Wallace [Cambridge, Mass.: MIT Press, 1983]).

humans as animals with special organs and abilities (e.g., certain features of the human throat, hand, and brain that let humans coordinate their actions by batting marks and noises back and forth). According to this story, these organs and abilities have a lot to do with who we are and what we want, but have no more of a *representational* relation to an intrinsic nature of things than does the anteater's snout or the bowerbird's skill at weaving. I see Dewey as having used this story to start freeing us from representationalist notions, and I see Putnam and Davidson as continuing this Deweyan initiative.[19] I regard Putnam's continuing insistence on using the term "representation" as a mistake. I follow Davidson in thinking that "it is good to be rid of representations, and with them the correspondence theory of truth, for it is thinking that there are representations which engenders thoughts of relativism."[20]

Putnam, however, does not feel comfortable with this picture of humans-as-slightly-more-complicated-animals. It strikes him, as does physicalism, as scientistic and reductionist. But these latter epithets would apply only to someone who argued, "Because Darwin tells us how things really and truly are, it behooves us to adjust our self-image to suit." I do not wish to argue in this realist, scientistic, reductionist way. Rather, I am suggesting, in the spirit of Deweyan experimentalism, that it behooves us to give the self-image Darwin suggested to us a whirl, in the hope of having fewer philosophical problems on our hands.

The antinaturalist self-images suggested to us by, among others, Plato and Kant have served us well, but they are hard to reconcile with Darwin's account of our origins. I think Dewey was right to suggest that we should try to get along without the remnants of those earlier self-images. We should see what happens if we (in Sartre's phrase) "attempt to draw the full con-

19 Davidson, unlike Putnam, explicitly repudiates representationalism. I discuss this difference between them in my introduction to Joseph Murphy, *Pragmatism: From Peirce to Davidson* (Boulder, Colo.: Westview Press, 1990). I suggest there that Dewey's unsuccessful attempt to construct a "metaphysics of empiricism" held him back from following out the implications of his pragmatism and of his Darwinism, but that Davidson has now enabled us to drop James's and Dewey's claim to have "described experience as it really is" (as opposed to the – supposedly inaccurate – way in which Locke and Hume described it). He has done this by showing how we can eliminate the middle man ("experience") that was supposed to intervene between language and the world, and also by showing how to drop the notion of language as a medium that intervenes between "subject" and "object." This view of Davidson is developed in my "Non-Reductive Physicalism," included in *Objectivity, Relativism, and Truth*, 113–25. I discuss the relation between Darwin and Dewey at some length in my "Dewey Between Hegel and Darwin," in this volume.

20 Donald Davidson, "The Myth of the Subjective," in *Relativism: Interpretation and Confrontation*, ed. Michael Krause (Notre Dame, Ind.: Notre Dame University Press, 1989), 165–6.

clusions from a consistently atheist position," one in which such phrases as "the nature of human life" no longer distract us from the absence of a God's-eye view. We can pursue this experiment by setting aside the subject–object, scheme–content, and reality–appearance distinctions and thinking of our relation to the rest of the universe in purely causal, as opposed to repre-sentationalist, terms (the same way we think of the anteater's and the bower-bird's relation to the rest of the universe). I suspect that many of my differ-ences with Putnam come down, in the end, to his unhappiness with such a purely causal picture.[21]

After listing the two leading ideas I have already discussed, Putnam suggests that he and I have different concepts of "warrant" and that it would help if I indicated "which of the following principles . . . he [Rorty] can accept." His list of principles goes like this:

(1) In ordinary circumstances, there is usually a fact of the matter as to whether the statements people make are warranted or not.

(2) Whether a statement is warranted or not is independent of whether the majority of one's cultural peers would *say* it is warranted or unwarranted.

(3) Our norms or standards of warranted assertibility are historical prod-ucts; they evolve in time.

(4) Our norms and standards always reflect our interests and values. Our picture of intellectual flourishing is part of, and only makes sense as part of, our picture of human flourishing in general.

(5) Our norms and standards of *anything* – including warranted assert-ibilty – are capable of reform. There are better and worse norms and stan-dards.[22]

I have no trouble with (3)–(5), but Putnam says that I am "certain to dis-agree" with (1). I am not sure whether I do or not, and I am equally unsure about (2). As to (1), I certainly agree that it is usually as "objective" (in the sense of "objective" that – in (III) above – Putnam distinguishes from "ab-solute") whether or not S is warranted in asserting p as whether or not S is

21 This suspicion is confirmed by Putnam's enthusiastic reaction to John McDowell's *Mind and World* (Cambridge, Mass.: Harvard University Press, 1994). (See Putnam's Dewey Lectures, *Journal of Philosophy* 87, no. 6 [1990], 279–328.) McDowell's principal target is the David-sonian thesis that language and inquiry can be explained in terms of causal interactions with the world alone. McDowell defends a notion of "answerability to the world," which he sees as essential and which the Davidsonian view cannot accommodate. I discuss this no-tion later in this volume, in "The Very Idea of Human Answerability to the World: John McDowell's Version of Empiricism."

22 Putnam, *Realism with a Human Face,* 21.

bald. This is because I view warrant as a sociological matter, to be ascertained by observing the reception of S's statement by his peers.

But the term "matter of fact" gives me pause. Does "There is a matter of fact about . . ." just mean that we can observe the behavior of S's peers and determine whether . . .? If so, I can happily embrace (1). But it must mean something more than that, or Putnam would not be so sure that I would disagree with it. There being a fact of the matter about warranted assertibility must, for Putnam, be something *more* than our ability to figure out whether S was in a good position, given the interests and values of himself and his peers, to assert *p*.

But what more, given (I)–(V), can it be? Presumably it is whatever makes it possible for a statement not to be warranted even though a majority of one's peers say it is. *Is* that possible? Is (2) true? Well, maybe a *majority* can be wrong. But suppose everybody in the community, except for one or two dubious characters notorious for making assertions even stranger than *p*, thinks S must be a bit crazy. They think this even after patiently listening to S's defense of *p*, and after making sustained attempts to talk him out of it. Might S still be *warranted* in asserting *p*? Only if there were some way of determining warrant *sub specie aeternitatis*, some natural order of reasons that determines, quite apart from S's ability to justify *p* to those around him, whether he is *really* justified in holding *p*.[23] I do not see how one could reconcile the claim that there is this nonsociological sort of justification with (I)–(V).

Of course, *p* might be *true*. S may be the unhonored prophet of some social movement or intellectual revolution whose time has not yet come. But *warranted*? I cannot see how Putnam would support (2) except by running "warranted" together with "true" – running together a claim supported by examining the behavior of S's peers and a claim to which this behavior is irrelevant. He and I presumably agree that many (praiseworthy and blameworthy) social movements and intellectual revolutions get started by people making *un*warranted assertions, assertions that begin to get warranted only as (in Putnam's words) "our norms and standards of warranted assertibility . . . evolve."

Putnam's discussion of his five principles[24] is a bit confusing, because he switches targets, substituting "the Relativist" for me. I entirely agree with,

---

23 On the skepticism-inducing role of the belief that there is such a natural order of reasons – a pattern of justification or warranting which is that of no particular human community but is somehow nature's own – see the sustained polemic against the very idea of "context-independent relations of epistemological priority" in Michael Williams, *Unnatural Doubts: Epistemological Realism and the Basis of Scepticism* (Oxford: Blackwell, 1991).

24 See Putnam, *Realism with a Human Face*, 22.

and fervently applaud, his relativist-bashing remark: "Relativism, just as much as Realism, assumes that one can stand within one's language and outside it at the same time."[25] But I do not see how this remark is relevant to my own, explicitly ethnocentric position.[26]

Things get clearer, however, when Putnam, later on the same page, zeroes in on my claim that reforms in our standards of warranted assertibility are not "better by reference to a previously known standard, but just better in the sense that they come to seem clearly better than their predecessors."[27] He says this passage amounts "to a rejection, rather than a clarification, of the notion of 'reforming' the ways we are doing and thinking invoked in my fifth principle."[28] Putnam sees me as relativistic because I can appeal to no "fact of the matter" to adjudicate between the possible world in which the Nazis win out, inhabited by people for whom the Nazis' racism seems common sense and our egalitarian tolerance crazy, and the possible world in which we win out and the Nazis' racism seems crazy.

I cannot, indeed, appeal to such a "fact of the matter," any more than a species of animal that is in danger of losing its ecological niche to another species, and thus faces extinction, can find a "fact of the matter" to settle the question of which species has the right to the niche in question. But neither, as far as I can see, can Putnam.

The problem for Putnam is that he must both maintain his anticonvergence thesis ((V) above) and make sense of the notion of "truth as idealized rational acceptability." He has invoked the latter notion as a defense against my evil twin, "the Relativist," for years and does so again in *Realism with a Human Face*.[29] But I cannot see what "idealized rational acceptability" can mean except "rational acceptability to an ideal community." Nor can I see how,

25 Ibid., 23.
26 For the difference between relativism and ethnocentrism, see my 1984 paper "Solidarity or Objectivity?" reprinted in *Objectivity, Relativism, and Truth*, 21–34. See esp. ". . . there is no truth in relativism, but this much truth in ethnocentrism: we cannot justify our beliefs (in physics, ethics, or any other area) to everybody, but only to those whose beliefs overlap ours to some appropriate extent" (30 n. 13). This essay was, in part, a reply to Putnam's criticism of my "relativism" in his *Reason, Truth, and History* (Cambridge University Press, 1981), 216. My reply was based on taking seriously Putnam's famous rhetorical question "We should use somebody *else's* conceptual scheme?"
27 This quote is from the following passage in my *Consequences of Pragmatism* (Minneapolis: University of Minnesota Press, 1982): "[The pragmatist] does think that in the process of playing vocabularies and cultures off against each other, we produce new and better ways of talking and acting – not better by reference to a previously known standard, but just better in the sense that they come to *seem* clearly better than their predecessors" (xxxvii).
28 Putnam, *Realism with a Human Face*, 23.
29 See ibid., 41.

given that no such community is going to have a God's-eye view, this ideal
community can be anything more than *us* as we should like to be. Nor can I
see what "us" can mean here except: us educated, sophisticated, tolerant, wet
liberals,[30] the people who are always willing to hear the other side, to think
out all the implications, and so on – the sort of people, in short, whom both
Putnam and I hope, at our best, to be. Identifying "idealized rational acceptability" with "acceptability to *us* at our best" is just what I had in mind
when I said that pragmatists should be ethnocentrists rather than relativists.[31]

If this is not the ideal community Putnam has in mind, then he must either propose another one or give some sense of "idealized rational acceptability" that is not acceptability to an ideal community. I cannot see any
promise in the latter alternative. The former alternative seems to leave him
with no option but to fall back on Peirce and the notion of "the community
of inquirers at the ideal end of inquiry" – the speakers of Peircish, the people whose norms and standards of warranted assertibility embody what Sellars called "CSP" (short for "Conceptual System Peirce"). But his refusal to
grant to Williams that the notion of knowledge entails that of convergence
to a single result forbids Putnam to make this Peirce-like move.[32] For once
we strip "idealized" of reference to some process built into any and every inquiry – something like Peirce's own "growth of Thirdness," something that
will guide us toward CSP along convergent lines – "idealized" adds nothing
to "rational acceptability." If there is no such guidance system built into human beings *qua* human, then the terms "warranted," "rationally acceptable,"

30 Putnam grants that I am as wet a liberal as they come, but adds that I seem, at times, "ever
    so slightly decadent" ("Liberation Philosophy," *London Review of Books* 8, no. 5 [1986], 5).
    I am here concerned to show that, as far as decadence goes, there is little to choose between
    us. Our common commitment to (I)–(IV) makes it impossible for either of us to find an
    Archimedean fulcrum. Our commitment to (V) makes it impossible to substitute a Peircean
    focus imaginarius for such a fulcrum.
31 This sort of ethnocentrism comes out in my discussion of Davidson's explication of "true"
    in terms of "language I know" and of the ineluctability of self-referential indexicals, in *Ob-
    jectivity, Relativism, and Truth*, 157–9. It comes out again when I argue that Habermas's term
    "ideal communication situation" is just an abbreviation for "the way of deciding public is-
    sues characteristic of free twentieth-century constitutional democracies, when they are at
    their rare best." See my *Contingency, Irony, and Solidarity* (Cambridge University Press, 1989),
    84, and "Habermas, Derrida and the Functions of Philosophy," this volume.
32 For details about the problems encountered by such a Peirce-like move (a move Putnam
    and I both made in our salad days), see Michael Williams, "Coherence, Justification and
    Truth," *Review of Metaphysics* 34 (1980), 243–72. I agree with Davidson that Putnam should
    apply his own "naturalistic fallacy argument" to his own definition of truth as idealized ra-
    tional acceptability. The only way this argument would not apply would be if "such as to hit
    the truth" were built into "idealized," thereby denaturalizing Putnam's definition at the cost
    of making it circular.

and so on will always invite the question "to whom?" This question will always lead us back, it seems to me, to the answer "*us,* at our best." So all "a fact of the matter about whether *p* is a warranted assertion" can mean is "a fact of the matter about our ability to feel solidarity with a community that views *p* as warranted."

Putnam says that in the possible world in which the Nazis win, "Rorty himself would not feel 'solidarity' with the culture that results." But neither would Putnam, nor the rest of the "us" just described. The presence or absence of such a sense of solidarity is, on my view, the heart of the matter. Part of the force of the Darwinian picture I am suggesting is that the spirit of Sartre's famous remark about a Nazi victory was right, though the letter is a bit off. Sartre said:

> Tomorrow, after my death, some men may decide to establish Fascism, and the others may be so cowardly or slack as to let them do so. If so Fascism will then be the truth of man, and so much the worse for us.[33]

Sartre should not have said that Fascism will be "the truth of man." There is no such thing. What he should have said is that the truth (about certain very important matters, like whom one can kill when) might be forgotten, become invisible, get lost – and so much the worse for *us.* "Us" here does not mean "us humans" (for Nazis are humans too). It means something like "us tolerant wet liberals."

So much the worse for truth too? What does that question mean? I take the force of the antiabsolutism embodied in (I)–(V) to be that it doesn't mean *anything* – that we cannot find a purpose for this additional lament. When we go, so do our norms and standards of rational assertibility. Does truth go too? Truth neither comes nor goes. That is not because it enjoys an atemporal existence, but because "truth," in this context, is just the reification of an approbative adjective, an adjective whose use is mastered once we grasp, as Putnam puts it, that "a statement is true of a situation just in case it would be correct to use the words of which the statement consists in that

---

33 Jean-Paul Sartre, "Existentialism Is a Humanism," in *Existentialism from Dostoevsky to Sartre,* ed. Walter Kaufmann (New York: New American Library, 1975), 358. I have quoted this passage in the past, leading Jeffrey Stout to remark that he usually takes it "as a sign of backsliding or an invitation to misreading when favorable references to Sartre and existentialism appear in Rorty's work" (*Ethics after Babel* [Boston: Beacon Press, 1988], 260). Stout thinks that the absence of a third thing, a neutral tribunal, to render judgment on us and the Nazis, does not imply "that there is no moral truth of the matter" (259). I agree, but Putnam does not. Putnam's argument is based on the presupposition that no third thing means no truth.

way in describing the situation."[34] Correct by whose standards? *Ours.* Who else's? The *Nazis'*?

Isn't this like the Homeric heroes (Nietzsche's "brave, strong, happy ones") denying truth to the Christians whom they might, in their nightmares, see inheriting the Mediterranean world? Isn't it like some imaginary language-using and prescient dinosaurs denying beauty to their foreseen successors, the mammals? Yes, it's *exactly* like that. The only difference is that we are right about charity being a virtue and Achilles was wrong, and we are right about our own beauty and my imaginary dinosaurs wrong. Once God and his view goes, there is just us and our view. What Sartre calls "a consistent atheism" would prevent us from inventing God surrogates like Reason, Nature, CSP, or a Matter of Fact about Warrant.

Applying what I have been saying to the phrase Putnam finds objectionable, I want to gloss "come to seem clearly better than their predecessors" as "come to seem *to us* clearly better than their predecessors." But "us" here doesn't mean "us humans – Nazis or not," any more than it means "whatever otherworlders take over the earth from humans" or "whatever nonhuman dominant species evolution next throws up to rule the earth." Rather, it means "language users whom we can recognize as better versions of ourselves."

Is this circular? That is, does "recognize them as better versions of ourselves" require recognizing them as people who still agree with us on the central issue in question (e.g., racism)? No. It means, rather: recognize them as people who have come to hold beliefs that are different from ours by a process that we, by *our present* notions of the difference between rational persuasion and force, count as rational persuasion.[35] Among the interests and values we have recently evolved into having are an interest in avoiding brainwashing and a positive valuation of literacy, liberal education, a free press, free universities, and genial tolerance of Socratic gadflies and Feyerabendian tricksters. When we picture a better version of ourselves, we build into this picture the evolution of this better version out of our present selves through a process in which actualizations of these values played an appropriate part.[36] If we did not build this process into the picture, we should not

---

34 Hilary Putnam, *Representation and Reality* (Cambridge, Mass.: MIT Press, 1988), 115.

35 The importance of "our present standards of what constitutes rational persuasion" is that we need to cover the possibility that the Nazis, or the nonhuman Galactics, have different ways of distinguishing persuasion and force than ours. It is our ways that count in deciding whether to apply the term "came to seem better" rather than, for example, "were brainwashed into."

36 Does this mean that we have to hold open the possibility that we might come to be Nazis by a process of rational persuasion? Yes. This is no more dangerous than holding open the

call the result "a version of ourselves," but something like "an unfortunate replacement for ourselves."

Putnam suggests that I am proposing a different, novel concept of "better" to replace our present concept. He says that

> *this* concept of 'coping better' is not the concept of there being *better* and *worse* norms or standards at all. . . . [I]t is internal to our picture of warrant that warrant is logically independent of the majority of our cultural peers. . . . [37]

Again, this last sentence would have been paradoxical if "the majority of" had been omitted. (Incidentally, I do not recall that I have ever, even at my worst, spoken of either warrant or truth being determined by *majority* vote.) Putting aside Quinean doubts (of the sort Putnam and I share) about notions like "internal" and "logically independent" for the moment, I claim that, as non-Quineans use these notions, they would *not* say that *warrant* (unlike truth) was independent of the opinion of our peers, any more than they would say that weight is logically independent of pressure exerted on surrounding objects.

But I shall waive this point. I shall also set aside the problem of how Putnam, who thirty years ago popularized the notion of "cluster concepts," can be so confident about the self-identity of concepts. Let me just grant that, in some suitably broad sense, I *do* want to substitute new concepts for old. I want to recommend explaining "better" (in the context "better standards of warranted assertibility") as "will come to seem better to *us*," not as a piece of "meaning-analysis," but as an answer to "What do you mean by 'better'?" which is more in accord with (I)–(V) than, for example, "closer to the way the world really is" or "closer to the way God sees it," or "closer to the facts of the matter," or "closer to idealized rational accceptability."

For the usual "naturalistic fallacy" reasons, neither these latter explications nor my preferred alternative will do as statements of necessary and sufficient conditions for a view, theory, policy, or practice being better. But once we give up the quest for such conditions – once we recognize that normative terms like "true" and "better" are not susceptible to definition – there is plenty of room for debate about which explications raise more difficulties than they solve. I see my explication of "better" (as applied to standards of warranted assertibility) in terms of "us at our best" (where "us" and "best"

---

possibility that we might revert to an Aristotelian–Ptolemaic cosmology by a process of rational persuasion. Neither possibility is very plausible, but to close off either of them is – as the ACLU keeps reminding us – part of what we mean by "intolerance."

37 Putnam, *Realism with a Human Face*, 24.

are spelled out along the lines suggested earlier) as raising fewer problems than Putnam's in terms of "idealized rational acceptability."

Putnam considers the possibility that my metaphilosophical stance might be: sure my concept is new and different, but the old feature of our old concept that you prize is a *bad* feature. His reaction to "But it is a bad feature" is to ask, "But what can 'bad' possibly mean here but 'based on a wrong metaphysical picture'? And how can a relativist speak of *right* or *wrong* metaphysical pictures?"[38] I quite agree that the relativist cannot, and that I cannot either. But why should either I, or this patsy called "the Relativist," explicate "bad" in terms of metaphysical pictures? There are all sorts of occasions on which we say that our concept of X needs to be changed and old intuitions thrown overboard, not for metaphysical reasons, but for reasons that are called, depending on context, "ethical" or "practical" or "political." Consider, for example, feminists' suggestion that we change, in initially counterintuitive ways, the concepts we use in allotting social roles, for the sake of a richer, fuller, happier nonsexist society. Or consider any other social movement that meets the objection "But what you are saying conflicts with our customary ways of thinking!" with "So what? Let's try some new ways of thinking! We might like them! Our interests and values – both old familiar interests and values and some new ones that we may not yet be quite conscious of having – may turn out to be better served by these new ways."[39]

This analogy to social movements that suggest shoving old concepts aside is my reply to an anti-Rorty argument attributed to Putnam by Bernard Williams:

> [Rorty's views] simply tear themselves apart. If, as Rorty is fond of putting it, the correct description of the world (for us) is a matter of what we find it convenient to say, and if, as Rorty admits, we find it convenient to say that science discovers a world that is already there, there is simply no perspective from which Rorty can say, as he also does, that science does not really discover a world that is already there, but (more or less) invents it.[40]

---

38 Ibid., 22.

39 My reference to interests and values of which we are not yet conscious is an invocation of Dewey's doctrine of "the means–end continuum" – the idea that you change what you want as you find out what happens when you try getting what you once wanted. Putnam and I are both enthusiastic proponents of this doctrine.

40 The quotation is from Williams's review of *Realism with a Human Face* in *London Review of Books* 13 (February 1991), 12. This passage from Williams is said by Ronald Dworkin to summarize "Hilary Putnam's devastating critique [of Rorty]." For Dworkin's additional reasons for thinking my view "philosophically a dog's dinner," see his "Pragmatism, Right Answers and True Banality," in *Pragmatism in Law and Politics*, ed. Michael Brint and William Weaver (Boulder, Colo.: Westview Press, 1991), 359–88.

Williams here, of course, runs the Goodman–Putnam claim that there is no Way the World Is together with the straw-man claim that there were no dinosaurs or atoms before we "invented" them; the latter claim is not entailed by anything in (I)–(V). But that conflation is a separate issue. I want to address, instead, the question Williams raises about convenience. It seems to me that all his point requires me to do is to distinguish between what is presently found convenient to say and what might be still more convenient to say. The convenience of the idea that there is a Way the World Is would, in a culture convinced of (I)–(V), be superseded by the still greater convenience of the idea that there is not.

The perspective from which I can say that the latter idea might be still more convenient is the familiar one of the tinkerer or the pragmatic social reformer: the person who says, "Let's see what happens if we try it this way." The metaphilosophical question about pragmatism is whether there is something other than convenience to use as a criterion in science and philosophy. Williams and (at least in the passage I am discussing) Putnam both seem to assume that the only lever that could pry us out of present convenience is something that has nothing to do with convenience – something like a "metaphysical picture." But what pries us out of present convenience is just the hope of greater convenience in the future. "Convenience" in this context means something like: ability to avoid fruitless disagreements on dead-end issues.

In short, my strategy for escaping the self-referential difficulties into which "the Relativist" keeps getting himself is to move everything over from epistemology and metaphysics to cultural politics, from claims to knowledge and appeals to self-evidence to suggestions about what we should try. This seems to me just the strategy one would want to adopt if one were a pragmatist in a sense contextually defined by (I)–(V). But Putnam does not adopt it, and I honestly do not see why he does not. At the last moment, it seems to me, he turns intuitionist. Even though he rejects, for the same reasons I should, appeals to intuition as a way of reinvigorating metaphysics (see his criticisms of Saul Kripke and David Lewis),[41] he seems quite happy with such appeals when he confutes "the Relativist."

In one passage, Putnam acknowledges the possibility that we might "behave better if we became Rortians – we may be more tolerant, less prone to fall for various varieties of religious intolerance and political totalitarianism."[42] This is exactly the possibility I have in mind. It is also, if I read Dewey

---

41 Putnam, *Realism with a Human Face*, 38–40. See also my own remarks on Lewis's notion of "elite objects" in *Objectivity, Relativism, and Truth*, 7–12.
42 Putnam, *Realism with a Human Face*, 24–5.

correctly, Dewey's pragmatic justification of pragmatism – and, specifically, of the views summarized in (I)–(V). But Putnam does not take this "political" stance seriously. He asks, "If our aim is tolerance and the open society, would it not be better to argue for these directly, rather than to hope that these will come as the by-product of a change in our metaphysical picture?" But surely I cannot, any more than Dewey, be accused of thinking that fiddling around with concepts like "fact of the matter," "better," and "rational acceptability" – doing the sort of thing we philosophy professors do – is the only, or even a principal, means of commending, or helping to bring about, tolerance and the open society. It is just one more nudge in the right direction – the sort of modest little contribution to social progress to which a somewhat peripheral academic discipline may aspire. Surely only someone who thought of philosophy as the pedestal on which culture rests would ask for more.

Putnam concludes, on what seems to me very little evidence, that it is "more likely" that,

> most of the time anyway, Rorty really thinks that metaphysical realism is *wrong*. We will be better off if we listen to him in the sense of having fewer false beliefs; but this, of course, is something he cannot admit he really thinks. I think, in short, that the attempt to say that *from a God's-Eye View there is no God's-eye view* is still there, under all that wrapping.[43]

I cannot figure out what the difference in metaphilosophical status between what I say (e.g., about "better" in the passage Putnam finds so wildly counterintuitive) and Putnam's own (I)–(V) is supposed by Putnam to be. Why is the former an attempt to give a God's-eye view and the latter not? Is Putnam painting a "metaphysical picture" when he puts forward (I)–(V)? I should have thought he was doing what he calls "criticizing accepted cultural norms and standards" by suggesting some alternative cultural norms and standards: suggesting, for example, that we clean out the last remnants of metaphysical realism from our conversational and pedagogical practices. I should have thought I was doing much the same thing.

Putnam, however, says that when I recommend a new cultural practice and claim that such a new practice is more rational, or enables us to hold more true beliefs, than its predecessors, I am using "these semantic and epistemic adjectives . . . *emotively*."[44] For, he says, when I argue that my own views "are more helpful philosophically" than the views I criticize, I am engaging in "hermeneutic discourse (which is to say, in rhetoric)." Again, I can only ask what the difference between his metaphilosophical stance and mine is

43 Ibid., 25.   44 Ibid., 24.

supposed to be. We seem, both to me and to philosophers who find the views of both of us absurd, to be in much the same line of business. But Putnam sees us as doing something quite different, and I do not know why.

So far I have been picking apart Putnam's *ipsissima verba* – a strategy that has its uses but that distracts from larger, less precise, but more important issues. So I shall conclude by returning to my earlier suggestion that what lurks in the background of Putnam's criticisms of me is his dislike of, and my enthusiasm for, a picture of human beings as just complicated animals. I can develop this suggestion by looking back to Putnam's 1983 essay "Why Reason Can't be Naturalized."

In this essay, Putnam takes as one example of "a naturalistic account of reason" the "appeal to Darwinian evolution." What he has in mind is the idea that we are constructed by evolution so as to be capable of tracking truth – that Nature has cleverly contrived an organism that represents it accurately, as opposed to merely coping with it cleverly. Putnam dismisses this idea for the same reasons ((I)–(V) again) as I would. My sense of "Darwinian" has nothing to do either with the notion of truth tracking or with that of arriving at some goal Nature has set for us.[45]

But after disposing of the evolutionary epistemologists, Putnam goes on to criticize Foucault and me as cultural relativists, people who want to reduce "better" to consensus, and thus are unable to offer rational criticism of a prevailing consensus. I will not take up the question of whether this gets Foucault or me right, but instead turn quickly to the morals Putnam draws in the final paragraphs of his essay, morals that sum up the view which results once one rejects the error common to evolutionary epistemologism and cultural relativism, to both "reductionism and historicism." Putnam says:

> Let us recognize that one of our fundamental self-conceptualizations, one of our fundamental 'self-descriptions', in Rorty's phrase, is that we are *thinkers,* and that *as* thinkers we are committed to there being *some* kind of truth, some kind of correctness which is substantial and not merely 'disquotational'. That means that there is no eliminating the normative.[46]

45 Dewey effectively criticized Spencer's doctrine that there was such a goal, in "Philosophical Work of Herbert Spencer": "Since his [Spencer's] 'environment' was but the translation of the 'nature' of the metaphysicians, its workings had a fixed origin, a fixed quality, and a fixed goal. Evolution still tends in the minds of Spencer's contemporaries to 'a single, far-off, divine event,' to a finality, a fixity" (*The Middle Works of John Dewey* [Carbondale: Southern Illinois University Press, 1977], 3: 208). In this respect, Peirce (and perhaps Bernard Williams also) can be counted among "Spencer's contemporaries."

46 Hilary Putnam, *Realism and Reason*, 246. For a criticism of Putnam's criticism of disquotational accounts of truth, and Putnam's reply to this criticism, see the exchange between us in *Philosophy and Phenomenological Research* 52, no. 2 (1992), 415–18, 431–47.

The idea of "some kind of correctness which is substantial" is the point at which I break off from Putnam. I have no use for either evolutionary epistemology or reductionism, but I think that Putnam runs together the question "Can we give necessary and sufficient conditions for the application of normative expressions?" with the question "Does our familiar use of normative expressions show that there is 'some kind of correctness which is substantial' (or that, as Putnam goes on to say, 'the rightness or wrongness of what we say is not *just* for a time and a place')?"[47]

My answer to *both* questions is no. I think that nothing about the substantiality or atemporality of correctness follows from the irreducibility of a set of expressions to one another. Further, I think that the rightness or wrongness of what we say *is* just for a time and a place. Without falling back into metaphysical realism – into the denial of one or more of propositions (I)–(V) – I cannot give any content to the idea of nonlocal correctness of assertion. If we shift from correctness and warrant to truth, then I suppose we might say, noncontroversially if pointlessly, that the *truth* of what we say is not just for a time or place. But that high-minded platitude is absolutely barren of consequences, either for our standards of warranted assertibility or for any other aspect of our practices. It is the sort of vacuity that pragmatists should avoid.

As I see it, the only aspect of our use of "true" that is captured neither by a commonsensical account of its approbative force nor by a disquotational account is what I have previously called the "cautionary" use of "true."[48] This is the use found in sentences such as "Your arguments satisfy all our contemporary norms and standards, and I can think of nothing to say against your claim, but still, what you say might not be true." I take this cautionary use to be a gesture toward future generations – toward the "better us" to

---

47 Putnam, *Realism and Reason,* 247.
48 See my "Pragmatism, Davidson and Truth," in *Objectivity, Relativism, and Truth,* 128. Davidson has recently said ("The Structure and Content of Truth," *Journal of Philosophy* [June 1990], 287–8) that I have misconstrued him as being a disquotationalist, and more generally that I and others have missed that part of "the content of the concept of truth" which is captured by T-theories. While agreeing with Davidson about the importance of theories "for describing, explaining, understanding and predicting a basic aspect of verbal behavior" (ibid., 313) – theories of the sort from which T-sentences are a fallout – I am not sure why it is important to call such theories "truth-theories," or why Davidson thinks that "the concept of truth" is central to such theories. I am unsure why Davidson thinks "truth" is more central to explanations of verbal behavior than are the other concepts ("meaning," "belief," "assent," etc.) used in formulating such explanations. I am also puzzled by Davidson's seemingly un-Quinean notion of "conceptual content" and by the un-Quinean conceptual–empirical distinction that he draws throughout his Dewey Lectures.

whom the contradictory of what now seems unobjectionable may have come, via appropriate means, to seem better. Putnam takes it as something more than that – the same mysterious "something more" as causes him to take seriously realistic talk about the presence or absence of a "matter of fact."[49]

I see no problem about the place of norms in a world of fact, since I think that the emergence of language-using organisms, and the development of norm-governed practices by those organisms, is readily explicable in Darwinian terms. This explicability, and the consequent naturalization of reason, has nothing to fear from the irreducibility of normative to descriptive sentences, any more than the utility of taking what Dennett calls "the intentional stance" toward certain organisms and machines has anything to fear from the irreducibility of intentional to nonintentional discourse (or, to use Putnam's famous example, than the utility of talking about square pegs and round holes has anything to fear from particle physics). So Putnam's claim that "reason can't be naturalized" seems to me ambiguous between an uncontroversial but inconsequential truth about irreducibility and a false claim that the Darwinian story leaves a gap in the fabric of causal explanation.

When Putnam says that "reason is both transcendent and immanent," I can agree with him. But this is because all I can mean by "transcendent" is "getting beyond our present practices by a gesture in the direction of our possibly different future practices." But this is not what Putnam means, for he takes this claim to entail that "philosophy, as culture-bound reflection and argument about eternal questions, is both in time and eternity."[50]

I see Putnam, in making this inference, as confusing the possible transcendence of the present by the future with the necessary transcendence of time by eternity. More generally, I see him as confusing our ability to use tensions within our present body of beliefs or desires to put anything (including our present norms and standards for warranted assertibility) up for grabs with our ability to achieve a rightness that is "not just for a time and a place."

This is how I would try to confirm my preliminary suggestion that what Putnam and I really disagree about is how much can be saved from the realist tradition once we affirm positions (I)–(V). Putnam thinks that these

49 The popularity of Michael Dummett's question "Is there a matter of fact about . . .?" has, alas, reinvigorated the flabby old controversy between realism and antirealism. Since I regret the survival of the controversy, I regret the popularity of the term "matter of fact." Explaining the nature of the old controversy by invoking this term seems to me a striking case of explaining the obscure by the more obscure.

50 Putnam, *Realism and Reason*, 247.

positions leave room for something like the Apel–Habermas notion of a "universal validity claim," something like the nonlocal and nontransient rightness with which religion and realist philosophy provided us. I think that these positions are of interest only insofar as they call on us to do without that notion, to experiment with what Sartre called "a consistent atheism" – with an image of ourselves (i.e., us wet liberals) as just as local and transient as any other species of animal, yet none the worse for that.

Putnam, a philosopher from whose writings I have benefited immeasurably for some thirty years, generously calls our debates "a very fruitful ongoing exchange."[51] I hope that this essay will help continue that exchange.

51 Putnam, *Realism with a Human Face*, 19.

3

JOHN SEARLE ON REALISM AND RELATIVISM

As North Americans use the term, "academic freedom" names some complicated local folkways that have developed in the course of this century, largely as a result of battles fought by the Canadian and American Associations of University Professors. These customs and traditions insulate colleges and universities from politics and from public opinion. In particular, they insulate teachers from pressure exerted by the public bodies or private boards that pay their wages.

One way to justify such customs is to start from the premise that the search for objective truth is something quite distinct from politics, and indeed distinct from almost all other cultural activities. So, the argument goes, if politics or passion intrudes on that search, the purposes of colleges and universities – the accumulation of knowledge – will not be served. In particular, if universities are politicized, they will no longer be worthy of trust, just as doctors who care more for their fees than for their patients, or judges who care more about popularity than about justice, are no longer worthy of trust. A politicized university will be likely to produce merely opinion rather than knowledge.

A number of contemporary philosophers, including myself, do their best to complicate the traditional distinctions between the objective and the subjective, reason and passion, knowledge and opinion, science and politics. We offer contentious reinterpretations of these distinctions, draw them in nontraditional ways. For example, we deny that the search for objective truth is a search for correspondence to reality and urge that it be seen instead as a search for the widest possible intersubjective agreement. So we are often accused of endangering the traditions and practices that people have in mind when they speak of "academic freedom" or "scientific integrity" or "scholarly standards."

This charge assumes that the relation between a belief about the nature of truth and certain social practices is presuppositional. A practice presupposes a belief only if dropping the belief constitutes a good reason for altering the practice. For example, the belief that surgeons do not perform operations merely to make money for themselves or their hospitals, but do so only if there is a good chance the operation will benefit the patient, is presupposed by current practices of financing health care. The belief that many diseases are caused by bacteria and viruses, and that few can be cured by acupuncture, is presupposed by current practices of disbursing public funds for medical research.

The question of whether academic freedom rests on philosophical presuppositions raises the general question of whether *any* social practice has *philosophical,* as well as empirical, presuppositions. Beliefs about surgeons' motives and about the causes and cures of diseases are empirical presuppositions. Although the empirical–philosophical distinction is itself pretty fuzzy, it is generally agreed that a belief is on the empirical end of the spectrum to the extent that we are clear about what would falsify it. In the medical examples I have used, we are clear about this. Various specific revelations about the success rate of acupuncture, or about the secret protocols of the American College of Surgeons, could have an immediate, devastating effect on current practices. But when it comes to a philosophical belief like "The truth of a sentence consists in its correspondence to reality" or "Ethical judgments are claims to knowledge rather than mere expressions of feeling" nobody is very clear about what it would take to make us believe or disbelieve it. Nobody is sure what counts for or against such propositions.

The reasons for this are the same as the reasons why it is unclear whether, if we stopped believing these propositions, we should need to change our practices. Philosophical views are just not tied very closely either to observation and experiment or to practice. This is why they are sometimes dismissed as *merely* philosophical, where "merely" suggests that views on these subjects are optional – that most people, for most purposes, can get along without any. But precisely to the extent that such views are in fact optional, social practices do *not* have philosophical presuppositions. The philosophical propositions said to be presuppositional turn out to be rhetorical ornaments of practice rather than foundations of practice. This is because we have much more confidence in the practice in question than in any of its possible philosophical justifications.

In a culture that regards debates among philosophers with appropriate insouciance, purported philosophical foundations would suffer the same fate as has, in the two centuries since the Enlightenment, overtaken theological foundations. As North American society has become more and more secular, the conviction has grown that a person's religious beliefs, and perhaps even her lack of such beliefs, are irrelevant to her participation in most of our social practices. But it was not always that way. Article Six of the Constitution of the United States, which forbids religious tests for office, was hardly uncontroversial. The conservatives who had doubts about Jefferson's Virginia Statute of Religious Freedom were convinced that participation in many of our institutions and practices presupposed Christian belief. They had a plausible case. But Jefferson, we now say with the benefit of hindsight, had a better case.

One useful example of the change in the relation between religious and other social practices is the gradual shift in attitudes toward oath taking between Jefferson's time and our own. Taking oaths has always been integral to legal practice, but there has been considerable disagreement about what an oath is, what sort of people can take it, and what presuppositions taking it involves. At the beginning of our century the *Encylopaedia Britannica* still defined an oath as "an asseveration or promise made under non-human penalty or sanction." The author of the relevant article offered dozens of instances of the relevance of belief in such sanctions – for example, Siamese Buddhists who made themselves eligible as witnesses in court by praying that, if they lied, they be punished by five hundred reincarnations as a beast and five hundred more as a hermaphrodite.

Nowadays most of us who are called upon to be witnesses in court, atheists and theists alike, solemnly and sincerely swear to tell the whole truth without giving much thought to the existence or nature of nonhuman penalties or sanctions. We atheists no longer even bother to distinguish between swearing and affirming, although that distinction was of great concern to the British House of Commons when the atheist Charles Bradlaugh asked to be seated, and was written into British law in 1888 only after anguished debate. No bailiff asks us about our religious beliefs before administering the oath. The suggestion that she do so would be regarded by the court as an absurd waste of time. Truthfulness under oath is, by now, a matter of our civic religion, our relation to our fellow citizens rather than our relation to a nonhuman power. The relation between belief in the existence of a certain kind of God and the practice of oath taking used to be presuppositional, but now it is not.

As I see it, it is with truth as it is with truth telling: philosophical debates about the nature of truth should become as irrelevant to academic practices as debates about the existence and forms of postmortem punishment are to present-day judicial practices. Just as we have much more confidence in our judicial system than we do in any account of the afterlife, or the workings of Divine Providence, so we have, or at least should have, much more confidence in our colleges and universities than we do in any philosophical view about the nature of truth or objectivity or rationality.

more

More specifically, I shall argue in what follows that philosophers who deny that there is any such thing as the correspondence of a belief to reality, and who thus seem to many nonphilosophers to have denied the existence of truth, are no more dangerous to the pursuit of truth than theologians who deny the existence of hellfire. Such theologians put neither morality nor Christianity in danger, and such philosophers endanger neither the university nor society. Those theologians did, however, change our sense of what Christianity is – of what it takes to be a good Christian. We now have a conception of Christianity that would have seemed perverse and outrageous to many of our eighteenth-century ancestors, though not to Jefferson. Analogously, these philosophers may gradually change our sense of what a university is and what its role in society is. We may wind up with a conception of the university and its social role that would have seemed outrageous to Wilhelm von Humboldt and to Nicholas Murray Butler, though not to John Dewey.

I view it as a mark of moral and intellectual progress that we are more fully prepared to judge institutions, traditions, and practices by the good they seem to be doing than by the philosophical or theological beliefs invoked in their defense. More generally, I view it as a mark of such progress that we are coming to think of such beliefs as abbreviations of practices rather than as foundations for practices and that we are learning to see many different beliefs as equally good abbreviations for the same practice. My view of the nonpresuppositional relation of any given set of philosophical convictions to academic freedom is of a piece with President Eisenhower's famous dictum that the United States is firmly founded in religious belief and that it doesn't matter which religion it is. I think that many different philosophical beliefs about the nature of truth and rationality can be invoked to defend the traditions and practices we call "academic freedom" and that in the short run, at least, it does not greatly matter which ones we pick.[1]

---

1 Eisenhower might have added that any religion that is dubious about U.S. democratic institutions must have something wrong with it. I should claim that any philosophy that is dubious about the folkways we call "academic freedom" must have something wrong with it.

A distinguished fellow philosopher, John Searle, sharply disagrees with me on this point. Outside of philosophy, Searle and I agree on a great deal. We are equally suspicious of the mannered posturing and resentful self-righteousness of the academic Left in the United States. We are equally suspicious of attempts to require courses that will shape students' sociopolitical attitudes, the sort of courses students at Berkeley now refer to as "compulsory chapel." We are equally nostalgic for the days when leftist professors concerned themselves with issues in real politics (such as the availability of health care to the poor or the need for strong labor unions) rather than with academic politics. But Searle and I disagree over the relevance of our professional speciality – philosophy – to the phenomena we both dislike.

In an article entitled "Rationality and Realism: What Is at Stake?" Searle describes what he calls "the Western Rationalistic Tradition" and says that it is under attack from such philosophers as Thomas Kuhn, Jacques Derrida, and myself.[2] Searle goes on to say that

> the biggest single consequence of the rejection of the Western Rationalistic Tradition is that it makes possible an abandonment of traditional standards of objectivity, truth, and rationality, and opens the way for an educational agenda one of whose primary purposes is to achieve social and political transformation.[3]

Searle lists a number of philosophical positions that he regards as central to the Western Rationalistic Tradition, but I shall discuss only two: the claim that, in Searle's words, "knowledge is typically of a mind-independent reality" and the claim that knowledge is expressed in "propositions which are true because they accurately represent that reality." I disagree with both claims. I agree with Kuhn that we should

> deny all meaning to claims that successive scientific beliefs become more and more probable or better and better approximations to the truth and simultaneously suggest that the subject of truth claims cannot be a relation between beliefs and a putatively mind-independent or 'external' world.[4]

I agree with Hilary Putnam that

> elements of what we call 'language' or 'mind' *penetrate so deeply into what we call 'reality' that the very project of representing ourselves as being 'mappers' of something*

2 John Searle, "Rationality and Realism: What Is at Stake?" *Daedelus* 122, no. 4 (Fall 1992), 55–84.
3 Ibid., 72.
4 T. S. Kuhn, "Afterwords," in Paul Horwich, ed., *World Changes: Thomas Kuhn and the Nature of Science* (Cambridge, Mass.: MIT Press, 1993), 330.

'language-independent' is fatally compromised from the start. Like Relativism, Realism is an impossible attempt to view the world from Nowhere.[5]

Kuhn, Putnam, Derrida, and I would all, I think, agree with Donald Davidson that

> it is futile either to reject or to accept the idea that the real and the true are
> "independent of our beliefs." The only evident positive sense we can make of
> this phrase, the only use that derives from the intentions of those who prize it,
> derives from the idea of correspondence, and this is an idea without content.[6]

The detailed arguments that go on among philosophers like Davidson,
Putnam, Derrida, Kuhn, and myself – philosophers who think that "correspondence to reality" is a term without content – and philosophers like
Searle are as baffling to nonspecialists as are those among theologians who
debate transubstantiation or who ask whether it is worse to be reincarnated
as a hermaphrodite or as a beast. The technical, nit-picking character of
both sets of arguments is itself a reason for suspecting that the issues we debate are not very closely tied in with our social practices.

If what Searle calls "traditional standards of objectivity, truth and rationality" are simply the normal practices of the academy – or, to give Searle
the benefit of the doubt, those practices as they were before people like
Kuhn, Derrida, and me began to muddy the waters – then I see no more reason to think that abandoning a belief in correspondence will make one a
less honest scholar than to think that abandoning a belief in God will make
one a less honest witness. The loyalty of philosophers on both sides of the
argument about the nature of truth to these "traditional standards" is much
greater than their attachment to the significance, or the insignificance, of
the idea of "correspondence."

Searle is right, however, that the bad guys tend to favor my side of the argument. There really are people who have no qualms about converting academic departments and disciplines into political power bases. These people
do not share Searle's and my reverence for the traditions of the university,
and they would like to find philosophical support for the claim that such
reverence is misplaced. Here is an example of the kind of rhetoric Searle
quotes with relish as an illustration of the evil influence of views like mine:

---

5 Hilary Putnam, *Reality with a Human Face* (Cambridge, Mass.: Harvard University Press,
  1990), 28. For my differences with Putnam, who considers me a "cultural relativist" and has
  some sympathy with Searle's criticisms of me and Derrida, if not those of Kuhn, see my "Putnam and the Relativist Menace," in this volume.
6 Donald Davidson, "The Structure and Content of Truth," *Journal of Philosophy* 87, no. 6
  (1990), 305.

"As the most powerful modern philosophies and theories have been demonstrating, claims of disinterest, objectivity and universality are not to be trusted, and themselves tend to reflect local historical conditions."[7] I have to admit to Searle that the committee which produced that dreadful sentence actually did include people who believe that the philosophical views I share with Kuhn and Derrida entail that the universities have no further use for notions like "disinterest" and "objectivity."

But these people are wrong. What we deny is that these notions can be explained or defended by reference to the notion of "correspondence to mind-independent reality." Philosophers on my side of the argument think that we can explain what we mean when we say that academic research should be disinterested and objective only by pointing to the ways in which free universities actually function. We can defend such universities only by pointing to the good these universities do, to their role in keeping democratic government and liberal institutions alive and functioning.

The distinction I am drawing is analogous to that between saying "We have no further use for Christianity" and saying "We cannot explain the Eucharist by reference to Aristotelian notions of substance and accident." At the time of the Council of Trent, many intelligent people thought that if we gave up on the Aristotelian–Thomistic account of the Eucharist, then the Christian religion, and thus the stability of the European sociopolitical order, would be endangered. But they were mistaken. Christianity survived the abandonment of this account, and survived in what Protestants think of as a desirably purified form.

Philosophers on my side of the argument think that if we stop trying to give epistemological justifications for academic freedom, and instead give sociopolitical justifications, we shall be both more honest and more clearheaded. We think that disinterested, objective inquiry would not only survive the adoption of our philosophical views, but might survive in a desirably purified form. One result of the adoption of our views might be, for example, that physics-envy will become less prevalent and that distinctions between disciplines will no longer be drawn in phallogocentric terms, such as "hard" and "soft." Biologists and historians might stop looking down their noses at colleagues in other departments who cannot produce experimental or archival data in support of their conclusions. We might stop debating the pointless and tiresome question of whether doctoral dissertations in English literature constitute contributions to knowledge, rather than being

---

7 The American Council of Learned Societies, *Speaking for the Humanities,* ACLS Occasional Paper no. 7 (1989), 18; quoted by Searle in "Rationality and Realism," 69.

merely expressions of opinion. Sociologists and psychologists might stop asking themselves whether they are following rigorous scientific procedures and start asking themselves whether they have any suggestions to make to their fellow citizens about how our lives, or our institutions, should be changed.

The crucial move made by people on my side of the argument about the nature of objectivity is that, just as the only difference between unconsecrated and consecrated bread lies in the social practices appropriate to each, so the only difference between desirable objectivity and undesirable politicization is the difference between the social practices conducted in the name of each. The point, we say, is not whether Christ is Really Present in the bread, but whether we should treat a consecrated host as we would a snack. The point is not whether disinterested and objective inquiry will lead to correspondence to mind-independent reality, but how to keep the Old Guard from freezing out the Young Turks while simultaneously preventing the Young Turks from wrecking the university.

A healthy and free university accommodates generational change, radical religious and political disagreement, and new social responsibilities, as best it can. It muddles through. There are no rules for this muddling through, any more than there are rules that our appellate judges follow when they accommodate old constitutional provisions to new sociopolitical situations. Debate at English department faculty meetings is no less, and no more, rational than at the conferences where justices of the Supreme Court discuss pending cases. As pragmatist judges and philosophers of law have reminded us, attempts to draw nice clean lines between law and morality, or between jurisprudence and politics, have met with little success.[8] The question about whether the judges of the higher courts explain what the law already is, or instead make new law, is as idle as the philosophical question about whether literary criticism produces knowledge or opinion. But recognizing the idleness of the first question does not make these philosophers, or the rest of us, value the ideal of a free and independent judiciary any the less. Nor does it make us less capable of telling good judges from bad judges, any more than our lack of an epistemology of literary criticism makes us less capable of telling good critics from bad critics, boring pedants from original minds.

More generally, the experience that we professors have had with decisions about curriculum and appointments should persuade us that the distinction between academic politics and the distinterested pursuit of truth is

8 See the chapters by Richard Posner and Thomas Grey in *The New Pragmatism*, ed. Morris Dickstein (Durham, N.C.: Duke University Press, forthcoming).

pretty fuzzy. But that fuzziness does not, and should not, make us treasure free and independent universities any the less. Neither philosophers nor anyone else can offer us nice sharp distinctions between appropriate social utility and inappropriate politicization. But we have accumulated a lot of experience about how to keep redrawing this line, how to adjust it to meet the needs of each new generation. We have managed to do so in ways that have kept our colleges and universities healthy and free.

One of the things this accumulated experience has taught us is that universities are unlikely to remain healthy and free once people outside them take a hand in redrawing this line. The one thing that has proved worse than letting the university order its own affairs – letting its members quarrel constantly and indecisively about what shall count as science or as scholarship – is letting somebody else order those affairs. As long as we keep this lesson in mind, and manage to keep the traditions of civility alive within the academy, what Searle calls "traditional standards of objectivity, truth and rationality" will take care of themselves. These standards are not under the guardianship of philosophers, and changes in opinion among philosophy professors will not cause us to abjure, or change, them. As Nelson Goodman said about logic, all the logician can do is tell you what deductive arguments people usually accept as valid; she cannot correct their notions of deductive validity. Similarly, all we philosophers can do when asked for standards or methods of disinterested and objective inquiry is to describe how the people we most admire conduct their inquiries. We have no independent information about how objective truth is to be obtained.

So much for the overall argument I am putting forward. I want to turn now to the more technical aspects of the disagreement between myself and Searle. The central question Searle raises is whether, if you do not believe in mind-independent reality, you can still believe in, and insist upon, objectivity.[9] Philosophers on my side of the argument answer that objectivity is

9 Compare Thomas Haskell's remark: "[A]s long as there is no respectable sense (not even a largely social and conventional one) in which we are entitled to say that there is a 'nature of things' for inquirers to 'get right,' then one cannot help wondering what the community of inquirers is for" ("Justifying the Rights of Academic Freedom in the Era of 'Power/Knowledge,'" in Louis Menand, ed., *The Future of Academic Freedom* [Chicago: University of Chicago Press, 1996] 70).

Later in his essay Haskell describes me as differing from Peirce, Lovejoy, and Dewey in that I am unable to say, as they did, that some interpretations were better than others, "better in a strong sense that did not depend on correspondence and yet was not reducible to perspective" (73). But all I am interested in is getting rid of correspondence and the notion of

not a matter of corresponding to objects but a matter of getting together with other subjects – that there is nothing to objectivity except intersubjectivity. So when Searle says, "If there is no such thing as objective truth and validity, then you might as well discuss the person making the statement and his motives for making it," we rejoin that nobody ever said there was no such thing as objective truth and validity. What we say is that you gain nothing for the pursuit of such truth by talking about the mind dependence or mind independence of reality. All there is to talk about are the procedures we use for bringing about agreement among inquirers.

One reason the question of mind-independent reality is so vexed and confusing is an ambiguity in the notion of "independence." Searle sometimes writes as if philosophers who, like myself, do not believe in "mind-independent reality" must deny that there were mountains before people had the idea of "mountain" in their minds or the word "mountain" in their language. But nobody denies that. Nobody thinks there is a chain of causes that makes mountains an effect of thoughts or words. What people like Kuhn, Derrida, and I believe is that it is pointless to ask whether there really are mountains or whether it is merely convenient for us to talk about mountains.

We also think it pointless to ask, for example, whether neutrinos are real entities or merely useful heuristic fictions. This is the sort of thing we mean by saying that it is pointless to ask whether reality is independent of our ways of talking about it. Given that it pays to talk about mountains, as it certainly does, one of the obvious truths about mountains is that they were here before we talked about them. If you do not believe that, you probably do not know how to play the language games that employ the word "mountain." But the utility of those language games has nothing to do with the question of whether Reality as It Is in Itself, apart from the way it is handy for human beings to describe it, has mountains in it. That question is about the other, *non*-causal sense of "independence." My side thinks nothing could possibly turn on the answers to questions of independence in *that* sense and that therefore we can get along quite nicely without the notion of Reality as It Is in Itself.

Davidson says that the question of whether the real is "independent of our beliefs" should not be asked, because he thinks that the only relevant sense of independence is not "causal antecedence" but "existence in itself." He thinks that the notion of "correspondence to reality" is useless, because

the intrinsic nature of things that is needed to make sense of correspondence. I do not want to reduce anything to perspective and would not know how to do so. See my remarks on relativism in "Solidarity or Objectivity?" in my *Objectivity, Relativism, and Truth* (Cambridge University Press, 1991), 21–34, and in my "Hilary Putnam and the Relativist Menace," in this volume.

the relevant reality is reality "as it is in itself." We who agree with Davidson think that the whole project of distinguishing between what exists in itself and what exists in relation to human minds – the project shared by Aristotle, Locke, Kant, and Searle – is no longer worth pursuing.[10] This project, like the project of underwriting the sanctity of the Eucharist, once looked interesting, promising, and potentially useful. But it did not pan out. It has turned out to be a dead end.

Another semitechnical point I wish to make concerns an ambiguity lurking in the notion of "accurate representation." Searle says, you recall, that the Western Rationalistic Tradition holds that knowledge is expressed in "propositions which are true because they accurately represent that [mind-independent] reality." We Davidsonians want to distinguish between two senses of the phrase "represent accurately." In the nonphilosophical sense, to ask a witness if she has accurately represented a situation is to ask about her truthfulness or her carefulness. When we say that good historians accurately represent what they find in the archives, we mean that they look hard for relevant documents, do not discard documents tending to discredit the historical thesis they are propounding, do not misleadingly quote passages out of context, tell the same historical story among themselves that they tell us, and so on. To assume that a historian accurately represents the facts as she knows them is to assume that she behaves in the way in which good, honest historians behave. It is not to assume anything about the reality of past events, or about the truth conditions of statements concerning such events, or about the necessarily hermeneutical character of the *Geisteswissenschaften*, or about any other philosophical topic.[11]

---

10 For Searle's clearest statement of this distinction, see his *Rediscovery of the Mind* (Cambridge, Mass.: MIT Press, 1992), 211: ". . . it is essential to understand the distinction between features of the world that are *intrinsic* and features that are *observer relative*. The expressions 'mass,' 'gravitational attraction,' and 'molecule' name features of the world that are intrinsic. If all observers and users cease to exist, the world still contains mass, gravitational attraction, and molecules. But expressions such as 'nice day for a picnic' . . . name objects by specifying some feature that has been assigned to them, some feature that is relative to observers and users."

For pragmatists like me, the feature of being a molecule is just as much or as little "relative to observers and users" as the suitability of a day for a picnic. So we are not sure whether, as Searle goes on to say, "if there had never been any users or observers, there would be no such features as being a nice day for a picnic." We see no useful purpose served by this attempt to distinguish intrinsic from observer-relative features of reality. "Essential," we ask Searle, "for what?"

11 Here I find myself in disagreement with Joyce Appleby, Lynn Hunt, and Margaret Jacob, in their *Telling the Truth about History* (New York: Norton, 1994). They say, "The most distinctive of historians' problems is that posed by temporality itself. . . . The past, insofar as it exists at

But when philosophers discuss the question of whether knowledge consists in accuracy of representation, they are not concerned with honesty or carefulness. The question at issue between representationalists like Searle and antirepresentationalists like me is merely this: Can we pair off parts of the world with parts of beliefs or sentences, so as to be able to say that the relations between the latter match the relations between the former? Can true beliefs or sentences be treated on the model of realistic portraiture? Obviously some sentences can, at least prima facie, be so treated – for example, "The cat is on the mat."[12] There are many other cases, such as the sentence "Neutrinos have no mass" or "The pursuit of scholarly truth requires academic freedom," to which the notion of "parts of the world" has no evident application. We philosophers haggle endlessly about whether the notions of "correspondence" and "representation" can be extended to these harder cases. When we are tired of haggling about that, we start haggling over whether there is any criterion for whether a belief accurately represents reality other than its coherence with the rest of our beliefs, and if not,

---

all, exists in the present; the historian too is stuck in time present, trying to make meaningful and accurate statements about time past. Any account of historical objectivity must provide for this crucial temporal dimension" (253). I am not sure who has had the "debilitating doubts that the past is knowable" (270) of which they speak, or why we should take such doubts more seriously than Descartes's doubt about the existence of matter. I do not think that there is something called "temporality" that poses a big problem, or that we require either "a theory of objectivity for the twenty-first century" (254) or a "revitalized and transformed practise of objectivity" (237).

One of the morals of what Kuhn says about the difference between textbook accounts of inquiry, written by people with philosophical axes to grind, and the actual processes of initiation into a disciplinary matrix (such as historiography) seems to me to be that we never have had much of a "theory of objectivity" and that we do not need a new one now. What we have had, and will with luck continue to have, is what Thomas Haskell (following Francis Abbot) calls "communities of the competent," communities that can muddle their way through an unending process of self-transformation without philosophical assistance.

Appleby and her colleagues think philosophy does help, and so they offer, as part of a "combination of practical realism and pragmatism," an "epistemological position that claims that people's perceptions of the world have some correspondence with that world." Philosophers like me think that "correspondence to reality" is just an uncashable and obsolete metaphor. So for us the term "some correspondence" is like "somewhat pregnant"; we do not think the issue is about *how much* correspondence perception or historiography might have. The epistemological position these three historians propose seems to us to fall between two irreconcilable philosophical alternatives rather than providing a useful synthesis or compromise.

12 See the cat. See the "cat." See the mat. See the "mat." See the isomorphism between the sentence and the fact? No? You are worried by "on" and "is"? So was Wittgenstein. Eventually these worries drove him to the view that using sentences was more like making moves in a game than like flashing pictures on a screen.

whether we should distinguish between the *criterion* of true belief and the *nature* of true belief.

Searle's claim that the correspondence theory of truth has moral or social importance runs together the philosophical and nonphilosophical senses of "accurate representation." If we antirepresentationalists and anticorrespondentists ever win our argument with Searle, that will give historians and physicists no reason to behave differently than they presently do. Nor, I suspect, will their morale or their efficiency improve if Searle and his fellow representationalists should win. Honesty, care, truthfulness, and other moral and social virtues are just not that closely connected to what we philosophy professors eventually decide to be the least problematic way of describing the relationship between human inquiry and the rest of the universe.

The claim about a lack of close connection that I have just made is not put forward as a philosophical truth about the necessary, ahistorical relation of philosophy to the rest of culture. It is simply a sociological truth about the lack of interest that most people, intellectuals as well as nonintellectuals, currently have in philosophy. It is like the truth that the adoption of the ethics of love suggested by St. Paul does not depend upon the Orthodox, as opposed to the Arian, position on the relation between the First and Second Persons of the Trinity. That is a sociological truth about contemporary Christians, not an ahistorical truth about the relation between ethics and theology. Things were otherwise in the days when not only your physical safety but your choice of which charioteers to cheer for in the hippodrome depended upon your theological allegiances.

If Searle has his way – if he succeeds in persuading us (or even in persuading funding agencies) that the relation between the Western Rationalistic Tradition and current academic practices is in fact presuppositional, and that refuting Kuhn, Derrida, and me is an urgent social need – then the academy will divide up into those who cheer for the representationalist philosophical team and those who (selflessly sacrificing grants for the sake of philosophical correctness) cheer for their opponents. Scholars and scientists will go around asking each other, and being asked by grant givers, "Which side are you on?"

I think that would be unfortunate, if only because it would be a waste of people's time and emotional energy. It would be better to distinguish the ethics of the academy – the customs and practices that help to determine the attitude of students to books, faculty to students, administrators to faculty and donors, and so on – from the private theological or philosophical convictions of any of the persons involved. To help keep the academy free and depoliticized, we should, for example, make sure that professors do not

But they might not make interesting physical discoveries. Gödel could not have pursued his views on truth vs morality. He accepted the Vienna Circle's view of mathematics.

mock the beliefs of their fundamentalist students, that donors do not designate particular persons to fill the chairs they endow, and that a scholar's conclusions about controversial issues within her field, or about political or philosophical matters, continue to be irrelevant to her membership in the university. But we should not worry about whether true sentences accurately represent mind-independent reality.

So far I have argued that philosophy does not make much difference to our practices and that it should not be allowed to do so. But this may seem a strange position for somebody who calls himself a pragmatist. We pragmatists say that every difference must make a difference to practice. We think that it is important to argue that the Western Rationalistic Tradition, as Searle defines it, is *wrong*. We insist on trying to develop another, better tradition. So how can we, without dishonesty, say that philosophical controversies do not matter all that much?

We pragmatists can make our position consistent, I think, by saying that although they don't matter much in the short run, they may well matter in the long run. The Christian who believes that God will punish him with hellfire if he lies under oath will, in the short run, do the same thing as the atheist who believes that he will be unable to live with himself if he betrays the social compact by committing perjury. But in the long run it may make a lot of difference whether a society is regulated by its members' fear of nonhuman sanctions or by secular sentiments of pride, loyalty, and solidarity. The physicist who describes himself as uncovering the absolute, intrinsic, in-itself character of reality and his colleague who describes herself as assembling better instruments for prediction and control of the environment will, in their race to solve the currently salient problems, do much the same things. But in the long run physicists whose rhetoric is pragmatist rather than Western Rationalistic might be better citizens of a better academic community.

Deep emotional needs are fulfilled by the Western Rationalistic Tradition, but not all such needs should be fulfilled. Deep emotional needs were fulfilled by belief in nonhuman judges and nonhuman sanctions. These were the needs Dostoyevsky evinced when he said that if God did not exist, everything would be permitted. But these needs should be, and to some extent have been, sublimated or replaced rather than gratified. I have pressed the analogies between theological and philosophical belief because I see the Western Rationalistic Tradition as a secularized version of the Western Monotheist Tradition – as the latest twist on what Heidegger calls "onto-theology." We pragmatists take the same dim view of Absolute Truth and of Reality as It Is in Itself as the Enlightenment took of Divine Wrath and Divine Judgment.

John Dewey once quoted G. K. Chesterton's remark that "[p]ragmatism is a matter of human needs and one of the first of human needs is to be something more than a pragmatist."[13] Chesterton had a point, and Dewey granted it. Dewey was quite aware of what he called "a supposed necessity of the 'human mind' to believe in certain absolute truths." But he thought that this necessity had existed only in an earlier stage of human history, a stage we might now move beyond. He thought that we had reached a point at which it might be possible, and helpful, to wrench ourselves free of it. He recognized that his suggestion was counterintuitive and would meet the kind of opposition Searle mounts. But he thought that the long-run good done by getting rid of outdated needs would outweigh the temporary disturbance caused by attempts to change our philosophical intuitions.

As Dewey saw it, the need to distinguish between the pursuit of truth "for its own sake" and the pursuit of what Bacon called "the improvement of man's estate" arose out of particular social conditions.[14] These conditions prevailed in ancient Greece and made it useful to draw certain distinctions that became, in the course of time, part of our common sense. These included, for example, the distinctions between theory and practice, mind and body, objective and subjective, morality and prudence, and all the others Derrida groups together as "the binary oppositions of Western metaphysics."

Dewey was happy to admit that these distinctions had, in their time, served us well. In their time, they were neither confusions nor repressive devices nor mystifications. On the contrary, they were instruments that Greek thinkers used to change social conditions, often for the better. But over a couple of millennia, these instruments outlived their usefulness. Dewey thought that, just as many Christians had outgrown the need to ask whether the sentences of the Creed correspond to objective reality, so civilization as a whole might outgrow the supposed necessity to believe in absolute truths.

Dewey learned from Hegel to historicize everything, including Hegel's own picturesque but outdated story of the union of subject and object at the end of History. Like Marx, Dewey dropped Hegel's notion of Absolute Spirit, but kept his insight that ideas and movements that had begun as instruments of emancipation (Greek metaphysics, Christianity, the rise of the bourgeoisie, the Hegelian System) had typically, over the course of time, turned

---

13 John Dewey, "A Short Catechism Concerning Truth," *The Middle Works of John Dewey* (Carbondale: Southern Illinois University Press, 1978), 6: 11.
14 See, on this point, the opening chapters of Dewey's *The Quest for Certainty*, in *The Later Works of John Dewey* (Carbondale: Southern Illinois University Press, 1984), vol. 4.

into instruments of repression – into parts of what Dewey called "the crust of convention." Dewey thought that the idea of "absolute truth" was such an idea and that the pragmatic theory of truth was "true in the pragmatic sense of truth: it works, it clears up difficulties, removes obscurities, puts individuals into more experimental, less dogmatic, and less arbitrarily sceptical relations to life." "The pragmatist," he continued, "is quite content to have the truth of his theory consist in its working in these various ways, and to leave to the intellectualist the proud possession of [truth as] an unanalyzable, unverifiable, unworking property."[15]

Dewey said that Chesterton's remark "has revealed that the chief objection of absolutists to the pragmatic doctrine of the personal (or 'subjective') factor in belief is that the pragmatist has spilled the personal milk in the absolutist's cocoanut [sic]."[16] His point was that Chesterton had implicitly admitted that the best, and perhaps the only, argument for the absolutist view of truth was that it satisifed a human need. Dewey saw that need as one we could outgrow. Just as the child outgrows the need for parental care and the need to believe in parental omnipotence and benevolence, so we may in time outgrow the need to believe in divinities that concern themselves with our happiness and in the possibility of allying ourselves with a nonhuman power called the Intrinsic Nature of Reality. In doing so, we might outgrow both the need to see ourselves as deeply sinful and guilty and the need to escape from the relative to the absolute. Eventually, Dewey thought, the subjective–objective and relative–absolute distinctions might become as obsolete as the distinction between the soul and the body or between natural and supernatural causes.

Dewey was quite aware, however, that the good work still being done by old distinctions would have to be taken over by new distinctions. He was also quite aware of what Berkeley called the need to "speak with the vulgar and think with the learned," to apply different strokes to different folks. So his writings are a sometimes confusing mixture of invocations of familiar distinctions with counterintuitive philosophical reinterpretations of those distinctions. His reformulations were often, at least to the vulgar, merely bewildering. So we should not be surprised to find Dewey, at the same time that he was energetically defending the pragmatic theory of truth against his

15 Ibid., 9.
16 Ibid., 11. Robert Westbrook (*John Dewey and American Democracy* [Ithaca, N.Y.: Cornell University Press, 1991], 137–8) cites this passage and points out that it applies to Bertrand Russell's criticisms of pragmatism as well as to Chesterton's. Pragmatism's radicalism and originality are nicely instanced by its ability to question a presupposition common to Chesterton and Russell, writers who had very little else in common.

absolutist opponents, writing such sentences as "The university function is the truth-function" and "The one thing that is inherent and essential [to the idea of the university] is the idea of truth."[17]

The nonphilosophers who read these sentences, which appeared in 1902 in an article called "Academic Freedom," probably took "the idea of truth" to mean something like "the idea of an accurate representation of the intrinsic nature of reality." Most people still take it to mean something like that. They automatically contrast the attempt to get such representations – to attain objective truth – with the attempt to make people happy, to fulfill human needs. The latter, they say, involves an element of subjectivity that should be excluded from science and scholarship. When such people are told by Searle and others that Kuhn, Derrida, and I deny that true beliefs represent anything and that reality has an intrinsic nature, they may well believe that the university is endangered and that the need to preserve academic freedom requires the refutation of these dangerous philosophers.[18]

Dewey, I think, would say that if it ever comes down to a choice between the practices and traditions that make up academic freedom and antirepresentationalist theories of truth and knowledge, we should go for academic freedom. We should put first things first. Change in philosophical opinion is, on Dewey's view, in the service of sociopolitical progress. He would have

17 John Dewey, "Academic Freedom," *The Middle Works*, 2: 55.
18 Searle is, of course, only one of a great number of philosophers who take this line. John Silber, president of Boston University and a well-known Kant scholar, reported to his trustees that "[s]ome versions of critical theory, radical feminism and multiculturalism, among other intellectual positions, are ideological in character and inhospitable to free intellectual inquiry" and that "[w]e [at Boston University] have resisted relativism as an official intellectual dogma, believing that there is such a thing as truth, and if you can't achieve it, at least you can approach it" (see "New Eruption at Boston U.," *Chronicle of Higher Education*, December 8, 1993). Nineteen philosophers signed a letter to the *Times* of London (May 9, 1992) saying that Derrida should not receive an honorary degree from Cambridge because his work offers "little more than semi-intelligible attacks upon the values of reason, truth and scholarship."

It is instructive to compare such assaults with those written, in the 1930s and 1940s, against logical positivism by C. E. M. Joad, Mortimer Adler, Brand Blanshard, and other philosophers. In its brief heyday, logical positivism was as fanatical, intolerant, and brutal as any intellectual movement has ever been, but by now the cries of "Civilization in danger!" that were raised against it seem a bit overwrought. Many of the slogans of "poststructuralism" now current in our universities, the slogans Searle sees as exemplifying literary frivolity and dangerous politicization, will come to seem as patently silly and self-righteously snotty as the youthful excesses of the first generation of logical positivists now seem to us. But the brief reign of poststructuralism will probably do a bit of good, just as the brief reign of logical positivism did. Poststructuralism claims far too much for literature and for politics, just as positivism claimed far too much for science and for philosophy. But intellectual progress is often made by just such violent pendulum swings.

had no interest in sacrificing free universities to his philosophical convictions. But, of course, he did not think that it would ever come down to any such choice. He saw no tension between his philosophical and his political work. I think he would have accepted my distinction between the short-run and the long-run effects of change in philosophical opinion.

Nothing, including the nature of truth and knowledge, is worth worrying about if this worry will make no difference to practice. But there are all sorts of ways of making a difference. One of them is by slowly, over a long period of time, changing what Wittgenstein called the pictures that hold us captive. We will always be held captive by some picture or other, for this is merely to say we shall never escape from language or from metaphor – never see either God or the Intrinsic Nature of Reality face to face. But old pictures may have disadvantages that can be avoided by the sketching of new pictures. Escape from prejudice and superstition, Dewey thought, was not escape from appearance to reality, but escape from the satisfaction of old needs to the satisfaction of new needs. It was a process of maturation, not progress from darkness to light. On his view, escape from the Western Rationalistic Tradition would indeed be an escape from error to truth, but it would not be an escape from the way things appear to the way things really are. It would merely be an escape from immature needs: the needs Chesterton felt and Dewey did not.

By way of conclusion, I shall put Dewey aside and come back to Searle. Searle sees the difference between himself and me as the difference between someone with a decent respect for hard fact, and other associated intellectual virtues, and someone who relishes, and helps encourage, what he calls "the general air of vaguely literary frivolity that pervades the Nietzscheanized Left."[19] He sees as presuppositional the relationships I see as largely ornamental. He says that the only argument for his own realist representationalist view is that

> it forms the presupposition of our linguistic and other sorts of practices: You cannot coherently deny realism and engage in ordinary linguistic practices, because realism is a condition of the normal intelligibility of those practices. You can see this if you consider any sort of ordinary communication. For example, suppose I call my car mechanic to find out if the carburetor is fixed. . . . Now suppose I have reached a deconstructionist car mechanic and he tries to explain to me that a carburetor is just a text anyway, and that there is nothing to talk about except the textuality of the text. . . . Whatever else is clear about

19 Searle, "Rationality and Realism," 78.

such situations, one thing is clear: communication has broken down. . . . Give me the assumption that these sorts of communication are even possible between human beings and you will see that you require the assumption of an independently existing reality.[20]

I do not think that this frivolously literary car mechanic is a plausible product of the overthrow of the Western Rationalistic Tradition. The deconstructionist Ph.D.'s in English who, after finding themselves unemployable in the academy, lucked into jobs as car mechanics have no trouble telling where their job stops and their philosophy begins. They would presumably say that the difference deconstruction has made to their lives is, like the difference Methodism or atheism made to their ancestors' lives, atmospheric and spiritual. They might even quote Dewey and say, as I myself would, that they have found Derrida's writings useful for getting "into more experimental, less dogmatic, and less arbitrarily skeptical relations to life."[21]

20 Ibid., 81. Searle goes on to say, "One interesting thing about the present theorists who claim to have shown that reality is a social construct, or that there is no independently existing reality, or that everything is really a text, is that they have denied one of the conditions of intelligibility of our ordinary linguistic practices without providing an alternative conception of that intelligibility." Pragmatists do not think there are such things as conditions of intelligibility. There are only tacit agreements to continue with certain social practices.

21 Searle's phrase "literary frivolity," like his reference (quoted later) to "the more scientific portions of our civilization" is characteristic of the traditional alliance of analytic philosophy with the natural sciences against the humanities. In the 1930s, the seedtime of analytic philosophy, the contrast between Carnap's respect for scientists and Heidegger's respect for poets was seen as a contrast between responsibility and frivolous irresponsibility.

   If you say that "the university function is the truth function," and if you think of truth as something about which you can expect to get a consensus, then, as Louis Menand has remarked, "the criticism of literature has the weakest case for inclusion in the professional structure of the research university." The books of F. R. Leavis or Harold Bloom are not happily described as "contributions to knowledge." But this apparent weakness is a product of the mistaken idea that consensus among inquirers – consensus of the sort Leavis and Bloom knew better than to hope for – is the goal of any responsible intellectual activity.

   I hope that this latter idea, and the resulting split between Snow's "two cultures," will sooner or later become obsolete. We might hasten the process of obsolescence by reflecting that we are much more certain of the value of departments of English literature than we are about the nature of the research university, or of knowledge. One can always make English departments look silly by asking them what they have contributed to knowledge lately. But humanists can make biology or mathematics departments look bad by asking what they have done lately for human freedom. The best thing about our universities is the live-and-let-live spirit that lets us wave such pointless questions aside. When, however, outside pressure makes us nervous and self-conscious, we start asking bad questions like "What *is* a university, anyway?" That question is almost certain to be answered by invidious comparisons among disciplines, and especially between the sciences and the humanities.

The more serious question, however, is, as I said earlier, the one about presuppositions. I can go some way with Searle on this question. Thus, I agree with him when he makes the Wittgensteinian point that

> [f]or those of us brought up in our civilization, especially the scientific por-
> tions of our civilization, the principles that I have just presented as those of
> the Western Rationalistic Tradition do not function as a *theory*. Rather, they
> function as part of the taken-for-granted background of our practices. The
> conditions of intelligiblity of our practices, linguistic and otherwise, cannot
> themselves be demonstrated as truths within those practices. To suppose they
> could was the endemic mistake of foundationalist metaphysics.[22]

I break off from Searle only at the point where he suggests that our practices would somehow become unintelligible if we described what we are doing in different ways – and in particular if we described them in the nonrealist, nonrepresentationalist terms commended by philosophers like Davidson and Derrida.

Searle and I recognize that certain propositions are intuitively obvious, indemonstrable, and taken for granted. But whereas he thinks that they cannot be questioned without the practices themselves (or, at least, their "intelligibility") being questioned, I see them as optional glosses on those practices. Whereas he sees conditions of intelligibility, presuppositions, I see rhetorical flourishes designed to make practitioners feel they are being true to something big and strong: the Intrinsic Nature of Reality. On my view, the comfort derived from this feeling is, at this stage in the maturation of Western humanity, as unnecessary and as potentially dangerous as the comfort derived from the conviction that one is obeying the Will of God.

It is unnecessary and dangerous because our maturation has consisted in the gradual realization that, if we can rely on one another, we need not rely on anything else. In religious terms, this is the Feuerbachian thesis that God is just a projection of the best, and sometimes the worst, of humanity. In philosophical terms, it is the thesis that anything that talk of objectivity can do to make our practices intelligible can be done equally well by talk of intersubjectivity. In political terms, it is the thesis that if we can just keep democracy and reciprocal tolerance alive, everything else can be settled by muddling through to some reasonable sort of compromise.

To adopt these various theses, it helps to reflect that nothing in your practices requires you to distinguish an intrinsic from an extrinsic feature of

22 Searle, "Rationality and Realism," 80.

reality.[23] If you give up the intrinsic–extrinsic distinction, the distinction between what things are like apart from human needs and interests and what they are like in relation to those needs and interests, you can also give up the idea that there is a great big difference between seeking human happiness and seeking scholarly or scientific truth. For now you will think of the latter search not as attempting to represent the intrinsic features of reality, without regard to human needs, but as finding descriptions of reality that satisfy particular human needs – those your fellow scientists and scholars have agreed need to be satisfied. The difference between bad subjectivity and sound scholarship will now be glossed as that between the satisfaction of private, idiosyncratic, and perhaps secret needs and the satisfaction of needs that are widely shared, well publicized, and freely debated.

This substitution of objectivity-as-intersubjectivity for objectivity-as-accurate-representation is the key pragmatic move, the one that lets pragmatists feel they can have moral seriousness without "realist" seriousness. For moral seriousness is a matter of taking other human beings seriously, and not taking anything else with equal seriousness. It turns out, pragmatists say, that we can take each other very seriously indeed without taking the intrinsic nature of reality seriously at all. We will not change our practices – either political or academic – merely because we have ceased to concern ourselves with epistemology or because we have adopted nonrepresentationalist philosophies of language and mind. But we may change our attitudes toward these practices, our sense of why it is important to carry them out. Our new sense of what we are doing will be itself as indemonstrable, and as intuitive, as was the Western Rationalistic Tradition. But pragmatists think it will be better, not just because it will free philosophers from perpetual oscillation between skepticism and dogmatism, but because it will take away a few more excuses for fanaticism and intolerance.

---

23 But you can still happily agree with common sense that there were dinosaurs and mountains long before anybody described them as dinosaurs and mountains, that thinking doesn't make it so, and that bank accounts and gender roles are social constructions in a sense in which giraffes are not. There would have been no bank accounts or gender roles had there been no human societies, whereas there would have been giraffes. But that is not to say that giraffes are part of Reality as It Is in Itself, apart from human needs and interests. In a wider sense of "social construction," everything, including giraffes and molecules, is socially constructed, for no vocabulary (e.g., that of zoology or physics) cuts reality at the joints. Reality has no joints. It just has descriptions – some more socially useful than others.

4

CHARLES TAYLOR ON TRUTH

The most basic disagreement between Charles Taylor and myself is over whether poetry should be seen as "a means of arranging the order of our internal lives by making an harmonious pattern of extremely complex attitudes, once thought to refer to an external order of metaphysics but now seen to be a symbolic ordering of our inner selves."[1] Taylor says that "such a self-enclosed reading manifestly will not do" for such writers as "Eliot, Pound, Mann, Lawrence, Joyce, Proust or Rilke."[2] I think that it will do admirably. I welcome every sign of increased willingness to see such writers as edifying examples of how to be merely human, rather than as the people who open us up to something other than themselves, and perhaps other than human.

If Taylor and I tried to argue about whether one should encourage a tendency to envisage what he calls "hypergoods," rather than simply arranging and balancing ordinary goods, we would probably end up talking about the details of our favorite poems and novels. For I suspect that different literary canons, and disagreement about how to read the works that appear in both our canons, lie at the bottom of our disagreement about the nature of moral experience. My reading of my canon makes me doubt Taylor's claim that we can make sense of our moral life only with "something like a hypergood perspective."[3] Taylor reads his favorite authors in the light of his conviction that

---

1 This is a formulation, by Stephen Spender, of a view Spender attributes to I. A. Richards. It is quoted by Taylor in *The Sources of the Self* (Cambridge, Mass.: Harvard University Press, 1989), 490–1.
2 Ibid., 491.
3 Ibid., 71.

"the poet, if he is serious, is pointing to something – God, the tradition – which he believes to be there for all of us." I read some of these same writers in the light of my conviction that seriousness can, and should, swing free of any such universalistic belief.

Instead of attempting to discuss these deeper differences, however, I shall stick to a narrow, specifically philosophical, disagreement. I shall confine myself to a parochial topic, one that only philosophy professors take seriously: truth. Taylor thinks of his own attachment to hypergoods as entailing a need to defend some form of the correspondence theory of truth. I reject all forms of that theory, except those that are so shallow and trivial as to be noncontroversial.

I think that Taylor would do better to split off universalism – the belief in hypergoods that are there for all of us – from this theory. He and I would doubtless continue to disagree about moral experience even if we came to agreement on what to say about truth, and about such related issues as the relation of language and thought to the rest of the universe. In the hope of facilitating such limited agreement, I shall bracket, in what follows, everything in Taylor's work except his rejection of what he calls "Rorty's nonrealism."[4]

I have frequently urged, in the course of polemics against attempts to resuscitate the correspondence theory of truth, that any such theory requires the idea that the world is divided into facts and that facts are what Strawson calls "sentence-shaped items," items having the shape of sentences in "Nature's Own Language." Taylor deplores my use of "rhetorical flourishes" such as "Nature's Own Language" to describe the view of my realist (or, as I should prefer to say, representationalist) opponents. He thinks that I should not pretend, as he puts it, that "believers in the correspondence theory are 'Raving Platonists'" – people who believe that "a vocabulary is somehow already out there in the world."[5]

To avoid starting unnecessary hares, I am prepared henceforth to abjure all references to "Nature's Own Language." I should insist, however, that this was no more farfetched a rhetorical flourish than Putnam's "God's-eye point of view"; both flourishes are just ways of saying that correspondence theorists need to have criteria for the adequacy of vocabularies as well as of statements, need the notion of one vocabulary somehow "fitting" the world better than

---

4 This phrase occurs in Taylor's "Rorty in the Epistemological Tradition," in *Reading Rorty*, ed. Alan Malachowski (Oxford: Blackwell, 1990), 258.
5 Ibid., 268–9; also see 262.

another. So perhaps the chastest, least rhetorical way of making my point is to restate it as: believers in the correspondence theory have to claim that some vocabularies (e.g., Newton's) do not just work better than others (e.g., Aristotle's) but do so because they represent reality more adequately. Taylor thinks that good sense can be made of this claim, and I do not.

Taylor says that there will be "no further problem with the proposition that the reality independent of my representations makes them true or false" once one drops the absurd notion of "the thing-in-itself" and, with Heidegger and Wittgenstein, refuses to let an "*ex ante* theory of knowledge" dictate to ontology. For once one has done so, once one recognizes the primacy of the *Zuhanden* over the *Vorhanden,* and realizes that to agree on a language is to agree on a form of life, one will find oneself "at grips with a world of independent things."[6]

But none of us antirepresentationalists have ever doubted that most things in the universe are causally independent of us. What we question is whether they are representationally independent of us. For X to be representationally independent of us is for X to have an intrinsic feature (a feature that it has under any and every description) such that it is better described by some of our terms rather than others. Because we can see no way to decide which descriptions of an object get at what is "intrinsic" to it, as opposed to its merely "relational," extrinsic features (e.g., its description-relative features), we are prepared to discard the intrinsic–extrinsic distinction, the claim that beliefs represent, and the whole question of representational independence or dependence. This means discarding the idea of (as Bernard Williams has put it) "how things are *anyway,*" apart from whether or how they are described.

Taylor seems to think that neither I nor any one else would feel any "serious temptation to deny that the no chairs claim ["There are no chairs in this room"] will be true or false in virtue of the way things are, or the nature of reality." But I do, in fact, feel tempted to deny this. I do so because I see two ways of interpreting "in virtue of the way things are." One is short for "in virtue of the way our current descriptions of things are used and the causal interactions we have with those things."[7] The other is short for "*simply* in virtue of the way things are, quite apart from how we describe them." On

---

6 Ibid., 264, 270.

7 This is a paraphrase of Davidson's "the truth of an utterance depends on just two things, what the words mean and how the world is arranged." I expatiate on the point of this latter formulation in my "Pragmatism, Davidson and Truth," in *Truth and Interpretation: Perspectives on the Philosophy of Donald Davidson,* ed. Ernest LePore (Oxford: Blackwell, 1986), 344–6.

the first interpretation, I think that true propositions about the presence of chairs, the existence of neutrinos, the desirability of respect for the dignity of our fellow human beings, *and everything else* are true "in virtue of the way things are." On the second interpretation, I think that *no* proposition is true "in virtue of the way things are."

Taylor cannot really believe that the ways we describe things, the words that make up our truth-value candidates, are simply irrelevant to the truth of our sentences and beliefs. So he might accept the first interpretation. But if he does, he opens himself to the question: can we distinguish the role of our describing activity, our use of words, and the role of the rest of the universe, in accounting for the truth of our true beliefs? I do not see how we can. To say that we cannot is to say, with Davidson, that we need to drop "the third dogma of empiricism," the distinction between scheme and content. This means dropping the attempt to sort out propositions by whether they are "made" true by "the world" or by "us" – dropping the problematic of realism and antirealism by dropping the representationalist presuppositions of that problematic.

On my view, if we drop that distinction and that problematic, we cannot explain what we mean by "correspondence" unless we posit something like "the world as it is in itself" or "the features that a thing has intrinsically, independent of how we describe it." That is why I think that when the thing-in-itself goes, correspondence goes too. So I think Taylor's attempt to keep the latter without the former is doomed to failure. Although the idea of the thing-in-itself is in disrepute, it seems to me to survive, in disguise, in the purportedly noncontroversial idea that things have intrinsic, non-description-relative features. That idea is quite distinct from the claim that most things, under most descriptions, have the features they do in entire causal independence from the way they are described.

Take dinosaurs. Once you describe something as a dinosaur, its skin color and sex life are causally independent of your having so described it. But before you describe it as a dinosaur, or as anything else, there is no sense to the claim that it is "out there" having properties. *What* is out there? The thing-in-itself? The world? Tell us more. Describe it in more detail. Once you have done so, but only then, are we in a position to tell you which of its features are causally independent of having been described and which are not. If you describe it as a dinosaur, then we can tell you that the feature of being oviparous is causally independent of our description of it, but the feature of being an animal whose existence has been suspected only in recent centuries is not. That is not a distinction between "intrinsic" and "merely relational" features of dinosaurs. It is just a distinction between their

(1) But this is an epistemological requirement, + it cannot be met.

causal-relations-under-a-description to some things (eggs) and their causal-relations-under-a-description to other things (us).

It was once thought (e.g., by Kripke) that causal relations are not under a description, whereas intentional relations are. The popularity of this belief was enhanced by Davidson's slogan that causation, unlike explanation, is not under a description. But I think that this slogan is not quite right. What Davidson should have said is that the same causal-relationship-under-a-description can be explained in many different ways, as many as there are ways of describing the things related.[8] This amounts to saying: no matter which way you describe the things between which you are trying to find causal relations, you should be able to see (find, envisage, posit) the very same such relations between them under every description of them. (If you describe them as dinosaurs and eggs, for example, you should be able to spot the same causal relations between them as when you describe them as batches of molecules or as space-time bumps.)

In other words, Davidson's point is (or should be) not that causal relations are more "intrinsic" to things than their descriptions, or that describing things as causally related to one another gets closer to the way they are "anyway" than describing them in other ways. It is (or should be) simply that *they cannot* causal relations must be kept constant under redescription.

However, people who pride themselves on being realists may ask: *Why* do they need to be kept constant? Because they *really and truly are* invariant or merely because unity is a desirable feature of science, a useful regulative idea that would be endangered if we let causal relations vary with descriptions? I see this as a bad question, because it presupposes one more version of the scheme–content distinction. It is one more example of the fatal temptation to hold on to the distinction between "in itself" and "for us." This latter distinction (which is *not* the same as the harmless and necessary distinction between "is" and "seems")[9] lurks at the bottom of most of the fruitless controversies in this area of philosophy.

Putnam's well-known criticisms of Kripke's (and his own) efforts to develop a causal theory of reference make clear why describing something's causal relations to other things is describing features that are no more and

---

Davidson is right

8 I am not sure, however, that Davidson would be willing to say this. For there are passages in his work in which he seems to suggest that only at the microstructural level, the level where there are "strict laws" and no "ceteris paribus" clauses, is there causal efficacy. I have trouble with this suggestion and hope that it is only apparently present in his writings.

9 The difference is that "is"–"seems" is a distinction that applies to objects under a description, whereas "in itself"–"for us" is an attempt to distinguish between an object under no description and a described object.

no less "intrinsic" or "extrinsic" to the thing than any other features of it, including its having been described by human beings. Once we drop the scheme–content distinction, we have no use for the distinction between the "intrinsic" and the "relational" features of things.

I can dramatize my basic disagreement with Taylor by taking up his contrast between our *self*-understanding and our understanding of "independent objects." Taylor brings up this contrast after suggesting that I might wish to say that I "agree perfectly well with [Taylor's] post-epistemological, intra-framework notion of truth as correspondence" but think that such an intra-framework notion of correspondence is "trivial" and "empty."[10]

So I do, and I also resist Taylor's claim that "this kind of truth (the post-epistemological kind) contrasts with something. It's not all the truth there is." "What it contrasts with," Taylor says, "is the truth of self-understanding. Just because we are partly constituted by our self-understandings, we can't construe them as of an independent object, in the way our descriptions of things are. . . . There isn't a single independent reality, staying put through all the changes in description, like the solar system stayed there, waiting for Kepler."[11]

I claim that we cannot make sense of the claim that "the solar system stayed there, waiting for Kepler," or at least not the sense that Taylor needs to make of it. As I see it, the only difference between redescribing the solar system and redescribing myself is that I use the redescription to make true statements about the solar system before I redescribed it, whereas, in some cases, I do not use my redescriptions to make true statements about my earlier self. Thus, in the case of a "Sartrean" redescription that changes the redescriber (e.g., when I redescribe myself as a coward or a homosexual, thus becoming something different), I make a predicate (e.g., "self-confessed

---

10 By "intra-framework" Taylor here means a notion of truth provided by our nonrepresentational dealings with the *Zuhanden*. He thinks these dealings not only "show us as being at grips with a world of independent things" but provide us with the insight that "our representations of [the world] are true or false by correspondence" ("Rorty in the Epistemological Tradition," 270). (As a Sellarsian psychological nominalist, who believes that all awareness is a linguistic affair, I of course am suspicious of the notion of "nonrepresentational dealings with the world." But the matter is complicated by the fact that, unlike Sellars, I do not see language as *representing* anything.) As I say in more detail later when I refer to the *Zuhanden* versus *Vorhanden* distinction, I think that our dealings with things give us at most a sense of the causal independence of objects, but do *not* give us any notion of truth as correspondence. Taylor thinks (ibid., 271) that "ordinary people" are believers in the correspondence theory of truth and that my views "might surprise and scandalize them." I do not think that nonphilosophers have any theory of truth, although I happily grant that they believe in a world of causally independent things.

11 Ibid., 272.

coward," "self-aware homosexual") true of my present self which was not true of my old self. But there are no scientifically interesting "Sartrean" re-descriptions of the solar system; large-scale astrophysical descriptions of it are, if true at all, always true. So if Kepler's description is right now, it was right before Kepler thought it up.

Is this difference helpfully explicated by Taylor's phrase "staying put through all changes in description"? If this just means "the solar system be-haved the same way before and after Kepler" it is merely a remark about the causal relations between Kepler and the solar system – just as "Pierre became a new man after he admitted his cowardice to himself" is simply a remark about the causal relations between the young Pierre's beliefs and behavior and those of the slightly older Pierre. We do not need the idea of two kinds of truth, or that of two kinds of reality (e.g., *Vorhandensein* and *Dasein*), to ex-plicate the difference between these two sets of causal relationships. But if "staying put" means "there was a world, consisting of a multiplicity of objects differentiated by intrinsic, non-descriptive-relative features, waiting for somebody to come along and develop a language that cut it at the joints by assigning a word to each object," or if it presupposes or entails that claim, things get controversial.

The strength of Taylor's position is that people like Goodman, Putnam, and myself – people who think that there is no description-independent way the world is, no way it is under no description – keep being tempted to use Kantian form–matter metaphors. We are tempted to say that there were no objects before language shaped the raw material (a lot of ding-an-sichy, all-content-no-scheme stuff). But as soon as we say anything like this we find ourselves accused (plausibly) of making the false causal claim that the in-vention of "dinosaur" caused dinosaurs to come into existence – of being what our opponents call "linguistic idealists." Davidson, however, has shown us how to make our point without saying anything susceptible to that mis-interpretation. He suggests that we stop trying to say *anything* general about the relation between language and reality, that we stop falling into our op-ponents' trap by taking seriously problems that owe their existence to the scheme–content distinction. We should just refuse to discuss such topics as "the nature of reference."

This suggestion amounts to saying: answer questions about word–world relations for particular words used in a particular ways by particular people, but don't answer any more general questions about such relations.[12] Treat,

---

[12] See Davidson's "Reality Without Reference" on this point, especially the following passage: "If the name 'Kilimanjaro' refers to Kilimanjaro, then no doubt there is *some* relation

as Davidson advises, "words, meanings of words, reference and satisfaction" as "posits we need to implement a theory of truth"[13] — a Tarski-style theory of truth for a particular, used language.[14] Such a theory is a theory that enables us to predict the behavior of speakers of that language in various situations. It is constructed by inspecting the apparent causal relations between speakers and their environment with the hope of eventually mapping their behavior onto ours. Such an empirical theory is entirely irrelevant to questions about "realism" or "the nature of reference."

This strategy dictates that whenever we are asked a question like "*Was* the solar system waiting around for Kepler?" we decline to answer. We insist that, in return for our abandoning our Kantian form–matter metaphors, our opponents abandon their anthropomorphic, pathetic-fallacy metaphors: no more inorganic objects hoping desperately that somebody will finally find language in which to pick them out, wistfully waiting for somebody to locate the joints that divide them from their neighbors. We think that the only way to get beyond this sterile clash of uncashable metaphors is to put the burden of argument on our opponents by asking them to answer two questions: (1) Can you find some way of getting between language and its object (as Wittgenstein sardonically put it) in order to suggest some way of telling which joints are nature's (part of the content) and which merely "ours" (just part of the scheme)? (2) If not, can you see any point in the claim that some descriptions correspond to reality better than others?[15]

This brings me to Taylor's distinction between matters "arbitrable by reason" and other matters. If there were a distinction between a sentence being just plain true and a sentence being true because it corresponded to reality, then there might be some point to a distinction between "believed because it suits our purposes better than any available alternative" and "believed

between English (or Swahili) speakers, the word, and the mountain. But it is inconceivable that one should be able to explain the relation without first explaining the role of the word in sentences; and if this is so, there is no chance of explaining reference directly in non-linguistic terms" (*Inquiries into Truth and Interpretation* [Oxford: Clarendon Press, 1984], 220).

13 Ibid., 222.

14 I take Davidson's claim (in "A Nice Derangement of Epitaphs," in *Truth and Interpretation*, ed. LePore, 445) that "there is no such thing as a language" to mean simply that there are no sets of conventions to be learned when one learns how to talk, no abstract structure to be internalized. The phrase "truth-theory for a language" just means "theory that enables you to predict, fairly successfully, what noises or marks a speaker or group of speakers will produce in what situations."

15 Readers familiar with Davidson will recognize this second question as a reformulation of his point that "the notion of fitting the totality of experience, like the notion of fitting the facts, or of being true to the facts, adds nothing intelligible to the simple concept of being true" ("On the Very Idea of a Conceptual Scheme," in *Inquiries,* 195).

because it has survived the arbitration of reason." For we could say that sentences believed true but not believed to correspond to reality are not arbitrable by reason, whereas those whose truth involved such correspondence are appropriate candidates for rational arbitration. If I understand him correctly, this is in fact Taylor's way of aligning these two distinctions.

Taylor pictures me as saying, by contrast, "either true by correspondence to reality or not true at all, so moral judgements (and other *Dasein*ish beliefs) can't be true."[16] This picks me up by the wrong handle. Taylor sees me as interpreting "all differences between 'alternative language-games' non-realistically,"[17] whereas I want to discard the whole project of distinguishing

16 See Taylor, "Rorty in the Epistemological Tradition." "He [Rorty] seems to be as always drawing his inference that a representation which is not made true by some independent reality might just as well not be considered a candidate for truth at all" (272). My inference is rather: since no proposition is "made" true by anything and since no sentence is a representation of anything, all candidates for truth are on a par in respect to their relation to an independent reality. Taylor takes me to have something like a correspondence view when it comes to normal, routine physical science, but as unwilling to grant that moral reflection or revolutionary, paradigm-changing physical science arrives at truth in the way normal physics does. I have no such attachment. My point is that the difference between doing physics (either normal or revolutionary) and reflecting on one's moral character is not a matter of truth vs. no truth, or of different kinds of truth, but *just* the difference between finding sentences that, if true, are (usually) always true and finding sentences that either have to include dates or else have to be seen as changing their truth-value. The only other difference is degree of controversiality – a sociological matter without philosophical significance.

I have to admit, however, that something like the view which Taylor attributes to me, and which I am here repudiating, can be found in certain passages of my *Philosophy and the Mirror of Nature*. There was an only half-erased decisionism in that book – an unhappy tendency to make existentialist noises, noises that presuppose a usable distinction between *Wille* and *Vorstellung*. By slowly coming to understand the thoroughgoing antirepresentationalism of Davidson's approach to language, I have been helped to reach what I hope is a more consistent view. I should think that decisionism was hard to find in most of the texts Taylor cites in "Rorty in the Epistemological Tradition." But I confess that as late as 1986 it still reared its ugly head. For I was still making the unhappy distinction between "demonstrating that previous philosophers were mistaken" and "offering redescriptions in an alternative language" instead of briskly saying that to say that one's predecessors used a bad language is just to say that they made a certain kind of mistake. (This lapse is cited by Taylor in "Rorty in the Epistemological Tradition," 259.) Whatever dumb things I may have said in the past, I am now heartily in accord with Taylor that "there is no automatic inference from lack of consensus to unarbitrability" (ibid., 263) and that there is no plausibility to the "scenario of closed pictures" (ibid., 260). I also am happy to say that when I put forward large philosophical views I am making "claims to truth" (see ibid., 266–7) rather than simply a recommendation to speak differently. After a good deal of wobbling and weaseling on the point, I am now prepared to go all the way with Quine in saying that there is no epistemic, methodological, or "status" line between science and philosophy (though, of course, I am still not willing to privilege the vocabulary of physics in the way in which Quine does).

17 Ibid., 273.

between what is to be treated "realistically" and "non-realistically." This is why I cannot see that notions like "corresponding" and "representing" have anything to do with the distinction between rational arbitrament and alternative ways of settling disputes. I see that distinction as needing no fancier philosophical explication than is offered by the distinction between persuasion and force (suitably fleshed out with Foucauldian warnings about insidious "capillary" uses of power).[18] I think of all instances of persuasion, of onself or of others, as equally cases of "the arbitration of reason."[19] Debates about astrophysics, how to read Rilke, the desirability of hypergoods, which movie to go to, and what kind of ice cream tastes best are, in this respect, on a par. There is no point to asking in which of these cases there is "a fact of the matter" or "a truth of the matter," though there may be a point in asking whether any useful purpose is served by spending much time in debate.

So far I have been talking about passages in which Taylor employs notions I refuse to use, and so asks questions I refuse to answer. I turn now to the differing stories we tell about what has happened in twentieth-century philosophy, the differing narratives we construct within which to place ourselves. Taylor and I both pride ourselves on having escaped from the collapsed circus tent of epistemology – those acres of canvas under which many of our colleagues still thrash aimlessly about. But each of us thinks that the other is still, so to speak, stumbling about among the tangled guy ropes rather than having escaped altogether.

Taylor thinks that once one gets out from under epistemology one comes

18 But not so padded as to eclipse the distinction altogether. Some overenthusiastic Foucauldians, alas, have tried to make the term "rational persuasion" inapplicable to *anything;* they have done so by treating even the most judicious, courteous, and apparently unfettered parliamentary or academic debate as an instance of "violence," because certain alternatives that the participants consider unworthy of serious consideration are "marginalized." This is as pointless as saying that the debates between Democriteans and Aristotelians did violence to the alternatives that Einstein would eventually propose.

19 Taylor, in "Rorty in the Epistemological Tradition" (262), criticizes me for saying that the world doesn't "decide between" language games and for reinterpreting issues (e.g., between Aristotle and Newton) that "have been quite conclusively decided rationally" as having been "settled on pragmatic grounds." What I meant by saying that the world doesn't decide is that we didn't have a criterion for choosing between Aristotle and Newton in the sense in which poker players have one for deciding who takes the pot. The decision was taken in the same way all large, complex, non-criterion-governed, rational decisions are taken – on pragmatic grounds. What could be more rational than to say that it is no longer worth the trouble to add new epicycles, reinterpret gravitational attraction as natural motion, and otherwise shore up Aristotle's cosmology? Why bother to make a big *Vorhandensein* vs. *Dasein* distinction to separate that sort of decision from Pierre's decision that it is no longer worth the trouble to distinguish between his behavior and that of a coward?

But this is a "persuasive definition" of "pragmatic"!

to an "uncompromising realism."[20] I think one comes to a position in which the only version of "realism" one has left is the trivial, uninteresting, and commonsensical one which says that all true beliefs are true because things are as they are. This is uninteresting because it says only that the production of true beliefs is a matter of causal relations between language users and the rest of the universe, and that if either were different, their relations would be different. Realism becomes interesting only when we supplement plain speech and common sense with the "in itself" versus "to us" distinction. Taylor sees me as bearing the burden of argument because he thinks that this latter distinction cannot simply be walked away from but must be dealt with.[21] I think that neither he nor anyone else has explained why we cannot just walk away from it. Such an explanation would have to tell us more than we have ever before been told about what good this distinction is supposed to do us. I keep hoping that Taylor, as fervent an anti-Cartesian as I, will join me in abandoning it. Alas, he persists in agreeing with Bernard Williams, Barry Stroud, and other admirers of Descartes that it is indispensable.

Taylor thinks that the early Heidegger helps us to avoid both a reductionistic naturalism and the boring epistemological problematic of Cartesian skepticism. He sees me (particularly because of my sympathies with Daniel Dennett and my reluctance to admit that "there really is something it is like to be a human or a bat, but not to be a fifth-generation computer")[22] as inclined toward reductionism. I see myself as a wholehearted naturalist, but one who is as antireductionist as Taylor himself. I define naturalism as the claim that (a) there is no occupant of space-time that is not linked in a single web of causal relations to all other occupants and (b) that any explanation of the behavior of any such spatiotemporal object must consist in placing that object within that single web. I define reductionism as the insistence that there is not only a single web but a single privileged description of all entities caught in that web. The reductionist thinks we need explanatory unity as well as causal unity – a way of commensurating all explanatory vocabularies, one that will give us true nomologicals connecting all these entities (thoughts and neurons, vices and hormones, actions and motions, persons and organisms). Having learned from Davidson to be satisfied with token–token identities between entities differently described, I regard myself as cleansed of reductionist sin.[23]

---

20 Ibid., 258.   21 See ibid., 273.   22 Ibid., 265.

23 One of the things for which I am grateful to Davidson is having shown us how to distinguish what is alive in naturalism from what is dead in reductionism. For more on this point, see "Non-Reductive Physicalism," in my *Objectivity, Relativism, and Truth* (Cambridge University Press, 1991), 113–25.

But this redemption makes me all the more eager to insist, against Taylor, that Heidegger and Merleau-Ponty do not show us how to avoid naturalism, but merely caution us against letting naturalism slide over into reductionism.

Taylor and I agree that epistemology is something to get beyond, but he thinks me still "a prisoner of the epistemological world-view."[24] He thinks this because, as he put it in an earlier essay, "Overcoming Epistemology,"

> the whole epistemological construal of knowledge is mistaken. It doesn't just consist of inner pictures of outer reality, but grounds in something quite other. . . . We can draw a neat line between my picture of the object and that object, but not between my dealing with the object and that object. . . . The notion that our understanding of the world is grounded in our dealings with it is equivalent to the thesis that this understanding is not ultimately based on representations at all, in the sense of depictions which are separately identifiable from what they are of.[25]

Whereas Taylor thinks Heidegger on *Zuhandensein*, and Merleau-Ponty on action and the body, help us out of epistemology, I think these two philosophers keep us within it just insofar as they allow a place, however derivative, for pictures (and thus for the notions of "representation" and "correspondence").[26] They also help keep us within it by treating our nonlinguistic causal interaction with the rest of the universe as "grounding" knowledge rather than just plain helping to cause it. Following Robert Brandom and Mark Okrent, I want to see the *Vorhanden* as merely a special case of the *Zuhanden* by seeing words as merely a special case of tools.[27] So I do not see our dealings with the world as the framework (what Searle calls "the Background") that makes picturing possible; I do not think that either language

24 Taylor, "Rorty in the Epistemological Tradition," 258.
25 Charles Taylor, "Overcoming Epistemology," in *After Philosophy*, ed. Kenneth Baynes, James Bohman, and Thomas McCarthy (Cambridge, Mass.: MIT Press, 1987), 477.
26 In *Sources of the Self*, Taylor says that Heidegger and Merleau-Ponty help us see that "radical objectivity is only intelligible and accessible through radical subjectivity" (176). I do not believe there is such a thing as radical objectivity; that is, I reject Bernard Williams's idea that physics can assume a point of view that ignores human needs and interests – an idea Taylor accepts. I think that the subjective–objective distinction can be as safely and profitably neglected as the distinction between "for us" and "in itself."
27 Note that this is quite compatible with saying that "language speaks us," as Heidegger does at the outset of "Letter on Humanism." We self-creating tool users cause new predicates to be true of ourselves whenever we create new tools with which to create ourselves. Language can speak us even though a language is just a bunch of marks and noises thrown about in more or less predictable ways by human beings. Poets can be the unacknowledged legislators of world-historical epochs even though they are merely human beings who use marks and noises in unpredictable ways.

or knowledge has anything to do with picturing, representing, or corresponding, and so I see formulating and verifying propositions as just a special case of what Taylor calls "dealing" and I call "coping."

Where Taylor sees a relation with the world more primordial than representation, I see no break between nonlinguistic and linguistic interactions of organisms (or machines) with the world. The only difference between such interactions is that we call interactions "linguistic" when we find it helpful to correlate the marks and noises being produced by other entities with the ones we ourselves make – to engage in translation, as well as in other ways of explaining the behavior of the beings we are observing.[28] So, *pace* Taylor, we cannot draw a line between the object and our picture of the object, for what Taylor calls "picturing" the object is just more dealing with it. It is just interacting with it in a more complex way than we did before we thought up a linguistic description of it. All that we can draw a line between is the object and some other objects (the marks, noises, brain states, or whatever that are helping us cope with the object). The latter are usually neither pictures nor representations.[29]

I hope that what I have been saying shows that I am not a "nonrealist" in the sense in which Taylor takes me to be one and that my pragmatism cannot be criticized for many of the sins Taylor found in it when he wrote "Rorty in the Epistemological Tradition."[30] But I realize that even if we put all ques-

---

28 For what it is worth, I agree with Dreyfus, Taylor, and Searle that mark-and-noise-making robots which, in Drefyus's phrase, "lack the flexibility of a six-month-old child" cannot be viewed as using a language. In particular, they cannot be viewed as having "internalized" the language used by their programmer in her flowcharts. To use a language requires interacting with the rest of the world in such a way that a radical interpreter could figure out how to translate the marks and noises one makes into sentences of the interpreter's language. It is one thing to say, with Dennett, that we can hardly avoid taking the intentional stance when trying to predict the behavior of robots and another thing to say that they are thinking or have "inner representations" (except in the trivial sense in which the retina bears an inner representation of what is before the eye or that inside a thermostat there is a representation of the temperature of the room). The basic anti-MIT thrust of the arguments about intentionality that Dreyfus, Taylor, and Searle have been offering all these years now seems to me right, even though I do not see the use either of Searle's notion of "intrinsic intentionality" or of Nagel's notion that robots lack a vital ingredient called "something it is like to be."

29 Sometimes, of course, they are pictures or representations, as when we use an illustrated dictionary or field guides to identify birds or wanted posters to identify criminals. Then we have representations in the proper sense – items some of whose parts can be correlated one-to-one with parts of the thing being represented (a condition that obviously does not hold for most sentences or beliefs).

30 I should like to think that my current, updated (see note 16 above), more thoroughly and explicitly Davidsonian and antirepresentationalist version of pragmatism gives me a better set of replies to Taylor than the slightly earlier version he criticized in that essay.

tions about truth, realism, and correspondence to one side, Taylor would still find my pragmatism too entrenched in the Enlightenment tradition, too unaware of the need for hypergoods. I am one of those who lack a sense of (in Taylor's words) "how deep the roots are of our fragile consciousness, and how mysterious and strange its emergence is."[31] I am also one of those who, like Aristotle and Dewey, think that the moral life is a series of compromises.[32] But at least I can try to clear myself of the charge Taylor levels at "theories of Enlightenment materialist utilitarianism." Such theories, Taylor says, "have two sides – a reductive ontology and a moral impetus."[33] Like Dewey, I am trying to keep the moral impetus while discarding the ontology (*any* ontology, reductive or otherwise).[34] I hope that this essay has shown that, whatever the other defects of my philosophical position, I am not someone who, as Taylor puts it, "allows epistemology to command ontology."[35]

---

31 Taylor, *Sources of the Self*, 347.   32 See ibid., 66–7.   33 Ibid., 337.
34 Even the neutral monist ontology of "experience" that Dewey developed in *Experience and Nature*.
35 Taylor, "Rorty in the Epistemological Tradition," 264.

5

DANIEL DENNETT ON INTRINSICALITY

The Battle over Intrinsicality

How do we tell when a complete causal explanation of X must include statements about X and when it is enough for it simply to explain why people think there is such a thing as X, explain why "X" is in the language? The Copernicans thought they did not have to explain the sun's motion, because it was enough to explain why the sun was *believed* to move. Their Aristotelian critics suggested they were confusing the predictive utility of a heliocentric model with the requirements of a genuine causal account. Dennett thinks it enough to explain why there *seems* to be phenomenology – why it seems as if "there's a difference between thinking . . . something seems pink to you and something *really seeming* pink to you."[1] His critics think this strategy shows that *Consciousness Explained* merely explains consciousness away.

It seems reasonable for Dennett to reply that explaining something away – explaining why we do not have to make a place for *it* in our picture, but only for the belief in it – is often a good thing to do. The road of inquiry would have been disastrously blocked if we had forbidden this move to the Copernicans or to those other seventeenth-century thinkers who attacked traditional beliefs about witches. On Dennett's account, we believe that there is phenomenology, and we believe in qualia, because we adopted a certain set of metaphors for talking about people, just as Aristotelians believed in solar motion, and witch-hunters in witches, because a certain picture of the cosmos held them captive. The use of these metaphors produced talk about "phenomenological data" – about, for example, what it is like to have

---

1 Daniel Dennett, *Consciousness Explained* (Boston: Little, Brown, 1991), 364.

*(1) "Conclusion" to Searle's Mystery of Consciousness
uses the "intrinsic" properties to defend his own
form of dualism. (as I argued in lecture April 1998)*

DANIEL DENNETT ON INTRINSICALITY   99

something pink on display in the Cartesian Theater. But if we can explain
people's linguistic and other behavior with the help of other metaphors –
for example, those that make up Dennett's Multiple Drafts Model – then we
are relieved of the obligation to explain qualia. As with the Copernicans, a
historicophilosophical gloss on our theory, one explaining why people once
talked about things that our theory need talk about no longer, is all that is
required.

To those whom Dennett, following Owen Flanagan, calls "the new mysterians," this strategy seems ludicrous. One cannot save the appearances
by tossing out phenomenological data, they argue, for those data *are* the
appearances. Reviewing *Consciousness Explained,* Thomas Nagel says, "A
theory of consciousness that doesn't include mental data is like a book
about Picasso that doesn't mention his paintings." On Nagel's view, the
claim that "there are no qualities, only judgements," is a product of Dennett's "Procrustean conception of scientific objectivity." Nagel thinks that
a non-Procrustean conception would make room for phenomenological
data by allowing for "objective standards that combine the first- and third-
person points of view."[2]

The cash value of the term "first-person point of view," as it is used by
Nagel, Searle, and others, is: a point of view that produces knowledge of *intrinsic,* nonrelational properties of mental events. Nagel and Searle see
clearly that if they accept the maxim "To explain all the relational properties something has – all its causes and all its effects – is to explain the thing
itself," then they will lose the argument. So nonrelational properties, and
the irreducibility of those properties to relational ones, are essential to their
case. When Nagel says, "Of course we would believe that anything that func-
tioned physically and behaviorally like a grown human being was conscious,
but the belief would be a conclusion from the evidence, rather than just a
belief in the evidence," he is saying that the intrinsic, nonrelational character of an explanandum cannot be reduced to the relational features that
permit us to have evidence of its presence. The gap Nagel sees between the
evidence and the conclusion from the evidence is the gap between the totality of the relations of consciousness to the rest of the universe and what
consciousness is *intrinsically.*

Searle sees the same gap as Nagel. He thinks we can refute the question-
begging claim that "mental states can be entirely defined in terms of their
causal relations" by pointing out that no such claim has ever been reached

2 Thomas Nagel, "What We Have in Mind When We Say We're Thinking," *Wall Street Journal,*
November 7, 1991.

by a close scrutiny of the phenomena in question. No one ever considered his own terrible pain or his deepest worry and concluded that they were just Turing machine states or that they could be entirely defined in terms of their causes and effects or that attributing such states to themselves was just a matter of taking a certain stance toward themselves.[3]

But for holists like Dennett, suggesting that we can "scrutinize the phenomena closely" is itself question-begging. That phrase presupposes just the idea of intrinsic, nonrelational features that Dennett questions – the idea of features that were clearly and distinctly scrutable, right up there on the screen of the Cartesian Theater, before you ever learned to talk. It begs the question of whether the behavior Searle describes as the result of scrutiny is best explained by saying that such scrutiny in fact occurs, or whether the appearance of scrutiny is as illusory as the appearance of phenomenology.

Dennett accepts, as Nagel and Searle do not, the Wittgensteinian dictum that ostensive definition requires a lot of stage setting in the language and that ostention without that stage setting (as when one says, "Forget about how it might be described; just concentrate on the *feel* of it – on what it's *like*") does not pick out an entity. Holists like Wittgenstein, Ryle, and Dennett – people who specialize in replacing intrinsic features with relational features – recognize their obligation to explain everything anybody has ever talked about. But they think that, just as it counts as an explanation of solar motion to explain why people used the term "solar motion," so it should count as an explanation of qualia to explain why people talk about intrinsic, nonrelational features of conscious experience. If the latter explanation succeeds, then the attribution of consciousness to other people (or nonpeople) can be viewed not as the result of an inference from behavioral evidence (as Nagel views it) but simply as a reformulation of that evidence.

This contrast between inferences from evidence and reformulations of evidence is, however, not quite the contrast we holists want. For putting it this way suggests an un-Quinean, unholistic contrast between fact and language – between inferring from one fact to another and changing one's description of the same fact. Holists cannot allow themselves the distinction between description and fact that this suggestion presupposes. They cannot

---

3 John Searle, *Intentionality* (Cambridge University Press, 1983), 262–3. The analogy between the Aristotle–Copernicus switch and the Descartes–Dennett switch that I am pursuing is reinforced by Dennett's allusion to Wittgenstein's famous question, "How would it look if the sun stood still and the earth moved?" In *Consciousness Explained*, discussing qualia, he follows U. T. Place and J. J. C. Smart in asking, "Well, what do you think it would seem like if it *were* just a combination of electrochemical happenings in your brain?"

allow questions like: is the organism's actual and possible behavior one fact and its consciousness another, or are they the same fact? For such questions try to do what Wittgenstein told us not to attempt: to get between language and its object. Holists can allow only questions like: should our best causal account of how things work include the relations of X to Y or merely an account of the relations of X to Y-talk? In the case at hand: should our account include the relations between brains, behavior, and events in the Cartesian Theater or just the relations between brains, behavior, and talk about such events?

Nagel would defend his conviction that what Dennett calls "heterophenomenology" is not enough by appealing to his metaphilosophical view that "the sources of philosophy are preverbal and often precultural, and one of its most difficult tasks is to express unformed but intuitively felt problems in language without losing them."[4] This metaphilosophical thesis epitomizes the nonholist, anti-Wittgensteinian picture of language according to which the limits of language are not the limits of thought. For on this picture, as Nagel says, "the content of some thoughts transcend every form they can take in the human mind."[5] This content–form distinction is essential to attempts to resist the encroachments of holism. For the holist wins if he can get you to drop what Davidson calls "the scheme–content distinction," and in particular to admit that what cannot be said cannot be thought. He wins if he can get you to accept Sellars's claim that "the appearances" which scientific explanation must save are themselves language-relative: that what appears to you is a matter of how you have been accustomed to talking. The psychological nominalism common to Sellars and Davidson – the view that, as Sellars said, "all awareness is a linguistic affair" – is just holism applied to the relation between language and thought. One will be able to defend the claim that there are intrinsic, nonrelational features of objects only if one can claim that knowledge of those features is *not* the same as knowledge of how to use the words one employs to describe those features.

Early in *Consciousness Explained* Dennett quotes Nagel as saying that "the attempt to give a complete account of the world in objective terms . . . inevitably leads to false reductions or to outright denial that certain patently real phenomena exist at all."[6] Dennett then suggests that Nagel might be won over to Dennett's own view after grasping the details of the theory that Dennett will proceed to develop. He further suggests that Nagel ought to accept heterophenomenology as a "neutral way of *describing the data*." Both suggestions

4 Thomas Nagel, *The View from Nowhere* (New York: Oxford University Press, 1986), 11.
5 Ibid., 102.
6 Dennett, *Consciousness Explained*, 71, quoting from Nagel, *The View from Nowhere*, 7.

are misleading and misguided. This becomes clear a bit later in the book when the heterophenomenologist starts claiming the ability to discover that what Nagel thought ineffable is not really ineffable. Nagel can reasonably regard this claim as begging all the interesting questions. From Nagel's point of view it is not good enough, because not neutral enough, to say, as Dennett says,

> If you retort "I'm not just saying that *I* can't describe it; I'm saying that it's indescribable!" we heterophenomenologists will note that at least you can't describe it *now*, and since you're the only one in a position to describe it, it is at this time indescribable. Later, perhaps, you will come to be able to describe it, but of course at that time it will be something different, something describable.[7]

Nagel can reasonably rejoin that he isn't interested in "something different, something describable." Rather, he is interested in preventing people from substituting the effable for the ineffable, for the *intrinsically* ineffable. Telling Nagel that he may become able, thanks to mastering Dennett's theory, to describe what he has previously been unable to describe is like telling Kant that he may become able, after mastering somebody else's theory (Hegel's, perhaps, or Sellars's), to describe what he had previously claimed was the indescribable thing-in-itself.

In "What Is It Like to Be a Bat?" Nagel says,

> Certainly it *appears* unlikely that we will get closer to the real nature of human experience by leaving behind the particularity of our human point of view and striving for a description in terms accessible to beings that could not imagine what it was like to be us.[8]

Nagel does not think that "the real nature of human experience" could be grasped in language by telling us that what we were *really* talking about when we used metaphors of a Cartesian Theater was something better described without those metaphors. He would presumably agree that the formula invoked by the Copernicans and by Dennett – "What you were describing as *A* was really *B*" – makes sense for things identified by nonintrinsic properties, but not for things identified by intrinsic properties. However, when we holists ask Nagel what "intrinsic" means, we are led around in a circle: the intrinsic properties are all and only those that we know we can never explain away. That is, they are properties we know things to have independently of our knowledge of how to describe those things in language.

---

7 Dennett, *Consciousness Explained*, 97.
8 Thomas Nagel, *Mortal Questions* (New York: Oxford University Press, 1979), 174.

This may seem an odd definition of "intrinsic property," since it is epistemological, as opposed to metaphysical definitions such as "property whose presence is necessary for the object being the object it is." But it is the only definition we holists can accept. For to avoid making a fatal concession to Nagel's essentialism, we must insist that "identity" is always identity under a description. Holists can countenance the notion of "property whose presence is necessary for the application of a certain description to the object," but not that of "property necessary for the object's self-identity, a self-identity it possesses apart from any particular description of it by us." When the nonholist says that the former notion does not capture the relevant sense of "intrinsic," the holist must reply that the only other sense of "intrinsic" she can make sense of is the one given above – a definition that is still epistemological but that presupposes the nonholist idea of nonlinguistic awareness.

The question of whether metaphysics and epistemology are distinct areas of inquiry is yet another about which holists must disagree with nonholists. It is as useless for a nonholist to tell a holist that she has confused metaphysics and epistemology as for an Aristotelian to tell a seventeenth-century corpuscularian that she has confused substantial change with local motion. The antiholist, antiverificationist notion that things have real essences apart from our knowledge of them, a notion shared by Kripke and Nagel and invoked by both in defense of Cartesianism, is required to keep the epistemology–metaphysics distinction – the distinction between objects and the sentences true of them – sharp. The holism and antiessentialism common to Wittgenstein, Quine, and Sellars breaks down this distinction by telling us that the only way to pick out an object is as that which most of a certain set of sentences are true of. I explore the implications of this latter claim – which I take to be central to the holist's case – in the following section.

Notice that if we once admit that there are such things as intrinsic properties, in the sense of properties knowledge of which is independent of the language we use – we can no longer think of heterophenomenology as a neutral method. For the heterophenomenologist's privilege of telling you what you were *really* talking about is not compatible with the claim that our knowledge of some things – for example, of the existence of qualia – is knowledge that cannot be affected by changing the way we talk, abandoning the pictures we have previously used language to sketch. So Dennett's suggestion that he has found neutral ground on which to argue with Nagel is wrong. By countenancing, or refusing to countenance, such knowledge, Nagel and Dennett beg all the questions against each other.

How could Dennett make his refusal to countenance such knowledge look like more than the blinkered stubbornness that Nagel and he must occasionally be tempted to attribute to each other? I do not think he can. At the depth of disagreement that separates these two philosophers, both their spades are turned. It is pointless for Dennett to say, "The more you look at the details of the Multiple Draft Theory, the more plausible my metaphilosophical presuppositions will become." That would be like a Galilean telling an Aristotelian that she will gradually become willing to settle for a world without final and formal causes, a world of atoms and the void, a world with only nominal essences, as she learns more about the elegant explanations of eclipses, parallax, and so on that a heliocentric model makes possible. Maybe she will, but it is not clear that she should – that there is any compelling reason for her to do so. This is because it is hardly clear when and whether to change one's mind about what to expect explanatory theories to do – and, in particular, about how paradoxical science has a right to be, how far it can go in substituting explanations of *X*-talk for explanations of *X*. There is no *general* way of answering the question with which I began this essay. For there is no overarching, ahistorical, context-free criterion to which one can appeal when asked to shift from one paradigm of explanation to another.

Things become even less clear, and neutral ground even harder to locate, when we leave philosophy of science and ascend to more abstract, more explicitly metaphilosophical levels. We ascend thither when we stop asking about the best explanation of the appearance of phenomenology and start asking whether there are such things as intrinsic, nonrelational properties *at all*, whether *any* ascription of any feature to any object is not an implicit description of its relations to something else. Wittgenstein and Sellars assume that it is, because for them becoming aware of qualia is the same thing as learning how to make judgments about qualia – a process that involves relating qualia to nonqualia. But the question of whether Wittgenstein and Sellars are right takes us back to the same old clash between holist and nonholist intuitions. For some of us, it is *obvious* that ostensive definition presupposes a lot of stage setting. For Nagel, on the other hand, the Wittgenstein-like claim that "it makes sense to say that someone is or is not using a concept correctly only against the background of the possibility of agreement and identifiable disagreement in judgments employing the concept" presages disaster. For accepting that claim would mean that "what there is or what is true" is limited to what we "could discover or conceive of or describe in some extension of human language."[9] To believe that is to give up what Nagel calls "the ambition of transcendence." Nagel thinks that the will-

---

9 Nagel, *The View from Nowhere*, 105–6.

ingness of recent philosophers (such as Wittgenstein, Ryle, Sellars, Davidson, and Dennett) to renounce this ambition is a sign of spiritual degeneration.

Centers of Descriptive Gravity

Even though metaphilosophy is just one more forum in which intuitions clash, I think it may serve the holist cause to which Dennett and I are both devoted to restate our holism in that forum. The high metaphilosophical ground should not be surrendered by default. So I want to commend some dashing metaphilosophical claims to Dennett, claims he might wish to make in an attempt to capture this ground from Nagel.

My principal suggestion is that Dennett put his claim that the self is a "center of narrative gravity"[10] in the context of the more general claim that *all* objects resemble selves in being centers of *descriptive* gravity. Narratives are just a particular form of description – the one employed by novelists and autobiographers – but the sort of thing novelists do is not all that different from the sort of thing logicians, physicists, and moralists do. All these people are weaving or reweaving sets of descriptions of objects. The only general truth we know, and the only one we need to know, about the relation between the objects and the descriptions is that the object X is what most of the beliefs expressed in statements using the term "X" are true of.[11] Like heroines whose stories are told by novelists, and selves whose self-consciousness about their own past character results in the acquisition of a quite different future, objects change as our descriptions of them change. That is to say, their center of descriptive gravity shifts as inquiry proceeds. Just as, for the usual Sartrean reasons, there is no perduring, intrinsic character of a human self – no "real me," no me *en soi*, for myself to grasp – so there is, for the usual Wittgensteinian–Sellarsian psychological nominalist reasons, no intrinsic character of *any* object to grasp.[12] So Nagel's ambition of transcendence is not the tough-minded commitment to intellectual honesty he thinks it, but rather a tender-minded yearning for an impossible stability and order – the kind of yearning William James deplored in the opening chapter of his *Pragmatism*.[13]

---

10 "Selves as Centers of Narrative Gravity" is the title of chapter 11 of *Consciousness Explained.*
11 I develop some of the implications of this dictum in my *Objectivity, Relativism, and Truth* (Cambridge University Press, 1991), 96–7.
12 Here I am reiterating a point made in "Charles Taylor on Truth," in this volume.
13 Accusations of tender-mindedness and boasts of tough-mindedness are, of course, cheap. I do not wish to make anything of these epithets, but merely to remind the reader how easily such accusations and boasts can be made by either side, and how little is ever settled by making them. It is, however, useful to point out the parallel between Dennett's advocacy of

The view I am suggesting has obvious resemblances to that of the ideal-ists – the founders of the holist tradition in modern philosophy, the first peo-ple to question the distinction between the intrinsic and the relational fea-tures of objects. The idealists' thesis of the internality of all relations amounts to the suggestion that we think of all objects as physicists think of centers of gravity. On this view, all objects are what they are in virtue of all their relations to everything else in the universe. That was why the idealists often said that "really" there was only One Big Object – the Absolute, the ob-ject that wasn't related to anything because it was nonspatiotemporal, a *to-tum simul*.

To retain the idealists' holism while junking their metaphysics, all we need do is renounce the ambition of transcendence. We can stop suggest-ing that the four-dimensional All is more of an object, or is "realer," than a dust mote or a patch of pink or Dennett's lost-sock center (the center of the smallest sphere that encompasses all the socks Dennett has lost in his life-time). We can do this if we cease to think in terms of Appearance and Real-ity, as Bradley and Royce did, or in terms of sentences made true by Us and sentences made true by the World, as Dummett and his followers do. If we drop such representationalist notions as "appearance" and "making true," then we can let numbers and tables, quarks and stars, lost socks and moral values share the same "objective" status. The interesting differences among them will be those made by our (often fluctuating) notions of what is rele-vant and irrelevant to the truth of beliefs about each different sort of object. These notions will not be responsible to something called "the intrinsic

the "sort of anti-essentialism that is comfortable with penumbral cases and the lack of strict dividing lines" (*Consciousness Explained*, 421) – an antiessentialism encouraged, as Dennett remarks, by Darwin's reinterpretation of biological specification – and James's joy in the fuzziness of the pragmatist's view of things, its lack of sharp outlines. Note also Dewey's re-mark that "[t]he influence of Darwin upon philosophy resides in his having conquered the phenomena of life for the principle of transition," thereby enabling us to renounce the sort of explanation that "only abstracts some aspect of the existing course of events in order to reduplicate it as a petrified eternal principle by which to explain the very changes of which it is the formalization" (John Dewey, "The Influence of Darwin on Philosophy," in *The Mid-dle Works of John Dewey* [Carbondale: Southern Illinois University Press, 1977], 4: 7, 11). Dewey would have admired Dennett's denunciation of the idea that "consciousness is a special all-or-nothing property that sunders the universe into two vastly different categories: the things that have it (the things that it is like something to be, as Nagel puts it) and the things that lack it" (*Consciousness Explained*, 447). Both James and Dewey thought of them-selves as following out the antiessentialist consequences of Peirce's "principle of pragma-tism" ("To attain perfect clearness in our thoughts of an object, then, we need only con-sider what conceivable effects of a practical kind the object may involve . . ."), a principle entailing the antiessentialist insistence on relationality that Peirce called "synechism."

character of the object in question," but only to the ordinary process of reweaving our webs of belief and desire, often in unpredictable ways (as when we begin to think of Riemann's axioms as relevant to interstellar distances or of the origin of the human species as irrelevant to moral values).[14]

Idealism sank under the burden of its residual attachment to the idea that philosophical reflection might provide a shortcut to transcendence, and for a time it took holism down with it. But holism bobbed up again as we gradually freed ourselves from the analytic–synthetic and language–fact distinctions with which neoempiricist anti-idealist polemics (such as Russell's and Ayer's) had lumbered us. Quine, White, Putnam, Wittgenstein, Kuhn, and the other liberators suggested we drop the idea of frozen sets of statements (the "analytic" ones, the ones that picked out the "intrinsic" features of an object).

Quine's notion of "the web of belief," like Putnam's notion of "cluster concepts" and Wittgenstein's image of overlapping strands, helped break the hold of the idea that we have, in the back of our heads, semantical rules that should enable us to give nice definite answers to questions like "Is it the same sock after being redarned so much?" and "Was Dalton talking about the same atoms Democritus was talking about?" The idea of an Official List of Semantic Rules for using the word "sock" or the word "atom" was an attempt to do for the meanings of "sock" and of "atom" what we do for Sherlock Holmes and the number 17 – keep them stable by not letting new Holmes stories into the canon and not letting physics touch mathematics. Something called "the language" by Carnap and "the eidetic structures" by Husserl was supposed to play the role of canon fixer, the sort of role Conan Doyle played for Holmes. Once this entity was set aside – and especially once Davidson started showing us how to erase "the boundary between knowing a language and knowing our way around in the world generally"[15] – we were in a fair way to eliminating the last refuge of a distinction that helps make

---

14 Here, for example, is how the "physical object" vs. "nonphysical object" distinction looks once it is separated from the distinction between Us and the World. We group Sherlock Holmes, Middle Earth, the number 17, the rules of chess, and the interstate commerce clause of the U.S. Constitution together as "nonphysical," not because they are all nonspatiotemporal (what's nonspatiotemporal about Middle Earth?), or because they are all somehow "subjective" or "conventional" objects, but because we do not expect our beliefs about them to be altered by the range of cultural activity known as "physical science." We might be wrong in this expectation, but that is all right. Holism and fallibilism go hand in hand, and the object known as "physical objecthood" (also known as "the meaning of the term 'physical object'") is no less a center of descriptive gravity than is any other object.

15 Donald Davidson, "A Nice Derangement of Epitaphs," in *Truth and Interpretation: Perspectives on the Philosophy of Donald Davidson*, ed. Ernest LePore (Oxford: Blackwell, 1986), 445–6.

the ambition of transcendence possible, the distinction between Us and What We May Not Be in Touch With.

There may seem to be a residue of the bad, metaphysical side of idealism in the claim that all objects are centers of descriptive gravity. For this may seem to entail saying that objects change not by being battered or moved about or discolored by other objects, but only by our changing our descriptions of them. Further, the suggestion that they change in the latter way may seem to go against our intuition that "objects exist independently of thought," the intuition the idealists tried to put in question. But once we think of our uses of words, and of our beliefs, as just worldly objects in constant causal interaction with other worldly objects, battering and being battered, it is no longer clear what "independence" might mean. Obviously it cannot mean "causal independence." But the only other gloss ever offered on "independent of thought" is "having intrinsic qualities unchangeable by our descriptions."

To forswear intrinsicality is to renounce the realists' ambition of transcending "the human point of view" and reaching objects whose relation to our descriptions of them is utterly external. But it is not thereby to become either an "idealist" or an "antirealist." It is merely to say that, just as Quine replaced "analyticity" with "centrality to our belief system," so we should replace "intrinsic feature of X" with "feature unlikely to be woven out of our descriptions of X." To insist on a stronger sense of "intrinsic," one that would allow for the gap Nagel sees between behavioral evidence and the attribution of consciousness, the sort of gap that inspires us with an ambition of transcendence, would be like insisting that "life" might have an intrinsic character to which all this newfangled talk about DNA is quite irrelevant.[16] Such insistence can, for us holists, mean no more than "Some day we may have ways of talking about life that we cannot now imagine" – but this gesture toward the future enlargement of the language is not the sort of thing that could gratify Nagel's or Royce's ambitions of transcendence. For they want to transcend themselves in the direction of something that is already *there*, not merely in the direction of a future contingency.

It may seem as if running the "soft" and the "hard" ways of changing things together confuses real and intentional objects. But if we are holist enough to follow Davidson in giving up the scheme–content distinction (the distinction, e.g., between what language contributes to the object and what the world contributes, what the mind does by way of constituting the object

---

16 See Dennett, *Consciousness Explained*, 25, on *élan vital*.

and what nonminds do to it once it has been constituted), then we no longer have a use for the intentional–real distinction. Once we agree with Davidson that only beliefs can make belief true, then we can get along quite well with what we used to call intentional objects. But we will no longer call them so, because we shall have no use for the real–intentional contrast. We shall just call them "objects" *tout court*. Analogously, we shall drop the idealists' claim that all relations are internal, for we will have no use for the external–internal contrast.

Isn't this to drop some useful, necessary distinctions? No. It is to drop some useless distinctions, distinctions that have made more trouble than they were worth. The ambition of transcendence, in the form it took in modern philosophy, gave us the distinction between the world and our conception of the world, between the content and the scheme we applied to that content, between the truly objective and the merely intersubjective. These distinctions brought with them such nuisances as epistemological skepticism, transcendental idealism, absolute idealism, logical constructionism, and phenomenology. Habitual use of these distinctions made us think that if we once gave up on intrinsicality – on the content as something distinct from the scheme – we should no longer have what Nagel calls "a robust sense of reality."[17] But once we are free of the scheme–content distinction, we are free to think of robustness as the willingness to let centers of descriptive gravity keep changing. The issue about who is more spiritually degenerate than whom depends on whether you think it more robust to describe yourself in the Darwinian terms that Dewey, Davidson, and Dennett use to describe themselves, or whether you think it more robust to keep your eyes on something on the other side of a gap, the sort of object that is "more" than just a center of descriptive gravity.

Which seems to you more robust will in part be decided by, and will in part decide, your reaction to Dennett's discussion of Searle's Chinese Room, to Frank Jackson's example of Mary the Color Scientist, and to all the other intuition pumps that have been designed to enhance or diminish your sense of the importance of phenomenology, qualia, and intrinsicality. Whether you keep or give up the ambition of transcendence is not determined by finding "confusions" or "mistakes" in the work of Nagel or Searle or Dennett

17 See *The View from Nowhere*, where Nagel says that the "present intellectual climate," created both by people who do not regard objectivity "as a method of understanding the world as it is in itself" and by those who think that objectivity "can provide a complete view of the world on its own," is due to "an insufficiently robust sense of reality and of its independence of any particular form of human understanding" (5).

or Davidson.[18] Diagnoses of illusion or confusion are just polemical ways of describing your opponents' distinctions, or their failure to make your distinctions. But distinctions are as much up for grabs as anything else. There are no quick fixes. There is only the continual passage back and forth between small intuition pumps like Jackson's description of Mary or Dennett's redescription of Mary[19] and large intuition pumps – for example, large metaphilosophical generalities like those I have cited from Nagel and those I have been formulating in opposition to his. All we can do is hope to attain reflective equilibrium by trekking back and forth between the low ground, where we haggle about how to describe the Chinese Room, and the high ground, on which we elaborate competing, self-serving definitions of such virtues as robustness.

The Mind as the Last Refuge of Intrinsicality

Full-strength holism, when applied to issues in the philosophy of mind, produces the radical antidualism espoused by Davidson.[20] "The most promising and interesting change that is occurring in philosophy today," Davidson says, "is that these dualisms [of scheme and content and of the objective and the subjective] are being questioned in new ways." These dualisms, he continues, have their common origin in "a concept of the mind with its private states and objects."[21] Commenting on Fodor, Davidson writes:

> [I]t is instructive to find the effort to make psychology scientific turning into
> a search for internal propositional states that can be detected and identified
> apart from relations to the rest of the world, much as earlier philosophers

18 Both Nagel and Dennett occasionally accuse their opponents of "confusions," "mistakes," and "illusions." In his review of *Consciousness Explained,* Nagel says that Dennett "confuses consciousness with self-consciousness" and is guilty of "a confusion about objectivity." In *Consciousness Explained,* Dennett says that "the illusion that consciousness is the exception [to the rule that whatever is, is explicable by being related to other things] comes about, as I suspect, because of a failure to understand this general feature of successful explanation [that explanation is in terms of things other than the explanandum]" (455). Such talk is probably inevitable, but its prevalence encourages the continuation of what Janice Moulton calls "the adversarial culture" of analytic philosophy. This is a culture whose inhabitants are impatient with the inconclusiveness of the search for reflective equilibrium and dream of finding unanswerable arguments – arguments that cannot be vitiated by a new set of distinctions.
19 Dennett, *Consciousness Explained,* 399.
20 Portions of this section are adapted from my "Consciousness, Intentionality and Pragmatism" in *Modelos de la Mente,* ed. José Quiros (Madrid, 1990). That essay offers an account of the recent disagreements between Fodor and Dennett, and a more extended account of Dennett's position in the development of philosophy of mind since Ryle.
21 Donald Davidson, "The Myth of the Subjective," in *Relativism: Interpretation and Confrontation,* ed. Michael Krausz (Notre Dame, Ind.: Notre Dame University Press, 1989), 163.

sought for something 'given in experience' which contained no necessary clue to what was going on outside. The motive is similar in the two cases: it is thought that a sound footing, whether for knowledge or for psychology, requires something inner in the sense of being non-relational.[22]

Suppose we become convinced (by reading Dennett's *Consciousness Explained,* perhaps) that persons have no states, propositional or otherwise, which meet this description – that all the properties truly ascribable to people are relational in the relevant respects, and none of them intrinsic. Davidson points out that despite this conviction we should still be able to specify various states of the organism about which the organism had epistemic access and authority of various special sorts. However, we should not explain this access or authority by reference to the "subjective" or "mental" character of the state, for these terms would themselves be explicated entirely by reference to such authority or access.

I have argued in the past that we might well have become convinced of this point a few hundred years ago, in the course of assimilating the implications of Galilean mechanics for the nature of scientific explanation. Had that happened, we would now neither be captivated by the metaphor of the Cartesian Theater nor have a use for Fodor's notion of "psychologically real states." Indeed, we would never have encouraged attempts to develop a science called "psychology" that took itself to be distinct both from the wisdom of the folk and from neurophysiology. In the days when corpuscularians were busy draining planets and rocks and animals of their intrinsic natures, busy driving out formal and final causes, Cartesian philosophers had to work fairly hard (in the face of incredulous stares from people like Hobbes and Gassendi) to create "consciousness" as a refuge for Aristotelian notions of substance, essence, and intrinsicality. But they succeeded. Thanks to their efforts, even after the colorfully diverse contents of Aristotelian nature were smeared together into one big swirl of corpuscles – one big substance called "matter" – there remained, here below, one other substance: the mind. The mind that these philosophers invented was its own place – in the sense that, as Davidson says, it contained "an ultimate source of evidence the character of which can be wholly specified without reference to what it is evidence for."[23] This mind knew both its own contents and its own intrinsic nature independently of its knowledge of anything else.

The cash value of the claim that the mind is its own place is that the mind is capable of swinging free of its environment – capable of standing in relations

22 Ibid., 170.   23 Ibid., 162.

of "aboutness" or "evidence for" to all kinds of things that have nothing to do with that environment – such things as unicorns and transfinite cardinals. But this ability to swing free of the environment – an ability Husserl thought was the Achilles' heel of all forms of naturalism – is, on the view of those who (like Dennett and Davidson) think intentionality extrinsic,[24] just as "naturalistic" as the ability to reflect light or to exert gravitational force. For although unicorns do not exist, sentences using the word "unicorn" do, and tokenings of such sentences are no more mysterious or unnatural than collisions of atoms. To attribute a belief in unicorns to someone is to describe her as standing in a relation to a proposition, just as to attribute a dollar value to her is to describe her as standing in a certain relation to a slave trader or an organ bank. The former attribution is no more "non-natural" than the latter. It is useful to talk about beliefs in unicorns, and thus about unicorns, in order to account for what we find in medieval books and tapestries, just as it is useful to talk about dollar values in order to account for the behavior of businessmen, to talk about propositions in order to account for the linguistic behavior of foreigners, and to talk about atoms to account for, say, chemical reactions. We do not talk about the internal structure or the evolutionary niche of unicorns, because we have no need to talk about unicorns when we do biology. We do not ask about the intrinsic nature of dollar values or of the dollar itself or of propositions, any more than about the intrinsic nature of transfinite cardinals. For values and propositions, like numbers, are *obviously* merely slices out of vast webs of relationships.[25]

To see things from Davidson's naturalistic perspective, it helps to consider the analogy between attributing states to a brain and to a mind. Nobody wants to suggest that a *brain* is its own place or that it could lose touch with the external world. For whether a brain is hooked up to wires, computers, and photoelectric cells, or instead to the rest of a central nervous system and some protoplasmic sense organs, is irrelevant.[26] It is always hooked up to *some* external world. If it ceased to be so hooked, it would cease to be a functioning brain. It would just be a heap of cells. Similarly, if a central

---

24 See Dennett's classification of contemporary philosophers of mind according to whether or not they take intentionality to be intrinsic in "Evolution, Error and Intentionality," *The Intentional Stance* (Cambridge, Mass.: MIT Press 1991) 287–321.

25 I owe the analogy between assigning intentional states and assigning dollar values to Dennett. See *The Intentional Stance,* 208.

26 The difference between these two alternatives creates the familiar problem of how we know that we are not brains in a vat. Davidson's solution is to say that a brain that has always been in a vat will have a lot of beliefs about the vat-cum-computer environment that in fact surrounds it, no matter what input it receives from the computer. For discussion and criticism

processor made of metal, silicon, and plastic were not hooked up to some input and output devices, it would not be a functioning central processor, but just a heap of chips. So one can imagine Davidson arguing as follows: if the mind is just the brain under another description, then both mind and brain are equally incapable of failure to hook up. The most that redescription in mentalistic rather than neural terms could do would be to describe more and more complicated hookups, not eliminate them altogether.[27]

Davidson's explanation of why the mind is not its own place hooks up nicely with Dennett's quasi-neurological account of consciousness in terms of parallel distributed processing. The work of these two holists, taken in tandem, should be thought of as the final stage of the attack on Cartesianism that began with Ryle. If this attack succeeds, our descendants will think it unfortunate that the seventeenth century did not carry through on its project of recontextualizing everything by seeing the mind too as just one more slice of a vast web of relationships. If the seventeenth century had treated Descartes's *Meditations* as just an unfortunate bit of residual Aristotelianism, forgiveable in the author of a great treatise on corpuscularian mechanics, we might never have had the notion of "consciousness," or the science of psychology,[28] to worry about.

of this Davidsonian line of argument, see Colin McGinn, "Radical Interpretation and Epistemology," in *Truth and Interpretation*, ed. LePore, 369–86. It is significant that McGinn thinks that, to refute Davidson, we need to resurrect the distinction between "experience" and "belief" which Dennett tries to bury. McGinn thinks it necessary, in order to make "interpretation respect the premises on which scepticism rests," to say that "the (phenomenological) content of experience is fixed by the intrinsic condition of the brain" (362). Davidson, by contrast, takes it as his aim to get rid of the premises on which scepticism rests. So for him, both "the problem of the external world" and "the problem of other minds" repose on a traditional but wrongheaded distinction between "the phenomenological content of experience" and the intentional states attributed to a person on the basis of his causal interactions with his environment.

27 For a defense of the idea of intrinsic mental states against Davidson, see Mark Johnston, "Why Having a Mind Matters," in *Truth and Interpretation*, ed. LePore, 408–26. Johnston is right to say that Davidson's "anomalous monism" takes "the propositional attitudes as constitutive of the mental" (424). He points out that one could take the absence of lawlike connections between mental and physical events, of which Davidson makes much, as showing "that the vocabulary of propositional attitudes is not made to carve out the natural mental properties which stand in lawlike relations to physical properties" (p. 425). One *could*, indeed, so take it. But then one *could* take the incommensurability of Aristotelian and corpuscularian explanations to show that a corpuscularian vocabulary is not suitable for carving out *verae causae*.

28 I am not suggesting that Wundt, Helmholz, and James would not have conducted the experiments they conducted, but merely that they would have described what they were doing as Freud described what he was doing (in his *Project*): namely, as providing placeholders to be filled in by the neurology of the future.

Dennett on Realism

In order to accept the metaphilosophical position I sketched in the second section (Centers of Descriptive Gravity) and in order to complete the "sea change" in philosophical thinking that Davidson foresees,[29] we have to stop worrying about realism and antirealism. Dennett, alas, still takes controversy over these topics seriously. So in this final section I turn to Dennett's residual attachment to ontology (forgivable in the author of a great treatise on the brain), and in particular to his distinction between illata and abstracta.

I shall begin by trying to rebut something Dennett says about my own views. Dennett describes me as believing that the difference between folk psychology and astrology is "not a significant difference."[30] He also says that I would not grant to users of folk psychology that their use of this tool gives them "power to understand and anticipate the animate world." I am puzzled to find these views ascribed to me and puzzled that Dennett should think either view entailed by my denial that "any brand of 'realism' could *explain* the (apparent?) success of the intentional stance." Dennett's argument for ascribing these views to me seems to be this: (1) Rorty must admit that if folk psychology is a tool that gives us the power in question, it does so by virtue of accurate representation of the real rather than of the merely apparent. (2) Admitting that it does so by virtue of accurate representation would contradict his denial of the explanatory denial of realism. (3) So he must deny that it gives us that power.

I would not admit what (1) claims I must admit. But Dennett thinks that move is not open to me, since

> [e]ven someone who has transcended the scheme/content distinction and has seen the futility of correspondence theories of truth [like Rorty] must accept the fact that *within* the natural ontological attitude we sometimes explain success by correspondence: one does better navigating off the coast of Maine when one uses an up-to-date nautical chart than one does when one uses a road map of Kansas. Why? Because the former accurately respresents the hazards, markers, depths and coastlines of the Maine coast, and the latter does not. Now why does one do better navigating the shoals of interpersonal relations using folk psychology than using astrology?[31]

The force of Dennett's analogy depends upon whether "accurately represents" can mean the same thing in the case of charts and in the case of the

---

29 See Davidson, "The Myth of the Subjective," 159.
30 Daniel Dennett, "Real Patterns," *Journal of Philosophy* 89 (1991), 50.
31 Ibid.

patterns we folk psychologists, taking the intentional stance, discern in human behavior. In the former case, accuracy of representation can be determined by matching bits of one thing (the chart) with bits of something else (Maine) and finding a procedure for predicting features of the one on the basis of features of the other. My argument for the inability of "any brand of 'realism'" to explain the success of things like particle physics or folk psychology in empowering us to understand and anticipate the world is just that no analogous matching seems possible.

To rehearse once again the hackneyed argument against such matching common to idealists and pragmatists: we cannot go back and forth between our statements about electrons and electrons, or our ascriptions of belief and beliefs, and pair them off as we pair off bits of the chart and bits of Maine. This would be, as Wittgenstein said, like checking what is said in the newspaper against another copy of the same paper. Whereas we have different tests for the presence of a curve on the chart and a curve on the coast, we do not have different procedures for ascribing beliefs and detecting the presence of the beliefs ascribed. That is why "folk psychology represents accurately" seems to me to add nothing to "folk psychology enables us to anticipate the world." *good* (handwritten)

Dennett does nothing to tighten the analogy between mariners and folk psychologists by showing what the relevant sort of pairing or matching would be. Nor does he do much to explain what it is to "tie reality to the brute existence of pattern" – something he says that he and Davidson do but Paul Churchland and I do not. The only construal I can make of this phrase is "apply, ceteris paribus, the term 'real' to any pattern that helps us anticipate and understand the world." I am as willing to do this as Dennett or Davidson, but I still need an answer to the question: what does thinking of a pattern as *real* do *except* remind us that that pattern has been found useful in anticipating the world? A genuine explanation ought to appeal to something whose presence or absence we can test independently of our tests for the presence of the explanandum, but the pseudo-explanations offered by philosophical "realism" do not.[32]

I also need to know what Dennett mean by "depends on" when he writes, "The success of folk-psychological prediction, like the success of any prediction, depends on there being some order or pattern in the world to exploit."

---

[32] See Michael Williams, "Do We (Epistemologists) Need a Theory of Truth?" *Philosophical Topics* 14 (1986), 223–42, and Arthur Fine, "Unnatural Attitudes: Realist and Instrumentalist Attachments to Science," *Mind* 95 (1986), 149–79, for further defense of the claim that these are pseudo-explanations.

Is this sort of "depends on," as they used to ask in Oxford, the "depends on" in "Whether he will show up depends on the weather"? No, because that sort of dependence is a matter of spotting predictively useful regularities. Nobody has ever spotted predictively useful regularities, established by correlating independently isolatable objects, between a bit of success and a bit of exploitable order in the world, any more than anyone has ever spotted such regularities connecting wealth with the possession of material goods. Good Quineans like Dennett and me cannot, of course, speak of "conceptual as opposed to empirical" connections, but we can speak of unhelpful rather than helpful explanations. "That theory is successful because it gets at something real" seems to me as unhelpful as (to use Dennett's example) "We laugh because of the hilarity of the stimulus."[33]

I should have thought that the same verificationist impulses which lead Dennett to say that "if we are not urbane verificationists, we shall be burdened with all sorts of nonsense: epiphenomenalism, zombies, indistinguishable inverted spectra . . ."[34] would lead him to dismiss the notion of "real patterns as opposed to very useful, but merely apparent, patterns." But he never quite does. Though he often tells us that the terms "realist" and "instrumentalist" are too unclear to be of much use, he is nevertheless prepared to classify himself as more realistic than I, less realistic than Davidson, and so on. He never decides whether he is delicately balanced on a fence that has "irrealists" like (supposedly) me on one side and "realists" like (supposedly) Davidson on the other, or whether he wants (as I do) to help tear down the fence by refusing to use the "irrealist–realist" distinction at all. He sits, so to speak, on a metafence.

Pragmatists like myself think that once we stop thinking of true beliefs as representations of reality and instead, with Bain and Peirce, view them as habits of action, we have no use for "real" except as an uninformative, nonexplanatory honorific – a pat on the back for the patterns we have come to rely upon. Nor, consequently, do we have a use for "only in the eye of the beholder" (a phrase that Dennett, alas, puts in my mouth).[35] I should think that our shared verificationist fervor would lead Dennett to agree with me on these points. But he never quite does. Instead, when asked, "Are pains real?" he tells us that "they are as real as haircuts and collars and opportunities and persons, but how real is that?"

Nobody would ask "how real is that?" unless he had some invidious con-

33 Dennett, *Consciousness Explained*, 32.
34 Ibid., 246.
35 Dennett, "Real Patterns," 50.

trast in mind between things that are *really* real and things that are (as Royce put it) "not so damned real." Dennett does have such a contrast in mind – the Reichenbachian contrast between illata and abstracta. Haircuts, pains, and persons[36] are, for Dennett, like centers of gravity – presumably alike in that they are all abstracta. They differ in this respect from electrons, which enjoy the status of illata. I have never seen Dennett put this abstract–concrete distinction to any use, except to answer questions about his ontological commitments.[37] But if one adopts Fine's "natural ontological attitude," as both Dennett and I do, then one should not answer such questions. A person with that attitude does not *have* "ontological commitments" and never talks, as Dennett still does, about "the furniture of the physical world." Once she has finished anticipating and understanding the world, she feels no impulse to take up a new topic – ontology – or to make invidious contrasts between the various tools (between, e.g., centers of gravity and electrons) that she has been using.

What does the difference between an illatum and an abstractum come to?[38] In "Real Patterns" Dennett says that "abstracta are definable in terms of physical forces and other properties."[39] This chimes with a passage from Reichenbach he quotes in *The Intentional Stance* which says that "the existence of abstracta is reducible to the existence of concreta" because "inferences to abstracta" are "equivalences, not probability inferences."[40] Elsewhere Reichenbach refers to abstracta as "combinations of concreta" and

36 Dennett, *Consciousness Explained*, 246.
37 See, e.g., *The Intentional Stance*, where Dennett invokes the notion of "abstracta" in the course of saying why he does not think that beliefs are "part of the 'furniture of the physical world'" and that attributions of belief are "*true* only if we exempt them from a certain familiar standard of literality" (72). Since I think Dennett would be hard-pressed to explain what that standard is, I wish he would fend off questions about his ontological views by saying, as I would, that he no longer has any such views. Someone who has, as Nietzsche says, "actively forgotten" the outworn creed on which she was suckled no longer has any theological convictions; someone who has actively forgotten Quine's distinction between canonical and merely handy notations no longer has any ontological commitments.
38 I once thought that Dennett distinguished the abstracta from "the furniture of the physical world" by the inability of the former to function as causes. But if he ever made the distinction in that way, he no longer seems inclined to do so. In "Real Patterns," he says that "if one finds a predictive pattern of the sort just described [the sort that helps you anticipate the world] one has *ipso facto* discovered a causal power" (43n). He now seems inclined to grant causal power to anything that appears in a predictively useful explanation, including a belief or a center of gravity (as in "The airplane crashed because the rush of passengers to the bar altered its center of gravity").
39 Dennett, "Real Patterns," 28.
40 Dennett, *The Intentional Stance*, 53n.

① Typically stupid Dennettian remark

gives "prosperity" as an example of a term that "refers to a totality of observable phenomena . . . [and] is used as an abbreviation which sums up all those observations in their interrelationship."[41] By contrast, Reichenbach continues, unobservable illata like electrons are "not combinations of concreta, but separate entities inferred from concreta, whose existence is merely made probable by the concreta."

Reichenbach puts forward two distinctions as if they were coextensive. First, there is the distinction between the referents of terms that you know how to use after being given a short snappy definition phrased mostly in terms of observables and mathematical relations – terms like "the typewriter's center of gravity" or "Dennett's lost sock center" – and terms like "electron," "belief," "pain," "person," and "gene." You can learn how to use the latter terms only by getting the hang of a whole mini language game.[42] Second, there is the distinction between terms whose referents are such that "their existence is reducible to the existence of concreta" and those whose referents are not so reducible. The first is a pedagogic distinction, the latter a metaphysical one.

We post-Quinean and post–*Philosophical Investigations* holists are not as much at ease with the second distinction as Reichenbach was. The problem is that "referent of a term whose existence is reducible to the existence of observables" sounds clear only as long as you think you have necessary and sufficient conditions for the applications of terms. You have such conditions, at most, only for terms that have short snappy definitions in terms of observables (like "Dennett's lost sock center"), and as long as you don't quibble about what counts as observable.

In Reichenbach's day, it seemed obvious that definability and ontological status had something to do with each other. But now it does not. Dennett is not entitled to help himself to the metaphysical part of the Reichenbachian illatum–abstractum distinction, but only to the pedagogical (what we used to call the "semantic") part. But, by itself, this part is no help to him. For pains, persons, and beliefs (I am not sure about haircuts) are not entities you can learn to talk about by being given short snappy definitions. From a pedagogical point of view, beliefs are much more like electrons than like lost sock centers.

Dennett wants to say that it is as silly to ask whether beliefs are real as to ask whether his lost sock center is real. I quite agree, but not for Dennett's

---

41 See Hans Reichenbach, *The Rise of Scientific Philosophy* (Berkeley: University of California Press, 1951), 263.

42 Recall Putnam's distinction between "single-criterion concepts" and "cluster concepts" – a somewhat fuzzy distinction but good enough for present purposes.

reasons. My reason is that it is silly to ask whether *anything* is real – as opposed to asking whether it is useful to talk about, spatially locatable, spatially divisible, tangible, visible, easily identified, made out of atoms, good to eat, and so on. Reality is a wheel that plays no part in any mechanism, once we have adopted the natural ontological attitude. So is the decision to be, or not be, "a realist about" something. So is the decision about what position to occupy on the spectrum that Dennett describes (with Fodor's industrial-strength realism at one end and what he calls, alas, "Rorty's milder-than-mild irrealism" at the other). Dennett should, on my view, drop his claim to have found "a mild and intermediate sort of realism" – the *juste milieu* along this spectrum. He should instead dismiss this spectrum as one of those things it is not useful to talk about – one of those metaphors that, like those which make up the image of the Cartesian Theater, looked promising but turned out to be more trouble than it was worth.[43]

Why am I quibbling at such length about how Dennett uses, and should use, words like "real" and "realism"? Why am I not as insouciant about Dennett's metaontological fence sitting as he is? Mainly because I would like to convince him that all the reasons we have for getting rid of a captivating but troublemaking picture of the mind, the Cartesian Theater, are also reasons for getting rid of a captivating but troublemaking picture of human inquiry: Penetrating the Veil of Appearances. All of the reasons why one would want to write a whole book developing a new set of metaphors for talking about consciousness are also reasons for writing a book that offers a new set of metaphors for talking about the goal of science, one that will replace the metaphors describing the Cartesian "project of pure inquiry" expounded by Bernard Williams – a book like Dewey's *Reconstruction in Philosophy*, for example. I think, in short, that Dennett's "urbane verificationism" is a bit *too* urbane. It stops short of the goal out of what seems to me misplaced courtesy to a half-defeated enemy.

I enjoy metaphilosophy in a way that Dennett seems not to enjoy it. That is why, in the second section of this essay, I tried to cloak Dennett's criticism of "the new mysterians" such as Nagel[44] in lofty metaphilosophical rhetoric. The rhetoric of mystery fans like Nagel, McGinn, and Gabriel Marcel – of

---

43 See the introduction to my *Objectivity, Relativism and Truth* for an expanded statement of this attempt to follow Fine to a position beyond realism and antirealism. I urge there that we drop notions like "fact of the matter," "bivalence," and "determinate reality" for the same sorts of reasons Quine dropped notions like "analyticity," "synonomy," "semantic rule," etc. The same point can be urged by saying that the kind of "determinate reality" that a center of gravity has is all the determinate reality any object could possibly have. To ask for more determinacy than that is to surrender to the ambition of transcendence.

44 For this criticism, see Dennett, *The Intentional Stance*, 5–7.

antiverificationists who cherish ineffability – should, I think, be countered by an equal and opposite rhetoric, one denouncing the very idea of ineffability. This rhetoric should do what the positivists did in their day: it should make verificationism seem glamorous, exciting, and exactly what the age demands. We should not be so urbane as to leave this sort of rhetoric to our opponents.

The sort of rhetoric I commend is, in fact, hinted at in the closing paragraph of *Consciousness Explained*. This is one of my favorite passages, for there Dennett robustly resists the natural temptation to announce that he has finally gotten consciousness right – accurately represented it, gotten its intrinsic features straight. Instead he says that all he has done in his book "is to replace one family of metaphors and images with another." He goes on to say that "metaphors are not 'just' metaphors; metaphors are the tools of thought."

I wish that he had gone one step further and had added that such tools are all that inquiry can ever provide, because inquiry is never "pure" in the sense of Williams's "project of pure inquiry." It is always a matter of getting us something we want. What do we want out of a theory of consciousness? Not that the intrinsic nature of consciousness be revealed (as the metaphor of science and philosophy joining forces to pierce the veil of appearances would suggest), but that we have a way of talking which will, if widely adopted, change our intuitions. Why should we want to change our intuitions? For the usual Kuhnian reasons: our old intuitions are giving rise to too much sterile controversy, too many fancy theories that tack epicycles (such as "narrow content") onto epicycles, too much speculation (like Roger Penrose's) about the need for an as-yet-unimaginable breakthrough before we can hope to reach the light, too much defeatist guff about "the limits of science." In short, we want some new intuitions because the old ones haven't been getting us anywhere.

Mystery fans, of course, think that we haven't been getting anywhere because of (in a phrase of Colin McGinn's) "our own incurable cognitive poverty" and that philosophers who are content to change metaphors in order to free themselves of inconvenient intuitions are (as Nagel puts it) "sick of the subject and glad to be rid of its problems" and are "turning philosophy into something less difficult and more shallow than it is." Nagel sees attempts (such as Dennett's) to change the language in order to help us actively forget troublesome old intuitions as symptoms of a childish rebellion "against the philosophical impulse itself."[45]

45 Nagel, *The View from Nowhere*, 11–12.

Nagel identifies "the philosophical impulse" with what he elsewhere calls "the ambition of transcendence." By speaking in such terms, Nagel gears up the debate between himself and Dennett a further metaphilosophical notch. I think it is very helpful to do so. Within the tradition of analytic philosophy, Nagel's *The View from Nowhere* is one of the very few recent books that articulates its author's moral sensibility and that recognizes that philosophical argument will sooner or later run up against the limits set by such sensibility. My own sense of what it is worthwhile and important for human beings to do requires abjuration of the ambition of transcendence to which Nagel remains faithful. Since which intuitions you think have, or have not, been getting us somewhere depends in part upon where you want to go, your willingness to retain or give up certain intuitions interacts with your willingness to retain or give up certain ambitions. Neither intuition nor ambition, we holists maintain, can provide an Archimedean point.

6

ROBERT BRANDOM ON SOCIAL PRACTICES AND REPRESENTATIONS

Robert Brandom's *Making It Explicit* and John McDowell's *Mind and World* were both published in 1994. Both books help us see the overlap between the views of two important recent critics of empiricism – Wilfrid Sellars and Donald Davidson. These two philosophers never discussed each other's work, but they complement one another beautifully.

Though they share indebtedness to Sellars and Davidson, the two books differ dramatically. Brandom helps us to tell a story about our knowledge of objects that makes almost no reference to experience. He does not so much criticize empiricism as assume that Sellars has disposed of it. The term "experience" does not occur in the admirably complete index to Brandom's 700-page book; it is simply not one of his words.

By contrast, McDowell's book tries to defend empiricism against Sellars and Davidson – conceding most of their premises but dissenting from their conclusions. Brandom can be read as carrying through on "the linguistic turn" by restating pragmatism in a form that makes James's and Dewey's talk of experience entirely obsolete. McDowell can be read as arguing that pragmatists should not be allowed to banish the term "experience" from philosophy, because the price of such disappearance is much greater than Sellars, Davidson, or Brandom realizes.

The possibility of such disappearance raises the question of the place of British empiricism in the history of philosophy. The American pragmatists have usually been viewed as belonging to the same empiricist tradition to which the so-called logical empiricism of Russell, Carnap, and Ayer also belongs. The pragmatists' version of empiricism has seemed, to many historians of philosophy, to differ from others simply by being less atomistic in its description of the perceptual given. Yet carrying through on the antidualist and panrelationalist impulses that gave rise to James's and Dewey's critiques of Hume's and Mill's psychological atomism seems, in the light of Sellars and Davidson, to lead to a much more radical view – one that is no longer a version of empiricism at all.

Looked back upon in the light of the work of these two men, British empiricism may well seem a mere unfortunate distraction, a parochical and unimportant movement whose only impact on contemporary philosophy has been to provide piles of rubbish for us to sweep away. Those who have been convinced by Sellars and Davidson are led to wonder whether the epistemologico-metaphysical efforts of Locke, Berkeley, and Hume leave us with any useful residue at all (except perhaps for the protopragmatism that Berkeley formulated in response to Locke's unfortunate distinction between primary and secondary qualities). Sellars and Davidson can both be read as saying that Aristotle's slogan, constantly cited by empiricists, "Nothing in the intellect which was not previously in the senses," was a wildly misleading way of describing the relation between the objects of knowledge and our knowledge of them.

McDowell, however, though agreeing that this slogan is misleading, thinks we are now in danger of tossing the baby out with the bath. We need to recapture the insight that motivated the empiricists. He disagrees with Brandom's implicit suggestion that we simply forget about sense impressions and other putative mental contents that cannot be identified with judgments. The controversy between McDowell and Brandom is exciting wide interest because it is forcing philosophers to ask whether we still have any use for the notion of "perceptual experience." Brandom thinks that this notion was never of much use and that its place can be taken by that of "noninferential judgments caused by changes in the physiological condition of sense-organs." McDowell thinks that such a replacement would deprive us of an important empiricist insight – one that Locke and Aristotle shared, though both formulated it very badly indeed.

Brandom carries through on Sellars's criticism of "the Myth of the Given" by showing how the notion of "accurate representation of objective reality" can be constructed out of material provided by our grasp of the notion of "making correct inferential connections between assertions." He carries through on the "linguistic turn" by showing that if we understand how organisms came to use a logical and semantical vocabulary, we do not need to give any further explanation of how they came to have minds. For to possess beliefs and desires, on Brandom's view, is simply to play a language game that deploys such a vocabulary.

McDowell demurs from Brandom's conclusions while accepting many of his premises. He does not agree that we can reconstruct the notion of representation out of that of inference and thinks that Brandom's "inferentialist" account of concepts does not work. For McDowell, it is equally important to accept Sellars's point that something without conceptual structure cannot justify a belief and to insist, *pace* Sellars, that mental events which are not judgments can justify beliefs. So he pumps new life into the notion of "perceptual experience" by arguing that such experience *is* conceptually structured, but is nonetheless distinct from the belief that may result from it.

Reading McDowell's daring and original book side-by-side with Brandom's helps one to grasp the present situation in anglophone philosophy of mind and language. One way of describing that situation is to say that whereas Sellars and Davidson use Kantian arguments to overcome the Humean dogmas retained by Russell and Ayer, Brandom and McDowell supplement Kantian arguments with Hegelian ones. Most anglophone philosophers still do not take Hegel seriously, but the rise of what Brandom and McDowell refer to as their "Pittsburgh School of neo-Hegelians" may force them to. For this school holds that analytic philosophy still must pass over from its Kantian to its Hegelian moment.

I shall begin my discussion of Brandom by citing some of the Sellarsian and Davidsonian doctrines that he and I have found most inspiring.

Sellars is perhaps best known for a doctrine he called "psychological nominalism," formulated as follows:

> . . . all awareness of *sorts, resemblances, facts,* etc., in short all awareness of abstract entities – indeed, all awareness even of particulars – is a linguistic affair. . . . [Not] even the awareness of such sorts, resemblances and facts as pertain to so-called immediate experience is presupposed by the process of acquiring the use of language.[1]

Sellars's discussion of awareness in "Empiricism and the Philosophy of Mind" follows the same lines as Wittgenstein's discussion of sensation in his *Philosophical Investigations.* Wittgenstein says, when talking about private sensations, that "a nothing would be as good as a something about which nothing can be said." Sellars's version of this slogan is that a difference that cannot be expressed in behavior is not a difference that makes a difference. The pragmatism he shares with Wittgenstein can be summed up by saying: if you

---

1 Wilfrid Sellars, "Empiricism and the Philosophy of Mind," sec. 29. This essay was reprinted first in Sellars's *Science, Perception and Reality* (London: Routledge, 1963) and was reprinted in 1997, along with a commentary by Brandom, by Harvard University Press.

find people talking about something like "sentience" or "consciousness" or "qualia" which seems not to tie up with anything else, to be capable of varying even when everything stays the same, to be merely externally related to everything else, forget about it. Or, at least, do not regard it as a topic on which philosophers need to shed light.

Sellars's psychological nominalism paves the way for his claim that if you have semantical talk you have all the intentional talk you need. For, as Sellars says, "the categories of intentionality are, at bottom, semantical categories pertaining to overt verbal performances."[2] The force of this claim is that if you understand how we started using a metalinguistic vocabulary to comment on and criticize our overt verbal performances, you understand how intentionality came to exist. You can see intentionality, the ability to have beliefs and desires, and rationality, the self-conscious attempt to make those beliefs and desires more coherent, as emerging over the course of time, just as we see an ability to stand on two legs and to pick up sticks as emerging over the course of time. If you accept what Sellars says in the passages I have quoted, you can not only link cultural to biological evolution in the way Dewey hoped to link it, but do so far more perspicuously and convincingly than Dewey did.

The trick here is not to try, as Carnap once did, to give necessary and sufficient conditions for sentences like "The word 'red' refers, in English, to this color" or "That Spanish sentence is about the union of León and Castille" by describing how these sentences are used by the relevant sets of speakers. There is no reductionist impulse at work in Sellars, but there is a therapeutic impulse. The therapy consists in saying: imagine how a term like "refers to" or "is about" came to be used, and you will thereby know all you need to know about how reference, aboutness, and intentionality came into the world. The analogy here is with a term like "money": imagine how a barter economy transformed itself into one in which legal currency and commercial credit were in use, and you will know all you need to know both about how money came into existence and about what money is. No mystery remains for philosophers to puzzle about. The illusion of *depth* vanishes – an illusion caused, in this case, by the idea that only things that can be experienced through the senses are unproblematic.

The effect of focusing on intentionality rather than consciousness is to deflect attention from nonsentential sense impressions – the sort of thing that might cause a squawk of "Red!" in a parrot or a human – to beliefs and

---

2 Sellars, "Empiricism and the Philosophy of Mind," sec. 50.

desires, the sort of thing expressed in complete sentences. Focusing on consciousness leads to the question that intrigues Nagel and other defenders of the idea of "qualia": the question of how machines that respond differentially to a range of stimuli differ from animals that do the same. For Nagel, there is a thing called "consciousness" which such machines, and zombies, lack and which animals such as ourselves possess. For Sellars, it is not clear that machines lack anything except behavioral flexibility and complexity.

To put this point another way, almost all philosophers, from Aristotle through Locke to Hegel and Dewey, have assumed that there was a sort of quasi-intentionality called "sentience" present in nonhuman animals and that sentience was something more than merely an ability to respond differentially. Those who denied this, as Descartes did in his suggestion that nonhuman animals might be just complex machines, were thought to be insufficiently sympathetic to the situation of dogs – creatures that have feelings but no language. The most common objection to Sellars's psychological nominalism is that babies and dogs are aware of pain – and therefore have some sort of protoconsciousness – even though their awareness can obviously not be a "linguistic affair." Philosophers like Nagel and Searle still dismiss psychological nominalism on this ground alone: that Sellars failed to make a place for sentience.

As I say in the essay immediately following, McDowell wishes to revive the notion of sentience, even though he accepts psychological nominalism. But almost the only passage in Brandom's book in which sentience is mentioned reads as follows:

> Described in the language of physiology, our sensing may be virtually indistinguishable from that of nondiscursive creatures. But we not only sense, we also perceive. That is, our differential response to sensory stimulation includes noninferential acknowledgement of propositionally contentful doxastic commitments. . . . Our mammalian cousins, primate ancestors, and neonatal offspring – who are sentient and purposive but not discursive creatures – are interpretable as perceiving and acting *only in a derivative sense.* An interpreter can make sense of what they do by attributing propositionally contentful intentional states to them, but the interpreter's grasp of those contents and of the signficance of those states derives from mastery of the richer practices of giving and asking for reasons.[3]

On Brandom's and Sellars's view, the difference between complex animals like dogs or complex machines like computers, on the one hand, and sim-

---

3 Robert Brandom, *Making It Explicit* (Cambridge, Mass.: Harvard University Press, 1994), 276; emphasis added.

ple animals like amoebas or simple machines like thermostats, on the other, is simply that it pays to describe the former, but not the latter, as having beliefs and desires. We can predict and explain the behavior of dogs and computers on the basis of such descriptions better than we can without them. So we do what Daniel Dennett calls "taking the intentional stance" toward these more complexly behaving entities. There is not much profit in adopting the intentional stance toward amoebas and thermostats, but we can do so if we like.

For pragmatists, the question that looms large for Thomas Nagel and John Searle – "Yes, but do computers really *have* beliefs and desires?" – does not arise. For the question of the utility of a vocabulary is not distinct from the question of the real possession of properties signified by the descriptive terms of that vocabulary. Pragmatists agree with Wittgenstein that there is no way to come between language and its object. Philosophy cannot answer the question: is our vocabulary in accord with the way the world is? It can only answer the question: can we perspicuously relate the various vocabularies we use to one another, and thereby dissolve the philosophical problems that seem to arise at the places where we switch over from one vocabulary to another?

I read Sellars and Brandom as pragmatists, because I treat psychological nominalism as a version of the pragmatist doctrine that truth is a matter of the utility of a belief rather than of a relation between pieces of the world and pieces of language. If our awareness of things is always a linguistic affair, if Sellars is right that we cannot check our language against our nonlinguistic awareness, then philosophy can never be anything more than a discussion of the utility and compatibility of beliefs – and, more particularly, of the various vocabularies in which those beliefs are formulated. There is no authority outside of convenience for human purposes that can be appealed to in order to legitimize the use of a vocabulary. We have no duties to anything nonhuman.

Brandom puts this point by saying that philosophy's job is to make our practices, linguistic and other, explicit rather than to judge these practices in the light of norms lying outside them. He takes Wittgenstein's infinite-regress argument against the possibility of appealing to such outside norms as fundamental to his metaphilosophical position. "Pragmatic theories of norms are distinguished from platonist theories, in treating as fundamental norms *implicit* in *practices* rather than norms *explicit* in *principles*." [4] There is

4 Ibid., 23; see also 77 and 629.

no way for human beings to get beyond their own practices except by dreaming up better practices, and no way to judge these new practices better except by reference to their various advantages for various human purposes. To say that philosophy's task is to make human practices explicit rather than to legitimize them by reference to something beyond them is to say that there is no authority beyond utility for these purposes to which we can appeal.

So much, for the moment, for Sellars and psychological nominalism. I turn now to Davidson. Davidson's most pregnant and striking philosophical doctrine is his claim that most of our beliefs, most of the beliefs of any language user, must be true. This is also his most controversial doctrine, but I choose it because I think that expounding it is a good way of bringing out Davidson's central contribution to the philosophy of mind and language: his insistence that the idea of "accurate representation of reality" is as dispensable a notion as "sentience" or "experience" or "consciousness."

As I read him, Davidson does for the very idea of representation what Sellars does for the very idea of experience. Just as Sellars gets rid of the question "What is the relation between experience and knowledge?" by replacing experiences with noninferentially acquired beliefs, so Davidson gets rid of the question "How do we know that our knowledge represents the world accurately?" by replacing beliefs viewed as representations with beliefs viewed as states attributed to persons in order to explain their behavior. Both of these therapeutic moves are recommendations for changes in philosophers' linguistic practices, suggestions that we shall lose nothing except our grip on traditional philosophical problems by making these changes.

In an essay called "A Coherence Theory of Truth and Knowledge" Davidson says that

> a correct understanding of the speech, beliefs, desires, intentions and other propositional attitudes of a person leads to the conclusion that most of a person's beliefs must be true, and so there is a legitimate presumption that any one of them, if it coheres with most of the rest, is true.[5]

He sums this up as the doctrine that "belief is in its nature veridical."

If one understands true beliefs as accurate representations of something that would be as it is even if never represented adequately in any human language, then this claim will seem paradoxical. But if one takes beliefs to be

---

5 Donald Davidson, "A Coherence Theory of Truth and Knowledge," in *Truth and Interpretation: Perspectives on the Philosophy of Donald Davidson,* ed. Ernest LePore (Oxford: Blackwell, 1986), 314.

states ascribed to an organism or a machine in order to explain and predict its behavior, then one will find oneself agreeing with Davidson that

> we can't in general first identify beliefs and meanings and then ask what causes them. The causality plays an indispensable role in determining the content of what we say and believe. This is a fact we can be led to recognize by taking up, as we have, the interpreter's point of view.[6]

Taking up that point of view amounts to being interested in what people believe, not because we want to measure their beliefs against what they purport to represent, but because we want to deal with these people's behavior. Dealing with that behavior may mean disregarding these people's beliefs as insufficiently coherent with our own, and thereupon treating them as we treat the uninformed and uneducated. Or it may mean blending ours and theirs in the course of instructive conversation. Or, in the most interesting case, it may mean being converted by those with whom we have been conversing to a new *Weltanschauung*, a fairly radical change in one's goals.

Davidson's coherentism amounts to the claim that the decision between these alternatives is never a matter of comparing these people's beliefs with nonbeliefs, thereby testing for accuracy of representation. It is always a matter of seeing how much coherence between new and old candidates for belief is possible.

Putting this point in Brandom's preferred terms of "social practices," decisions about truth and falsity are always a matter of rendering practices more coherent or of developing new practices. They never require us to check practices against a norm that is not implicit in some alternative practice, real or imagined. Davidson agrees with Sellars that the search for truth cannot lead us beyond our own practices into what Sellars called "an archē beyond discourse." It can only be a search for a discourse that works better than previous discourses, a discourse linked with those previous discourses by the fact that most of the beliefs had by any participant in discourse must be true.[7]

---

6 Ibid., 317.
7 See Davidson's remark that we do not "understand the notion of truth, as applied to language, independent of the notion of translation" ("On the Very Idea of a Conceptual Scheme," in *Inquiries into Truth and Interpretation* [Oxford: Clarendon Press, 1984], 194). Compare Sellars's claim that "semantic statements of the Tarski–Carnap variety do not assert relations between linguistic and extra-linguistic items" (*Science and Metaphysics* [London: Routledge, 1968], 82), but rather relate linguistic items we know how to manipulate, elements of a language we already know, to other linguistic items. (See also "Empiricism and the Philosophy of Mind," sec. 31.)

Brandom would like to fill in the details of Davidson's argument that a grasp of the distinction between true and false belief "can emerge only in the context of interpretation, which alone forces us to the idea of an objective, public truth."[8] He agrees with Davidson that interpretation comes first and objectivity later – that the distinction between intersubjective agreement and objective truth is itself only one of the devices we use to improve our social practices. But he thinks that Davidsonians should be more tolerant of notions such as "representation" and "correspondence to reality."

Brandom's attitude toward these notions is analogous to McDowell's attitude toward the notion of "experience." Just as McDowell thinks that one can be a psychological nominalist and still find something true and important in empiricism, so Brandom thinks that one can be a good pragmatist and a good Davidsonian and still find something true in the correspondence theory of truth and in the distinction between reality and appearance. This is the burden of chapter 8 of his book, which is titled "Ascribing Propositional Attitudes: The Social Route from Reasoning to Representing."

Brandom is, in this respect, to Davidson as McDowell is to Sellars. Each thinks that a distinguished precursor was unfortunately tempted to throw the baby out with the bath. Brandom wants to recuperate "representation" and McDowell wants to recuperate "perceptual experience." It is natural, therefore, that both Brandom and McDowell have doubts about my own version of pragmatism – a version that delights in throwing out as much of the philosophical tradition as possible and urges that philosophers perform their principal social function only when they change intuitions, as opposed to reconciling them. In the eyes of both Brandom and McDowell, I am a sort of aging *enfant terrible,* making the appropriation of Sellars and Davidson unnecessarily difficult by recasting the views of each in unnecessarily counterintuitive ways.

In what follows, I shall first summarize Brandom's treatment of objectivity and of representation. Then I shall discuss the relative advantages of abandoning and preserving the notion of "representation."

Davidson's view of representation is simple and dismissive: "Beliefs are true or false, but they represent nothing. It is good to be rid of representations, and with them the correspondence theory of truth, for it is thinking there are representations that engenders thoughts of relativism."[9] Brandom's view is more complex:

8 See Brandom, *Making It Explicit,* 152–3.
9 Donald Davidson, "The Myth of the Subjective," in *Relativism: Interpretation and Confrontation,* ed. Michael Krausz (Notre Dame, Ind.: Notre Dame University Press, 165–6.

The chief task [of chapter 8] is to explain the *representational dimension* of thought and talk. . . . The representationalist order of explanation, dominant since the seventeenth century, presents propositional contentfulness in representational terms from the outset. . . . This approach is objectionable if it is pretended that an account in these terms gives one an independent grip on what is expressed by the declarative use of sentences – as though one could understand the notions of states of affairs or truth conditions in advance of understanding claiming or judging. The representationalist semantic tradition embodies an undeniable insight: whatever is propositionally contentful does necessarily have such a representational aspect; nothing that did not would be recognizable as expressing a proposition.[10]

To grasp what Brandom is saying it is important to realize that he does not think that to call a belief true is to describe a property the belief has. A fortiori, it is not to impute the property of corresponding to reality. Brandom thinks that "the classical metaphysics of truth properties misconstrues what one is doing in endorsing the claim as *describing* it in a special way."[11] For Brandom, to call one's conversational partner's claim "true" is simply to endorse it, not to say something about its relation to nonlinguistic reality. So Brandom can heartily agree with Davidson that most of our beliefs must be true, if that simply means that translation and conversation require that interlocutors endorse most of each other's beliefs (not to mention their own).

This is a thoroughly pragmatist approach to ascriptions of truth. But Brandom thinks this approach is compatible with saying that "objects and the world of facts that comprises them are what they are regardless of what anyone takes them to be."[12] This latter claim is at odds with a view that I take to be basic to pragmatism, that nothing has any intrinsic properties, that there is, as Nelson Goodman says, no Way the World Is. Brandom thinks that "thought and talk give us a perspectival grip on a nonperspectival world."[13] For Nietzsche, Dewey, and Goodman there are perspectives all the way down, but for Brandom there seems to be something more.

It seems that way, but the appearance may be illusory. Brandom never suggests that inquiry will someday converge to this nonperspectival world. On the contrary, he insists that any and every grip on it will be perspectival, determined by some historically contingent set of human needs and interests. Brandom is not saying that there is, *pace* Goodman, a Way the World Is. He is saying that something like the idea of such a way is essential to our linguistic practices. He is, as he says,

---

10 Brandom, *Making It Explicit*, 495–6.   11 Ibid., 515.   12 Ibid., 594–5.   13 Ibid., 594.

reconstruing objectivity as consisting in a kind of perspectival *form*, rather than in a nonperspectival *content*. What is shared by all discursive practices is *that* there is a difference between what is objectively correct in the way of concept application and what is merely taken to be so, not *what* it is – the structure, not the content.[14]

Like Davidson – and unlike Peirce, Putnam, and Habermas – Brandom is not committed to defining "true" in epistemic terms. He follows Davidson's advice and does not try to define "true" by reference to "what is taken true by all the members of a community, or by the experts in a community, or what will always be taken true by them, or by what would be taken true by them under some ideal conditions for inquiry."[15] As he goes on to say, "There is no bird's-eye view above the fray of competing claims from which those that deserve to prevail can be identified, *nor from which even necessary and sufficient conditions for such deserts can be formulated.*"[16]

When I first read Brandom's book, it seemed to me that Brandom was abandoning hard-won ground by making the notions of "representation," "fact," and "making true" respectable. This was because I had gotten accustomed to Davidson's repudiation of all these notions. I no longer am sure about this, and now I am inclined to say that Brandom and Davidson pretty much agree on all the issues and are simply employing different rhetorical strategies to make essentially the same points. But rhetoric matters, especially if one sees, as I do, the pragmatist tradition not just as clearing up little messes left behind by the great dead philosophers, but as contributing to a world-historical change in humanity's self-image.

Consider the question of whether there are such things as facts that make true sentences true. Davidson thinks that one of the great contributions of Tarski was to show how we could avoid the notion of facts. He thinks that there is no need to talk of any sort of truth maker and that doing so is highly misleading. Brandom thinks that doing so is harmless and cheerfully says things that might make Davidson's hair stand on end. For example:

> [T]he nonlinguistic facts could be largely what they are, even if our discursive practices were quite different (or absent entirely) for what claims are true does not depend on anyone's claiming of them. But our discursive practices could not be what they are if the nonlinguistic facts were different.[17]

Again, Davidson thinks that one good reason never to talk about representation is that doing so encourages talk of relativism, and thus attempts to defeat relativism by cultivating what philosophers like Michael Devitt and Crispin Wright call "our realist intuitions" – our sense that we are committed to getting something out there, something that exists independently of our human needs and interests, *right*. Brandom, in an as yet unpublished reply to my doubts about his book, says that "a central enterprise of [his] book is an anti-relativist one: to offer an account of what it is to be committed to the correctness of our claims answering to how things actually *are*, rather than to how anyone or everyone *takes* them to be." He goes on to say that "our use of *de re* ascriptions of propositional attitudes" expresses our

> nonrelativist commitments to one way of talking being a *better* way of talking about what there really is – [as when we say things like] 'Ptolemy claimed *of* the orbital trajectories of the planets that they were the result of the motion of crystalline spheres.'

I think that Davidson's response to the passages I have just quoted from Brandom would run something like this: Certainly we should not think of our claims answering to how anyone or everyone takes things to be, but neither should we take them to answer to how things really are. The alternative is to take them as *about* things, but not as *answering to* anything, either objects or opinions. Aboutness is all you need for intentionality. Answering to things is what the infelicitous notion of representing adds to the harmless notion of aboutness: it is what differentiates good inferentialists like you and me from the representationalist bad guys. For as long as our beliefs are said to be answerable to something, we shall want to be told more about how this answering works, and the history of epistemology suggests that there is nothing to be said. Aboutness, like truth, is indefinable, and none the worse for that. But "answering" and "representing" are metaphors that cry out for further definition, for literalization.

Whether or not this would be Davidson's response, it is mine. It seems to me that when Brandom says he is offering us a nonrelativist view he is doing the same sort of thing Kant did when he said that he was not a skeptic, but an empirical realist. A lot of Kant's readers, including Hegel, decided that "transcendental idealism" was just a fancy new name for what they were used to calling "skepticism." Brandom says he is not a relativist, even though the objectivity he believes in is "a kind of perspectival form, rather than a non-perspectival content." But Brandom's readers who are accustomed to using "relativist" as a term of abuse are going to insist that being a relativist consists precisely in denying the existence of nonperspectival content. The shift from "about *X*" to "answering to *X*" is the same sort of shift Kant makes from "nonillusory" to "empirically real"; this shift did not give critics the full-blooded notion of reality they were demanding.

Brandom wants to get from the invidious comparison made in such *de re* ascriptions as "She believes *of* a cow that it is a deer" to the traditional distinction between subjective appearance and objective reality. It seems to me that all that such invidious comparisons give us is a distinction between better and worse tools for handling the situation at hand – the cow, the planets, or whatever. They do not give us a distinction between more and less accurate descriptions of what the thing really is, in the sense of what it is all by itself, apart from the utilities of human tools for human purposes. But only the latter sense of "what it really is" will satisfy people who worry about relativism. What Brandom calls "the fundamental distinction of *social* perspectives between commmitments one *attributes* to another and those one *undertakes* oneself" gives me a distinction between your bad tools and my better ones. But I doubt that it gives us a distinction between my representing reality accurately and your representing it inaccurately.

I can restate my doubts by considering Brandom's description of "intellectual progress" as "making more and more true claims about the things that are really out there to be talked and thought about." I see intellectual progress as developing better and better tools for better and better purposes – better, of course, by our lights. Philosophers like Searle, who find Kuhn's description of scientific progress intolerable, insist that we are making genuine intellectual progress only if we are getting closer and closer to the way things are in themselves. Brandom's perspectivalism prevents him from using the phrase "in themselves," but his phrase "more and more true claims about the things that are really out there" flirts with something like the "bird's-eye view above the fray of competing claims" that he has already repudiated.

To sum up, my hunch is that Brandom, like Kant, is trying too hard to find a compromise in an uncompromisable dispute, and so falls between two stools. When he says that "concern with getting things right is built into any practices that generate disposition-transcendent conceptual norms," aggressive realists like Searle will read "getting things right" in one way, while sympathetic pragmatists like me will read them in another way. It is hard to pour new wine into old bottles without confusing the customers.

I want to interpret the claim that Copernicus got right what Ptolemy got mostly wrong (the planets) or the claim that St. Paul got right what Aristotle got mostly wrong (virtue) as a claim about the greater suitability of the former figures for the various purposes I want to serve. But people who worry about realism versus antirealism – as I do not, but as the vast majority of anglophone philosophers do – will feel cheated if they think that that is *all* Brandom has in mind.

One way of putting the issue is to revert to the words I put in Davidson's mouth earlier and to say that one should just stop talking about "answering" altogether, thus avoiding the choice between answering to people and answering to nonpeople. As long as the latter choice is posed, one will count as a defender of objectivity merely by virtue of denying, as Brandom does, that truth can be identified with what people believe under certain conditions. But when Brandom then goes on to say that he identifies truth with answering to nonpeople, realists like Searle will ask him how he knows that he is giving these nonpeople the answers they expect and deserve.

The choice is between dropping the notions of "answering" and "representing" (though not those of "of" and "about") and keeping them. My argument for dropping them is that they preserve an image of the relation between people and nonpeople that might be called "authoritarian" – the image of human beings being subject to a judgment other than that of a consensus of other human beings. I see both Brandom's identification of calling an assertion "true" with endorsing it and Davidson's refusal to define "true" as tools for persuading us to abandon this authoritarian image. But I see Brandom's persistence in using the terms "getting right," "really is," and "making true" as tools that will fall into authoritarian hands and be used for reactionary purposes.

In the controversy between authoritarians and antiauthoritarians, Brandom's heart is certainly in the right place. This is clear from his insistence that reality has no norms of its own to offer, apart from those that we develop. But his rhetoric will not convey the state of his heart to those who still hanker after answerability.

I shall conclude with some remarks on a neologism that Brandom invents in order to legitimize his use of the word "fact." This is the word "claimable." I quote from another unpublished paper of his ("Vocabularies of Pragmatism"):

> . . . we should distinguish between two senses of 'claim'; on the one hand there is the act of *claiming*, and on the other there is what is *claimed*. I want to say that facts are true claims in the sense of what is claimed (indeed, of what is claimable), rather than in the sense of true claimings. With this distinction on board, there is nothing wrong with saying that facts *make* claims true – for they make claimings true. This sense of 'makes' should not be puzzling, it is inferential. "John's remark that *p* is true because it is a fact that *p*" just tells us that the first clause follows from the second.

false

Consider a parallel case. I claim that what makes opium put people to sleep is its dormitive power. When Molière and others jeer at my suggestion, I explain that the sense of "makes" which I am using should not be puzzling, for it is inferential. "The doctor's remark that opium puts people to sleep because it has dormitive power" just tells us that the first clause follows from the second – that if something has dormitive power it will put people to sleep.

It seems to me that the notion of a claimable is as useless for explanatory purposes as that of dormitive power. Unless we are given some details about how opium's dormitive power does the trick, what it consists in, we will not find the term "dormitive power" useful. It is not rendered useful just because clauses referring to it can be given an inferential role. I find the notion of "a claimable" useless, except to encourage a rhetoric which suggests that human inquiry is "answerable" to something, a rhetoric that seems to me better avoided.

Brandom points out that to deny the existence of facts and truths about protons long before the term "photon" appeared in language leads to paradox. This is because it seems reasonable to infer as follows:

(1) There were photons five million years ago.
(2) It was the case then that there were photons.
(3) It is true that it was the case then that there were photons.
(4) It was true then that there were photons.

It seems reasonable, but of course philosophers have, paradoxically, denied it. Heidegger notoriously said that "before Newton, Newton's laws were neither true nor false." Brandom quotes me as having said, "Since truth is a property of sentence, since sentences are dependent for their existence upon vocabularies, and since vocabularies are made by human beings, so are truths."

Paradox, however, is sometimes a small price to pay for progress, as the examples of Copernicus, Kant, and Freud may suggest. Further, it is a price Brandom himself is willing to pay, at least in the eyes of Searle, Nagel, and others, when he follows Sellars in casting sentience to the winds and denying that dogs and babies have beliefs "except in a derivative sense." I am not sure that the paradox of which Heidegger and I are guilty is any more paradoxical than the paradox of which many people think Sellars and Brandom guilty when they assert that all awareness is a linguistic affair.

I am willing to say that facts make beliefs true in a derivative sense of "make" – namely, the inferential sense. The force of saying that this sense is derivative and metaphorical is to decline responsibility for giving further details about how the making gets done. Analogously, the force of saying that babies and dogs have beliefs only in a derivative and metaphorical sense is to decline responsibility for explaining how they differ from thermostats. Reference to such derivative senses should, however, be avoided where possible – if only because employing them will seem a cop-out to one's philosophical critics.

David Lewis once said that philosophy is a matter of collating our intuitions and then finding a way to keep as many of them as possible. I think that it is a matter of treating both intuitions and accusations of paradox as the voice of the past, and as possible impediments to the creation of a better future. Of course the voice of the past must always be heeded, since rhetorical effectiveness depends upon a decent respect for the opinions of mankind. But intellectual and moral progress would be impossible unless people can sometimes, in exceptional cases, be persuaded to turn a deaf ear to that voice.

7

THE VERY IDEA OF HUMAN ANSWERABILITY TO THE WORLD: JOHN McDOWELL'S VERSION OF EMPIRICISM

I shall begin by summarizing some of the most prominent features of John McDowell's *Mind and World*, a task made easier by his introduction to the paperback edition of that book, from which I shall borrow heavily.

McDowell's central notion is that of "answerability to the world." He says that

> to make sense of a mental state's or episode's being directed towards the world, in the way in which, say, a belief or judgment is, we need to put the state or episode in a normative context. A belief or judgment to the effect that things are thus and so . . . must be a posture or stance that is *correctly or incorrectly* adopted according to whether or not things are indeed thus and so. . . . This relation between mind and world is normative, then, in that thinking that aims at judgment, or the fixation of belief, is answerable to the world – to how things are – for whether or not it is correctly executed.[1]

Before going on, let me note that McDowell here does something that critics of the correspondence theory of truth have always complained about: he treats perceptual judgments as a model for all judgments. To say that "This is red" is "directed towards the world" or "answerable to the world" is intuitively plausible. But such phrases seem less applicable if one's paradigm of a belief is "We ought to love one another," or "There are many transfinite cardinals," or "Proust was only an effete petit bourgeois."

Another way of making the same point is to remark that there are vast areas of culture in which "a belief or judgment that things are thus and so" is indeed "a posture or stance that is *correctly or incorrectly* adopted," but in

1 John McDowell, *Mind and World*, paperback ed. (Cambridge, Mass.: Harvard University Press, 1996), xi–xii.

which it would be strange to say that it is "*correctly or incorrectly* adopted according to whether or not things are indeed thus and so." The addition of this latter phrase may go unnoticed if one's paradigm of a belief or judgment is one of Newton's laws, but it will seem pointless when one is describing beliefs such as "Blake is a better role model for poets than Byron" or "Heidegger's philosophy was better than his politics." In art, morals, and politics we want to judge correctly, but talk of "world-directedness" and of things "indeed [being] thus and so" sounds hollow.[2]

This point recalls one of the differences between the sort of anglophone thinking that harks back to Bacon and Locke and philosophical traditions that regard anglophone empiricism as a notable example of cultural lag. When anglophone philosophers think of a cultural achievement, a triumph of the human intellect, they typically think first of modern physical science and of the saga that links Newton to Gell-Mann. Nonanglophone philosophers may as easily think first of the European novel from Cervantes to Nabokov or of socialist politics from Fourier to Helmut Schmidt. For these philosophers are more inclined than their anglophone colleagues to follow Nietzsche's advice and to "look at science through the optic of art."

Philosophers who take this advice will find Brandom's *Making It Explicit* more attractive than McDowell's *Mind and World*. For Brandom is content to think of normativity, of the possibility of correctness and incorrectness, in terms of human beings' answerability to one other. Brandom could, I have argued in the preceding essay, say everything he needs to say about objectivity, about the possibility that any given judgment we make, no matter how unanimously, could be wrong, without ever talking about "answerability to the world" or "world-directedness." Brandom's account of objectivity works just as well for mathematics as for physics. It is as applicable to literary criticism as to chemistry.

The centrality of perception and of natural science to his treatment of the topic of answerability becomes explicit when McDowell goes on to say

> Even if we take it that answerability to how things are includes more than answerability to the empirical world, it nevertheless seems right to say this: since

---

2 This, of course, is the point at which people begin to quarrel about whether to be "realists" about artistic, moral, and political judgments. The recent prevalence of quarrels about when and where there is "a fact of the matter" – quarrels whose participants have never been able to say what difference in practice would be made by the victory of one side or the other – seems to me to give us good reason to banish the term "fact of the matter" from philosophy. I fear that if "world-directedness" becomes popular, it will provide yet another way to prolong the tedious controversies about realism vs. antirealism.

our cognitive predicament is that we confront the world by way of sensible intuition (to put it in Kantian terms), our reflection on the very idea of thought's
directedness at how things are must begin with answerability to the empirical
world.[3]

When discussing literature or politics, however, it is a bit strained to say that
we are in a cognitive predicament. It is even more obviously strained to say
that this predicament is caused by the need to confront the world by way of
sensible intuition.

McDowell's choice of Kantian terms is a choice of visual metaphors,
metaphors that Kant used to lament our lack of the faculty of intellectual intuition that Aristotle had described, overoptimistically, in *De Anima*. It is also
a choice of natural science as the paradigm of rational inquiry, a Kantian
choice that Hegel explicitly repudiates. When one switches from Kant to
Hegel, the philosopher whom Sellars described as "the great foe of immediacy," these metaphors lose much of their appeal. So it is not surprising that
it is among anglophone philosophers, who read far more Kant than they do
Hegel, that these metaphors should remain most prevalent.

From a Sellarsian, Davidsonian, Brandomian, or Hegelian viewpoint,
there is no clear need for what McDowell describes as

'a minimal empiricism': the idea that experience must constitute a tribunal,
mediating the way our thinking is answerable to how things are, as it must be
if we are to make sense of it as thinking at all.[4]

For Sellars, Davidson, and Brandom, we are constantly interacting with
things as well as with persons, and one of the ways in which we interact with
both is through their effects on our sensory organs and other parts of our
bodies. But none of these three philosophers needs the notion of experience as a mediating tribunal. They can be content with an account of the
world as exerting control on our inquiries in a merely causal way, rather than
as exerting what McDowell calls "*rational* control." What McDowell says of
Davidson is true of Sellars and Brandom as well: all three think "a merely
causal, not rational, linkage between thinking and independent reality will
do, as interpretation of the idea that empirical content requires friction
against something external to thinking."[5] That such an account will *not* do
is the first, and largely unargued, premise of McDowell's book.

McDowell is a devoted reader of Sellars, Davidson, and Brandom and is
fully aware of "a frame of mind . . . that makes it hard to see how experience

3 McDowell, *Mind and World*, xii.   4 Ibid.   5 Ibid., 68.

could function as a tribunal, delivering verdicts on our thinking."[6] But he sees these three philosophers as so infatuated with the need to repudiate the Myth of the Given – to avoid the British empiricists' traditional confusion of causation with justification – as to be willing to give up world-directedness and rational answerability to the world.

McDowell develops his account of how these three demythologizing philosophers fell into error by distinguishing between the "logical space of nature" and "the logical space of reasons." The former he defines as "the logical space in which the natural sciences function, as we have been enabled to conceive them by a well-charted, and in itself admirable, development of modern thought."[7] He uses the term "the realm of law" as a synonym for "the logical space of nature" and often states the problem raised by abandoning the Myth of the Given as that of understanding the relation between the realm of law and the realm of reason.

As McDowell sees it, Sellars and Davidson are so impressed by nature as described by physics – the realm of law as the realm of atoms and void – that they feel impelled to give an account of experience that "disqualifies it from intelligibly constituting a tribunal." "For these purposes," McDowell says,

> Sellars and Davidson are interchangeable. Sellars' attack on the Given corresponds . . . to Davidson's attack on what he calls "the third dogma of empiricism" – the dualism of conceptual scheme and empirical "content."[8]

Sellars and Davidson both think that adopting psychological nominalism, and thereby avoiding a confusion between justification and causation, entails claiming that only a belief can justify a belief. This means drawing a sharp line between experience as the cause of the occurrence of a justification, and the empiricist notion of experience as itself justificatory. It means reinterpreting "experience" as the ability to acquire beliefs noninferentially as a result of neurologically describable causal transactions with the world.

One can restate this reinterpretation of "experience" as the claim that human beings' only "confrontation" with the world is the sort that computers also have. Computers are programmed to respond to certain causal transactions with input devices by entering certain program states. We humans program ourselves to respond to causal transactions between the higher brain centers and the sense organs with dispositions to make assertions. There is no epistemologically interesting difference between a machine's program state and our dispositions, and both may equally well be called "beliefs" or "judgments." There is no more or less intentionality, world-directedness, or rationality in the one case than in the other. We can describe both ourselves and machines in normative, programming terms or in non-normative, hardware terms. No problem arises, in either case, about the interface between software and hardware, the intentional and the nonintentional, the space of reasons and the space of laws.

McDowell regards Sellars, Davidson, and Brandom as "renouncing empiricism" because they renounce the idea of experience as a tribunal. Brandom and Sellars agree with Davidson that, as McDowell puts it, "we cannot take experience to be epistemologically significant without falling into the Myth of the Given."[9] But McDowell thinks that this renunciation of empiricism simply will not work. He thinks that doing so will "leave the [traditional] philosophical questions still looking as if they *ought* to be good ones," so that "the result is continuing philosophical discomfort, not an exorcism of philosophy."[10]

Like me, McDowell regards himself as a therapeutic philosopher. He hopes, as I do, to create a "frame of mind in which we would no longer seem to be faced with problems that call on philosophy to bring subject and object back together again."[11] We both want to "achieve an intellectual right to shrug our shoulders at sceptical questions"[12] and to "disown an obligation to try to answer the characteristic questions of modern philosophy."

But McDowell believes, as I do not, that "a real insight is operative in seeming to be faced with that obligation." So he thinks that empiricism, expelled with a pitchfork, will return again through the window. He thinks that we can "trace some distinctive anxieties of modern philosophy to a tension between two forces": the "attractiveness of a minimal empiricism on the one hand" and the fact that "all awareness is a linguistic affair" on the other.[13] In McDowell's picture, the linguistic turn in philosophy helped us see that nothing is part of the process of justification which does not have a linguistic shape. It did not, however, take away the need to "make sense of the world-directedness of empirical thinking." "So long as the attractions of empiricism are not explained away," he says, the incoherence of the Myth of the Given will be "a source of continuing philosophical discomfort."

I take the linguistic turn in philosophy, the turn that made it possible for Sellars to envisage his doctrine of psychological nominalism, to be a turn

---

9 Ibid., xvii.
10 Ibid., 142n. In this footnote McDowell criticizes me rather than Sellars and Davidson. But what he says goes for them too, if they are interpreted as I interpret them: as saying that renouncing empiricism will leave us in Wittgensteinian peace and Humean good spirits – able to walk away from the traditional epistemological problematic with a good conscience.
11 Ibid., 86.   12 Ibid., 143.   13 Ibid., xvi.

away from the very idea of human answerability to the world. I agree with Heidegger that there is a straight line between the Cartesian quest for certainty and the Nietzschean will to power. So I think that modern European philosophy amounts to an attempt by human beings to wrest power from God – or, more placidly put, to dispense with the idea of human answerability to something nonhuman. It involves what Heidegger lamented as "forgetfulness of Being." Like Nietzsche and Derrida, I think of such forgetfulness as a thoroughly good thing, and of what Heidegger called the "humanism" of modern philosophy as an equally good thing. I regard the need for world-directedness as a relic of the need for authoritative guidance, the need against which Nietzsche and his fellow pragmatists revolted.

I suspect that our differing accounts of the genesis and development of modern philosophy provide the most fruitful locus of debate between McDowell and myself. But before returning to these accounts, and to our differing metaphilosophical strategies, I shall sketch McDowell's own bold and ingenious resolution of the dilemma he believes to be posed by Sellars's and Davidson's antiempiricist polemic. To do so, I shall discuss three notions central to his thinking: (1) "bald naturalism," (2) "second nature," and (3) "rational freedom."

Bald Naturalism

McDowell sees, as I have already noted, a sharp dichotomy between the realm of nature and that of law. Bald naturalists are philosophers who deny this sharp dichotomy; they are people with reductionist instincts, such as Quine. Quine would like to think that the language of physics has some sort of priority and that everything which does not fit into that language must be regarded as a concession to practical convenience rather than as part of an account of how things really are.

McDowell sometimes rephrases his nature–law dichotomy as a dichotomy between two kinds of intelligibility, as in the following passage:

> The modern scientific revolution made possible a newly clear conception of the distinctive kind of intelligibility that the natural sciences allow us to find in things. . . .We must sharply distinguish natural scientific intelligibility from the kind of intelligibility something acquires when we situate it in the logical space of reasons. That is a way of affirming the dichotomy of logical spaces, as bald naturalism refuses to do.[14]

14 Ibid., xix.

In his picture, people like Quine (and sometimes even Sellars) are so impressed with natural science that they think the first sort of intelligibility is the only genuine sort.

I think that it is important, when discussing the achievements of the scientific revolution, to make a distinction McDowell does not make: a distinction between particle physics, together with those microstructural parts of natural science that can easily be linked up with particle physics, and all the rest of natural science. Particle physics, unfortunately, fascinates many contemporary philosophers, just as corpuscularian mechanics fascinated John Locke. Quine once said that the reason the indeterminacy of translation was distinct from the indeterminacy of theory was that the differences in psychological explanation, unlike those in biological explanation, made no difference to the motion of elementary particles. David Lewis thinks that all objects in the universe are gerrymandered artifacts except these elementary particles. Sellars himself was all too inclined to describe nature in Democritean terms as "atoms and void" and to invent pseudo-problems about how to reconcile the "scientific" with the "manifest" image of human beings.

To guard against this simpleminded and reductionistic way of thinking of nonhuman nature, it is useful to remember that the form of intelligibility shared by Newton's primitive corpuscularianism and contemporary particle physics has no counterpart in, for example, the geology of plate tectonics or in Darwin's and Mendel's accounts of heredity and evolution. What we get in those areas of natural science are narratives, natural histories, rather than the subsumption of events under laws.

So I think that McDowell should not accept the bald naturalists' view that there is a "distinctive form of intelligibility" found in the natural sciences and that it consists in relating events by laws. It would be better to say that what Davidson calls "strict laws" are the exception in natural science – nice if you can get them, but hardly essential to scientific explanation.[15] It would be better to treat "natural science" as a name of an assortment of useful gimmicks rather than of a natural kind. It would be even better to stop using terms like "forms of intelligibility," for one might then avoid worrying, as McDowell worries, about whether "what we experience is [or is] not external to the realm of the kind of intelligibility which is proper to meaning."[16]

15 For criticism of Davidson on this point, see my "Davidson's Mental–Physical Distinctions," in *The Philosophy of Donald Davidson*, ed. Lewis Hahn, The Library of Living Philosophers (La Salle, Ill.: Open Court, forthcoming).
16 McDowell, *Mind and World*, 72.

If you are fascinated by the kind of natural science that does give you nice strict laws, you will be inclined to overdramatize the contrast between nature and reason by saying, as McDowell does, that the "logical space of reasons" is sui generis. I would argue that it is no more or less sui generis than the logical space of political argument or biological explanation or soccer or carpentry. *All* language games are sui generis. That is, that they are irreducible to one another, where the test of "reducibility" is something like the discovery of material conditionals relating statements made in one game to statements made in another. But this sense of "sui generis" – the sense in which baseball is sui generis over against soccer, jai alai, basketball, chess, and poker – is philosophically sterile.

If we are trying to give philosophy Wittgensteinian peace, we should do what Dewey did: try to make all the traditional philosophical "dichotomies" look like overdramatizations of the banal fact that different tools serve different purposes. We should treat the fact that you cannot use intentional talk and particle talk simultaneously as just as philosophically sterile as the fact that you cannot play baseball and jai alai simultaneously. We should not allow this fact to make us wonder, as McDowell wonders, how to "bring understanding and sensibility, reason and nature, back together."[17]

To sum up, McDowell thinks that we need to keep a big reason–nature, law–reason dichotomy in place, as bald naturalists do not. I think that both bald naturalists and McDowell make too great a fuss about this dichotomy and use it to engender pseudo-problems. One reason they make too great a fuss is that both talk about intelligibility rather than convenience.

Quine thinks that particle physics gives us the one true paradigm of intelligibility. McDowell thinks that we have two such paradigms. I think we would do better to rid ourselves of the notion of "intelligibility" altogether.[18] We should substitute the notion of techniques of problem solving. Democritus, Newton, and Dalton solved some problems with particles and laws. Darwin, Gibbon, and Hegel solved others with narratives. Carpenters

---

17 Ibid., 108.
18 Another way of putting this point is to say that intelligibility is cheap: you can get it just by training people to talk in a certain way. That a view is intuitive, or a phrase intelligible, shows very little about the utility of either. By way of contrast, consider McDowell's claim that "the sheer intelligibility of the idea [of openness to facts] is enough" for his purposes (of finding a middle way between bald naturalism and the renunciation of empiricism) (ibid., 113). He thinks that the idea of our being open to facts has an advantage in "intelligibility" over that of "the fact itself impressing itself on a perceiver." But any greater plausibility of metaphors of transparency over metaphors of impression is entirely a function of the rhetoric by which one has previously been charmed.

solve others with hammers and nails, and soldiers still others with guns. Philosophers' problems are about how to prevent the words used by some of these problem solvers from getting in the way of other words used by other problem solvers. These problems are not posed by dichotomies between realms of being, but by cultural imperialists, people with monotheistic delusions of grandeur, such as Quine and Fichte.

Second Nature

If, like McDowell, you are concerned with the question of whether there is rational as opposed to merely causal control of human inquiry by the world, you will want to concentrate on the interface between the space of reasons and the space of nature and to find something that can be described as in both. To make room for something of that sort, you will need to say, as McDowell does, that "we need not equate the very idea of nature with the idea of instantiations of concepts that belong in the logical space . . . in which the natural-scientific kind of intelligibility is brought to light."

"Human beings," McDowell goes on to say, "acquire a second nature in part by being initiated into conceptual capacities, whose interrelations belong in the logical space of reasons." Elsewhere he uses the analogy of being initiated into a moral community, and thereby acquiring a moral character. The acquisition of a moral character and the acquisition of the ability to have perceptual experiences are both examples of "initiation into conceptual capacities." Further:

> Such initiation is a normal part of what it is for a human being to come to maturity, and that is why, although the structure of the space of reasons is alien to the layout of nature conceived as the realm of law, it does not take on the remoteness from the human that rampant platonism envisages. If we generalize the way Aristotle conceives the moulding of ethical character, we arrive at a notion of having one's eyes opened to reasons at large by acquiring a second nature. I cannot think of a good short English expression for this, but it is what figures in German philosophy as *Bildung*.[19]

Having one's eyes opened to reasons gives one the ability to be rationally controlled by the world, and thereby the ability to be in world-directed states and the ability to have judgments that are answerable to the world. It also gives one rational freedom. All these endowments become unintelligible,

19 Ibid., 84.

McDowell thinks, if we describe encounters with the world through our sensory apparatus in the terms used by Sellars, Davidson, and Brandom.

For the latter three philosophers, *Bildung* is a matter of intrahuman relationships – the acquisition of the ability to interact with other human beings by asking for and giving reasons. The more *gebildet* you are, the more complex and interesting are the kinds of reasons you can ask for and give. But at no point do these three philosophers describe the *world* as a sort of conversational partner, offering you candidates for belief, nominations you are free to accept or decline. The world thrusts beliefs on you, in the course of causal interactions between the program you have internalized in the course of becoming *gebildet* and your sense organs. So for these philosophers it is not felicitous to describe *Bildung* as opening your eyes to reasons for belief offered you by the nonhuman world.

By contrast, for McDowell the idea that the world is a sort of conversational partner is all-important. He wants to conceive of experience as "openness to the world" or "openness to reality,"[20] in the same sense of openness in which a conversable person is open to new ideas. It is essential for him to describe perceptual illusions (the Müller-Lyon illusion, the woman with her head in a black bag whom the unwary take to be headless, etc.), *not* as causing us to have true or false beliefs depending on our programming, but as presenting us with candidates for belief that we are free to accept or reject depending on our degree of intellectual sophistication.

McDowell likes to talk about the world doing you favors, showing you a kindness, vouchsafing facts. He says, for example, that

> the particular facts that the world does us the favor of vouchsafing to us, in the various relevant modes of cognition, actually shape the space of reasons as we find it. The effect is a sort of coalescence between the idea of the space of reasons as we find it and the idea of the world as we encounter it.
>
> Of course we are fallible in our judgments as to the shape of the space of reasons as we find it, or – what comes to the same thing – as to the shape of the world as we find it. That is to say that we are vulnerable to the world's playing us false; and when the world does not play us false we are indebted to it.[21]

Brandom, Sellars, and Davidson can all agree that the space of reasons as we find it is also, by and large, the shape of the world. Because most of our beliefs must be true, we can make no sense of the idea that a great gulf might separate the way the world is and the way we describe it. Unlike McDowell,

---

20 Ibid., 111.
21 John McDowell, "Knowledge and the Internal," *Philosophy and Phenomenological Research* 55, 4 (1995), 887.

however, they think that the world shapes the space of reasons not by "vouch-safing facts" to us but by exercising brute causal pressure on us. Just as the brute pressure of the environment led to successive stages of biological evolution, so it led to the successive stages of cultural evolution.

These three philosophers and McDowell agree that if you cannot use words you do not have conceptual capacities. To have a conceptual capacity just *is* being able to use a word. But the first three see no reason to think of the nonhuman world as a conversational partner. But for McDowell things are not so simple. He says that "conceptual capacities . . . can be operative not only in judgments . . . but already in the transactions in nature that are constituted by the world's impacts on the receptive capacities of a suitable subject."[22] McDowell agrees that rocks and trees do not talk, but they do not *just* cause us to make judgments either. He thinks of a perceptual appearance as a request to you by the world to make a judgment, but as not yet itself a judgment, even though it has the conceptual form of a judgment.

So rocks and trees offer us reasons to believe by, so to speak, borrowing our ability to use words – an ability they did not have before humans developed language. McDowell's "impressions" are neither physiological states that produce noninferential beliefs nor those noninferential beliefs themselves, but something in between the two – the ingredients of *second* nature. McDowell says:

> Once we remember second nature, we see that operations of nature can include circumstances whose descriptions place them in the logical space of reasons, *sui generis* though that logical space is. This makes it possible to accommodate impressions in nature without posing a threat to empiricism. From the thesis that receiving an impression is a transaction in nature, there is now no good inference to the conclusion drawn by Sellars and Davidson, that the idea of receiving an impression must be foreign to the logical space in which concepts such as that of answerability function. . . . In receiving impressions, a subject can be open to the way things manifestly are.[23]

Rational Freedom

McDowell says that "responsiveness to reasons" is a good gloss on one notion of freedom. But, he continues, there may be philosophical puzzlement about how such responsiveness fits into the natural world. Humean compatibilists like Davidson, Dennett, and myself, people who want to dissolve rather than solve the problem of freedom and determinism, think that such

22 McDowell, *Mind and World*, xx.   23 Ibid.

puzzlement should disappear once we see that the tools we use to apply and change our norms are often different from those we use to predict what will happen next. So we do not see the need to do what McDowell calls "looking for a conception of our nature that includes a capacity to resonate to the structure of the space of reasons."[24]

But for McDowell the notions of "rational freedom," "openness to the world," and "answerabilty to the world" stand or fall together. So does the notion of "spontaneity," in Kant's sense of "the spontaneity of the understanding." So also does that of "empirical content." McDowell thinks that Davidson does not see that a merely causal account of our responses to the nonhuman threatens our empirical judgments with "emptiness," in the sense of contentlessness: "If we are to avert the threat of emptiness, we need to see intuitions as standing in rational relations to what we should think."[25]

On McDowell's understanding of "content," some uses of words to classify visible and tangible things – such as "witch" and "Boche" and "phlogiston" – turn out not to have empirical content. They are pseudo-concepts. As we learn more and more about the world, the fewer pseudo-concepts we have and the more real, contentful empirical concepts. As we make intellectual progress, we become more and more open to the world. The world manages to fill our beliefs up with more and more empirical content and thus, so to speak, to tell us more and more about itself.[26]

Davidson, Sellars, and Brandom have no use for this contrast between uses of words that have content and uses of those that do not. As good inferentialists and panrelationalists, they think that all a concept needs to have content is for the word to function as a node in a pattern of inferences. All the words ever systematically bandied about, by superstitious cavemen as well as by sophisticated physicists, are on a par as far as content or lack of content goes. Whereas McDowell wants to revive a version of Russell's idea that nonreferring singular terms are only pseudo-singular terms, Davidson, Sellars, and Brandom all want to claim that any singular term that has a use is as good a singular term as any other.

Just because the notion of "rational freedom" is, as McDowell uses it, so interlocked with other notions I have no use for – notions like answerability and content – I have no use for it. So I construe "rational freedom" as

24 Ibid., 109.   25 Ibid., 68.
26 Davidsonians like me explicate Kant's slogan "Concepts without intuitions are empty" as "Linguistic behavior that is not interpreted, eventually, by reference to its causal interaction with the speaker's environment is not interpretable at all." So we drop the metaphors of fullness and emptiness in favor of metaphors of causal relatedness and lack of causal relatedness.

"that funny thing McDowell thinks we would not have if Davidson were right that there is 'a merely causal, not rational, linkage between thinking and independent reality.'" I find it hard to associate this sense of the term "free" with the only one Hume was interested in: the sense in which you are not free if there is a gun at your child's head or if you are under hypnosis – the one we invoke when ascribing moral responsibility. I also find it hard to associate it with Hegel's claim that history is the story of increasing freedom. It seems to me a specifically Kantian sense of the term "freedom" – one we could discard if we were willing to abandon the Kantian dichotomy between kinds of intelligibility and to talk instead about techniques of problem solving.

So much for the three McDowellian notions I have been using as pegs on which to hang my account of McDowell's solution to his problem: how to avoid both bald naturalism and the view, common to Sellars, Davidson, and Brandom, that the notion of "perceptual experience" can simply be discarded.

I think that this solution is brilliantly original and completely successful. McDowell is just the philosopher you want if you fear losing your grip on the notion of "perceptual experience." He does a splendid job of reconciling common turns of speech such as "a glimpse of the world" and "openness to the world" and "answerability to the world" with a repudiation of the confusion between causation and justification embodied in the Myth of the Given. His conception of "second nature" is just what is needed for this job of reconciliation. He has rehabilitated empiricism.

But, of course, I do not *want* such a reconciliation or such a rehabilitation. I think that most of the common turns of speech McDowell invokes should be discarded rather than given philosophical backup. I see nothing worth saving in empiricism. I think that saving the notion of answerability to the world saves an intuition that clashes with the romanticism which animated both Dewey and Nietzsche. For this notion retains the figure of "the world" as a nonhuman authority to whom we owe some sort of respect.

In his discussion of my views in *Mind and World*, McDowell quotes me as saying that "there seems no obvious reason why the progress of the language-game we are playing should have anything in particular to do with the way the rest of the world is." He rebuts this by saying, "It is the whole point of the idea of norms of inquiry that following them ought to improve our chances of being right about the way the world is."[27]

---

27 McDowell, *Mind and World*, 151.

I think that this view of the function of norms of inquiry will lead one back to the distinction between scheme and world and to the notion that the progress of inquiry consists in an increasingly tight "fit" with the world. McDowell, who accepts Davidson's critique of the scheme–content distinction, denies this. "The world that I invoke here," he says, "is not the world that . . . [Rorty thinks] well lost. . . . It is the perfectly ordinary world in which there are rocks, snow is white, and so forth. It is that ordinary world on which our thinking bears in a way that Rorty's separation of viewpoints leaves looking mysterious, precisely because it separates relatedness to the world from the normative surroundings that are needed to make sense of the idea of bearing – rational bearing – on anything." My own thinking, McDowell says, makes these problems urgent, so my "refusal to address them can only be an act of will, a deliberate plugging of the ears."[28]

I, of course, think that McDowell has been seduced by an empiricist siren song and that my deafness to that song is an example of hard-won intellectual virtue rather than the result of a perverse act of will. But I also think that there is very little neutral ground for the two of us to stand on while we debate our disagreements. In particular, I do not think that more rigorous formulation of the issue is going to help. For I simply cannot believe that anything important hangs on saying, with McDowell, that we should lose our Kantian freedom unless perceptual appearances were distinct from judgments, rather than saying, with Brandom, that Kantian freedom consists simply in being able to withhold an "is-claim" and make a "looks-claim" instead.

Crackerbarrel pragmatists like me always ask, as William James did, "What difference to practice is that funny little difference in theory supposed to make?" So I find myself asking how that nice clean-cut disagreement between Brandom and McDowell about the nature of looks could possibly tie in with the politicocultural hopes that led Kant, Hegel, and Dewey to write their books. One lesson we should have learned from the revolt against medieval scholasticism is that when philosophers start quarreling about whether there is a third thing intermediate between two other things (Aquinas's "materia signata," for example, an intermediary between prime matter and substantial form), they may have traded cultural significance for professional rigor.

So my inclination is to turn away from the admirably precise formulations of the issue that McDowell offers and to continue talking in fuzzy world-historical-cum-psychoanalytic terms about the need to bring humanity to

28 Ibid., 51.

full maturity by discarding the image of the fierce father figure. When I succumb to this inclination, I seek out the passages in McDowell in which he
offers *his* version of world history. The most pregnant of these passages is his
remark that "our philosophical anxieties are due to the intelligible grip on
our thinking of a modern naturalism" and his suggestion that we "work on
loosening that grip."[29]

I read this passage in McDowell as echoing similar passages in Gadamer
and in Charles Taylor – two other philosophers who think that Aristotle
grasped something important, something we began to lose our grip on after corpuscularian mechanics had made Aristotelianism seem obsolete. I
also read it in the light of McDowell's remark to me, in correspondence, that
a "Darwinian tone" pervades much of my writing. McDowell expands on this
point by saying that my suspicion of pre-Darwinian ways of talking "reflects
a precisely *non*-pragmatist favoring of Darwinian vocabulary, as the only
linguistic apparatus that we can genuinely see as permitting us to describe
reality."

I stoutly deny thinking that Darwin describes reality, or even just us human beings, better than anybody else. But his way of describing human beings, when supplemented (as Dewey and Dennett supplement it) by a story
about cultural evolution, does give us a useful gimmick to prevent people
from overdramatizing dichotomies and thereby generating philosophical
problems. By pressing an analogy between growing a new organ and developing a new vocabulary, between stories about how the elephant got its trunk
and stories about how the West got particle physics, we neo-Darwinians hope
to fill out the self-image sketched by the Romantic poets and partially filled
in by Nietzsche and Dewey.

29 Ibid., 177.

8

ANTISKEPTICAL WEAPONS: MICHAEL WILLIAMS VERSUS DONALD DAVIDSON

Michael Williams's *Unnatural Doubts: Epistemological Realism and the Basis of Scepticism*[1] offers us something I would not have imagined possible before reading it: a genuinely novel, and very powerful, line of argument against epistemological skepticism. It also purports to show that competing antiskeptical arguments fail. I am enthusiastic about the new antiskeptical weapon that Williams has added to our arsenal, but dubious about his claim that the weapons previously on the market were ineffective. So I shall first try to show off Williams's new weapon in the most advantageous possible light. Then I shall argue that Williams has not shown that there is anything wrong with the alternative weapon purveyed by Donald Davidson, one of his principal competitors in the antiskepticism business. Finally, I shall argue that, although Williams's and Davidson's weapons embody the same basic design, there are reasons for preferring Davidson's version.

Barry Stroud, the leading contemporary exponent of the view that epistemological skepticism is a serious and important issue, says that skepticism "appeals to something deep in our nature." Stroud tries to show "how closely Descartes' requirement that the dream-possibility be eliminated corresponds to our ordinary standards or requirements for knowledge in daily life."[2] He claims that "the sources of Descartes' requirement . . . illuminate something about our actual conception of knowledge."[3]

---

1 Published in 1991 by Blackwell (Oxford). A paperback edition has appeared from Princeton University Press (1996). All parenthetical page references are to the Blackwell edition.
2 Barry Stroud, *The Significance of Philosophical Scepticism* (Oxford: Oxford University Press, 1984), 39.
3 Ibid., 43.

Williams rejoins that we do not have an "actual conception of knowledge" to be illuminated. Williams thinks that there is no such thing as "human knowledge" or "our epistemic position" or "our view of reality." As he puts it, there may be "fewer things in heaven and earth than are dreamt of in our epistemology" (102).

Williams thinks, however, that we can dismiss Stroud's claims only if we find "the correct theoretical diagnosis of skepticism." He says that the clue to this correct diagnosis lies in "the context-sensitivity of both skeptical doubts and everyday certainties" (35). Once we realize that the skeptic has created a new context of inquiry by inventing a topic called "our epistemic situation," we can say, with Williams, that the skeptic has indeed discovered that "knowledge is impossible under the conditions of philosophical reflection." But we can add that this discovery does nothing to show that "under the conditions of philosophical reflection, knowledge is generally impossible" (xx).

Williams sees the skeptic as needing to defend his epistemological realism – his claim that there is something called "human knowledge" to be investigated – by means of an argument that "the deep demands of our ordinary ways of thinking only come to the surface in the context of his [the skeptic's] extraordinary investigation into the status of human knowledge in general" (35). Williams does not doubt that this extraordinary investigation creates a context – a context in which skeptical doubts make sense – but he claims that Stroud and his ilk owe us an explanation of why this context should be created.

Williams makes a very helpful distinction between theoretical diagnoses of skepticism and therapeutic diagnoses. Therapeutic diagnoses claim that skepticism somehow does not make sense, because it is somehow based on a misuse of words. This therapeutic strategy has always been subject to the objection that anything has a sense if you give it a sense. Williams agrees with this objection, and responds that he will "never accuse the skeptic of incoherence" and will not argue that his problems are pseudo-problems (37). Rather, he will "grant that they are fully genuine, but only given certain theoretical ideas about knowledge and justification." This means that we must abandon hope for a "definitive refutation" of the skeptic (35) and be content with criticism of the skeptic's "implicit theory of the relation of philosophical reflection to ordinary life" (35). We must recognize that "commonsense certainty and philosophical doubt" are distinct contexts, and equally "context-bound" (12). Philosophical reflection of the Cartesian sort does not make us context-free, but simply creates a new, and seemingly pointless, context. Near the end of his book, Williams sums up by saying:

I have never denied that the skeptic is conditionally correct, in the sense that, by the standards he insists on applying, we never know anything about the world. My point has always been that these standards . . . are not built into the human condition, but into a particular intellectual project. (354)

In *The Significance of Philosophical Scepticism*, Stroud spends most of his time arguing that antiskeptics, such as transcendental idealists and verificationists, have failed to show the incoherence of the skeptic's position. Williams concedes the point and gives up on the attempt to demonstrate incoherence. Nor does he fall back on what he calls "a bluff pragmatism," a pragmatism that would argue that "we don't have to respond to skepticism because it makes no difference whether we do or not" (12). Rather, he admits that it will make a difference whether or not we work within the context of philosophical doubt. But he insists that Stroud has not shown the need for such a context.

Williams notes that many philosophers see the context within which Stroud works as created by what Williams calls "the objectivity requirement": "the requirement that the knowledge we want to explain is knowledge of an objective world, a world that is the way it is independently of how it appears to us to be or what we are inclined to believe about it" (91). Such philosophers, as he says, typically "see the objectivity requirement as the deep source of skeptical problems" (91). Williams is strikingly original in pointing out that it is only the "fatal interaction" of the objectivity requirement with "the totality condition" that gives rise to such problems. He defines the latter as the condition that all our knowledge be examined at once.

I shall return later to the topic of the relation between the totality condition and the objectivity requirement, when I contrast Williams with Davidson. But first I want to describe Williams's alternative to epistemological realism – to the doctrine that "human knowledge" or "our knowledge of the external world" is a suitable topic of assessment. That alternative is "contextualism" – the doctrine that "the epistemic status of a proposition is liable to shift with situational, disciplinary and other contextually variable factors" and that, "independently of all such influences, a proposition has no epistemic status whatsoever" (119). A contextualist denies what the epistemological realist asserts: that every belief, by virtue of its content, has "an inalienable epistemic character which it carries with it wherever it goes and which determines where its justification must finally be sought" (116).

Williams sums up the issue between contextualism and epistemological realism by saying that contextualism is "not offered as a question-begging direct answer to an undeniably compelling request for understanding, but as

a challenge to justify the presumption that there is something to understand" (119). The skeptic creates this presumption by assuming that "experiential knowledge is generally prior to knowledge of the world." But,
Williams points out, the only reason for so taking it is that otherwise there
would be no way to go about assessing our knowledge of the world. As he
says, "the sceptic's foundationalism, together with the realism it embodies,
is a brute metaphysical commitment" (134).

Williams has, I think, succeeded in showing that you do not have to agree
with Stroud when he says that "it must be shown or explained *how* it is possible for us to know things about the world, given that the sense-experiences
we get are compatible with our merely dreaming."[4] You will agree with him
only if you are already a foundationalist. You will see his problem as urgent
only if you have already partitioned your beliefs into beliefs about the external world and experiential beliefs, and assumed that the former must be
inferred from the latter. But you will partition them in this way only if you
have already come to believe that there is what Descartes called "a natural
order of reasons" (117), and therefore a context-free epistemic status that
is intrinsic to the content of a belief (121). Williams has thus shown that it
is not enough to criticize epistemological foundationalism and to substitute
a coherentist epistemology for a foundationalist one. One gets to the bottom of the issue only if one asks why one might think that there is a discipline called epistemology or a topic called "human knowledge."

So much for my sympathetic account of Williams's powerful new antiskeptical weapon. I have less sympathy for his claim to have made "the correct
theoretical diagnosis." He says in his preface that

> many theoretical diagnoses have been put forward. Skepticism has been
> traced to a misguided 'spectator theory' of knowledge, to the dualism of sub-
> ject and object, to the quest for certainty, to thinking of 'experience' as a kind
> of impenetrable veil between ourselves and 'reality', and to the correspon-
> dence theory of truth. . . . I agree with the New Skeptics: these familiar diag-
> noses, in their usual forms, are all inadequate, when not simply mistaken. That
> said, however, I continue to believe that the threat of skepticism is intimately
> linked to a foundational conception of knowledge, which I distinguish from
> all the suggestions just alluded to. (xviii)

I want to question whether Williams *should* distinguish a foundational conception of knowledge from all these other suggestions about how to dispose

---

4 Ibid., 13.

of the skeptic, and in particular from the suggestion that we get rid of the dualism of subject and object. For the foundationalist's break between experiential belief and beliefs about the world looks very much like that very dualism.

I think that Williams does not adequately appreciate the most radical recent criticism of that dualism: Davidson's attack on the scheme–content distinction. Williams grants that Davidson has something important to say, but thinks that

> it is best to see him [Davidson] as offering a way of thinking about belief and meaning that comes into its own after we have seen our way beyond traditional skeptical worries. (316)

In other words, Williams thinks that the weapons Davidson purveys are useful only for the mopping-up operations that will follow the final, decisive battle with the skeptic. Davidson will be useful only after we have won that battle, a battle we can win only by employing Williams's new antiskeptical superweapon.

But I think that Williams picks up Davidson by the wrong handle, and therefore misunderstands Davidson's strategy. Williams is wrong in thinking that Davidson tries to answer the skeptic *directly* – an impossible task – and also in thinking that Davidson does not rise to the level of his own theoretical diagnosis, the only level at which the skeptic can be countered. Williams is working with an exhaustive division of philosophers into contextualists like himself – who realize that the skeptic cannot be answered directly but does not need to be – and epistemological realists like Davidson. The latter do not realize this, and so they proceed to give direct answers to the skeptic, answers that necessarily fail (272).

But it is not plausible to think of Davidson as an epistemological realist. He is not one of those who believe that every belief, by virtue of its content, "has an inalienable epistemic character which it carries with it wherever it goes and which determines where its justification must finally be sought." Davidson is as contextualist as you can get. For him, the content of a belief is what an interpreter takes it to be, and that will vary depending upon the interpreter's own beliefs. Justification is as variable as interpretation. There is simply no room in Davidson's system for the sort of "natural order of reasons" to which Williams defines epistemological realists as being committed.

Williams wrongly takes Davidson's 1984 essay "A Coherence Theory of Truth and Knowledge"[5] to show that Davidson does have an epistemological

---

5 Donald Davidson, "A Coherence Theory of Truth and Knowledge," in *Truth and Interpretation: Perspectives on the Philosophy of Donald Davidson,* ed. Ernest LePore (Oxford: Blackwell, 1986), 307–19.

theory – a coherentist one – to offer. He brushes off (379) Davidson's subsequent regret at having used the term "coherence," doubts that culminate in his 1990 Dewey Lectures.[6] He says that Davidson, "when it comes to justification, is a radical holist" – that is, somone who holds that "epistemic justification supervenes on features of our belief system taken as a whole" (379, 275).

I do not think it is plausible to ascribe radical holism to Davidson – who could happily echo Williams's own contextualist and externalist view. He could also happily join Williams in saying that there is, indeed, no profitable subject to be discussed under the topic "our knowledge of the world." The interesting disagreement between them arises when Davidson says that, since he has already shown that most of ours, or anybody's, beliefs are bound to be *true*, the skeptic has been defeated before the topic of *justification* comes up.

Williams does not think that Davidson has shown that belief is in its nature veridical. To see why not, consider the different things Williams and Davidson say about brains in vats. Davidson thinks that brains in vats are mostly right about the things they think about. Davidson would argue that a brain that grows up in a vat, and has no causal contact with chairs and fires, is not able to wonder whether it is indeed, as it believes, sitting in a chair before a fire. Davidson thinks you can wonder only about what you know about already and that much of what this particular brain knows about is its vat-cum-computer environment. Analogously, a dreamer is dreaming about mostly real things, and believing mostly true things about them, even though he is wrong about, for example, which particular real things surround him at this particular moment.

Williams responds to this line of thought by saying that Davidson wants to "derive both coherence and correspondence from charity." But, Williams objects,

> the appeal to charity turns out to involve the idea of unproblematic access to certain causal relations between speakers and objects in the world. If, in the context of the skeptic's question, we grant ourselves this access, the game is over before it starts. (313)

This objection is misguided. If Davidson were, as Williams thinks he is, offering a direct answer to the skeptic, then indeed he would not be able to invoke such unproblematic access. But Davidson is not doing that. Rather, he is trying to undermine the skeptic's idea that we can know what our be-

---

6 See Davidson's "The Structure and Content of Truth," *Journal of Philosophy* 87 (June 1990), 279–328.

liefs are without already having a lot of true beliefs about the causal relations between those beliefs and the world.

Like Williams, Davidson is offering a theoretical diagnosis of skepticism. This diagnosis says that the reason the skeptic thinks she needs an inference from experience to the world is that she does not understand that ascription of experience to herself requires ascribing intentional states and that that is possible only for somebody who has many true beliefs about the world. There is no such thing as knowing what you believe without knowing a great deal about the objects of your belief. "Causality," Davidson says, "plays an indispensable part in determining the content of what we say and believe."[7] Williams objects to this Davidsonian line of thought by saying that

> unless we already have some way of connecting coherence with truth, thus assuring ourselves of the existence of an objective world, we will have no way of knowing that our beliefs are interpretable, in this [Davidsonian] sense of 'interpret'. (314)

To bolster his objection, Williams cites, and implicitly endorses, an argument of Peter Klein's to the effect that all Davidson can show is that "*if* there are beliefs, then they are true in the main." But, Klein says,

> in order to know that there are any beliefs, we would have to know at least one very important truth about our environment, namely, that there are events outside of our bodies which are causally correlated with states of ourselves.[8]

I suspect that Davidson would be happy to settle for saying that "if there are beliefs, they are true in the main." He need not trouble himself with the question of whether his belief that there are beliefs, and therefore extracorporeal causes of beliefs, is justified.

Williams might riposte that Davidson, by taking this insouciant attitude, has granted his point that a causal account of the nature of belief comes into its own only after one has polished off the skeptic with a weapon on which Williams holds the patent. He might reiterate that without a theoretical diagnosis of skepticism "Davidson's argument will be ineffective while, with one, it will be unnecessary" (316). But this riposte would succeed only if Williams's own theoretical diagnosis, but not Davidson's, applied to a skeptic who thought we are unjustified in assuming the existence of beliefs. It is hard to tell whether it would or not, because it is hard to know how such a

---

7 Davidson, "A Coherence Theory," 317.
8 Peter Klein, "Radical Interpretation and Global Skepticism," in *Truth and Interpretation,* ed. LePore, 386.

skeptic would formulate her skepticism. Presumably she has to say that she doubts whether she has any beliefs, and therefore doubts whether she has the doubt that she might seem to be expressing. This sort of skepticism is not Descartes's or Stroud's sort. Both Williams's and Davidson's weapons were designed for use against Descartes and Stroud. They would produce oversophisticated overkill when used on so weak an opponent. Were one in fact confronted with so helpless a skeptic, I am not sure that anything except a bluff pragmatism would serve.

Williams, however, has another line of argument against Davidson's claim to have shown that most of everybody's beliefs are true. This is his claim that, if we use only Davidsonian weaponry, "the skeptic's problem concerning the justifiability of beliefs tends less to be solved than transformed into a problem about the inscrutability of reference" (316). Williams's point is that the external interpreter of the brain in the vat's linguistic behavior will have no reason to think that his idea of what the vat is talking about "matches the self-understanding" of the brain. He puts the point as follows:

> For example, if we were brains in vats . . . the omniscient interpreter would take our utterances to be about events in the computer that controls our simulated sensory input, though presumably we would not. . . . But why should I be comforted by the thought that, if I were a brain in a vat, I should not have mostly false beliefs about the world as I now conceive it but mostly true beliefs about the vat-environment? (314)

Davidson, however, would ask, "Why do you think we would not think our utterances were about events in the computer?" As Davidson sees it, the "self-understanding" that Williams here attributes to envatted brains, and thinks might not be matched from the outside, is just another version of the "epistemic situation" that Williams decries elsewhere. Both "our epistemic situation" and "our self-understanding" are, in Davidson's eyes, versions of the "scheme" half of the "scheme–content dualism."

When Williams says that "presumably we would not" take our beliefs to be about events in the computer, Davidson would say that he presumes this only because he has bought in to the idea that we can know the content of our intentional states without knowing what causes them. But to buy in to this is to buy in to the very foundationalism which Williams takes to be an infallible symptom of epistemological realism: a foundationalism that says my beliefs may swing free from their causes.

Williams is taking for granted that the self-understanding of a brain in a vat can swing free of the vat and its associated computer. Davidson is insisting that having beliefs about things cannot swing free from the way things are, because such beliefs are part of a web of causal interactions with those things. He thinks the only way to get rid of the dualism of subject and object is to say that the purported gap between the two is an arbitrary line drawn across this web – a line that serves no purpose except to create a context within which Descartes and Stroud can get to work.

In this concluding section, I shall try to be ecumenical. As I see it, Williams is right that skepticism requires both the totality condition and the objectivity requirement. The only difference between him and Davidson is that he wants to treat the objectivity condition as harmless and forestall skepticism by getting rid of the totality requirement. For his part, Davidson wants to get rid of the objectivity requirement. He thinks that once it is gone the totality condition will not cross anyone's mind. Williams's theoretical diagnosis says: stop drawing a line around a purported natural kind called "human knowledge" and then asking about the relation of this to the rest of the universe. Davidson's theoretical diagnosis says: stop drawing a line across the universe and contrasting something called "our beliefs about the world" or "the subject" with something on the other side of the line called "the world" or "the object." It is not clear that we need to choose between these two diagnoses. Either seems to provide sufficient reason to ignore the epistemological context within which Descartes and Stroud work.

The resemblances between these two diagnoses are, however, obscured by an ambiguity in Williams's formulation of the objectivity requirement, which I cited earlier as "the requirement that the knowledge we want to explain is knowledge of an objective world, a world that is the way it is independently of how it appears to us to be or what we are inclined to believe about it" (91). This formulation might suggest that Davidson and Williams are irreconcilably at odds, since Davidson thinks that the notion of "independence" is a broken reed. It is, he says, an idea that "derives from the idea of correspondence, and this is an idea without content."[9]

It turns out, however, that, at least part of the time, all Williams means by the world being independent of what we are inclined to believe about it is that "an objective proposition's being true is one thing and our believing it to be true, or being justified in believing it true, something else again" (238). He thinks this is all there is to realism, to the idea of "reality's being 'independent' of thought" (238). On this construal of the objectivity requirement, of course, even Davidson can accept it, for the distinction

9 Davidson, "Structure," 305.

between being justified and being true will not by itself suffice to reinstate a dualism of subjective scheme and objective content.

But just because it does not, the objectivity requirement, glossed in this vegetarian way, will not serve the skeptic's purposes. Because he does gloss it in this way, Williams thinks that those who, like Davidson, train their fire on the objectivity requirement ignore the important target: the totality condition. But those whom Williams criticizes for wasting energy on the objectivity requirement respond that his is not the usual gloss. The usual gloss on the notion of "independence" is that, to quote Williams, "our experience could be just as it is and all our beliefs about the world could be false" (74).

Puzzlingly, Williams seems to think these two glosses of the term "independent" are equivalent. But they are not. To take them as equivalent is to make precisely the inference from "any one of our beliefs about the world could be false" to "all our beliefs about the world could be false," which Davidson sees as the all-important conjuring trick that made skepticism seem plausible in the first place. I conclude that if Williams were content to gloss the objectivity thesis in the first, vegetarian way, then he and Davidson could join forces. They both say that the skeptic is drawing an unnecessary line, creating an unnecessary context by creating an unnecessary gap. They would disagree, at most, about which comes first, the chicken or the egg: the totality condition or the scheme–content picture that makes both foundationalism and the totality condition seem plausible.

On the other hand, if Williams glosses the objectivity thesis in the second, more dubious way, then we shall have to choose between his theoretical diagnosis and Davidson's. Faced with this choice, I would gravitate to Davidson's side.

One reason I would do so is that Williams still seems to me a bit bewitched by epistemology, by the idea that there is something interesting to be said about human knowledge. Davidson almost never, except in the unfortunate title of his essay on coherence, discusses the topic of knowledge. He is not interested in when we have knowledge and when we do not. This seems to me a good thing not to be interested in. Williams, on the other hand, gets involved with debates about closure with Dretske and Nozick, and flirts with reliabilism when he says that "questions about the truth-induciveness of justification procedures will have to be asked case by case and, when they are so asked, they will have to be answered empirically" (265–6). This last passage chimes with Philip Kitcher's attempt to isolate procedures and test them for reliability.

I do not think that Kitcher, or any other philosopher of science, has shown how to isolate procedures of justification in such a way as to make invidious comparisons between bad scientists and good scientists. I do not think that Williams should buy in to that enterprise. But Williams still seems to hanker after some modest sort of naturalized epistemology, even after urging us to give up the idea that human knowledge is a natural kind.

I think that after one gives up this notion, one should say that the only question anywhere in the area is the historicosociological question of how and why patterns of justification change. This is *not* a question about the truth-induciveness of justification procedures. For the reasons I offered in the first essay in this volume, that question should not be raised. If, with Sellars and Brandom, one takes the principal use of the adjective "true" to be endorsement rather than description, one can drop the notion that there are propositions out there that have a property called truth, as well as questions about whether we are using the right means of separating these from the ones that have another property called falsity. If, with Davidson, we take "true" as a primitive predicate, we will not be tempted to think that there is a topic called "knowledge," the name of the result of the compresence of justified belief with truth, which is distinct from the topic of justification.

Williams's tolerance for Kitcher-like questions about which of our procedures of justification are truth-inducing seems to me a hangover of the scheme–content picture. On this picture, truth is over there, where the object is, and justification over here, where we are. So there seems to be a question about whether we are managing to cross the gap. Part of Davidson's attempt to erase this picture is his attempt to prevent our nominalizing the blameless, indispensable, and unanalyzable adjective "true" into a far-off object called Truth. On Davidson's substitute picture, wherever you have either justification or true beliefs or rationality, you automatically have a lot of the other two. There is a human activity called "justifying beliefs" that can be studied historically and sociologically, but this activity does not have a goal called Truth or, therefore, a goal called Knowledge. So the question of whether and how we reach this goal does not arise.

II

MORAL PROGRESS: TOWARD MORE
INCLUSIVE COMMUNITIES

9

HUMAN RIGHTS, RATIONALITY, AND SENTIMENTALITY

In a report from Bosnia, David Rieff said, "To the Serbs, the Muslims are no longer human. . . . Muslim prisoners, lying on the ground in rows, awaiting interrogation, were driven over by a Serb guard in a small delivery van."[1] This theme of dehumanization recurred when Rieff said:

> A Muslim man in Bosansi Petrovac . . . [was] forced to bite off the penis of a fellow-Muslim. . . . If you say that a man is not human, but the man looks like you and the only way to identify this devil is to make him drop his trousers – Muslim men are circumcised and Serb men are not – it is probably only a short step, psychologically, to cutting off his prick. . . . There has never been a campaign of ethnic cleansing from which sexual sadism has gone missing.

The moral to be drawn from Rieff's stories is that Serbian murderers and rapists do not think of themselves as violating human rights. For they are not doing these things to fellow human beings, but to *Muslims*. They are not being inhuman, but rather are discriminating between true humans and pseudo-humans. They are making the same sort of distinction the Crusaders made between humans and infidel dogs, and Black Muslims make between humans and blue-eyed devils. The founder of my university was able both to own slaves and to think it self-evident that all men were endowed by their creator with certain inalienable rights. This was because he had convinced himself that the consciousness of blacks, like that of animals, "participates more of sensation than of reflection."[2] Like the Serbs, Mr. Jefferson did not think of himself as violating *human* rights.

---

1 David Rieff, "Letter from Bosnia," *New Yorker,* November 23, 1992, 82–95.
2 "Their griefs are transient. Those numberless afflictions, which render it doubtful whether heaven has given life to us in mercy or in wrath, are less felt, and sooner forgotten with

Serbs take themselves to be acting in the interests of true humanity by purifying the world of pseudo-humanity. In this respect, their self-image resembles that of moral philosophers who hope to cleanse the world of prejudice and superstition. This cleansing will permit us to rise above our animality by becoming, for the first time, wholly rational and thus wholly human. Serbs, moralists, Jefferson, and Black Muslims all use the term "men" to mean "people like us." They all think that the line between humans and animals is not simply the line between featherless bipeds and the rest. Rather, this line divides some featherless bipeds from others: there are animals walking about in humanoid form. We and those like us are paradigm cases of humanity, but those too different from us in behavior or custom are, at best, borderline cases. As Clifford Geertz puts it, "Men's most importunate claims to humanity are cast in the accents of group pride."[3]

We here in the safe, rich democracies feel about Serbian torturers and rapists as they feel about their Muslim victims: they are more like animals than like us. But we are not doing anything to help the Muslim women who are being gang-raped or the Muslim men who are being castrated, any more than we did anything in the 1930s when the Nazis were amusing themselves by torturing Jews. Here in the safe countries we find ourselves saying things like "That's how things have always been in the Balkans," suggesting that, unlike us, those people are used to being raped and castrated. The contempt we always feel for losers – Jews in the 1930s, Muslims now – combines with our disgust at the winners' behavior to produce the semiconscious attitude: "a pox on both your houses." We think of Serbs or Nazis as animals, because ravenous beasts of prey are animals. We think of Muslims or Jews being herded into concentration camps as animals, because cattle are animals. Neither sort of animal is very much like us, and there seems no point in human beings getting involved in quarrels between animals.

The human–animal distinction, however, is only one of three main ways in which we paradigmatic humans distinguish ourselves from borderline cases. A second is by invoking the distinction between adults and children. Ignorant and superstitious people, we say, are like children; they will attain true humanity only if raised up by proper education. If they seem incapable

them. In general, their existence appears to participate more of sensation than reflection. To this must be ascribed their disposition to sleep when abstracted from their diversions, and unemployed in labor. An animal whose body is at rest, and who does not reflect must be disposed to sleep of course." Thomas Jefferson, "Notes on Virginia," *Writings*, ed. Andrew A. Lipscomb and Albert Ellery Bergh (Washington, D.C., 1905), 1: 194.

3 Clifford Geertz, "Thick Description," in his *The Interpretation of Culture* (New York: Basic Books, 1973), 22.

of such education, that shows that they are not really the same kind of being as we educable people are. Blacks, the whites in the United States and
in South Africa used to say, are like children; that is why it is appropriate to
address black males, of whatever age, as "boy." Women, men used to say, are
permanently childlike; that is why it is appropriate to spend no money on
their education and to refuse them access to power.

When it comes to women, however, there are simpler ways of excluding
them from true humanity: for example, using "man" as a synonym of "human being." As feminists have pointed out, such usages reinforce the average male's thankfulness that he was not born a woman, as well as his fear of
the ultimate degradation: feminization. The extent and depth of the latter
fear are evidenced by the particular sort of sexual sadism Rieff describes. His
point that such sadism is never absent from attempts to purify the species or
cleanse the territory confirms Catharine MacKinnon's claim that, for most
men, being a woman does not count as one way of being human. Being a
nonmale is the third main way of being nonhuman.

Philosophers have tried to help straighten out this confusion by specifying what is special about featherless bipeds, explaining what is essential to
being human. Plato suggested that there is a big difference between us and
animals, a difference worthy of respect and cultivation. He thought that human beings have a special added ingredient that puts them in a different
ontological category than brutes. Respect for this ingredient provides a reason for people to be nice to each other. Anti-Platonists like Nietzsche reply
that attempts to get people to stop murdering, raping, and castrating one
another are, in the long run, doomed to failure – for the real truth about
human nature is that we are a uniquely nasty and dangerous kind of animal.
When contemporary admirers of Plato claim that all featherless bipeds –
even the stupid and childlike, even the women, even the sodomized – have
the same inalienable rights, admirers of Nietzsche reply that the very idea
of "inalienable human rights" is, like the idea of a special added ingredient,
a laughably feeble attempt by the weaker members of the species to fend off
the stronger members.

As I see it, one important intellectual advance that has been made in our
century is the steady decline in interest in this quarrel between Plato and
Nietzsche about what we are really like. There is a growing willingness to neglect the question "What is our nature?" and to substitute the question
"What can we make of ourselves?" We are much less inclined than our ancestors were to take "theories of human nature" seriously, much less inclined
to take ontology or history or ethology as a guide to life. We are much less
inclined to pose the ontological question "What *are* we?" because we have

come to see that the main lesson of both history and anthropology is our extraordinary malleability. We are coming to think of ourselves as the flexible, protean, self-shaping animal rather than as the rational animal or the cruel animal.

One of the shapes we have recently assumed is that of a human rights culture. I borrow the term "human rights culture" from the Argentinean jurist and philosopher Eduardo Rabossi. In an article called "Human Rights Naturalized" Rabossi argues that philosophers should think of this culture as a new, welcome fact of the post-Holocaust world. Rabossi wants them to stop trying to get behind or beneath this fact, stop trying to detect and defend its so-called philosophical presuppositions. On Rabossi's view, philosophers like Alan Gewirth are wrong to argue that human rights cannot depend upon historical facts. "My basic point," Rabossi says, is that "the world has changed, that the human rights phenomenon renders human rights foundationalism outmoded and irrelevant."[4]

Human rights foundationalism is the continuing attempt by quasi-Platonists to win, at last, a final victory over their opponents. Rabossi's claim that this attempt is *outmoded* seems to me both true and important; it is my principal topic in this essay. I shall enlarge upon, and defend, Rabossi's claim that the question of whether human beings really *have* the rights enumerated in the Helsinki Declaration is not worth raising. In particular, I shall defend the claim that nothing relevant to moral choice separates human beings from animals except historically contingent facts of the world, cultural facts.

This claim is sometimes called "cultural relativism" by those who indignantly reject it. One reason they reject it is that such relativism seems to them incompatible with the fact that our human rights culture is morally superior to other cultures. I quite agree that ours is morally superior, but I do not think that this superiority counts in favor of the existence of a universal human nature. It would only do so if we assumed that a claim of moral superiority entails a claim to superior knowledge – assumed that such a claim

---

4 See Edwardo Rabossi, "La teoría de los derechos humanos naturalizada," *Revista del Centro de Estudios Constitucionales* (Madrid), no. 5 (January–March 1990), 159–79. Rabossi also says that he does not wish to question "the idea of a rational foundation of morality." I am not sure why he does not. Rabossi may perhaps mean that in the past – e.g., at the time of Kant – this idea still made a kind of sense, but makes sense no longer. That, at any rate, is my own view. Kant wrote in a period when the only alternative to religion seemed to be something like science. In such a period, inventing a pseudo-science called "the system of transcendental philosophy" – setting the stage for the show-stopping climax in which one pulls moral obligation out of a transcendental hat – might plausibly seem the only way of saving morality from the hedonists on one side and the priests on the other.

is ill-founded if not backed up by knowledge of a distinctively human attribute. But it is not clear why "respect for human dignity" – our sense that the differences between Serb and Muslim, Christian and infidel, gay and straight, male and female should not matter – must presuppose the existence of any such attribute.

Traditionally, the name of the shared human attribute that supposedly "grounds" morality is "rationality." Cultural relativism is associated with irrationalism because it denies the existence of morally relevant transcultural facts. To agree with Rabossi one must, indeed, be irrationalist in that sense. But one need not be irrationalist in the sense of ceasing to make one's web of belief as coherent, and as perspicuously structured, as possible. Philosophers like myself, who think of rationality as simply the attempt at such coherence, agree with Rabossi that foundationalist projects are outmoded. We see our task as a matter of making our own culture – the human rights culture – more self-conscious and more powerful, rather than of demonstrating its superiority to other cultures by an appeal to something transcultural.

We think that the most philosophy can hope to do is to summarize our culturally influenced intuitions about the right thing to do in various situations. The summary is effected by formulating a generalization from which these intuitions can be deduced, with the help of noncontroversial lemmas. That generalization is not supposed to ground our intuitions, but rather to summarize them. John Rawls's "Difference Principle" and the U.S. Supreme Court's construction, in recent decades, of a constitutional "right to privacy" are examples of this kind of summary. We see the point of formulating such summarizing generalizations as increasing the predictability, and thus the power and efficiency, of our institutions, thereby heightening the sense of shared moral identity that brings us together in a moral community.

Foundationalist philosophers, such as Plato, Aquinas, and Kant, have hoped to provide independent support for such summarizing generalizations. They would like to infer these generalizations from further premises, premises capable of being known to be true independently of the truth of the moral intuitions that have been summarized. Such premises *are* supposed to justify our intuitions, by providing premises from which the content of those intuitions can be deduced. I shall lump all such premises together under the label "claims to knowledge about the nature of human beings." In this broad sense, claims to know that our moral intuitions are recollections of the Form of the Good, or that we are the disobedient children of a loving God, or that human beings differ from other kinds of animal by having dignity rather than mere value are all claims about human nature. So are such counterclaims as that human beings are merely vehicles for selfish genes or merely eruptions of the will to power. To claim such knowledge is to claim to know something that, though not itself a moral intuition, can *correct* moral intuitions. It is essential to this idea of moral knowledge that a whole community might come to *know* that most of its most salient intuitions about the right thing to do were wrong.

But now suppose we ask: *is* there this sort of knowledge? What kind of question is *that?* On the traditional view, it is a philosophical question, belonging to a branch of epistemology known as "metaethics." But on the pragmatist view I favor, it is a question of efficiency: a question about how best to grab hold of history – how best to bring about the utopia sketched by the Enlightenment. If the activities of those who attempt to achieve this sort of knowledge seem of little use in actualizing this utopia, that is a reason to think there is no such knowledge. If it seems that most of the work of changing moral intuitions is being done by manipulating our feelings rather than by increasing our knowledge, that is a reason to think there is no knowledge of the sort that philosophers like Plato, Aquinas, and Kant hoped to get.

This pragmatist argument against the Platonist has the same form as an argument for cutting off payment to the priests who perform purportedly war-winning sacrifices – an argument which says that all the real work of winning the war seems to be done by generals and admirals, not to mention foot soldiers. This argument does not say: since there seem to be no gods, there is probably no need to support the priests. It says instead: since there is apparently no need to support the priests, there probably are no gods. We pragmatists argue from the fact that the emergence of the human rights culture seems to owe nothing to increased moral knowledge, and everything to hearing sad and sentimental stories, to the conclusion that there is probably no knowledge of the sort Plato envisaged. We go on to argue that since no useful work seems to be done by insisting on a purportedly ahistorical human nature, there probably is no such nature, or at least nothing in that nature that is relevant to our moral choices.

In short, my doubts about the effectiveness of appeals to moral knowledge are doubts about causal efficacy, not about epistemic status. My doubts have nothing to do with any of the theoretical questions discussed under the heading of "metaethics": questions about the relation between facts and values, or between reason and passion, or between the cognitive and the noncognitive, or between descriptive statements and action-guiding statements. Nor do they have anything to do with questions about realism and antirealism. The difference between the moral realist and the moral antirealist seems to pragmatists a difference that makes no practical difference.

Further, such metaethical questions presuppose the Platonic distinction between inquiry that aims at efficient problem solving and inquiry that aims at a goal called "truth for its own sake." That distinction collapses if one follows Dewey in thinking of all inquiry – in physics as well as ethics – as practical problem solving or if one follows Peirce in seeing *every* belief as action-guiding.[5]

Even after the priests have been pensioned off, however, the memories of certain priests may still be cherished by the community – especially the memories of their prophecies. We remain profoundly grateful to philosophers like Plato and Kant, not because they discovered truths but because they prophesied cosmopolitan utopias – utopias most of whose details they may have gotten wrong, but utopias we might never have struggled to reach had we not heard their prophecies. As long as our ability to *know* and in particular to discuss the question "What is man?" seemed the most important thing about us human beings, people like Plato and Kant accompanied utopian prophecies with claims to know something deep and important – something about the parts of the soul or the transcendental status of the common moral con-

---

5 The present state of metaethical discussion is admirably summarized by Stephen Darwall, Allan Gibbard, and Peter Railton, "Toward Fin de Siècle Ethics: Some Trends," *Philosophical Review* 101 (January 1992), 115–89. This comprehensive and judicious article takes for granted that there is a problem about "vindicating the objectivity of morality" (127), that there is an interesting question as to whether ethics is "cognitive" or "noncognitive," that we need to figure out whether we have a "cognitive capacity" to detect moral properties (148), and that these matters can be dealt with ahistorically.

When these authors consider historicist writers such as Alasdair MacIntyre and Bernard Williams, they conclude that they are "[*meta*] *théoriciens malgré eux*" who share the authors' own "desire to understand morality, its preconditions and its prospects" (183). They make little effort to come to terms with suggestions that there may be no ahistorical entity called "morality" to be understood. The final paragraph of the article does suggest that it might be helpful if moral philosophers knew some more anthropology or psychology or history. But the penultimate paragraph makes clear that, with or without such assists, "contemporary metaethics moves ahead, and positions gain in complexity and sophistication."

It is instructive, I think, to compare this article with Annette Baier's "Some Thoughts on the Way We Moral Philosophers Live Now" (*Monist* 67, no. 4 [1984], 490–7). There Baier suggests that moral philosophers should "at least occasionally, like Socrates, consider why the rest of society should not merely tolerate but subsidize our activity." She goes on to ask, "Is the large proportional increase of professional philosophers and moral philosophers a good thing, morally speaking? Even if it scarcely amounts to a plague of gadflies, it may amount to a nuisance of owls." The kind of metaphilosophical and historical self-consciousness and self-doubt displayed by Baier seems to me badly needed, but it is conspicuously absent in *Philosophy in Review* (the centennial issue of the *Philosophical Review* in which "Toward Fin de Siècle Ethics" appears). The contributors to this issue are convinced that the increasing sophistication of a philosophical subdiscipline is enough to demonstrate its social utility and are entirely unimpressed by murmurs of "decadent scholasticism."

sciousness. But this ability and those questions have, in the past two hundred years, come to seem much less important. It is this cultural sea change that Rabossi summarizes in his claim that human rights foundationalism is *outmoded*. In the remainder of this essay, I want to take up the following questions: *Why* has knowledge become much less important to our self-image than it was two hundred years ago? Why does the attempt to found culture on nature, and moral obligation on knowledge of transcultural universals, seem so much less important to us than it seemed in the Enlightenment? Why is there so little resonance, and so little point, in the question "Do human beings in fact *have* the rights listed in the Helsinki Declaration"? Why, in short, has moral philosophy become such an inconspicuous part of our culture?

A simple answer to these questions is: because between Kant's time and ours, Darwin argued most intellectuals out of the view that human beings contained a special added ingredient. He convinced most of us that we were exceptionally talented animals, animals clever enough to take charge of our own evolution. I think this answer is right as far as it goes. But it leads to a further question: Why did Darwin succeed, relatively speaking, so very easily? Why did he not cause the creative philosophical ferment that was caused by Galileo and Newton?

The revival by the New Science of the seventeenth century of a Democritean–Lucretian corpuscularian picture of nature scared Kant into inventing transcendental philosophy, inventing a brand-new kind of knowledge, one that could demote the corpuscularian world picture to the status of "appearance." Kant's example encouraged the idea that the philosopher, as an expert on the nature and limits of knowledge, can serve as a supreme cultural arbiter.[6] But by the time of Darwin this idea was already beginning to seem quaint. The historicism that dominated the intellectual world of the early nineteenth century had created an antiessentialist mood. So when Darwin came along, he fit into the evolutionary niche that Herder and Hegel had begun to colonize. Intellectuals who populate this niche look to the future rather than to eternity. They prefer new ideas about how to

---

6 Fichte's *Vocation of Man* is a useful reminder of the need that was felt, circa 1800, for a cognitive discipline called philosophy that would rescue utopian hope from natural science. It is hard to think of an analogous book written in reaction to Darwin. Those who couldn't stand what Darwin was saying tended to go straight back behind the Enlightenment to traditional religious faith. The unsubtle, unphilosophical opposition, in nineteenth-century Europe, between science and faith suggests that most intellectuals could no longer believe that philosophy might produce some sort of superknowledge, knowledge that might trump the results of physical and biological inquiry.

change things over stable criteria for determining the desirability of change. They are the ones who think much of both Plato and Nietzsche outmoded.

The best explanation both of Darwin's relatively easy triumph and of our own increasing willingness to substitute hope for knowledge is that the nineteenth and twentieth centuries saw, among Europeans and Americans, an extraordinary increase in wealth, literacy, and leisure. This increase made possible an unprecedented acceleration in the rate of moral progress. Such events as the French Revolution and the ending of the transatlantic slave trade helped nineteenth-century intellectuals in the rich democracies to say: It is enough for us to know that we live in an age in which human beings can make things better for ourselves.[7] We do not need to dig behind this historical fact to nonhistorical facts about what we really are.

In the two centuries since the French Revolution, we have learned that human beings are far more malleable than Plato or Kant had dreamed. The more we are impressed by this malleability, the less interested we become in questions about our ahistorical nature. The more we see a chance to recreate ourselves, the more we shall read Darwin not as offering one more theory about what we really are but as providing reasons why we do not need to ask what we really are. Nowadays, to say that we are clever animals is not to say something philosophical and pessimistic but something political and hopeful – namely, if we can work together, we can make ourselves into whatever we are clever and courageous enough to imagine ourselves becoming. This is to set aside Kant's question "What is man?" and to substitute the question "What sort of world can we prepare for our great-grandchildren?"

The question "What is man?" in the sense of "What is the deep ahistorical nature of human beings?" owed its popularity to the standard answer to that question: we are the *rational* animal, the one that can *know* as well as merely feel. The residual popularity of this answer accounts for the residual popularity of Kant's astonishing claim that sentimentality has nothing to do with morality, that there is something distinctively and transculturally hu-

---

7 Some contemporary intellectuals, especially in France and Germany, take it as obvious that the Holocaust made it clear that the hopes for human freedom which arose in the nineteenth century are obsolete – that at the end of the twentieth century we postmodernists know that the Enlightenment project is doomed. But even these intellectuals, in their less preachy and sententious moments, do their best to further that project. So they should, for nobody has come up with a better one. It does not diminish the memory of the Holocaust to say that our response to it should not be a claim to have gained a new understanding of human nature or of human history, but rather a willingness to pick ourselves up and try again.

man called "the sense of moral obligation" which has nothing to do with love, friendship, trust, or social solidarity. As long as we believe *that,* people like Rabossi are going to have a tough time convincing us that human rights foundationalism is an outmoded project.

To overcome this idea of a sui generis sense of moral obligation, it would help to stop answering the question "What makes us different from other animals?" by saying, "We can know and they can merely feel." We should substitute "We can feel *for each other* to a much greater extent than they can." This substitution would let us disentangle Christ's suggestion that love matters more than knowledge from the neo-Platonic suggestion that knowledge of the truth will make us free. For as long as we think there is an ahistorical power that makes for righteousness – a power called truth or rationality – we will not be able to put foundationalism behind us.

The best, and probably the only, argument for putting foundationalism behind us is the one I have already suggested: it would be more efficient to do so, because it would let us concentrate our energies on manipulating sentiments, on sentimental education. That sort of education gets people of different kinds sufficiently well acquainted with one another that they are less tempted to think of those different from themselves as only quasi-human. The goal of this sort of manipulation of sentiment is to expand the reference of the terms "our kind of people" and "people like us."

All I can do to supplement this argument from increased efficiency is to offer a suggestion about how Plato managed to convince us that knowledge of universal truths mattered as much as he thought it did. Plato thought that the philosopher's task was to answer questions like "Why should I be moral? Why is it rational to be moral? Why is it in my interest to be moral? Why is it in the interest of human beings as such to be moral?" He thought this because he thought that the best way to deal with people like Thrasymachus and Gorgias was to demonstrate to them that they had an interest of which they were unaware, an interest in being rational, in acquiring self-knowledge. Plato thereby saddled us with a distinction between the true and the false self. That distinction was, by the time of Kant, transmuted into a distinction between categorical, rigid moral obligation and flexible, empirically determinable self-interest. Contemporary moral philosophy is still lumbered with this opposition between self-interest and morality, an opposition which makes it hard to realize that my pride in being a part of the human rights culture is no more external to my self than my desire for financial or sexual success.

It would have been better if Plato had decided, as Aristotle was to decide, that there was nothing much to be done with people like Thrasymachus and Callicles and that the problem was how to avoid having children who would be like Thrasymachus and Callicles. By insisting that he could reeducate people who had matured without acquiring appropriate moral sentiments by invoking a higher power than sentiment, the power of reason, Plato got moral philosophy off on the wrong foot. He led moral philosophers to concentrate on the rather rare figure of the psychopath, the person who has no concern for any human being other than himself. Moral philosophy has systematically neglected the much more common case: the person whose treatment of a rather narrow range of featherless bipeds is morally impeccable, but who remains indifferent to the suffering of those outside this range, the ones he thinks of as pseudo-humans.[8]

Plato set things up so that moral philosophers think they have failed unless they convince the rational egotist that he should not be an egotist – convince him by telling him about his true, unfortunately neglected self. But the rational egotist is not the problem. The problem is the gallant and honorable Serb who sees Muslims as circumcised dogs. It is the brave soldier and good comrade who loves and is loved by his mates, but who thinks of women as dangerous, malevolent whores and bitches.

Plato thought that the way to get people to be nicer to each other was to point out what they all had in common – rationality. But it does little good to point out, to the people I have just described, that many Muslims and women are good at mathematics or engineering or jurisprudence. Resentful young Nazi toughs were quite aware that many Jews were clever and learned, but this only added to the pleasure they took in beating such Jews. Nor does it do much good to get such people to read Kant and agree that one should not treat rational agents simply as means. For everything turns on who counts as a fellow human being, as a rational agent in the only relevant sense – the sense in which rational agency is synonymous with membership in *our* moral community.

For most white people, until very recently, most black people did not so count. For most Christians, until the seventeenth century or so, most heathen did not so count. For the Nazis, Jews did not count. For most males in countries in which the average annual income is less than two thousand pounds, most females still do not so count. Whenever tribal and national rivalries become important, members of rival tribes and nations will not so count. Kant's

---

8 Nietzsche was right to remind us that "these same men who, amongst themselves, are so strictly constrained by custom, worship, ritual gratitude and by mutual surveillance and jealousy, who are so resourceful in consideration, tenderness, loyalty, pride and friendship, when once they step outside their circle become little better than uncaged beasts of prey"(*The Genealogy of Morals,* trans. Francis Golffing [Garden City, N.Y.: Doubleday, 1956], 174).

account of the respect due to rational agents tells you that you should extend the respect you feel for the people like yourself to all featherless bipeds. This is an excellent suggestion, a good formula for secularizing the Christian doctrine of the brotherhood of man. But it has never been backed up by an argument based on neutral premises, and it never will be. Outside the circle of post-Enlightenment European culture, the circle of relatively safe and secure people who have been manipulating one another's sentiments for two hundred years, most people are simply unable to understand why membership in a biological species is supposed to suffice for membership in a moral community. This is not because they are insufficiently rational. It is, typically, because they live in a world in which it would be just too risky – indeed, would often be insanely dangerous – to let one's sense of moral community stretch beyond one's family, clan, or tribe.

To get whites to be nicer to blacks, males to females, Serbs to Muslims, or straights to gays, to help our species link up into what Rabossi calls a "planetary community" dominated by a culture of human rights, it is of no use whatever to say, with Kant: notice that what you have in common, your humanity, is more important than these trivial differences. For the people we are trying to convince will rejoin that they notice nothing of the sort. Such people are *morally* offended by the suggestion that they should treat someone who is not kin as if he were a brother, or a nigger as if he were white, or a queer as if he were normal, or an infidel as if she were a believer. They are offended by the suggestion that they treat people whom they do not think of as human as if they were human. When utilitarians tell them that all pleasures and pains felt by members of our biological species are equally relevant to moral deliberation, or when Kantians tell them that the ability to engage in such deliberation is sufficient for membership in the moral community, they are incredulous. They rejoin that these philosophers seem oblivious to blatantly obvious moral distinctions, distinctions any decent person would draw.

This rejoinder is not just a rhetorical device, nor is it in any way irrational. It is heartfelt. The *identity* of these people, the people whom we should like to convince to join our Eurocentric human rights culture, is bound up with their sense of who they are *not*. Most people – especially people relatively untouched by the European Enlightenment – simply do not think of themselves as, first and foremost, a human being. Instead, they think of themselves as being a certain *good* sort of human being – a sort defined by explicit opposition to a particularly bad sort. What is crucial for their sense of who they are is that they are *not* an infidel, *not* a queer, *not* a woman, *not* an untouchable. Just insofar as they are impoverished, and as their lives are perpetually at risk, they have little else than pride in not being what they are not to sustain their self-respect. Since the days when the term "human being" was synonymous with "member of our tribe," we have always thought of human beings in terms of *paradigm* members of the species. We have contrasted *us*, the *real* humans, with rudimentary or perverted or deformed examples of humanity.

We Eurocentric intellectuals like to suggest that we, the paradigm humans, have overcome this primitive parochialism by using that paradigmatic human faculty, reason. So we say that failure to concur with us is due to "prejudice." Our use of these terms in this way may make us nod in agreement when Colin McGinn tells us, in the introduction to his recent book,[9] that learning to tell right from wrong is not as hard as learning French. The only obstacles to agreeing with his moral views, McGinn explains, are prejudice and superstition.

One can, of course, see what McGinn means: if, like many of us, you teach students who have been brought up in the shadow of the Holocaust, brought up believing that prejudice against racial or religious groups is a terrible thing, it is not very hard to convert them to standard liberal views about abortion, gay rights, and the like. You may even get them to stop eating animals. All you have to do is to convince them that all the arguments on the other side appeal to "morally irrelevant" considerations. You do this by manipulating their sentiments in such a way that they imagine themselves in the shoes of the despised and oppressed. Such students are already so nice that they are eager to define their identity in nonexclusionary terms. The only people such students find any trouble being nice to are the ones they consider irrational – the religious fundamentalist, the smirking rapist, or the swaggering skinhead.

Producing generations of nice, tolerant, well-off, secure, other-respecting students of this sort in all parts of the world is just what is needed – indeed, *all* that is needed – to achieve an Enlightenment utopia. The more youngsters like this we can raise, the stronger and more global our human rights culture will become. But it is not a good idea to encourage these students to label "irrational" the intolerant people they have trouble tolerating. For that Platonic–Kantian epithet suggests that with only a little more effort, the good and rational part of these other people's souls could have triumphed over the bad and irrational part. It suggests that we good people know something these bad people do not know and that it is probably their own silly

9 Colin McGinn, *Moral Literacy: or, How to Do the Right Thing* (London: Duckworth, 1992), 16.

fault that they do not know it. All they had to do, after all, was to think a little harder, be a little more self-conscious, a little more rational.

But the bad people's beliefs are not more or less "irrational" than the
belief that race, religion, gender, and sexual preference are all morally irrelevant – that these are all trumped by membership in the biological
species. As used by moral philosophers like McGinn, the term "irrational behavior" means no more than "behavior of which we disapprove so strongly
that our spade is turned when asked *why* we disapprove of it." So it would be
better to teach our students that these bad people are no less rational, no
less clear-headed, no more prejudiced than we good people who respect
Otherness. The bad people's problem is, rather, that they were not as lucky
in the circumstances of their upbringing as we were. Instead of treating all
those people out there who are trying to find and kill Salman Rushdie as irrational, we should treat them as deprived.

Foundationalists think of these people as deprived of truth, of moral
knowledge. But it would be better – more concrete, more specific, more sug-
gestive of possible remedies – to think of them as deprived of two more concrete things: security and sympathy. By "security" I mean conditions of life
sufficiently risk-free as to make one's difference from others inessential to
one's self-respect, one's sense of worth. These conditions have been enjoyed
by North Americans and Europeans – the people who dreamed up the human rights culture – much more than they have been enjoyed by anyone
else. By "sympathy" I mean the sort of reactions Athenians had more of after seeing Aeschylus's *The Persians* than before, the sort that whites in the
United States had more of after reading *Uncle Tom's Cabin* than before, the
sort we have more of after watching television programs about the genocide
in Bosnia. Security and sympathy go together, for the same reasons that
peace and economic productivity go together. The tougher things are, the
more you have to be afraid of, the more dangerous your situation, the less
you can afford the time or effort to think about what things might be like
for people with whom you do not immediately identify. Sentimental education works only on people who can relax long enough to listen.

If Rabossi and I are right in thinking human rights foundationalism outmoded, then Hume is a better adviser than Kant about how we intellectuals
can hasten the coming of the Enlightenment utopia for which both men
yearned. Among contemporary philosophers, the best adviser seems to me
to be Annette Baier. Baier describes Hume as "the woman's moral philoso-

---

10 Annette Baier, "Hume, the Women's Moral Theorist?" in *Women and Moral Theory*, ed. Eva
   Kitay and Diana Meyers (Totowa, N.J.: Rowman & Littlefield, 1987), 40.

pher" because Hume held that "corrected (sometimes rule-corrected) sympathy, not law-discerning reason, is the fundamental moral capacity."[10] Baier would like us to get rid of both the Platonic idea that we have a true self and the Kantian idea that it is rational to be moral. In aid of this project, she suggests that we think of "trust" rather than "obligation" as the fundamental moral notion. This substitution would mean thinking of the spread of the human rights culture not as a matter of our becoming more aware of the requirements of the moral law, but rather as what Baier calls "a progress of sentiments."[11] This progress consists in an increasing ability to see the similarities between ourselves and people very unlike us as outweighing the differences. It is the result of what I have been calling "sentimental education." The relevant similarities are not a matter of sharing a deep true self that instantiates true humanity, but are such little, superficial similarities as cherishing our parents and our children – similarities that do not distinguish us in any interesting way from many nonhuman animals.

To accept Baier's suggestions, however, we have to overcome our sense that sentiment is too weak a force and that something stronger is required. This idea that reason is "stronger" than sentiment, that only an insistence on the unconditionality of moral obligation has the power to change human beings for the better, is very persistent. I think this persistence is due mainly to a semiconscious realization that if we hand our hopes for moral progress over to sentiment, we are in effect handing them over to *condescension*. For we shall be relying on those who have the power to change things – people like the rich New England abolitionists or rich bleeding hearts like Robert Owen and Friedrich Engels – rather than relying on something that has power over *them*. We shall have to accept the fact that the fate of the women of Bosnia depends on whether television journalists manage to do for them what Harriet Beecher Stowe did for black slaves – whether these journalists can make us, the audience back in the safe countries, feel that these women are more like us, more like real human beings, than we had realized.

To rely on the suggestions of sentiment rather than on the commands of reason is to think of powerful people gradually ceasing to oppress others, or to countenance the oppression of others, out of mere niceness rather than

11 Baier's book on Hume is entitled *A Progress of Sentiments: Reflections on Hume's Treatise* (Cambridge, Mass.: Harvard University Press, 1991). Baier's view of the inadequacy of most attempts by contemporary moral philosophers to break with Kant comes out most clearly when she characterizes Allan Gibbard (in his book *Wise Choices, Apt Feelings*) as focusing "on the feelings that a patriarchal religion has bequeathed to us" and says that "Hume would judge Gibbard to be, as a moral philosopher, basically a divine disguised as a fellow expressivist" (312).

out of obedience to the moral law. But it is revolting to think that our only hope for a decent society consists in softening the self-satisfied hearts of a leisure class. We want moral progress to burst up from below, rather than waiting patiently upon condescension from the top. The residual popularity of Kantian ideas of "unconditional moral obligation" – obligation imposed by deep ahistorical noncontingent forces – seems to me almost entirely due to our abhorrence of the idea that the people on top hold the future in their hands, that everything depends on them, that there is nothing more powerful to which we can appeal against them.

Like everyone else, I too would prefer a bottom-up way of achieving utopia, a quick reversal of fortune that will make the last first. But I do not think this is how utopia will in fact come into being. Nor do I think our preference for this way lends any support to the idea that the Enlightenment project lies in the depths of every human soul.

So why does this preference make us resist the thought that sentimentality may be the best weapon we have? I think Nietzsche gave the right answer to this question: we resist out of resentment. We *resent* the idea that we shall have to wait for the strong to turn their piggy little eyes to the suffering of the weak, slowly open their dried-up little hearts. We desperately hope there is something stronger and more powerful that will *hurt* the strong if they do *not* do these things – if not a vengeful God, then a vengeful aroused proletariat or, at least, a vengeful superego or, at the very least, the offended majesty of Kant's tribunal of pure practical reason. The desperate hope for a noncontingent and powerful ally is, according to Nietzsche, the common core of Platonism, of religious insistence on divine omnipotence, and of Kantian moral philosophy.[12]

Nietzsche was, I think, right on the button when he offered this diagnosis. What Santayana called "supernaturalism," the confusion of ideals and power, is *all* that lies behind the Kantian claim that it is not only nicer, but more *rational*, to include strangers within our moral community than to exclude them. If we agree with Nietzsche and Santayana on this point, however, we do not thereby acquire any reason to turn our backs on the Enlightenment project, as Nietzsche did. Nor do we acquire any reason to be sardonically pessimistic about the chances of this project, in the manner of such admirers of Nietzsche as Santayana, Ortega, Heidegger, Strauss, and Foucault.

For even though Nietzsche was quite right to see Kant's insistence on un-

---

12 Nietzsche's diagnosis is reinforced by Elizabeth Anscombe's famous argument that atheists are not entitled to the term "moral obligation."

conditionality as an expression of resentment, he was quite wrong to treat Christianity and the age of the democratic revolutions as signs of human degeneration. He and Kant, alas, shared something with each other that neither shared with Harriet Beecher Stowe – something that Iris Murdoch has called "dryness" and Jacques Derrida has called "phallogocentrism." The common element in the thought of both men was a desire for purity. This sort of purity consists in being not only autonomous, in command of oneself, but also in having the kind of self-conscious self-sufficiency that Sartre describes as the perfect synthesis of the in-itself and the for-itself. This synthesis could be attained, Sartre pointed out, only if one could rid oneself of everything sticky, slimy, wet, sentimental, and womanish.

Although this desire for virile purity links Plato to Kant, the desire to bring as many different kinds of people as possible into a cosmopolis links Kant to Stowe. Kant represents, in the history of moral thinking, a transitional stage between the hopeless attempt to convict Thrasymachus of irrationality and the hopeful attempt to see every new featherless biped who comes along as one of us. Kant's mistake was to think that the only way to have a modest, damped-down, nonfanatical version of Christian brotherhood after letting go of the Christian faith was to revive the themes of pre-Christian philosophical thought. He wanted to make knowledge of a core self do what can be done only by the continual refreshment and re-creation of the self, through interaction with selves as unlike itself as possible.

Kant performed the sort of awkward balancing act that is required in transitional periods. His project mediated between a dying rationalist tradition and a vision of a new, democratic world, the world of what Rabossi calls "the human rights phenomenon." With the advent of this phenomenon, Kant's balancing act has become outmoded and irrelevant. We are now in a good position to put aside the last vestiges of the idea that human beings are distinguished by the capacity to know rather than by the capacities for friendship and intermarriage, distinguished by rigorous rationality rather than by flexible sentimentality. If we do so, we shall have dropped the idea that assured knowledge of a truth about what we have in common is a prerequisite for moral education, as well as the idea of a specifically moral motivation. If we do all these things, then we shall see Kant's *Foundations of the Metaphysics of Morals* as a placeholder for *Uncle Tom's Cabin* – a concession to the expec-

13 See Jane Tompkins, *Sensational Designs: The Cultural Work of American Fiction, 1790–1860* (New York: Oxford University Press, 1985), for a treatment of the sentimental novel that chimes with the point I am trying to make here. In her chapter on Stowe, Tompkins says that she is asking the reader "to set aside some familiar categories for evaluating fiction –

tations of an intellectual epoch in which the quest for quasi-scientific knowledge seemed the best response to religious exclusionism.[13]

Unfortunately, many philosophers, especially in the English-speaking world, are still trying to hold on to the Platonic insistence that the principal duty of human beings is to *know*. That insistence was the lifeline to which Kant and Hegel thought we had to cling.[14] Just as German philosophers in the period between Kant and Hegel saw themselves as saving reason from Hume, many English-speaking philosophers now see themselves as saving reason from Derrida. But with the wisdom of hindsight, and with Baier's help, we have learned to read Hume not as a dangerously frivolous iconoclast but as the wettest, most flexible, least phallogocentric thinker of the Enlightenment. Someday, I suspect, our descendants may wish that Derrida's contemporaries had been able to read him not as a frivolous iconoclast, but rather as a sentimental educator, as another of "the women's moral philosophers."[15]

If one follows Baier's advice, one will see it as the moral educator's task not to answer the rational egotist's question "Why should I be moral?" but

---

stylistic intricacy, psychological subtlety, epistemological complexity – and to see the sentimental novel not as an artifice of eternity answerable to certain formal criteria and to certain psychological and philosophical concerns, but as a political enterprise, halfway between sermon and social theory, that both codifies and attempts to mold the values of its time" (126).

The contrast that Tompkins draws between authors like Stowe and "male authors such as Thoreau, Whitman and Melville, who are celebrated as models of intellectual daring and honesty" (124), parallels the contrast I tried to draw between public utility and private perfection in my *Contingency, Irony, and Solidarity* (Cambridge University Press, 1989). I see *Uncle Tom's Cabin* and *Moby Dick* as equally brilliant achievements, achievements we should not attempt to rank hierarchically, because they serve such different purposes. Arguing about which is the better novel is like arguing about which is the superior philosophical treatise: Mill's *On Liberty* or Kierkegaard's *Philosophical Fragments*.

14 Technically, of course, Kant denied knowledge in order to make room for moral faith. But what is transcendental moral philosophy if not the assurance that the noncognitive imperative delivered via the common moral consciousness shows the existence of a "fact of reason" – a fact about what it is to be a human being, a rational agent, a being that is something more than a bundle of spatiotemporal determinations? Kant was never able to explain how the upshot of transcendental philosophy could be knowledge, but he was never able to give up the attempt to claim such knowledge. On the German project of defending reason against Hume, see Fred Beiser, *The Fate of Reason: German Philosophy from Kant to Fichte* (Cambridge, Mass.: Harvard University Press, 1987).

15 I have discussed the relation between Derrida and feminism in "Deconstruction, Ideology and Feminism: A Pragmatist View," *Hypatia* 8 (1993), 96–103, and also in my reply to Alexander Nehamas in *Lire Rorty* (Paris: Eclat, 1992). Richard Bernstein is, I think, basically right in reading Derrida as a moralist, even though Thomas McCarthy is also right in saying that "deconstruction" is of no political use.

rather to answer the much more frequently posed question "Why should I care about a stranger, a person who is no kin to me, a person whose habits I find disgusting?" The traditional answer to the latter question is "Because kinship and custom are morally irrelevant, irrelevant to the obligations imposed by the recognition of membership in the same species." This has never been very convincing, since it begs the question at issue: whether mere species membership *is*, in fact, a sufficient surrogate for closer kinship. Furthermore, that answer leaves one wide open to Nietzsche's discomfiting rejoinder: *that* universalistic notion, Nietzsche will sneer, would have crossed the mind of only a slave – or, perhaps, an intellectual, a priest whose self-esteem and livelihood both depend on getting the rest of us to accept a sacred, unarguable, unchallengeable paradox.

A better sort of answer is the sort of long, sad, sentimental story that begins, "Because this is what it is like to be in her situation – to be far from home, among strangers," or "Because she might become your daughter-in-law," or "Because her mother would grieve for her." Such stories, repeated and varied over the centuries, have induced us, the rich, safe, powerful people, to tolerate and even to cherish powerless people – people whose appearance or habits or beliefs at first seemed an insult to our own moral identity, our sense of the limits of permissible human variation.

To people who, like Plato and Kant, believe in a philosophically ascertainable truth about what it is to be a human being, the good work remains incomplete as long as we have not answered the question "Yes, but am I under a *moral obligation* to her?" To people like Hume and Baier, it is a mark of intellectual immaturity to raise that question. But we shall go on asking that question as long as we agree with Plato that it is our ability to *know* that makes us human.

Plato wrote quite a long time ago, in a time when we intellectuals had to pretend to be successors to the priests, had to pretend to know something rather esoteric. Hume did his best to josh us out of that pretense. Baier, who seems to me both the most original and the most useful of contemporary moral philosophers, is still trying to josh us out of it. I think Baier may eventually succeed, for she has the history of the past two hundred years of moral progress on her side. These two centuries are most easily understood not as a period of deepening understanding of the nature of rationality or of morality, but rather as one in which there occurred an astonishingly rapid progress of sentiments, in which it has become much easier for us to be moved to action by sad and sentimental stories.

10

RATIONALITY AND CULTURAL DIFFERENCE

In this essay I discuss some of the questions that come up when some cultures are said to be more rational, and therefore better, than others. These questions also arise when some cultures are said to be less rationalistic, and therefore better, than others. I shall begin by distinguishing three senses of the term "rationality."

Rationality$_1$ is the name of an ability that squids have more of than amoebas, that language-using human beings have more of than non-language-using anthropoids, and that human beings armed with modern technology have more of than those not so armed: the ability to cope with the environment by adjusting one's reactions to environmental stimuli in complex and delicate ways. This is sometimes called "technical reason" and sometimes "skill at survival." It is ethically neutral, in the sense that this ability, by itself, does not help one decide what species or what culture it would be best to belong to.

Rationality$_2$ is the name of an extra added ingredient that human beings have and brutes do not. The presence of this ingredient within us is a reason to describe ourselves in different terms than those we use to describe nonhuman organisms. This presence cannot be reduced to a difference in degree of our possession of rationality$_1$. It is distinct because it sets goals other than mere survival; for example, it may tell you that it would be better to be dead than to do certain things. Appeal to rationality$_2$ establishes an evaluative hierarchy rather than simply adjusting means to taken-for-granted ends.

Rationality$_3$ is roughly synonymous with tolerance – with the ability not to be overly disconcerted by differences from oneself, not to respond aggressively to such differences. This ability goes along with a willingness to alter one's own habits – not only to get more of what one previously wanted but to reshape oneself into a different sort of person, one who wants different things than before. It also goes along with a reliance on persuasion rather than force, an inclination to talk things over rather than to fight, burn, or banish. It is a virtue that enables individuals and communities to coexist peacefully with other individuals and communities, living and letting live, and to put together new, syncretic, compromise ways of life. So rationality in this sense is sometimes thought of, as by Hegel, as quasi-synonymous with freedom.[1]

The Western intellectual tradition has often run these three senses of "rationality" together. It is often suggested that we can use language, and thus technology, to get what we want – be as efficient as we are in gratifying our desires – only because we have the precious, quasi-divine ingredient, rationality$_2$, which our brute cousins lack. Equally often, it is assumed that the adaptability signaled by rationality$_1$ is the same virtue as the tolerance I have labeled rationality$_3$. That is, it is assumed that the cleverer we get at adapting to circumstances by increasing the range and complexity of our responses to stimuli, the more tolerant of other sorts of human beings we will become. When all three senses of "rationality" are lumped together, it may begin to seem self-evident that humans who are good at arming themselves with technical means for gratifying their desires will also automatically adopt the right desires – those "in accordance with reason" – and will exhibit tolerance to those with alternative desires because they will understand how and why these undesirable desires were acquired. This produces the suggestion that the place where most of the technology comes from – the West – is also the place to get one's moral ideals and one's social virtues.

There are familiar philosophical as well as familiar political reasons for doubting this assimilation and the consequent suggestion. The philosophical reasons are those shared by old-time American pragmatists like Dewey and newfangled poststructuralists like Derrida, and consist mostly in attacking the very idea of rationality$_2$. These reasons are those produced in the course of the familiar attacks on "rationalism," "phallogocentrism," "the

---

1 Milan Kundera has described a utopia pervaded by rationality$_3$ as the "paradise of individuals" envisaged by the European novel. I discuss Kundera's conception of the role of the novel in the context of East–West cultural comparison in my "Heidegger, Kundera and Dickens," *Essays on Heidegger and Others* (Cambridge University Press, 1991), 66–82. I sketch a version of this paradise as "an intricately-textured collage of private narcissism and public pragmatism," a "bazaar surrounded by lots and lots of exclusive private clubs," at the end of my "On Ethnocentrism: A Reply to Clifford Geertz," reprinted in my *Objectivity, Relativism, and Truth* (Cambridge University Press, 1991), 203–10.

metaphysics of presence," "Platonism," and so on. The political reasons are those shared by people who believe, as do Roger Garaudy and Ashis Nandy, that "[t]he Western countries are sick"[2] – and by those who, like myself, believe that, though not sick, the West may have boxed itself, and the rest of the world with it, into a very tight corner. For liberals who are also pragmatists, as I am, questions about rationality and cultural differences boil down to questions about the relation between $rationality_1$ and $rationality_3$. We just drop the whole idea of $rationality_2$.

Now I want to turn to the notion of "culture" and, once again, distinguish three senses of the term.

$Culture_1$ is simply a set of shared habits of action, those that enable members of a single human community to get along with one another and with the surrounding environment as well as they do. In this sense of the term, every army barracks, academic department, prison, monastery, farming village, scientific laboratory, concentration camp, street market, and business corporation has a culture of its own. Many of us belong to a lot of different cultures – to that of our native town, to that of our university, to that of the cosmopolitan intellectuals, to that of the religious tradition in which we were brought up, to those of the organizations to which we belong or groups with which we have dealings. In this sense, "culture" is not the name of a virtue, nor is it necessarily the name of something human beings have and other animals do not. Ethologists talk about the culture of a band of baboons as easily as ethnologists talk about the culture of a village, and both mean pretty much the same thing by the term. In respect to this neutrality between the nonhuman and the human, and in respect to a lack of evaluative force, $culture_1$ resembles $rationality_1$. There is a difference in complexity and richness between the culture of a farming village and that of Buddhism, the same sort of difference as separates the $rationality_1$ of the amoeba from that of the squid, but not a difference of kind.

$Culture_2$ is the name of a virtue. In this sense, "culture" means something like "high culture." Prisoners often don't have much or any of it but inhabitants of monasteries and universities often have quite a lot. Good indications of the possession of $culture_2$ are an ability to manipulate abstract ideas for the sheer fun of it, and an ability to discourse at length about the differing values of widely diverse sorts of painting, music, architecture, and writing. $Culture_2$ can be acquired by education and is a typical product of

2 Roger Garaudy, Foreword to Ashis Nandy, *Traditions, Tyranny and Utopias* (Oxford: Oxford University Press, 1987), x.

the sort of education reserved for the wealthier and more leisured members of a society. It is often associated with rationality$_3$, as in Matthew Arnold's suggestion that sweetness and light go together.

Culture$_3$ is a rough synonym for what is produced by the use of rationality$_2$. It is what supposedly has steadily gained ground, as history has gone along, over "nature" – over what we share with brutes. It is the overcoming of the base and irrational and animal by something universally human, something all persons and cultures are more or less able to recognize and respect. To say that one culture$_1$ is more "advanced" than another is to say that it has come closer to realizing "the essentially human" than another culture$_1$, that it is a better expression of what Hegel called "the self-consciousness of Absolute Spirit," a better example of culture$_3$. The universal reign of culture$_3$ is the goal of history.

It is often suggested these days that any culture$_1$ is worthy, ceteris paribus, of preservation. But this suggestion is usually tempered by the admission that there are some cultures – for example, those of concentration camps, criminal gangs, and international conspiracies of bankers – that we would be better off without. It is sometimes also modified by suggestions, like that cited earlier, that some very large and prominent culture$_1$ is "sick" or "decadent." There is a tension between the theoretical idea that anything that takes as long to develop and solidify as a culture$_1$ or a species of living thing is worth keeping around and the practical necessity to endanger or exterminate certain cultures (for example, the Mafia, thugs, Nazis) or certain species (for example, the smallpox bacillus, the anopheles mosquito, the fire ant, the krait).

I doubt that the suggestion that any and every culture$_1$ is prima facie worth preserving would ever have been made if there had not been a certain amount of confusion between the three senses of "culture" that I have distinguished. In particular, this suggestion would not have been made unless we had acquired the habit of seeing various cultures$_1$ as works of art, automatically worthy of appreciation as examples of the triumph of culture$_3$ over nature, and thus inferred that failure to appreciate and cherish any such triumph would count as a failure in culture$_2$. Such failure would be philistine, insensitive, a betrayal of both culture$_2$ and culture$_3$.

The suggestion that we treat every culture as a work of art, prima facie worthy of preservation in the way in which every work of art is so worthy, is a comparatively recent one, but it is very influential among leftist intellectuals in the contemporary West. It goes along with a sense of guilt about "Eurocentrism" and with rage at the suggestion that any culture might be seen as less "valid" than another. To my mind, this set of attitudes is an attempt to preserve the Kantian notion of "human dignity" even after one has given up on rationality$_2$. It is an attempt to re-create the Kantian distinction between value and dignity by thinking of every human culture, if not of every human individual, as having incommensurable worth – as surrounded by the aura that, for persons who are cultured$_2$, surrounds works of art.

This nonrationalist version of Kantianism, however, often tries to combine the claim that every culture is as valid as every other with the claim that some cultures$_1$ – or at least one, that of the modern West – are "sick" or "sterile" or "violent" or "empty" – empty of whatever it is that gives all other cultures$_1$ their "validity." Susan Sontag, for example, has urged that "the white race is the cancer of the planet" – a metaphor that suggests the need for radical surgery, for extirpation, the same sort of need as we feel in regard to the smallpox bacillus and the krait.

In the discourse of some contemporary leftist intellectuals, it sometimes seems as if only *oppressed* cultures count as "real" or "valid" cultures$_1$.[3] Analogously, there has been a tendency among modern Europeans who pride themselves on their culture$_2$ to think that only "difficult" and "different" works of art – preferably produced in garrets by rejected, marginalized artists – are "real" or "valid" instances of artistic creativity. This is accompanied by the suggestion that easily understood paintings by well-fed members of the Royal Academy, or much-watched soap operas produced by handsomely compensated hacks, fall short of the status of "art." To be cultured$_2$, among leftist intellectuals of the present day, is to be able to see all oppressed cultures – all victims of colonialism and economic imperialism – as more valuable than anything done by or in the contemporary West.

This exaltation of the non-Western and the oppressed seems to me just as dubious as the Western imperialists' assurance that all other forms of life are "childish" in comparison with that of modern Europe. The latter assurance depends on the idea that one's own power to suppress other forms of life is an indication of the value of one's own form. The former exaltation depends on a bad inference from the premise that what makes cultures valuable has nothing to do with power, to the conclusion that powerlessness, like poverty, is an index of worth, and indeed of something auratic, something like holiness. I shall try, in the next section of this essay, to sketch a pragmatist view of cultural difference that avoids both ideas.

---

3 This goes along with a tendency to try for a "theory of oppression," an attempt that seems to me as likely to be fruitless as are theories of evil or of power. I think that abstraction and generalization have, in such attempts, gone one step too far and that we need to get back to the rough ground.

In the form it took in the works of its most important exponent, John Dewey, American pragmatism was an attempt to make the categories of moral and political thought continuous with those used in a Darwinian–Mendelian account of biological evolution. Dewey tied Hegel and Darwin together. He blended Hegel's conception of history as the story of increasing human freedom with Darwin's account of evolution in order to get rid of the universalism common to Plato and Kant and of Hegel's sense of immanent teleology, the Hegelian idea that "the real is the rational and the rational is the real." Dewey dropped the notion of an ahistorical human nature and substituted the idea that certain mammals had recently become capable of creating a new environment for themselves rather than simply reacting to environmental exigencies.

I find it useful, in restating Dewey's adaptation of Darwin, to use the term "meme" – a term recently popularized by Richard Dawkins and Daniel Dennett. A meme is the cultural counterpart of a gene. Words of moral approbation, musical phrases, political slogans, stereotypical images, abusive epithets are all examples of memes. Just as the triumph of one species over another – its ability to usurp the space previously occupied by the other – can be viewed as a triumph of a set of genes, so the triumph of one culture over another can be viewed as the triumph of a set of memes. From a Deweyan point of view, neither sort of triumph is an indication of any special virtue – for example, of a "right" to triumph or of proximity to the goal of Nature or of History. Both are just the outcomes of concatenations of contingent circumstances. For Dewey, to speak of the "survival of the fittest" is merely to say, tautologously, that what survives survives. It is not to suggest that there is something outside the struggles of genes and memes that provides a criterion by which to sort out good outcomes from bad outcomes. The process of evolution has nothing to do with evaluative hierarchies, nor, *pace* Hegel, do the factors that determine the survival of memes. When a Deweyan describes history as the story of increasing human freedom, she is not saying that there is a power – rationality$_2$ – which somehow favors such freedom. She is merely saying that, given the evaluative hierarchy provided by *our* memes – the contingent historical outlook of a particular culture$_1$ – past events and future possiblities are usefully connected by a dramatic narrative of increasing freedom, increasing rationality$_3$.

Before Dewey, Spencer had attempted to assimilate a triumphalist story of cultural development to a Darwinian story about biological evolution. But Spencer tried to hold on to something like rationality$_2$ and something like culture$_3$. That is, he tried to hold on to the idea of an immanent teleology, one that provided a universalistic criterion of the "health" or "goodness" of an evolutionary or cultural development. As Dewey said in an essay on Spencer of 1904, Spencer's notion of "environment" was "but the translation of the 'nature' of the metaphysicians," and so for him evolution still tends to "'a single, far-off, divine, event' – to a finality, a fixity."[4] Spencer, Dewey said, believed "in nature as a mighty force, and in reason as having only to cooperate with nature, instead of thwarting it with its own petty, voluntary devices, in order to usher in the era of unbridled progress."[5] For Dewey, by contrast, "Nature" was the name not of a force, but simply of the results of a series of chances. "Reason" was the name neither of an extra added ingredient nor of what was "natural" and "essential" to our species. The term denotes nothing more than a high degree of rationality$_1$.

For Dewey, there was a connection, but not a necessary or unbreakable one, between the increase in rationality$_1$ that comes with modern science and technology and rationality$_3$ – between efficiency and tolerance. As we became more and more emancipated from custom – more and more willing to do things differently than our ancestors for the sake of coping with our environment more efficiently and successfully – we became more and more receptive to the idea that good ideas might come from anywhere, that they are not the prerogative of an elite and not associated with any particular locus of authority. In particular, the rise of technology helped break down the traditional distinction between the "high" wisdom of priests and theorists and the "low" cleverness of artisans – thus contributing to the plausibility of a democratic system of government.

For Dewey, the New Science of the seventeenth century, and the new technology and the liberal reforms of the eighteenth and nineteenth, did not arise out of rationality$_2$ and thus were not examples – as they were for Spencer – of human beings realizing their "natural" or "essentially human" abilities to better effect. They were simply exemplifications of a new flexibility and adaptability that some human communities had come to exhibit. This increasing flexibility led to profound social changes – the overthrow of feudal institutions, industrial capitalism, parliamentary government, colonialist expansion for the sake of cheap labor and new markets, female suffrage, two world wars, mass literacy, the possibility of environmental catastrophe and of nuclear holocaust, and a lot of other recent developments. The very mixed bag of results produced by this new flexibility – this increased ability to alter the environment rather than simply fending off its blows – meant, in Dewey's

---

4 John Dewey, "The Philosophical Work of Herbert Spencer," *The Middle Works of John Dewey* (Carbondale: Southern Illinois University Press, 1977), 3: 208.
5 Ibid., 203.

eyes, that we typically solve old problems at the cost of creating new problems for ourselves. (For example, we eliminate old forms of cruelty and intolerance only to find that we have invented new, more insidious forms thereof.) He had no wholesale solution to offer to the new problems we had created, only the hope that the same experimental daring which had created the new problems as by-products might, if combined with a will to decrease suffering, eventually produce piecemeal solutions to those new problems.

Obviously, increasing flexibility and efficiency can as easily be used to oppress as to free – to increase suffering as to decrease it, to decrease rationality$_3$ as to increase it. So there is nothing *intrinsically* emancipatory about a greater degree of rationality$_1$. There is no a priori reason why it should produce a greater degree of rationality$_3$. But in fact, for various historically specific reasons, it has sometimes done so. One such reason was the prevalence of Christian rhetoric – a rhetoric of human brotherhood – in the communities that were the first to develop modern technology. Another was the fact that religious tolerance – thanks to the role of refugees from religious persecution in the founding of the United States and the compromises effected in various European countries in the wake of the Wars of Religion – became part of the public rhetoric of some of the great imperialist and colonialist powers. Religious tolerance – tolerance about matters of ultimate importance – often paves the way for tolerance of other forms of difference.[6]

Unlike Kant, Hegel, and Spencer, Dewey had no arguments, based on claims about the nature of rationality$_2$, to show that the rhetorics of human brotherhood, and of tolerance of different opinions and styles of life, are good rhetorics to have – rhetorics that pick out the right goals. He did not think it the function of philosophy to provide argumentative backup, firm foundations, for evaluative hierarchies.[7] He simply took the rhetorics and goals of the social democratic movement of the turn of the century for granted and asked what philosophy might do to further them. His answer was that it could try to change our self-image so that we dropped the whole idea of rationality$_2$ and came to think of ourselves as continuous with amoebas

6 On the role of religious tolerance in Rawls's account of liberal justice, see my "The Priority of Democracy to Philosophy," reprinted in *Objectivity, Relativism, and Truth*, 175–96.

7 Dewey's attitude toward the idea that philosophers might provide foundations for social practices resembled that of Wittgenstein, who said, in reference to the Frege–Russell notion that the foundations of mathematics can be found in logic, "The *mathematical* problems of what is called foundations are no more the foundations of mathematics for us than the painted rock is the support of the painted tower" (*Remarks on the Foundations of Mathematics*, 8: 16). In other words, the philosophy of X (where X is something like mathematics, art, science, class struggle, or postcolonialism) is just more X and cannot *support* X – though it may expand, clarify, or improve X.

and squids, though also continuous with those unimaginably more flexible, free, and imaginative humanoids who may be our descendants. These descendants would inhabit a social democratic utopia in which humans caused one another far less suffering than they presently do – a utopia in which human brotherhood was realized in ways we can now barely imagine. The unifying social ideal of this utopia would be a balance between minimizing suffering and the maximization of rationality$_3$ – a balance between pressure not to hurt others and tolerance of different ways of living, between vigilance against cruelty and reluctance to set up a panoptic state. As good pragmatists, inhabitants of this utopia would not think of themselves as realizing the true nature of humanity, living in accordance with rationality$_2$, but simply as being happier and freer, leading richer lives, than the inhabitants of previous human communities.

What happens when we examine the topic of cultural differences from this Deweyan angle? When we try to do so, the following questions become salient: Would this Deweyan utopia preserve the geographically bounded cultural differences in place today – for example, the differences between Buddhist and Hindu, Chinese and Japanese, Islamic and Christian cultures, or would it throw all or most of these into a blender? If the latter, would that be a mistake? Would something very important have been irretrievably lost? Or would new cultural differences – the differences between new cultures$_1$ that would spontaneously form within such a tolerant utopia – compensate for the loss of the old differences?

When the question is posed in that way, the only plausible answer seems to be: nobody knows, but there seems no particular reason to hope for immortality for any contemporary set of cultural differences, as opposed to hoping that it may eventually be supplanted by a new and more interesting set. In modern Europe, we do not much miss the culture of Ur of the Chaldees or of pagan Carthage. Presumably modern Indians do not much miss the cultures that were displaced and gradually extirpated as the Aryan-speaking peoples descended from the North. In both cases, there is the feeling that we have a lot of cultural diversity now, maybe all we need, and that Ur and Harappa are no more to be regretted than are the eohippus, the mammoth, and the saber-toothed tiger. Given seven thousand species of birds, nobody mourns much for the archaeopteryx. Given the rich pluralism of modern Europe nobody much cares whether the last Gaelic or Breton speakers – or the last strict-rhyme-scheme poets or Palladian architects – die out. We regret the imminent loss of the birds of paradise and the great whales because we know it will take 10 million years for new species of equal grandeur to evolve, but when it comes to Christianity, Islam, Buddhism, and the secular humanism of the modern West, we suspect that – given peace, wealth, luck, and utopian rationality$_3$ – these cultures$_1$ will be extirpated only when new cultures, of at least equal grandeur, are available to take their places.

This rather facile answer suggests that I have picked up the topic of cultural difference by the wrong handle. For this topic is a live one today because of the suspicion that what I blithely refer to as "the secular humanism of the modern West" is a sort of omnivorous monster, one that swallows up all other cultures$_1$ and is incapable of producing diversity from within itself. This suspicion is linked to the further suspicion that the Deweyan views I hold – those that make up what Ashis Nandy calls an "evolutionist, technocratic, pragmatism"[8] – already beg all the important questions. For in the eyes of Nandy and many others, Dewey himself is simply one more representative of a non-self-critical culture$_1$ that, even as it prides itself on kindness and tolerance, is engaged in destroying all possibility of cultural difference – a culture$_1$ that is, at bottom, philistine, sterile, and violent, intrinsically opposed to the pursuit of culture$_2$ and to the development of rationality$_3$.

From Nandy's point of view, if I understand it, tolerance and pragmatism – rationality$_3$ and the view that rationality$_2$ does not exist – are like oil and water. Nandy would say that the pragmatic insistence on seeing human beings as simply one more organism, and human cultures as bearers of memes none of which are more closely related to something transhistorical (such as Nature or God) than others, is incompatible with the sort of tolerance of cultural differences that would allow a place for what is important in the Indian tradition. Nandy, I gather, accepts the views that, in the following passage, he describes Gandhi as holding:

> Gandhi rejected the modern West primarily because of its secular scientific worldview. To him a culture which did not have a theory of transcendence could not be morally or cognitively acceptable. He knew that the ideological core of the modern world was post-Galilean science which prided itself on being the only fully secular area of knowledge. He also knew that legitimation of the modern West as a superior culture came from an ideology which viewed secularized societies as superior to non-secular ones; once one accepted the ideology, the superiority of the West became an objective evaluation.[9]

Dewey would deny that there could be an objective evaluation of the West as superior *tout court*. For superiority is, for a pragmatist, always relative to the purpose something is being asked to serve. But he would insist on three

8 Nandy, *Traditions*, xvi. 9 Ibid., 129–30.

points. First, *some* of the West's achievements – controlling epidemics, increasing literacy, improving transportation and communication, standardizing the quality of commodities, and so on – are not likely to be despised by anybody who has had experience of them. Second, the West is better than any other known culture at referring questions of social policy to the results of future experimentation rather than to principles and traditions taken over from the past. Third, the West's willingness to go secular, to give up on transcendence, has done much to make this second achievement possible. For reasons I have already sketched, Dewey saw secularization as one of the forces that helped make a social democratic utopia plausible.

Dewey thought it unlikely that the West's achievements could be made compatible with any religious culture, any pursuit of transcendence, more specific and less vague than that suggested in his *Common Faith*. That book attempted to bring Darwin and religion together by seeing the pragmatist denial of rationality$_2$ as a way of uniting the human and the rest of nature, in the manner of Spinoza and Wordsworth. For Dewey, "the essentially irreligious attitude" is

> that which attributes human achievement and purpose to man in isolation from the world of physical nature and his fellows. Our successes are dependent upon the cooperation of nature. The sense of the dignity of human nature is as religious as is the sense of awe and reverence when it rests upon a sense of human nature as a cooperating part of a larger whole.[10]

Dewey wanted us to secularize nature by seeing it as nonteleological, as having no evaluative hierarchies of its own. But he wanted us to keep something vaguely like a sense of transcendence by seeing ourselves as just one more product of evolutionary contingencies, as having only (though to a much greater degree) the same sorts of abilities as squids and amoebas. Such a sense makes us receptive to the possibility that our descendants may transcend us, just as we have transcended the squids and the apes. Dewey had no sense of Wordsworth's "something far more deeply interfused," but he thought that "militant atheism" showed a lack of Wordsworthian "natural piety."[11] Dewey did not have what Nandy called "a theory of transcendence," except in the sense that he saw a utopia pervaded by rationality$_3$ as the sort of goal that makes possible what he called "the unification of the self through allegiance to inclusive ideal ends" – a phrase that was his highly secularized definition of "faith."[12]

---

10 John Dewey, *A Common Faith* (New Haven, Conn.: Yale University Press, 1934), 25.
11 Ibid., 53.   12 See ibid., 33.

How does one decide between Dewey and Nandy? As I see it, the conflict between them is a straightforward conflict of empirical predictions – predictions of what is likely to happen if "an evolutionist, technocratic pragmatism," even when combined with something like a Wordsworthian sense of community with nature, becomes dominant in a politically unified global community. Nandy thinks that this will lead to bad results, and Dewey thought that it would lead to good results – where "good results" means a utopia characterized by maximal rationality$_3$ and maximal elimination of what Nandy calls "man-made suffering."

Dewey would entirely agree with Nandy that "only by retaining a feel for the immediacy of man-made suffering can a utopia sustain a permanently critical attitude toward itself and other utopias."[13] But he would argue that the West is likely to be, relatively speaking and despite its manifest cruelties, pretty good at retaining such a feel. He would base his argument on the fact that the West has developed a culture$_1$ of hope – a hope of a better world as attainable here below by social effort – as opposed to the cultures$_1$ of resignation characteristic of the East. The Romantic social idealism that has pervaded European and North American thought since the French Revolution is obviously not the whole story about the culture of the West, but neither is it to be neglected. Nandy, it seems to me, largely neglects this Romantic strain.[14]

In a passage Dewey would have liked, Nandy writes:

> . . . human civilization is constantly trying to alter or expand its awareness of exploitation and oppression. Who, before the socialists, had thought of class as a unit of repression? How many, before Freud, had sensed that children needed to be protected against their own parents? How many believed, before Gandhi's rebirth after the environmental crisis in the West, that modern technology, the supposed liberator of man, had become his most powerful oppressor?[15]

Dewey would, however, pick up on the examples of the socialists and Freud to claim that the West had taken the lead in such expansion of awareness of

---

13 Nandy, *Traditions,* 9.

14 Nandy mentions this strain in *Traditions,* 82–3, but he seems to think that it cannot be reconciled, as Dewey tried to reconcile it, with an enthusiasm for technology. So he sees Thoreau, Ruskin, and Tolstoy as the true heirs of Wordsworth and Blake. He thus resembles the so-called Young American critics of Dewey – Van Wyck Brooks, Lewis Mumford, Waldo Frank, and Randolph Bourne – who had many of the same heroes. See the discussion of these four men's hostility to Dewey's technologism in Casey Blake, *Beloved Community* (Chapel Hill: University of North Carolina Press, 1990).

15 Nandy, *Traditions,* 22.

exploitation and oppression – and in particular that psychoanalysis and the Socialist International are as good representatives of the West as, say, the KGB and the Union Carbide Company. Further, Dewey would be dubious about the claim that modern science and technology have oppression built in, as opposed to being tools that are equally useful for oppression and for relief from oppression.

Nandy, however, believes that such a claim of neutrality is false. He decries the attempt to "operate as if the pathology of modern science lay only in its context"[16] – as if it were not modern science itself but only its use by particular people that is to blame. He insists that "violence lies at the heart of modern science"[17] and that "today science has a built-in tendency to be an ally of authoritarianism."[18] By contrast, he claims, "the traditional cultures, not being driven by the principles of absolute internal consistency and parsimony, did allow the individual to create a place for himself in a plural structure of authority." This, it seems to me, is Nandy's basic argument for the claim that "the main civilizational problem is not with irrational, self-contradicting superstitions, but with the ways of thinking associated with the modern concept of rationality."[19] Like Foucault, Nandy sees the culture created in the West by modern science as differing from "the traditional cultures" in that "modern science has already built a structure of near-total isolation where human beings themselves – including all their suffering and moral experience – have been objectified as things and processes, to be vivisected, manipulated or corrected."[20]

Both Foucault and Nandy see in the modern West a panoptic society in which individuality – and thus rationality$_3$ – is becoming increasingly impossible. Dewey, by contrast, sees the growing amount of leisure, wealth, and security available in technological societies as making individuality – and thus rationality$_3$ – increasingly easy.

Nandy may be right in his prediction that the forces within Western culture that promote panopticism and prevent individuality will, in the end, outweigh romantic hopes for a utopia pervaded by rationality$_3$. But I am not sure that we philosophers can do much to decide whether he is right. That is, I am not sure that there is much point in our debating what is "central" or "essential" to the culture of the West or that of India, or in debating whether, for instance, the presence of "a theory of transcendence" in the latter has done more or less for individuality than the forty-hour work week and the welfare state have done in the former.

16 Ibid., 111.   17 Ibid.   18 Ibid., 110.   19 Ibid., 106.   20 Ibid.

All we philosophers can do, I suspect, is to sharpen the issues a bit. Nandy sharpens them by insisting that we question the common Western idea that science is neutral between political and cultural alternatives. All I can do by way of sharpening them is to point out that Dewey suggests a way of hanging on to science and technology while dropping the notions of rationality$_2$ and of culture$_3$, thereby setting aside the claim of the West to "objective" superiority where "objective" has some ahistorical, transcultural sense. Further, Dewey's pragmatic, antirepresentationalist view that scientific beliefs are tools for the gratification of desires, together with his doctrine of the means–end continuum (the doctrine that new means continually engender new ends, and conversely), gives us a way of doing something Nandy recommends. It lets us, in Nandy's words, "refuse to partition cognition and affect" and thereby "blur the boundaries between science, religion, and the arts."[21] For on a pragmatic view science, religion and the arts are all, equally, tools for the gratification of desire. None of them can dictate, though any of them can and will suggest, what desires to have or what evaluative hierarchies to erect.

It would be in the spirit of his criticisms of Spencer for Dewey to agree with Nandy that nowadays "we must look elsewhere [than to science] to find support for democratic values."[22] But whereas Nandy apparently follows Gandhi in thinking of religion as a better place to find such support, Dewey, with an eye to the dangers of religious fundamentalism, prefers art. Dewey accepts the traditional account of Greek art – in particular, the art of Athenian sculptors and tragedians – as an important contribution to the process of secularization, thereby bringing human beings out of a culture of resignation into a culture of hope.[23] He shares the typically Western preference for art that is not a handmaiden to religion – a preference for the sort of plastic art that developed out of Renaissance humanism and out of nineteenth-century bohemianism rather than the sort of temple decoration found at Varanasi, Nara, and Chartres. He shares the typically Romantic idea that the artist's activity is less ancillary and more autonomous than anyone else's, that poets are the unacknowledged legislators of the world, the proper successors to priests and sages.

---

21 Ibid., 45.   22 Ibid., 110.

23 For an account of the West as the former sort of culture before the late Middle Ages and as the latter sort of culture thereafter, see Hans Blumenberg's *The Legitimacy of the Modern Age* (Cambridge, Mass.: MIT Press, 1985). Blumenberg argues that at a certain point (thanks to Ockhamite themes developed by Francis Bacon) the West switched from pinning its hopes on another world to pinning its hopes on the chance that future generations might be happier and freer than their ancestors.

I suspect that this difference about whether religion or art provides the safest and most reliable counterweight to science and technology may be the crucial difference between Nandy and Dewey, just as the difference about whether there is something called *denken* over against *dichten* is the crucial difference between Heidegger and Dewey.[24] For Dewey, it is the Romantic strain, rather the rationalist strain, that should be preserved from Hegel and Marx, and combined with a Darwinian naturalism. Such naturalism is fairly difficult to combine with traditional religions, but fairly easy to combine with the Romanticism that is the least common denominator of Wordsworth and Byron, of Emerson and Nietzsche.

If Dewey were asked what activities typical of culture$_2$ are in the best position to mediate encounters between cultures$_1$, in such a way as to promote rationality$_3$, I think he might look to the sorts of novels and memoirs written by people whose personal lives have involved a tension between cultures$_1$. I am thinking of books by people like Salman Rushdie, V. S. Naipaul, Kwame Anthony Appiah, Kazuo Ishiguro, and Gayatri Chakravorty Spivak.[25] Dewey would look to people who have had to find, in the course of self-creation and artistic creation, concrete, nontheoretical ways of blending the modern West with one or another non-Western culture.

Such a preference for small concrete compromises over large theoretical syntheses would accord with Dewey's pragmatic view that theory is to be en-

---

24 On the Heidegger–Dewey contrast, see the first two essays in my *Essays on Heidegger and Others*.
25 See, for an example of the attitude and the practice I have in mind here, Kwame Anthony Appiah, "Is the Post- in Post-Modernism the Post- in Post-Colonial?" *Critical Inquiry* 17 (Winter 1991), 336–57. Appiah says: "If there is a lesson in the broad shape of this circulation of cultures, it is surely that we are all already contaminated by each other, that there is no longer a fully autochthonous *echt*-African culture awaiting salvage by our artists (just as there is, of course, no American culture without African roots). And there is a clear sense in some postcolonial writing that the postulation of a unitary Africa over against a monolithic West – the binarism of Self and Other – is the last of the shibboleths of the modernizers that we must learn to live without" (354). Appiah quotes Sara Suleri as saying that she is tired of being an "otherness machine" and notes that one effect of colonialism has been to force postcolonial intellectuals to have "the manufacture of alterity as our principal role" (356). Appiah takes as the emblem of his essay a recent wooden Yoruba sculpture called *Man with a Bicycle*, a sculpture that, Appiah says, "is produced by someone who does not care that the bicycle is the white man's invention; it is not there to be Other to the Yoruba Self; it is there because someone cared for its solidity; it is there because it will take us further than our feet will take us; it is there because machines are now as African as novelists . . . and as fabricated as the kingdom of Nakem" (357).
        For another example of fruitful contamination, consider the kind of nation we may have in the middle of the next century, a period when U.S. yuppies may need not only to learn Japanese, but to know a lot about traditional Japanese culture, in order to get promoted within a U.S. economy owned and directed by Americanized Japanese.

couraged only when likely to facilitate practice. My own hunch is that attempts to erect large theoretical oppositions between, or effect large theoretical syntheses of, the "spirit" or the "essence" of distinct cultures$_1$ are only stopgaps and makeshifts. The real work of building a multicultural global utopia, I suspect, will be done by people who, in the course of the next few centuries,[26] unravel each culture$_1$ into a multiplicity of fine component threads and then weave these threads together with equally fine threads drawn from other cultures$_1$ – thus promoting the sort of variety-in-unity characteristic of rationality$_3$. The resulting tapestry will, with luck, be something we can now barely imagine – a culture$_1$ that will find the cultures$_1$ of contemporary America and contemporary India as suitable for benign neglect as we find those of Harappa or of Carthage.

26 Do we *have* a few centuries? Perhaps not. The possibility of nuclear holocaust or environmental catastrophe will not go away, if it ever does, for a long time – and if either happens, it will be fair, though a bit pointless, to blame "the West." But short odds seems no reason to stop constructing utopias.

FEMINISM AND PRAGMATISM

When two women ascended to the Supreme Court of Minnesota, Catharine MacKinnon asked, "Will they use the tools of law as women, for all women?" She continued as follows:

> I think that the real feminist issue is not whether biological males or biological females hold positions of power, although it is utterly essential that women be there. And I am not saying that viewpoints have genitals. My issue is what our identifications are, what our loyalties are, who our community is, to whom we are accountable. If it seems as if this is not very concrete, I think it is because we have no idea what women as women would have to say. I'm evoking for women a role that we have yet to make, in the name of a voice that, unsilenced, might say something that has never been heard.[1]

Urging judges to "use the tools of law as women, for all women" alarms universalist philosophers. These are the philosophers who think that moral theory should come up with principles that mention no group smaller than "persons" or "human beings" or "rational agents." Such philosophers would be happier if MacKinnon talked less about accountability to women *as* women and more about an ideal Minnesota or an ideal United States, one in which all human beings would be treated impartially. Universalists would prefer to think of feminism as Mary Wollstonecraft and Olympe de Gouges did, as a matter of rights that are already recognizable and describable, although not yet granted. This describability, they feel, makes MacKinnon's hope for a voice saying something never heard before unnecessary, overly dramatic, hyperbolic.

---

1 Catharine MacKinnon, "On Exceptionality," in her *Feminism Unmodified: Discourses on Life and Law* (Cambridge, Mass.: Harvard University Press, 1987), 77.

Universalist philosophers assume, with Kant, that all the logical space necessary for moral deliberation is now available – that all important truths about right and wrong can not only be stated but be made plausible, in language already to hand. I take MacKinnon to be siding with historicists like Hegel and Dewey and to be saying that moral progress depends upon expanding this space. She illustrates the need for such expansion when she notes that present sex-discrimination law assumes that women "have to meet either the male standard for males or the male standard for females. . . . For purposes of sex discrimination law, to be a woman means either to be like a man or to be like a lady."[2] In my terms, MacKinnon is saying that unless women fit into the logical space prepared for them by current linguistic and other practices, the law does not know how to deal with them. MacKinnon cites the example of a judicial decision that permitted women to be excluded from employment as prison guards because they are so susceptible to rape. The court, she continues, "took the viewpoint of the reasonable rapist on women's employment opportunities."[3] "The conditions that create women's rapeability as the definition of womanhood were not even seen as susceptible to change."[4]

MacKinnon thinks that such assumptions of unchangeability will be overcome only once we can hear "what women as women would have to say." I take her point to be that assumptions become visible *as* assumptions only if we can make the contradictories of those assumptions sound plausible. So injustices may not be perceived as injustices, even by those who suffer them, until somebody invents a previously unplayed role. Only if somebody has a dream, and a voice to describe that dream, does what looked like nature begin to look like culture, what looked like fate begin to look like a moral abomination. For until then only the language of the oppressor is available, and most oppressors have had the wit to teach the oppressed a language in which the oppressed will sound crazy – *even to themselves* – if they describe themselves *as* oppressed.[5]

---

2 Ibid., 71. See also Carolyn Whitbeck's point that "the category, lesbian, both in the minds of its male inventors and as used in male-dominated culture is that of a physiological female who is in other respects a stereotypical male" ("Love, Knowledge and Transformation," in *Hypatia Reborn*, ed. Azizah Y. al-Hibri and Margaret A. Simons [Bloomington: Indiana University Press, 1990], 220). Compare Marilyn Frye's reference to "that other fine and enduring patriarchal institution, Sex Equality" (*The Politics of Reality* [Trumansburg, N.Y.: Crossing Press, 1983], 108).

3 MacKinnon, "On Exceptionality," 38.   4 Ibid., 73.

5 Frye remarks, "For subordination to be permanent and cost effective, it is necessary to create conditions such that the subordinated group acquiesces to some extent in the subordination" (*Politics of Reality*, 33). Ideally, these will be conditions such that a member of the subordinate

MacKinnon's point that logical space may need to be expanded before justice can be envisaged, much less done, can be restated in terms of John Rawls's claim that moral theorizing is a matter of attaining reflective equilibrium between general principles and particular intuitions – particular reactions of revulsion, horror, satisfaction, or delight to real or imagined situations or actions. MacKinnon sees moral and legal principles, particularly those phrased in terms of equal rights, as impotent to change those reactions.[6] So she sees feminists as needing to alter the data of moral theory rather than needing to formulate principles that fit preexistent data better. Feminists are trying to get people to feel indifference or satisfaction where they once recoiled, and revulsion and rage where they once felt indifference or resignation.

One way to change instinctive emotional reactions is to provide new language that will facilitate new reactions. By "new language" I mean not just new words but also creative misuses of language – familiar words used in ways that initially sound crazy. Something traditionally regarded as a moral abomination can become an object of general satisfaction, or conversely, as a result of the increased popularity of an alternative description of what is happening. Such popularity extends logical space by making descriptions of situations that used to seem crazy seem sane. Once, for example, it would have sounded crazy to describe homosexual sodomy as a touching expression of devotion or to describe a woman manipulating the elements of the Eucharist as a figuration of the relation of the Virgin to her Son. But such descriptions are now acquiring popularity. At most times, it sounds crazy to describe the degradation and extirpation of helpless minorities as a purification of the moral and spiritual life of Europe. But at certain periods and places – under the Inquisition, during the Wars of Religion, under the Nazis – it did not.

---

group who does not acquiesce will sound crazy. Frye suggests that a person's sounding crazy is a good indicator that you are oppressing that person (112). See also MacKinnon, "On Exceptionality": "Especially when you are part of a subordinated group, your own definition of your injuries is powerfully shaped by your assessment of whether you could get anyone to do anything about it, including anything official" (105). For example, a noncrazy claim to have been raped is one acceptable to those (usually males) in a position to offer support or reprisal. Only where there is a socially accepted remedy can there have been a real (rather than crazily imagined) injury.

6   When Olympe de Gouges appealed in the name of women to the Declaration of the Rights of Men and Citizens, even the most revolution-minded of her male contemporaries thought she was crazy. When Canadian feminists argued, in the 1920s, that the word "persons" in an act specifying the conditions for being a senator covered women as well as men, the Supreme Court of Canada decided that the word in that context should not be so construed, because it never had been. (The Judicial Committee of the Privy Council, be it said, later ruled in the feminists' favor.)

Universalistic moral philosophers think that the notion of "violation of human rights" provides sufficient conceptual resources to explain why some traditional occasions of revulsion really are moral abominations and others only appear to be. They think of moral progress as an increasing ability to see the reality behind the illusions created by superstition, prejudice, and unreflective custom. The typical universalist is a moral realist, someone who thinks that true moral judgments are *made* true by something out there in the world. Universalists typically take this truth maker to be the intrinsic features of human beings *qua* human. They think you can sort out the real from the illusory abominations by figuring out what those intrinsic features are and that all that is required to figure this out is hard, clear thought.

Historicists, by contrast, think that if "intrinsic" means "ahistorical, untouched by historical change," then the only intrinsic features of human beings are those they share with brutes – for example, the ability to suffer and inflict pain. Every other feature is up for grabs. Historicists say, in Susan Hurley's words, that "the existence of certain shared practices, any of which might not have existed, is all that our having determinate reasons . . . to do anything rests on."[7] So they think that we are not yet in a position to know what human beings are, since we do not yet know what practices human beings may start sharing.[8] Universalists talk as if any rational agent, in any epoch, could somehow have envisaged all the possible morally relevant differences, all the possible moral identities brought into existence by such shared practices. But for MacKinnon, as for Hegel and Dewey, we know, at most, only those possibilities that history has actualized so far. MacKinnon's central point, as I read her, is that "a woman" is not yet the name of a way of being human – not yet the name of a moral identity, but, at most, the name of a disability.[9]

7 This passage is from Samuel Scheffler's quotation of Hurley in his review of her *Natural Reasons* (Oxford: Oxford University Press, 1989) in the *London Review of Books* 12 (September 13, 1990), 9–10. I have not yet been able to locate the page from which Scheffler is quoting. The view Hurley is summarizing is not her own but that of philosophers influenced by Wittgenstein.

8 In an article on Rawls ("Reason and Feeling in Thinking about Justice," *Ethics* 99 [1989], 248), Susan Moller Okin points out that thinking in Rawls's original position is not a matter of thinking like a "disembodied nobody" but rather of thinking like a lot of different people in turn – thinking from the point of view of "every 'concrete other' whom one might turn out to be." Hurley (*Natural Reasons*, 381) makes the same point. The historicity of justice – a historicity that Rawls has acknowledged in his essays of the 1980s – amounts to the fact that history keeps producing new sorts of "concrete others" whom one might turn out to be.

9 See the theme of "woman as partial man" in Carolyn Whitbeck's "Theories of Sex Difference," in *Women and Values,* ed. Marilyn Pearsall (Belmont, Calif.: Wadsworth, 1986), 34–50. This theme is developed in fascinating detail in Thomas Laqueur, *Making Sex: Body and Gender from the Greeks to Freud* (Cambridge, Mass.: Harvard University Press, 1990).

Taking seriously the idea of as yet unrealized possibilities, and of as yet unrecognized moral abominations resulting from failure to envisage those possibilities, requires one to take seriously the suggestion that we do not presently have the logical space necessary for adequate moral deliberation. Only if such suggestions are taken seriously can passages like the one I quoted from MacKinnon be read as prophecy rather than empty hyperbole. But this means revising our conception of moral progress. We have to stop talking about the need to go from distorted to undistorted perception of moral reality, and instead talk about the need to modify our practices so as to take account of new descriptions of what has been going on.

Here is where pragmatist philosophy might be useful to feminist politics. For pragmatism redescribes both intellectual and moral progress by substituting metaphors of evolutionary development for metaphors of progressively less distorted perception. By dropping a representationalist account of knowledge, we pragmatists drop the appearance–reality distinction in favor of a distinction between beliefs that serve some purposes and beliefs that serve other purposes – for example, the purposes of one group and those of another group. We drop the notion of beliefs being made true by reality, as well as the distinction between intrinsic and accidental features of things. So we drop questions about (in Nelson Goodman's phrase) the Way the World Is. We thereby drop the ideas of the Nature of Humanity and of the Moral Law, considered as objects that inquiry is trying to represent accurately or as objects that make true moral judgments true. So we have to give up the comforting belief that competing groups will always be able to reason together on the basis of plausible and neutral premises.

From a pragmatist angle, neither Christianity nor the Enlightenment nor contemporary feminism is a case of cognitive clarity overcoming cognitive distortion. Each is, instead, an example of evolutionary struggle – struggle guided by no immanent teleology. The history of human social practices is continuous with the history of biological evolution, the only difference being that what Richard Dawkins and Daniel Dennett call "memes" gradually take over the role of Mendel's genes. Memes are things like turns of speech, terms of aesthetic or moral praise, political slogans, proverbs, musical phrases, stereotypical icons, and the like. Memes compete with one another for the available cultural space as genes compete for the available *Lebensraum*.[10] No gene or meme is closer to the purpose of evolution or to

10 Michael Gross and Mary Beth Averill, in their "Evolution and Patriarchal Myths" (in *Discovering Reality*, ed. Sandra Harding and Merrill B. Hintikka [Boston: D. Reidel, 1983]), suggest that the term "struggle" is a specifically masculist way of describing evolution and ask,

the nature of humanity than any other – for evolution has no purpose and humanity no nature. So the moral world does not divide into the intrinsically decent and the intrinsically abominable, but rather into the goods of different groups and different epochs. As Dewey put it, "The worse or evil is a rejected good. In deliberation and before choice no evil presents itself as evil. Until it is rejected, it is a competing good. After rejection, it figures not as a lesser good, but as the bad of that situation."[11] On a Deweyan view, the replacement of one species by another in a given ecological niche, or the enslavement of one human tribe or race by another or of human females by human males, is not an intrinsic evil. The latter is a rejected good, rejected on the basis of the greater good that feminism is presently making imaginable. The claim that this good is greater is like the claim that mammals are preferable to reptiles, or Aryans to Jews; it is an ethnocentric claim made from the point of view of a given cluster of genes or memes. There is no larger entity which stands behind that cluster and makes its claim true (or makes some contradictory claim true).

Pragmatists like myself think that this Deweyan account of moral truth and moral progress comports better with the prophetic tone in contemporary feminism than do universalism and realism. Prophecy, as we see it, is all that non-violent political movements can fall back on when argument fails. Argument for the rights of the oppressed *will* fail just insofar as the only language in

---

"Why not see nature as bounteous, rather than parsimonious, and admit that opportunity and cooperation are more likely to abet novelty, innovation and creation than are struggle and competition?" (85). The question gives me pause, and I have no clear answer to it. All I have is the hunch that, with memes as with genes, tolerant pluralism will sooner or later, in the absence of interstellar travel, have to come to terms with shortage of space for self-expression.

    There is a more general point involved here, the one raised by Jo-Ann Pilardi's claim that Hegel, Freud, and others "were burdened with a notion of identity which defines it as oppositional, one which was derived from the psychosocial development of male children" ("On the War Path and Beyond," in *Hypatia Reborn*, ed. al-Hibri and Simons, 12). Just such a notion of identity is central to my claims in this essay – and particularly to the claims about the possible benefits of feminist separatism in the essay's later pages. So I am employing what many feminist writers would consider specifically male assumptions. All I can say in reply is that the notion of identity as oppositional seems to me hard to eliminate from such books as Frye's – and especially from her discussion of feminist anger. Anger and opposition seem to me the root of most moral prophecy, and it is the prophetic aspect of feminism that I emphasize in this essay.

11 John Dewey, *Human Nature and Conduct*, in *The Middle Works of John Dewey* (Carbondale: Southern Illinois University Press, 1983), 14: 193. See also "Outlines of a Critical Theory of Ethics," in *The Early Works of John Dewey* (Carbondale: Southern Illinois University Press, 1969), 3: 379: "Goodness is not remoteness from badness. In one sense, goodness is based upon badness; that is, good action is always based upon action good once, but bad if persisted in under changing circumstances."

which to state relevant premises is one in which the relevant emancipatory premises sound crazy. We pragmatists see universalism and realism as committed to the idea of a reality-tracking faculty called "reason" and an unchanging moral reality to be tracked, and thus unable to make sense of the claim that a new voice is needed. So we commend ourselves to feminists on the ground that we can fit that claim into *our* view of moral progress with relative ease.

We see it as unfortunate that many feminists intermingle pragmatist and realist rhetoric. For example, MacKinnon at one point defines feminism as the belief "that women are human beings in truth but not in social reality."[12] The phrase "in truth" here can only mean "in a reality that is distinct from social reality," one that is as it is whether or not women ever succeed in saying what has never been heard. Such invocations of an ahistoricist realism leave it unclear whether MacKinnon sees women as appealing from a bad social practice to something that transcends social practice, appealing from appearance to reality, or instead sees them as doing the same sort of thing as the early Christians, the early socialists, the Albigensians, and the Nazis did: trying to actualize hitherto-undreamt-of possibilities by putting new linguistic and other practices into play and erecting new social constructs.[13]

Some contemporary feminist philosophers are sympathetic to the latter alternative, because they explicitly reject universalism and realism. They do so because they see both as symptoms of what Derrida has called "phallogocentrism" – what MacKinnon calls "the epistemological stance . . . of which male dominance is the politics."[14] Other such philosophers, however,

12 MacKinnon, *Feminism Unmodified*, 126.
13 Suppose we define a moral abomination, with Jeffrey Stout, as something that goes against our sense of "the seams of our moral universe," one that crosses the lines between, as he puts it, "the categories of our cosmology and our social structure" (*Ethics after Babel* [Boston: Beacon Press, 1988], 159). Then the choice between a realist and pragmatist rhetoric is the choice between saying that moral progress gradually aligns these seams with the *real* seams and saying that it is a matter of simultaneously reweaving and enlarging a fabric that is not intended to be congruent with an antecedent reality. Giving an example of such a seam, Stout says, "The sharper the line between masculine and feminine roles and the greater the importance of that line in determining matters such as the division of labor and the rules of inheritance, the more likely it is that sodomy will be abominated" (153). Later he says, "The question is not whether homosexuality is intrinsically abominable but rather what, all things considered, we should do with the relevant categories of our cosmology and social structure" (158). As with the abominableness of homosexual sodomy, so, we pragmatists think, with the abominableness of the absence or presence of patriarchy. In all such cases, up to and including the abominableness of torturing people for the sheer pleasure of watching them writhe, pragmatists think that the question is not about intrinsic properties but about what we should do with the relevant categories – a question that boils down to what descriptions we should use of what is going on.
14 MacKinnon, "On Exceptionality," 50.

warn against accepting the criticisms of universalism and realism common to Nietzsche, Heidegger, and Derrida – against finding an ally in what is sometimes called "postmodernism." Sabina Lovibond, for example, cautions against throwing Enlightenment universalism and realism overboard. "How can anyone ask me to say goodbye to 'emancipatory metanarratives,'" she asks, "when my own emancipation is still such a patchy, hit-or-miss affair?"[15] Lovibond's universalism comes out when she says, "It would be arbitrary to work for sexual equality unless one believed that human society was disfigured by inequality *as such.*" Her realism comes out in her claim that feminism has a "background commitment . . . to the elimination of (self-interested) cognitive distortion."[16]

I share Lovibond's doubts about the apocalyptic tone and rhetoric of unmasking prevalent among people who believe that we are living in a "postmodern" period.[17] But, on all the crucial philosophical issues, I am on the

15 Sabina Lovibond, "Feminism and Postmodernism," *New Left Review* 178 (Winter 1989), 12. For a somewhat more tempered account of the relation of postmodernism to feminism see Kate Soper, "Feminism, Humanism and Postmodernism," *Radical Philosophy* 55 (Summer 1990), 11–17. In their "Social Criticism Without Philosophy: An Encounter Between Feminism and Postmodernism," in *Universal Abandon?* ed. Andrew Ross (Minneapolis: University of Minnesota Press, 1988), Nancy Fraser and Linda Nicholson argue that "a robust postmodern-feminist paradigm of social criticism without philosophy is possible" (100). I of course agree, but I am not as sure about the need for, and utility of, "social-theoretical analysis of large-scale inequalities" (90) as are Fraser and Nicholson.

This is because I am less sure than Fraser about the possibility that "the basic institutional framework of [our] society could be unjust" (Fraser, "Solidarity or Singularity?" in *Reading Rorty*, ed. Alan Malachowski [Oxford: Blackwell, 1990], 318), and hence about "the utility of a theory that could specify links among apparently discrete social problems via the basic institutional structure" (319). I suspect my differences with Fraser are concrete and political rather than abstract and philosophical. She sees, and I do not see, attractive alternatives (more or less Marxist in shape) to such institutions as private ownership of the means of production and constitutional democracy, attractive alternatives to the traditional social democratic project of constructing an egalitarian welfare state within the context of these two basic institutions. I am not sure whether our differences are due to Fraser's antifoundationalist theory hope (see note 17 below) or to my own lack of imagination.

16 Lovibond, "Feminism," 28. See Lovibond's reference to "remaking society along rational, egalitarian lines" (12). The idea that egalitarianism is more rational than elitism, rational in a sense that provides reasons for action *not* based on contingent shared practices, is central to the thinking of most liberals who are also moral realists.

17 A rhetoric of "unmasking hegemony" presupposes the reality–appearance distinction that opponents of phallogocentrism claim to have set aside. Many self-consciously "postmodern" writers seem to be trying to have it both ways – to view masks as going all the way down while still making invidious comparisons between other people's masks and the way things will look when all the masks have been stripped off. These postmodernists continue to indulge in the bad habits characteristic of those Marxists who insist that morality is a matter of class interest and then add that everybody has a moral obligation to identify with the interests of a particular class. Just as "ideology" came to mean little more than "other people's

side of Lovibond's postmodernist opponents.[18] I hope that feminists will continue to consider the possibility of dropping realism and universalism, dropping the notion that the subordination of women is *intrinsically* abominable, dropping the claim that there is something called "right" or "justice" or "humanity" that has always been on their side, making their claims true. I agree with those whom Lovibond paraphrases as saying, "[T]he Enlightenment rhetoric of 'emancipation', 'autonomy' and the like is complicit in a fantasy of escape from the embodied condition."[19] In particular, it is complicit in the fantasy of escape from a historical situation into an ahistoricist empyrean – one in which moral theory can be pursued, like Euclidean geometry, within an unalterable, unextendable, logical space. Although practical politics will doubtless often require feminists to speak with the universalist vulgar, they might profit from thinking with the pragmatists.

One of the best things about contemporary feminism, it seems to me, is its ability to eschew such Enlightenment fantasies of escape. My favorite passages in MacKinnon are ones in which she says things like "[W]e are not attempting to be objective about it, we're attempting to represent the point of view of women."[20] Feminists are much less inclined than Marxists were to fall back on a comfortable doctrine of immanent teleology. Much feminist writing can be read as saying: We are *not* appealing from phallist appearance to nonphallist reality. We are *not* saying that the voice in which women will some day speak will be better at representing reality than present-day masculist discourse. We are not attempting the impossible task of developing a nonhegemonic discourse, one in which truth is no longer connected with power. We are not trying to do away with social constructs in order to find something that is not a social construct. We are just trying to help women out of the traps men have constructed for them, help them get the power they do not presently have, and help them create a moral identity as women.

ideas," so "product of hegemonic discourse" has come to mean little more than "product of other people's way of talking." I agree with Stanley Fish that much of what goes under the heading of "postmodernism" exemplifies internally inconsistent "anti-foundationalist theory hope" (see Fish, *Doing What Comes Naturally: Change, Rhetoric and the Practice of Theory in Literary and Legal Studies* [Durham, N.C.: Duke University Press, 1989], 346, 437–8).

18 I am not fond of the term "postmodernism" and was a bit startled (as presumably was MacIntyre) to find Lovibond saying that Lyotard, MacIntyre, and I are "among the most forceful exponents of the arguments and values which constitute postmodernism within academic philosophy" ("Feminism," 5). Still, I recognize the similarities between our positions that lead Lovibond to group the three of us together. Some of these similarities are outlined by Fraser and Nicholson, "Social Criticism," 85–7.

19 Lovibond, "Feminism," 12.

20 MacKinnon, "On Exceptionality," 86. See also the "postmodernist" suggestion that the quest for objectivity is a specifically masculist one (50, 54).

I have argued in the past that Deweyan pragmatism, when linguistified along lines suggested by Hilary Putnam and Donald Davidson, gives you all that is politically useful in the Nietzsche–Heidegger–Derrida–Foucault tradition. Pragmatism, I claim, offers all the dialectical advantages of postmodernism while avoiding the self-contradictory postmodernist rhetoric of unmasking. I admit that insofar as feminists adopt a Deweyan rhetoric of the sort I have just described, they commit themselves to a lot of apparent paradoxes and incur the usual charges of relativism, irrationalism, and power worship.[21] But these disadvantages are, I think, outweighed by the advantages. By describing themselves in Deweyan terms, feminists would free themselves from Lovibond's demand for a general theory of oppression – a way of seeing oppression on the basis of race, class, sexual preference, and gender as so many instances of a general failure to treat equals equally.[22] They would thereby avoid the embarrassments of the universalist claim that the term "human being" – or even the term "woman" – names an unchanging essence, an ahistorical natural kind with a permanent set of intrinsic

21 We pragmatists are often told that we reduce moral disagreement to a mere struggle for power by denying the existence of reason or human nature, conceived of as something that provides a neutral court of appeal. We often rejoin that the need for such a court, the need for something ahistorical that will ratify one's claims, is itself a symptom of power worship – of the conviction that unless something large and powerful is on one's side, one shouldn't bother trying.

22 Developing this point would take too long. Were more time and space available, I would argue that trying to integrate feminism into a general theory of oppression – a frequent reaction to the charge that feminists are oblivious to racial and economic injustice – is like trying to integrate Galilean physics into a general theory of scientific error. The latter attempt is as familiar as it is fruitless. The conviction that there is an interesting general theory about human beings or their oppression seems to me like the conviction that there is an interesting general theory about truth and our failure to achieve it. For the same reasons that transcendental terms like "true" and "good" are not susceptible of definition, neither error nor oppression has a single neck that a single critical slash might sever.

Maria Lugones is an example of a feminist theorist who sees a need for a general philosophical theory of oppression and liberation. She says, for example, that "the ontological or metaphysical possibility of liberation remains to be argued, explained, uncovered" ("Structure/Antistructure and Agency under Oppression," *Journal of Philosophy* 87 [October 1990], 502). I prefer to stick to merely empirical possibilities of liberation. Although I entirely agree with Lugones about the need to "give up the unified self" (503), I see this not as a matter of ontology, but merely as a way of putting the familiar point that the same human being can contain different coherent sets of belief and desire – different roles, different personalities, etc. – correlated with the different groups to which she belongs or whose power she must acknowledge. A more important disagreement between us, perhaps, concerns the desirability of harmonizing one's various roles, self-images, etc., in a single unifying story about oneself. Such unification—the sort of thing I describe later as overcoming splits – seems to me desirable. Lugones, on the other hand, urges the desirability of "experiencing oneself in the limen" (506).

features. Further, they would no longer need to raise what seem to me unanswerable questions about the accuracy of their representations of "woman's experience." They would instead see themselves as *creating* such an experience by creating a language, a tradition, and an identity.

In the remainder of this essay I want to develop this distinction between expression and creation in more detail. But first I want to insert a cautionary remark about the relative insignificance of philosophical movements as compared with social-political movements. Yoking feminism with pragmatism is like yoking Christianity with Platonism, or socialism with dialectical materialism. In each case, something big and important, a vast social hope, is being yoked with something comparatively small and unimportant, a set of answers to philosophical questions – questions that arise only for people who find philosophical topics intriguing rather than silly. Universalists – of both the bourgeois liberal and the Marxist sort – often claim that such questions are in fact urgent, for political movements *need* philosophical foundations. But we pragmatists cannot say this. We are not in the foundations business. *All* we can do is to offer feminists a few pieces of special-purpose ammunition – for example, some additional replies to charges that their aims are unnatural, their demands irrational, or their claims hyperbolic.

So much for an overview of my reasons for trying to bring feminism and pragmatism together. I want now to enlarge on my claim that a pragmatist feminist will see herself as helping to create women rather than attempting to describe them more accurately. I shall do so by taking up two objections that might be made to what I have been saying. The first is the familiar charge that pragmatism is inherently conservative, biased in favor of the status quo.[23]

---

23 For a good example of this charge, see Jonathan Culler, *Framing the Sign: Criticism and Its Institutions* (Oklahoma City: University of Oklahoma Press, 1988): ". . . the humanities must make their way between, on the one hand, a traditional, foundationalist conception of their task and, on the other, the so-called 'new pragmatism' to which some critics of foundationalism have retreated. If philosophy is not a foundationalist discipline, argues Richard Rorty, then it is simply engaged in a conversation; it tells stories, which succeed simply by their success. Since there is no standard or reference point outside the system of one's beliefs to appeal to, critical arguments and theoretical reflections can have no purchase on these beliefs or the practices informed by them. Ironically, then, the claim that philosophers and theoreticians tell stories, which originates as a critique of ideology . . . becomes a way of protecting a dominant ideology and its professionally successful practitioners from the scrutiny of argument, by deeming that critique can have no leverage against ordinary beliefs, and that theoretical arguments have no consequences. This pragmatism, whose complacency seems altogether appropriate to the Age of Reagan, subsists only by a theoretical argument of the kind it in principle opposes, as an ahistorical 'preformism': what one does must be based on one's beliefs, but since there are no foundations outside the system of one's beliefs, the only thing that could logically make one change a belief is something one already believes" (55).
    Culler is right in saying that we pragmatists hold the latter view, but wrong in suggest-

The second objection arises from the fact that if you say that women need to be created rather than simply freed, you seem to be saying that in some sense women do not now fully exist. But then there seems no basis for saying that men have done women wrong, since you cannot wrong the nonexistent.

Hilary Putnam, the most important contemporary philosopher to call himself a pragmatist, has said that "a statement is true of a situation just in case it would be correct to use the words of which the statement consists in that way in describing the situation." Putting the matter this way immediately suggests the question: correct by whose standards? Putnam's position that "truth and rational acceptability are interdependent notions" makes it hard to see how we might ever appeal from the oppressive conventions of our community to something nonconventional, and thus hard to see how we could ever engage in anything like "radical critique."[24] So it may seem that we pragmatists, in our frenzied efforts to undercut epistemological

ing that we think that *logical* changes in belief are the only respectable ones. What I have called "creative misuses" of language are *causes* to change one's belief, even if not *reasons* to change them. See the discussion of Davidson on metaphor in various essays in my *Objectivity, Relativism, and Truth* (Cambridge University Press, 1991) for more on this cause–reason distinction and for the claim that most moral and intellectual progress is achieved by non-"logical" changes in belief. Culler is one of the people I had in mind in footnote 16 above – the people who want to hang on to the primacy of logic (and thus of "theoretical reflection" and "critique") while abandoning logocentrism. I do not think this can be done.

Culler's charge can be found in many other authors, e.g., Joseph Singer, "Should Lawyers Care about Philosophy?" *Duke Law Journal* (1989): " . . . Rorty . . . has marginalized the enterprise of philosophy, thereby depriving pragmatism of any critical bite" (1752). On my view, pragmatism bites other philosophies, but not social problems as such – and so is as useful to fascists like Mussolini and conservatives like Oakeshott as it is to liberals like Dewey. Singer thinks that I have "identified reason with the status quo" and defined "truth as coextensive with the prevailing values in a society" (1763). These claims are, I think, the result of the same inference Culler draws in the passage quoted above. Both Singer and Culler want philosophy to be capable of setting goals and not to be confined to the merely ancillary role I describe in note 26 below.

24 See Putnam's *Representation and Reality* (Cambridge, Mass.: MIT Press, 1988), 114–15. See also Robert Brandom's formulation of "phenomenalism about truth" as the view that "being true is to be understood as being *properly* taken-true (believed)." Brandom says that what is of most interest about the classical pragmatist stories (C. S. Peirce, William James) is "the dual commitment to a normative account of claiming or believing [Alexander Bain's and Peirce's account of belief as a rule for action] that does not lean on a supposedly explanatory antecedent notion of truth, and the suggestion that truth can then be understood phenomenalistically, in terms of features of these independently characterized takings-true" ("Pragmatism, Phenomenalism, Truth Talk," *Midwest Studies in Philosophy* 12 [1988], 80). Brandom, Davidson, and I would agree with Putnam that "truth does not transcend use," but I think all three of us might be puzzled by Putnam's further claim that "whether an epistemic situation is any good or not depends on whether many different statements are true" (*Representation and Reality*, 115). This seems to me like saying that whether a person is wealthy or not depends on how much money she has.

skepticism by doing away with what Davidson calls "the scheme–content distinction," have also undercut political radicalism.

Pragmatists should reply to this charge by saying that they cannot make sense of an appeal from our community's practices to anything except the practice of a real or imagined alternative community. So when prophetic feminists say that it is not enough to make the practices of our community coherent, that the very *language* of our community must be subjected to radical critique, pragmatists add that such critique can only take the form of imagining a community whose linguistic and other practices are different from our own. Once one grants MacKinnon's point that one can get only so far with an appeal to make present beliefs more coherent by treating women on a par with men, once one sees the need for something more than an appeal to rational acceptability by the standards of the existing community, then such an act of imagination is the only recourse.

This means that one will praise movements of liberation not for the accuracy of their diagnoses but for the imagination and courage of their proposals. The difference between pragmatism and positions such as Marxism, which retain the rhetoric of scientism and realism, can be thought of as the difference between utopianism and radicalism. Radicals think that there is a basic mistake being made, a mistake deep down at the roots. They think that deep thinking is required to get down to this deep level, and that only there, when all the superstructural appearances have been undercut, can things be seen as they really are. Utopians, however, do not think in terms of mistakes or of depth. They abandon the contrast between superficial appearance and deep reality in favor of the contrast between a painful present and a possibly less painful, dimly seen future. Pragmatists cannot be radicals, in this sense, but they can be utopians. They do not see philosophy as providing instruments for radical surgery or microscopes that make precise diagnosis possible.[25] Philosophy's function is rather to clear the road for

---

25 In "Should Lawyers Care?" Joseph Singer praises Elizabeth Spelman for "using the tools of philosophy to promote justice" and suggests that one such use is to show that "the categories and forms of discourse we use . . . have important consequences in channeling our attention in particular directions" (1771). Surely it is no disrespect to Spelman's achievement, or to philosophy, to insist that it takes no special tools, no special philosophical expertise, to make and develop this latter point. The use of notions like "powerful methods" and "precise analytical instruments" in the rhetorics of analytic philosophy and of Marxism constitutes, to my mind, misleading advertising. An unfortunate result of such mystification is that whenever a philosophy professor like Spelman or me does something useful, it is assumed that we were doing something distinctively philosophical, something philosophers are specially trained to do. If we then fail to go on to do something else that needs to be done, we are usually charged with using an obsolete and inadequate set of philosophical tools.

prophets and poets, to make intellectual life a bit simpler and safer for those
who have visions of new communities.[26]

So far I have taken MacKinnon as my example of a feminist with such a
vision. But of course she is only one of many. Another is Marilyn Frye, who
says in her powerful book, *The Politics of Reality,* that "there probably is really
no distinction, in the end, between imagination and courage." For, she continues, it takes courage to overcome "a mortal dread of being outside the
field of vision of the arrogant eye." This is the eye of a person who prides
himself on spotting the rational unacceptability of what is being said – that
is, its incoherence with the rest of the beliefs of those who currently control
life chances and logical space. So feminists must, Frye goes on to say, "dare
to rely on ourselves to make meaning and we have to imagine ourselves capable of . . . weaving the web of meaning which will hold us in some kind of
intelligibility."[27] Such courage is indistinguishable from the imagination it
takes to hear oneself as the spokesperson of a merely possible community,
rather than as a lonely, and perhaps crazed, outcast from an actual one.

MacKinnon and many other feminists use "liberalism" as a name for an
inability to have this sort of courage and imagination. "In the liberal mind,"
MacKinnon says, "the worse and more systematic one's mistreatment of it,
the more it seems justified. Liberalism . . . never sees power as power, yet can
see as significant only that which power does."[28] The phenomenon she is
pointing to certainly exists, but "liberalism" seems to me the wrong name
for it. So, of course, does "pragmatism." I think the main reason – apart from
some reflexes left over from early Marxist conditioning – why pejorative uses

---

26 See Dewey's "From Absolutism to Experimentalism," in *The Later Works of John Dewey* (Car-
    bondale: Southern Illinois University Press, 1984), 5: 160: "Meantime a chief task of those
    who call themselves philosophers is to help get rid of the useless lumber that blocks our
    highways of thought, and strive to make straight and open the paths that lead to the fu-
    ture." There is a lot of this road-clearing rhetoric in Dewey, rhetoric that is continuous with
    Locke's description of himself as an underlaborer to those who seemed to him the
    prophetic spirits of his time – corpuscularian scientists like Newton and Boyle. Both
    metaphors suggest that the philosopher's job is to drag outdated philosophy out of the way
    of those who are displaying unusual courage and imagination.

    In "Should Lawyers Care?" Singer says that "Dewey, unlike Rorty, saw the problems of
    philosophy as inseparable from the problems of collective life" and that "by separating phi-
    losophy from justice, Rorty's vision reinforces existing power relations" (1759). It is true
    that Dewey often speaks as if social problems and philosophical problems were interlocked,
    but I would argue that all these passages can best be interpreted in the road-clearing sense
    I have just suggested. Dewey never, I think, saw pragmatism in the way in which Marxists
    saw dialectical materialism – as a philosophical key that unlocks the secrets of history or of
    society.

27 This and the previous quote are from Frye, *Politics of Reality,* 80.

28 MacKinnon, "On Exceptionality," 221; cf. 137.

of the terms "liberal" and "pragmatist" are still common among political radicals is that if you say, with Putnam, that "truth does not transcend use," you
may easily be taken as referring to actual, present use. Again, if you deny that
truth is a matter of correspondence to reality, you may easily be taken as
holding that a true belief is one that coheres with what most people currently
believe. If you think that emancipatory moral or social thought requires penetrating to a presently unglimpsed reality beneath the current appearances,
and find pragmatists telling you that there is no such reality, you may easily
conclude that a pragmatist cannot help the cause of emancipation.

When, however, we remember that John Dewey – a paradigmatic liberal
as well as a paradigmatic pragmatist – spent a great deal of time celebrating
the sort of courage and imagination Frye describes, we may be willing to
grant that the relation between pragmatism and emancipation is more complex. Dewey said remarkably little about the situation of women, but one of
the few things he did say is worth quoting:

> Women have as yet made little contribution to philosophy, but when women
> who are not mere students of other persons' philosophy set out to write it, we
> cannot conceive that it will be the same in viewpoint or tenor as that composed
> from the standpoint of the different masculine experience of things. Institu-
> tions, customs of life, breed certain systematized predilections and aversions.
> The wise man reads historic philosophies to detect in them intellectual for-
> mulations of men's habitual purposes and cultivated wants, not to gain insight
> into the ultimate nature of things or information about the make-up of real-
> ity. As far as what is loosely called reality figures in philosophies, we may be
> sure that it signifies those selected aspects of the world which are chosen be-
> cause they lend themselves to the support of men's judgment of the worth-
> while life, and hence are most highly prized. In philosophy, "reality" is a term
> of value or choice.[29]

Suppose we think, as feminists often do, of "men's habitual purposes and
cultivated wants" as the habitual purposes and cultivated wants of males, the
half of the species that long ago enslaved the other half. This permits us to
read Dewey as saying: if you find yourself a slave, do not accept your masters' descriptions of the real; do not work within the boundaries of their
moral universe. Instead, try to invent a reality of your own by selecting aspects of the world that lend themselves to the support of *your* judgment of
the worthwhile life.[30]

29 John Dewey, "Philosophy and Democracy," *The Middle Works*, 11: 145.
30 To use an analogy suggested by Charlotte Perkins Gilman's poem "Similar Cases," it is as if
one said to the creatures that were eventually to become mammals: "Do not try to imitate

Dewey's doctrine of the means–end continuum might have led him to add: do not expect to know what sort of life is worthwhile right off the bat, for that is one of the things you will constantly change your mind about in the process of selecting a reality. You can neither pick your goals on the basis of a clear and explicit claim about the nature of moral reality, nor derive such a claim from clear and explicit goals. There is no method or procedure to be followed except courageous and imaginative experimentation. Dewey would, I think, have been quick to see the point of Frye's description of her own writing as "a sort of flirtation with meaninglessness – dancing about a region of cognitive gaps and negative semantic spaces, kept aloft only by the rhythm and momentum of my own motion, trying to plumb abysses which are generally agreed not to exist."[31] For meaninglessness is exactly what you have to flirt with when you are in between social, and in particular linguistic, practices – unwilling to take part in an old one but not yet having succeeded in creating a new one.

The import of Dewey's pragmatism for movements such as feminism can be seen if we paraphrase Dewey as follows: do not charge a current social practice or a currently spoken language with being unfaithful to reality, with getting things wrong. Do not criticize it as a result of ideology or prejudice, where these are tacitly contrasted with your own employment of a truth-tracking faculty called "reason" or a neutral method called "disinterested observation." Do not even criticize it as "unjust" if "unjust" is supposed to mean more than "sometimes incoherent even on its own terms." Instead of appealing from transitory current appearances to the permanent reality, appeal to a still only dimly imagined future practice. Drop the appeal to neutral criteria, and the claim that something large like Nature or Reason or History or the Moral Law is on the side of the oppressed. Instead, just make invidious comparisons between the actual present and a possible, if inchoate, future.[32]

So much for the relations between pragmatism and political utopianism.

the ways in which those larger and more powerful fish cope with their environment. Rather, find ways of doing things that will help you find a new environment." ("Similar Cases" is perhaps most easily found in Ann Lane, *To Herland and Beyond: The Life and Works of Charlotte Perkins Gilman* [New York: Pantheon, 1990], 363–4. The point of the poem is that if it were true that, as feminists were often told, "you can't change your nature," we would have had neither biological nor cultural evolution.)

31 Frye, *Politics of Reality*, 154.

32 As I suggested earlier, it is easy to bring together Dewey's claim that, in philosophy, "real" is as evaluative a term as "good" with "postmodernist" views – e.g., those found in Chris Weedon's book *Feminist Practice and Poststructuralist Theory* (New York: Blackwell, 1987). Pretty much the only difference between Weedon's criticism of the philosophical tradition and Dewey's is one that also separates contemporary pragmatists like Putnam and Davidson

I have been arguing that the two are compatible and mutually supporting. This is because pragmatism allows for the possibility of expanding logical space, and thereby for an appeal to courage and imagination rather than to putatively neutral criteria. What pragmatism loses when it gives up the claim to have right or reality on its side it gains in ability to acknowledge the presence of what Frye calls "abysses which are generally agreed not to exist." These are situations that give the universalist and the realist trouble – ones in which plenty of assent-commanding descriptions are available, but such that none of these descriptions does what is needed.

from Dewey – the use of "language" instead of Dewey's word "experience" as the name of what it is important for the oppressed to reshape. Weedon, like Putnam and Davidson and unlike Dewey, is what Wilfrid Sellars called a "psychological nominalist" – someone who believes that all awareness is a linguistic affair. She says, "Like Althusserian Marxism, feminist poststructuralism makes the primary assumption that it is language which enables us to think, speak and give meaning to the world around us. Meaning and consciousness do not exist outside language" (32). The difference with Dewey has few consequences, however, since Dewey would have heartily agreed with Weedon that one should not view language "as a transparent tool for expressing facts" but as "the material in which particular, often conflicting versions of facts are constructed" (131).

The only real advantage of psychological nominalism for feminists, perhaps, is that it replaces hard-to-discuss (I am tempted to say "metaphysical") questions about whether women have a different *experience* than men, or Africans a different experience than Europeans, or about whether the experience of upper-class African women more closely resembles that of lower-class European men than that of upper-class European women, with easier-to-discuss (more evidently empirical) questions about what *language* these various groups of people use to justify their actions, exhibit their deepest hopes and fears, etc. Answers to the latter questions are jumping-off places for practical suggestions about different languages they might use, or might have used. I share MacKinnon's skepticism about the idea that "viewpoints have genitals" and Sandra Harding's skepticism about the utility of notions like "woman's morality," "woman's experience," and "woman's standpoint." See Harding's "The Curious Coincidence of Feminine and African Moralities: Challenges for Feminist Theory," in *Women and Moral Theory*, ed. Eva Kittay and Diana Meyers (Totowa, N.J.: Rowman & Littlefield, 1987), 296–315.

Although most of the doctrines (e.g., essentialism, Cartesian individualism, moral universalism) that Weedon attributes to "liberal humanism" are doctrines that Dewey (a notorious liberal humanist) also targeted, Weedon does not seem able to eschew a longing for what Mary Hawkesworth calls "a successor science which can refute once and for all the distortions of androcentrism" ("Knowers, Knowing, Known: Feminist Theory and the Claims of Truth," in *Feminist Theory in Practice and Process*, ed. Micheline R. Malson et al. [Chicago: University of Chicago Press, 1989], 331). But once you put aside universalism, you should neither hope for knockdown refutations nor talk about "distortion." Hawkesworth goes on to criticize Harding for saying that "[f]eminist analytical categories *should* be unstable at this moment in history" (Harding, "The Instability of the Analytical Categories of Feminist Theory," in ibid., 19). But prophecy and unstable categories go together, and Harding's claim chimes with many of the passages I have quoted from Frye. Harding's further claim that "we [feminists] should learn how to regard the instabilities themselves as valuable resources" is one that Dewey would have cheered.

I turn now to the paradox I noted earlier: the suggestion that women are only now coming into existence rather than having been deprived of the ability to express what was deep within them all the time. I take MacKinnon's evocation of a "role that women have yet to make" as a way of suggesting that women are only now beginning to put together a moral identity *as* women. To find one's moral identity in being an *X* means being able to do the following sort of thing: make your *X*-ness salient in your justification of important uncoerced choices, make your *X*-ness an important part of the story you tell yourself when you need to recover your self-confidence, make your relations with other *X*s central to your claim to be a responsible person. These are all things men have usually been able to do by reminding themselves that they are, come what may, *men*. They are things men have made it hard for women to do by reminding themselves that they are women. As Frye puts it, men have assigned themselves the status of "full persons" – people who enjoy what she calls "unqualified participation in the radical 'superiority' of the species"[33] and withheld this status from women. The result of men constantly, fervently, and publicly thanking God that they are *not* women has been to make it hard for women to thank God that they are. For a woman to say that she finds her moral identity in being a woman would have sounded, until relatively recently, as weird as for a slave to say that he found his moral identity in being a slave.

Most feminists might agree that it was only with the beginnings of the feminist movement that women began to find their moral identities in being women.[34] But most feminists are probably still realist and universalist enough to insist that there is a difference between the claim that one cannot find one's moral identity in being an *X* and the claim that an *X* is not yet a full-fledged person, a person to whom injustice has been done by forbidding her to find her moral identity in her *X*-hood. For the great advantage of realism and universalism over pragmatism is that they permit one to say that women were everything they are now, and *therefore* were entitled to everything they are now trying to get – even when they did not know, and might even have explicitly denied, that they were entitled to it.

For us pragmatists, however, it is not so easy to say that. For we see personhood as a matter of degree, not as an all-or-nothing affair, something evenly distributed around the species. We see it as something that slaves typically have less of than their masters. This is not because there are such

33 Frye, *Politics of Reality*, 48–9.
34 I am too ignorant about the history of feminism – about how long and how continuous the feminist tradition has been – to speculate about when things began to change.

things as "natural slaves" but because of the masters' control over the language spoken by the slaves – their ability to make slaves think of their pain as fated and even somehow deserved, something to be borne rather than resisted. We cannot countenance the notion of a deep reality that reposes unrecognized beneath superficial appearances. So we have to take seriously the idea, made familiar by such writers as Charles Taylor, that interpretation goes all the way down: that what a human being is, for moral purposes, is largely a matter of how he or she describes himself or herself. We have to take seriously the idea that what you experience yourself to be is largely a function of what it makes sense to describe yourself as in the languages you are able to use. We have to say that the Deltas and Epsilons of Huxley's *Brave New World* and the proles of Orwell's *1984* were persons only in the sense in which fertilized human ova or human infants are persons – in the sense, namely, that they are capable of being made into persons. So we pragmatists have to identify most of the wrongness of past male oppression with its suppression of past potentiality rather than with its injustice to past actuality.

In order to say that women are only now in the process of achieving a moral identity as women, I do not need to deny that some women have, in every epoch, had doubts about, and offered alternatives to, the standard, androcentric descriptions of women. All I need to deny is that women have been able to *forget* the latter descriptions – the ones that make them seem incapable of being full persons. I am denying that women in previous epochs have been able to avoid being torn, split, between men's description of them and whatever alternative descriptions they have given to themselves. As an example of the sort of thing I have in mind – of the need to name, and thus to begin to bridge, what Frye calls "abysses generally agreed not to exist" – consider Adrienne Rich's description of her situation when young. She was, she says, "split between the girl who wrote poems, who defined herself as writing poems, and the girl who was to define herself by her relationships with men."[35] I want to interpret Rich's individual situation as an allegory of the more general situation in which women found themselves before feminism achieved liftoff – of their inability to stop defining themselves in terms of their relationships with men. To envisage this inability, consider how Rich's situation differed from that of a young man in a similar situation.

Since Byron and Goethe, men have thought of writing poems as one of

35 Adrienne Rich, *On Lies, Secrets, and Silence: Selected Prose, 1966–1978* (New York: Norton, 1979), 40.

the best ways to create an autonomous self, to avoid having to define oneself in the terms used by one's parents, teachers, employers, and rulers. Since 1820 or thereabouts, a young man has had the option of defining himself as a poet, of finding his moral identity in writing verse. But, Rich tells us, this is not easy for a young woman.

What is the difficulty? It is not that there is any dearth of true descriptions that Rich might have applied to herself. There were no well-formed – that is, generally intelligible – questions to which Rich could not have given true, well-formed answers. But nevertheless there was, she tells us, a split. The various true descriptions that she applied did not fit together into a whole. But, she implicitly suggests, a young male poet's descriptions would have fit together easily. Rich was, in her youth, unable to attain the kind of coherence or integrity we think of as characteristic of full persons. For persons who are capable of the full glory of humanity are capable of seeing themselves steadily and whole. Rather than feel that splits are tearing them apart, they can see tensions among their alternative self-descriptions as, at worst, necessary elements in a harmonious variety-in-unity.

Rich's account of herself as split rings true, for, as she shows in her essay on Emily Dickinson and elsewhere, the language games men have arranged that young women should play force them to treat the men in their lives (or the absence of men in their lives) as the independent variable and everything else – even their poems – as dependent variables. So insofar as Rich could not tie her poems in with her relationships with men, she had a problem. She was split. She could not be, so to speak, a full-time poet, because a language she could not forget did not let one be both a full-time poet and a full-time female. By contrast, since Byron, the language has let one be a full-time poet and a full-time hero (just as, since Socrates, it has been possible to be a full-time intellectual and a full-time hero).

What might solve Rich's problem? Well, perhaps nowadays it is a little easier for a young woman to define herself by and in her poems than when Rich was young – simply because she may have read books by Rich, Frye, and others. But only a little easier. What would make it *really* easy? Only, I would suggest, the sort of circumstance that made it easy for a young man in the generation after Byron to make his poetic activity the independent variable in the story he told himself about himself. In the preceding generation there was what now looks to us like a band of brothers – Hölderlin and Keats, Byron and Goethe, Shelley and Chamisso. Bliss was it in that dawn to be alive, and to be a young male with poetic gifts was to be able to describe oneself in heroic terms, terms one could not have used earlier without sounding crazy. That band of brothers founded an invisible club, a very good club, one that still gives new members a warm welcome.[36] So young male poets do not face abysses when they attempt self-definition. But, as Rich points out, Emily Dickinson was not allowed into that club.[37] So, to make things really easy for future Dickinsons and Riches, there would have to be a good, well-established club they could join.

Here, I take it, is where feminist separatism comes in. Rich asks that

> we understand lesbian/feminism in the deepest, most radical sense: as that love for ourselves and other women, that commitment to the freedom of all of us, which transcends the category of "sexual preference" and the issue of civil rights, to become a politics of *asking women's questions,* demanding a world in which the integrity of all women – not a chosen few – shall be honored and validated in every aspect of culture.[38]

Someone who tries to fit what Rich is saying into a map drawn on a universalist and realist grid will have trouble locating any space separate from that covered by "the category of 'sexual preference'" or by "the issue of civil rights." For justice, on this universalist view, is a matter of our providing one another with equal advantages. Nothing, in this vision, *could* transcend civil rights and the realization of those rights by institutional change. So, for example, lesbian separatism is likely to be seen simply as an arrangement by which those with a certain sexual preference can escape stigma until such time as the laws have been extended to protect lesbians' rights and the mores have caught up with the laws.

Frye offers a contrasting view of the function of separatism when she writes:

> *Re* the new being and meaning which are being created now by lesbian-feminists, we *do* have semantic authority, and, collectively, can and do define with effect. I think it is only by maintaining our boundaries through controlling concrete access to us that we can enforce on those who are not-us our definitions of ourselves, hence force on them *the fact of our existence* and thence open up the *possibility* of our having semantic authority with them.[39]

---

36 The continued attractions of this club in our own cynical century are evidenced by the fact that, even as Bernard Shaw was having Candida make fun of Marchbanks, Joyce had Stephen Dedalus write that he would "forge in the smithy of my soul the uncreated conscience of my race." Joyce was not making fun of Stephen, and even Shaw admitted that Candida "does not know the secret in the poet's heart."

37 "What might, in a male writer – a Thoreau, let us say, or a Christopher Smart or William Blake – seem a legitimate strangeness, a unique intention, has been in one of our two major poets [Dickinson] devalued into a kind of naïveté, girlish ignorance, feminine lack of professionalism, just as the poet herself has been made into a sentimental object. ('Most of us are half in love with this dead girl,' confesses Archibald MacLeish. Dickinson was fifty-five when she died.)" (Rich, *On Lies,* 167).

38 Ibid., 17.   39 Frye, *Politics of Reality,* 106n.

I take Frye's point to be, in part, that individuals – even individuals of great courage and imagination – cannot achieve semantic authority, *even semantic authority over themselves,* on their own. To get such authority you have to hear your own statements as part of a shared practice. Otherwise you yourself will never know whether they are more than ravings, never know whether you are a heroine or a maniac. People in search of such authority need to band together and form clubs, exclusive clubs. For if you want to work out a story about who you are – put together a moral identity – which decreases the importance of your relationships to one set of people and increases the importance of your relationships to another set, the physical absence of the first set of people may be just what you need. So feminist separatism may indeed, as Rich says, have little to do with sexual preference or with civil rights, and a lot to do with making things easier for women of the future to define themselves in terms not presently available. These would be terms that made it easy for "women as women" to have what Dewey calls "habitual purposes and cultivated wants" – purposes and wants that, as Rich says, only a chosen few women presently have.

To sum up: I am suggesting that we see the contemporary feminist movement as playing the same role in intellectual and moral progress as was played by, for example, Plato's Academy, the early Christians meeting in the catacombs, the invisible Copernican colleges of the seventeenth century, groups of workingmen gathering to discuss Tom Paine's pamphlets, and many other clubs that were formed to try out new ways of speaking and to gather the moral strength to go out and change the world. For groups build their moral strength by achieving increasing semantic authority over their members, thereby increasing the ability of those members to find their moral identities in their membership in such groups.

When a group forms itself in conscious opposition to those who control the life chances of its members and succeeds in achieving semantic authority over its members, the result may be its ruthless suppression – the sort of thing that happened to the Albigensians and that Margaret Atwood has imagined happening to feminists. But it may also happen that, as the generations succeed one another, the masters, those in control, gradually find their conceptions of the possibilities open to human beings changing. For example, they may gradually begin to think of the options open to their own children as including membership in the group in question. The new language spoken by the separatist group may gradually get woven into the language taught in the schools.

Insofar as this sort of thing happens, eyes become less arrogant and the members of the group cease to be treated as wayward children or as a bit

crazy (the ways in which Emily Dickinson was treated). Instead, they gradually achieve what Frye calls "full personhood" in the eyes of everybody, having first achieved it only in the eyes of members of their own club. They begin to be treated as full-fledged human beings rather than being seen, like
children or the insane, as degenerate cases – as beings entitled to love and
protection, but not to participation in deliberation on serious matters. For
to be a full-fledged person in a given society is a matter of double negation:
it is *not* to think of oneself as belonging to a group that powerful people in
that society thank God they do *not* belong to.

In our society, straight white males of my generation – even earnestly egalitarian straight white males – cannot easily stop themselves from feeling
guilty relief that they were not born women or gay or black, any more than
they can stop themselves from being glad that they were not born mentally
retarded or schizophrenic. This is in part because of a calculation of the obvious socioeconomic disadvantages of being so born, but not entirely. It is
also the sort of instinctive and ineffable horror that noble children used to
feel at the thought of having been born to non-noble parents, even very rich
non-noble parents.[40]

At some point in the development of our society, guilty relief over not
having been born a woman may not cross the minds of males, any more than
the question "noble or base-born?" now crosses their minds.[41] That would
be the point at which both males and females had *forgotten* the traditional
androcentric language, just as we have all forgotten the distinction between
base and noble ancestry. But if this future comes to pass, we pragmatists
think, it will not be because females have been revealed to possess something – namely, full human dignity – that everybody, even they themselves,
once mistakenly thought they lacked. It will be because the linguistic and
other practices of the common culture have come to incorporate some of
the practices characteristic of imaginative and courageous outcasts.

The new language that, with luck, will get woven into the language taught

---

40 This is the sort of ineffable horror that creates a sense of moral abomination (at, e.g., in-
    tercaste marriage), and thus furnishes the intuitions one tries to bring into reflective equi-
    librium with one's principles. To view moral abominableness as something we can produce
    or erase by changing the language taught to the young is the first step toward a nonuni-
    versalist conception of moral progress.

41 To realize how far away such a future is, consider Eve Klossofsky Sedgwick's point that we
    shall do justice to gays only when we become as indifferent to whether our children turn
    out to be gay or straight as we are to whether they become doctors or lawyers. Surely she is
    right, and yet how many parents at the present time can even imagine such indifference?
    For the reasons suggested by Stout (in *Ethics after Babel*), I suspect that neither sexism nor
    homophobia can vanish while the other persists.

to children will not, however, be the language the outcasts spoke in the old days, before the formation of separatist groups. For that was infected by the language of the masters. It will be, instead, a language gradually put together in separatist groups in the course of a long series of flirtations with meaninglessness. Had there been no stage of separation, there would have been no subsequent stage of assimilation. No prior antithesis, no new synthesis. No carefully nurtured pride in membership in a group that might not have attained self-consciousness were it not for its oppression, no expansion of the range of possible moral identities, and so no evolution of the species. This is what Hegel called the cunning of reason and what Dewey thought of as the irony of evolution.

Someone who takes the passage I quoted from Dewey seriously will not think of oppressed groups as learning to *recognize* their own full personhood and then gradually, by stripping away veils of prejudice, leading their oppressors to confront reality. For they will not see full personhood as an intrinsic attribute of the oppressed, any more than they see human beings having a central and inviolable core surrounded by culturally conditioned beliefs and desires – a core for which neither biology nor history can account. To be a pragmatist rather than a realist in one's description of the acquisition of full personhood requires thinking of its acquisition by blacks, gays, and women in the same terms as we think of its acquisition by Galilean scientists and Romantic poets. We say that the latter groups invented new moral identities for themselves by getting semantic authority over themselves. As time went by, they succeeded in having the language they had developed become part of the language everybody spoke. Similarly, we have to think of gays, blacks, and women inventing themselves rather than discovering themselves, and thus of the larger society as coming to terms with something new.

This means taking Frye's phrase "new *being*" literally and saying that there were very few female full persons around before feminism got started, in the same sense in which there were very few full-fledged Galilean scientists before the seventeenth century. It was, of course, *true* in earlier times that women should not have been oppressed, just as it was *true* before Newton said so that gravitational attraction accounted for the movements of the planets.[42] But, despite what Scripture says, truth will not necessarily prevail.

---

42 Pragmatists need not deny that true sentences are always true (as I have, unfortunately, suggested in the past that they might—notably in my "Waren die Gesetze Newtons schon vor Newton wahr? *Jahrbuch des Wissenschaftskollegs zu Berlin* [1987] 247–63). Stout (*Ethics after Babel*, chap. 11) rightly rebukes me for these suggestions and says that pragmatists should agree with everybody else that "Slavery is absolutely wrong" has always been true – even in periods when this sentence would have sounded crazy to everybody concerned, even slaves

"Truth" is not the name of a power that eventually wins through; it is just the nominalization of an approbative adjective. So just as a pragmatist in the philosophy of science cannot use the truth of Galileo's views as an explanation either of his success at prediction or of his gradually increasing fame,[43] so a pragmatist in moral philosophy cannot use the rightness of the feminist cause as an explanation either of its attraction for contemporary women or of its possible future triumph. For such explanations require the notion of a truth-tracking faculty, one that latches on to antecedently existing truth makers. Truth is ahistorical, but that is not because truths are made true by ahistorical entities.

Frye's term "new *being*" may seem even more unnecessarily hyperbolic than MacKinnon's "new voice," but we pragmatists can take it at face value and realists cannot. As I read Frye, the point is that before feminism began to gather women together into a kind of club, there were female eccentrics like Wollstonecraft and de Gouges, but these were not women who existed *as* women in MacKinnon's sense of "as." They were eccentric because they failed to fit into roles that men had contrived for them to fill and because there were as yet no other roles. For roles require a community – a web of social expectations and habits that define the role in question. The community may be small, but like a club as opposed to a convocation, or a new species as opposed to a few atypical mutant members of an old species, it exists only insofar as it is self-sustaining and self-reproducing.[44]

To sum up for the last time: prophetic feminists like MacKinnon and Frye

(who hoped that their fellow tribespeople would return in force and enslave their present masters). All that pragmatists need is the claim that this sentence is not *made* true by something other than the beliefs we would use to support it – and, in particular, not by something like the Nature of Human Beings.

43 I have criticized realists' claims to explain predictive success by truth in Part I of my *Objectivity, Relativism, and Truth*. A related point – that the success of a true theory needs just as much historicosociological explanation as the success of a false one – is made by Barry Barnes and other members of the so-called Edinburgh school of sociology of science.

44 It may seem that the view I am offering is the one Frye rejects under the name of "the institutional theory of personhood" – the theory that, as she puts it, "'person' denotes a social and institutional role and that one may be allowed or forbidden to adopt that role" (49). She says that this view "must be attractive to the phallist, who would fancy the power to create persons." But I do not want to say that men have the power to make full persons out of women by an act of grace, in the way in which sovereigns have the power to make nobles out of commoners. On the contrary, I would insist that men could not do this if they tried, for they are as much caught as are women in the linguistic practices that make it hard for women to be full persons. The utopia I foresee, in which these practices are simply forgotten, is not one that could be attained by an act of condescension on the part of men, any more than an absolute monarch could produce an egalitarian utopia by simultaneously enobling all her subjects.

foresee a new being not only for women but for society. They foresee a society in which the male–female distinction is no longer of much interest. Feminists who are also pragmatists will not see the formation of such a society as the removal of social constructs and the restoration of the way things were always meant to be. They will see it as the production of a better set of social constructs than the ones presently available, and thus as the creation of a new and better sort of human being.

12

THE END OF LENINISM, HAVEL,
AND SOCIAL HOPE

At the beginning of his *New Reflections on the Revolution of Our Time,* Ernesto Laclau says: "The cycle of events which opened with the Russian Revolution has definitively closed . . . as a force of irradiation in the collective imaginary of the international left. . . . The corpse of Leninism, stripped of all the trappings of power, reveals its pathetic and deplorable reality."[1] I agree with Laclau, and I hope that intellectuals will use the death of Leninism as an occasion to rid themselves of the idea that they know, or ought to know, something about deep, underlying forces – forces that determine the fates of human communities.

We intellectuals have been making claims to such knowledge ever since we set up shop. Once we claimed to know that justice could not reign until kings became philosophers or philosophers kings; we claimed to know this on the basis of a searching inspection of the human soul. More recently, we claimed to know that it will not reign until capitalism is overthrown and culture decommodified; we claimed to know this on the basis of a grasp of the shape and movement of History. I would hope that we have reached a time at which we can finally get rid of the conviction common to Plato and Marx that there *must* be large theoretical ways of finding out how to end injustice, as opposed to small experimental ways.

Laclau and Chantal Mouffe, in their much-discussed book, *Hegemony and Socialist Strategy,* suggest that the Left will have to settle for social democracy. Alan Ryan suggests that the best we can hope for is "a kind of welfare-capitalism-with-a-human-face, not easy to distinguish from a 'socialism' with

---

1 Ernest Laclau, *New Reflections on the Revolution of Our Time* (London: Verso, 1990), ix.

a big role for private capital and individual entrepreneurs."[2] Agreeing with these suggestions as I do, I think the time has come to drop the terms "capitalism" and "socialism" from the political vocabulary of the Left. It would be a good idea to stop talking about "the anticapitalist struggle" and to substitute something banal and untheoretical – something like "the struggle against avoidable human misery." More generally, I hope that we can banalize the entire vocabulary of leftist political deliberation. I suggest we start talking about greed and selfishness rather than about bourgeois ideology, about starvation wages and layoffs rather than about the commodification of labor, and about differential per-pupil expenditure on schools and differential access to health care rather than about the division of society into classes.

As one reason for such banalization, I would cite Laclau's thesis that "the transformation of thought – from Nietzsche to Heidegger, from pragmatism to Wittgenstein – has decisively undermined philosophical essentialism" and that this transformation enables us to "reformulate the materialist position in a much more radical way than was possible for Marx."[3] I think that the best way to be more radically materialist than Marx is to strip leftist political deliberation of Hegelian romance. We should stop using "History" as the name of an object around which to weave our fantasies of diminished misery. We should concede Francis Fukuyama's point (in his celebrated essay, *The End of History*)[4] that if you still long for total revolution, for the Radically Other on a world-historical scale, the events of 1989 show that you are out of luck. Fukuyama suggested, and I agree, that no more romantic prospect stretches before the Left than an attempt to create bourgeois democratic welfare states and to equalize life chances among the citizens of those states by redistributing the surplus produced by market economies.

Fukuyama, however, sees nothing but boredom ahead for us intellectuals once we have admitted that bourgeois democratic welfare states are the best polities we can imagine. He thinks that the end of romantic politics will have the same dampening effect on our collective imaginary as the admission that contemporary Athenian institutions were the best he could imagine would have had on Plato. As a follower of Strauss and Kojève, Fukuyama regrets this dampening. In the intellectual tradition to which he belongs, political philosophy is first philosophy. Utopian politics, the sort of politics whose paradigm is Plato's *Republic*, is the root of philosophical thought.

2 Alan Ryan, "Socialism for the Nineties," *Dissent* 37 (Fall 1990), 442.
3 Laclau, *New Reflections*, 112.
4 Francis Fukuyama, *The End of History and the Last Man* (New York: Free Press, 1992).

On a Straussian view, the hope of creating a society whose hero is Socrates, rather than Achilles or Themistocles, lies behind what Heidegger calls "Western metaphysics." So to damp down political romance is to impoverish our intellectual life, and perhaps make it impossible. Straussians tend to agree with Heideggerians that the end of metaphysics means the beginning of a nihilistic wasteland, a wasteland in which bourgeois freedoms and bourgeois happiness may become universal but in which there will be no appreciative readers of Plato. They tend to agree with Kojève that if we give up on "the Platonic–Hegelian *ideal* of the Wise Man," if we "deny that the supreme value is contained in Self-Consciousness," then we "take away the meaning of all human discourse whatsoever."[5]

Heartily disagreeing with Kojève as I do, I would urge that the Plato–Hegel–Marx–Heidegger brand of romance, the romance of world history, is something that intellectual life and leftist politics would now be much better off without – that this romance is a ladder we should now throw away. I distrust the way in which Kojève let his imagination be dominated by the Master–Slave section of Hegel's *Phenomenology* – and in particular by the passage which suggests that full moral seriousness, and perhaps full intellectual awareness, is possible only for those engaged in a life-and-death struggle. Kojève's use of that passage brings together Hegel's account of history as the story of increasing self-consciousness with the more bloodthirsty side of Marxism, the specifically Leninist side. Kojève, Strauss, Adorno, Nietzsche, and Heidegger are linked to Lenin and Mao by an urge to extirpate: either to abolish the bourgeoisie as a class or, at least, to root out bourgeois culture, the culture Nietzsche and Heidegger thought would turn Europe into a wasteland. That culture – the culture of Nietzsche's "last men" – is the contemporary counterpart of the culture that put Socrates to death: both are cultures for which self-consciousness is *not* the supreme virtue and for which the Platonic–Hegelian ideal of the Wise Man is not all that important.

Thanks to Marxism, the term "bourgeois culture" has become a way of lumping together anything and everything intellectuals despise. Calling that lump by that name was a way of linking the intellectual's romance of self-creation with the oppressed worker's desire to expropriate the expropriators. Such linkages help us intellectuals to associate ourselves with the ideals of democracy and human solidarity. These linkages let us have the best of both worlds: we have been able to combine the traditional disdain of the wise for the many with the belief that the present, degenerate bourgeois

5 Alexandre Kojève, *Introduction to the Reading of Hegel: Lectures on "The Phenomenology of Spirit,"* trans. J. H. Nichols, Jr. (Ithaca, N.Y.: Cornell University Press, 1969), 91.

many will be replaced by a new sort of many – the emancipated working class.

But now that we leftist intellectuals can no longer be Leninists, we have to face up to some questions Leninism helped us evade: Are we more interested in alleviating misery or in creating a world fit for Socrates, and thus for ourselves? What is behind the regret we feel when we are forced to conclude that bourgeois democratic welfare states are the best we can hope for? Is it sadness at the thought that the poor will never get all the way out from under the rich, that the solidarity of a cooperative commonwealth will never be attained? Or is it, instead, sadness at the thought that we, the people who value self-consciousness, may be irrelevant to the fate of humanity? That Plato, Marx, and we ourselves may just be parasitical eccentrics living off the surplus value of a society to which we have nothing in particular to contribute? Was our thirst for world-historical romance, and for deep theories about deep causes of social change, caused by our concern for human suffering? Or was it at least in part a thirst for an important role for ourselves?

So far I have been suggesting that what Fukuyama, like Nietzsche and Kojève before him, is worried about is not the end of history, but the end of the philosophy, and thus the romance, of history. What bothers him is our diminished ability to use History as an object around which we intellectuals can wrap our fantasies. This ability has, indeed, been diminished. To quote Laclau again: "If 'the end of history' is understood as the end of a conceptually graspable object encompassing the whole of the real in its diachronic spatiality, we *are* clearly at the end of 'history.'"[6] But if *that* is what we mean, then it would be better to say that what is over is our conviction that there is some object – the human soul, the will of God, the evolutionary process, History, or Language, for example – a better conceptual grasp of which will increase our chances of doing the right thing.

Laclau's attempt to be more radically materialist than Marx leads him to say that the loss of that conviction leaves us at "the beginning of history, at the point where historicity finally achieves full recognition."[7] I agree, but I think that to recognize historicity fully would mean sticking to small experimental ways of relieving misery and overcoming injustice. It would mean keeping the distinction between real leftist politics – that is, initiatives for the reduction of human misery – and cultural politics firmly in mind. It would mean being content to be concrete and banal when talking real politics, no

---

6 Laclau, *New Reflections*, 83; emphasis added.
7 Ibid., 84.

matter how abstract, hyperbolic, transgressive, and playful we become when we turn, in a mood of relaxation, to cultural politics.

A lot of fantasies can stand on their own without being twined around some large conceptually graspable object. These are the homely, familiar fantasies shared by the educated and the uneducated, by us middle-class intellectuals in U.S. and European universities and by people living in shantytowns outside of Lima. They are concrete fantasies about a future in which everybody can get work from which they derive some satisfaction and for which they are decently paid, and in which they are safe from violence and from humiliation. We intellectuals have, since Plato, supplemented these small concrete, local, banal fantasies with a larger, blurrier, more sophisticated set of fantasies. Between Plato and Hegel, these were fantasies that tied in the small concrete fantasies with a story about human beings' relation to something ahistorical – something like God or Human Nature or the Scientifically Knowable Nature of Reality. After Hegel, and especially after Lenin, we switched to a story about human beings' relation to History. History itself, reified into something that has a shape and a movement, took the place of an atemporal power. But we still explain why the small fantasies have not been realized by claiming that their fulfillment depended upon attaining a closer relation to something larger and more powerful than ourselves. We say, for instance, that our efforts have so far failed because the "right historical moment" has not yet come.

Our belief in such explanations has let us intellectuals feel that we can be useful to nonintellectuals by telling them how they can get what they want, what it would take to make some of the small fantasies we all share come true. Such explanations let us feel that our special gifts are good for more than giving ourselves sophisticated private pleasures – that these gifts have social utility, permit us to function as an avant-garde in a universal human struggle. Since Hegel, we have been able to think of ourselves as internalizing the Incarnate Logos, of becoming one with God's increasing self-consciousness, his realization of himself in the history of the human race. With Hegel, "World History" became the name of the inspiring blur produced by fudging the differences between the immaterial and the material, the atemporal and the temporal, the divine and the human. The Marxist–Leninist version of this blur called "History" helped us both overcome our fear of elitism and gratify our blood lust by letting us picture ourselves as swept up by the aroused masses – borne along toward the slaughter-bench of history, the altar where the bourgeoisie will be redemptively sacrificed.

As I see it, Hegel's switch from fantasies of individual salvation through contact with a blurry other world to fantasies of the blurry end of a historical sequence was a step forward. That is because it adumbrated a sort of pro-topragmatism. It helped us stop talking about the way things were always meant to be – God's will, Nature's way – and begin talking about the way things never were but might, with our help, become. With Hegel, intellectuals began to switch over from fantasies of contacting eternity to fantasies of constructing a better future. Hegel helped us to start substituting hope for knowledge.

This substitution was, of course, by no means complete in Hegel. Hegel still tried to break culture up into parts labeled "Philosophy," "Art," "Natural Science," and the like, and tried to give priority to philosophy. In particular, he insisted that there was something called "the System" or "Absolute Knowledge" – something so big and so finely structured as to eliminate any residual blurs. This insistence that there might be a completed object of knowledge provoked justified ridicule from, among others, Kierkegaard, Marx, and Dewey. Nobody since their time, with the possible exception of Kojève, has taken seriously the idea that there was something called "Philosophy" that reached its completion with Hegel. Rather, we have treated Hegel as a reductio ad absurdum of the idea of Absolute Knowledge and so have dropped the Platonic–Hegelian ideal of the Wise Man. We have become content to say what Hegel himself said once, and Marx and Dewey said pretty consistently: that philosophy is, at most, its time held in thought.

Marx went on to do what Hegel only rarely did. He tried to hold his time in thought by calculating just *how* it might be improved for the benefit of future generations. He took Hegel's historicism and protopragmatism more seriously than Hegel himself had managed to take them, because he blurred the distinction between understanding the world and knowing how to change it. His suggestion was that it could be changed for the better by replacing capitalism with communism and by replacing bourgeois culture with new forms of cultural life that would arise naturally from the emancipation of the working class. This Marxist suggestion has been the principal legacy of Hegel's work to the social imagination of the past two centuries. Switching from the World Spirit to the working class made it possible to save Hegelian hope, and the Hegelian narrative of History as the expansion of Freedom, from the Hegelian System.

This suggestion now has to be dropped. The events of 1989 have convinced those who were still trying to hold on to Marxism that we need a way of holding our time in thought, and a plan for making the future better than the present, which drops reference to capitalism, bourgeois ways of life, bourgeois ideology, and the working class. We must give up on the Marxist blur, as Marx and Dewey gave up on the Hegelian blur. We can no longer use the term "capitalism" to mean both "a market economy" and the "source of all contemporary injustice." We can no longer tolerate the ambiguity between capitalism as a way of financing industrial production and capitalism as the Great Bad Thing that accounts for most contemporary human misery. Nor can we use the term "bourgeois ideology" to mean both "beliefs suited for societies centered around market economies" and "everything in our language and habits of thought that, if replaced, would make human happiness and freedom more easily realized." Nor can we use the term "working class" to mean both "those who are given the least money and least security in market economies" and "the people who embody the true nature of human beings."

These ambiguities will no longer seem tolerable if one agrees, as I do, with Jürgen Habermas about the lesson of 1989. He writes as follows, in his volume of reflections on the events of that year, *Die nachholende Revolution:*

> . . . the revolutionary changes which are culminating under our eyes at the present time contain one unequivocal lesson: complex societies cannot reproduce themselves, if they do not leave intact the logic of self-regulation of a market economy.[8]

The leftist use of the terms "capitalism," "bourgeois ideology," and "working class" depends on the implicit claim that we can do *better* than a market economy, that we know of a viable alternative option for complex technologically oriented societies. But at the moment, at least, we know of no such option. Whatever program the Left may develop for the twenty-first century, it is not going to include nationalization of the means of production or the abolition of private property. Nor is it likely to include the detechnologization of the world, simply because nobody can think of a way to counter the effects of bad old technological-bureaucratic initiatives except the development of new and better technological-bureaucratic initiatives.

I agree with Habermas when he goes on to say that "the non-communist left has no reason to be depressed" and that there is no reason to abandon hope for "the emancipation of human beings from willed immaturity (*selbstverschuldeter Unmündigkeit*) and from degrading conditions of existence."[9] But I have no clear sense of what mechanisms might realize that hope. For example, when Alan Ryan says that "it is impossible to believe that we should give up on the hope that broad-brush planning reduces waste and at any rate diminishes the irrationalities of production and distribution," I would very

---

8 Jürgen Habermas, *Die nachholende Revolution* (Frankfurt: Suhrkamp, 1990), 196–7.
9 Ibid., 203.

much like to agree with him. But I feel no assurance. I no longer think I have much grasp of what options remain open to economic planners, nor of what can and cannot be safely turned over to the state. I detest the complacent satisfaction that admirers of Reagan and Thatcher have taken in the downfall of Marxism, and I am terrified by the tendency, among intellectuals in recently liberated Central European countries, to assume that free markets solve all social problems. But these reactions are not enough to give me any clear sense of how state power *should* be related to economic decisions. I do not think I am alone in this, and I refer to my own perplexity merely as an instance of what seems to me widespread bewilderment among leftist intellectuals. We have no reason to be depressed, but we also have little sense of how to make ourselves useful.

Since "capitalism" can no longer function as the name of the source of human misery, or "the working class" as the name of a redemptive power, we need to find new names for these things. But unless some new metanarrative eventually replaces the Marxist one, we shall have to characterize the source of human misery in such untheoretical and banal ways as "greed," "selfishness," and "hatred." We shall have no name for a redemptive power save "good luck." Speaking with the vulgar in this way makes it hard for us intellectuals to continue believing that our special gifts suit us for positions in the avant-garde of the struggle against injustice. For there seems to be nothing in particular that we know that everybody else doesn't also know. The old large blurry fantasies are gone, and we are left with only the small concrete ones – the ones we used to view as symptoms of petit bourgeois reformism.

This sense that we can no longer function as an avant-garde is, I think, what lies behind the widespread feeling, even among leftists who have no use for Strauss and Kojève, that Fukuyama was on to something. What he latched on to was the loss of "History" as a term we intellectuals could use in our self-descriptions, could use to reassure ourselves that we have a social function, that what we do is relevant to human solidarity. By inventing "History" as the name of an object that could be conceptually grasped, Hegel and Marx made it possible to keep both the romance of the Christian story about the Incarnate Logos, and the Christian sense of solidarity against injustice, even after we lost religious faith. But now we have either to spin some new metanarrative that does not mention capitalism, yet has the same dramatic power and urgency as the Marxist narrative, or else to give up the idea that we intellectuals are notably better at holding our time in thought than our fellow citizens. Since I have no idea how to do the former, I suggest we do the latter.

I want now to return to Laclau's sentence about Lenin and the Bolshevik Revolution having, for a long time, irradiated "the collective imaginary of the international left." No political movement can survive for long without such irradiation, irradiation by concrete events and heroic individuals. If there had been no Lenin and no Bolshevik Revolution, if we had had to settle simply for Marx's revision of Hegel's blurry story about the Incarnate Logos, our collective imaginary would have long since ceased to glow. So now we have to ask ourselves: What events might replace the Bolshevik Revolution, and what figure might replace Lenin, in the imaginations of the generation born around 1980, the people who will be leftist university students in the year 2000? What might irradiate the collective imaginary of leftists who take for granted that state ownership of the means of production is no longer an option?

One plausible answer to this question is: the sequence of events in Czechoslovakia in the last months of 1989 and the figure of Václav Havel. I have no idea how that revolution is going to proceed or any good guesses about whether the moral and political consensus that swept Havel to power will endure. But neither, I take it, does Havel. One of the most surprising and refreshing things about Havel is that he cheerfully admits that he does not. Havel seems prepared to go all the way in substituting groundless hope for theoretical insight. As he says in the interviews collected as *Disturbing the Peace*, "[H]ope is not prognostication." Throughout those interviews, he emphasizes his lack of interest in underlying forces, historical trends, and large, conceptually graspable objects. The following passage, describing the events of 1967–9, is typical:

> Who would have believed – at a time when the Novotny regime was corroding away because the entire nation was behaving like Švejks [Schweiks, as in Jaroslav Hašek's novel] – that half a year later that same society would display a genuine civic-mindedness, and that a year later this recently apathetic, skeptical and demoralized society would stand up with such courage and intelligence to a foreign power! And who would have suspected that, after scarcely a year had gone by, this same society would, as swiftly as the wind blows, lapse back into a state of demoralization far deeper than its original one! After all these experiences, one must be very careful about coming to any conclusions about the way we are, or what can be expected from us.[10]

"Us" here means "us Czechs and Slovaks," but what Havel is saying works just as well if we take it to mean "us human beings."[11]

---

10 Václav Havel, *Disturbing the Peace* (New York: Knopf, 1990), 109.
11 We can put Havel's refusal to prognosticate in a U.S. context by asking, "Who would have guessed that the white middle class which acknowledged the justice of Truman's desegre-

Lenin would not have agreed with Havel that "we have to be very careful about coming to any conclusions about the way we are, or what can be expected from us." Scientific socialism, Lenin thought, gave us the tools to formulate, and demonstrate the truth of, just such prognostications. Lenin would have expected Marxist theory at least to retrodict, if not predict, the varying behavior of the Czechs and Slovaks at various historical moments. But the end of Leninism will, with luck, rid us of the hope for anything like scientific socialism, for any similar source of theoretically based prognostication. It will, I hope, leave us with only what Martin Jay calls "fin-de-siècle socialists." These are people who think, as Jay puts it, that "[T]here is sufficient work to be done without being haunted by the need to measure what modest successes might be granted to us against the daunting model of a normatively totalized, fully redeemed, social order."[12]

Havel is, in Jay's sense, a fin-de-siècle thinker, but he is not a fin-de-siècle *socialist*. The revolution over which he is presiding has had no better ideas than to give back the expropriated properties and to sell off the nationalized factories to whatever private entrepreneurs will buy them. Timothy Garton Ash reported that the choice between Dubček and Havel for president became clear when people in Prague found themselves saying, "Dubček is a great man, of course, but he is, well – what can one say? – he is, after all . . . a *communist*." One reason why all of us in the international Left are going to have to weed terms like "capitalism," "bourgeois culture" (and, alas, even "socialism")[13] out of our vocabulary is that our friends in Central and Eastern Europe will look at us incredulously if we continue to employ them. The

gation of the military, the Supreme Court's reversal of the separate-but-equal doctrine, and King's freedom marches, the white middle class which turned King into a schoolbook hero, would now decide that it is more important to cut suburbanites' taxes than to protect ghetto children by building safe havens for them? Who can know whether, a decade further down the road, the same middle class may not become disgusted with its own greed and throw out the rascals who pandered to its selfishness?"

12 Martin Jay, *Fin-de-Siècle Socialism and Other Essays* (London: Routledge, 1988), 13. The line I take in this essay owes much to Jay's discussion of "totalization" in this book and in his *Marxism and Totality* (Berkeley: University of California Press, 1984).

13 Toward the end of his *Socialism in America* (San Diego, Calif.: Harcourt Brace Jovanovich, 1985), Irving Howe writes, "Suppose, indeed, we were to conclude that the socialist label creates more trouble than it's worth; we would then have to cast about for a new vocabulary, something not to be won through fiat. How much would actually change if our words were to change? If, say, we ceased calling ourselves socialists and instead announced that henceforth we are to be known as – what? 'Economic democrats' or 'democratic radicals'? The substance of our problems would remain, the weight of this century's burden still press upon us. We would still regard capitalist society as an unjust society, still find intolerable its inequities, still be repelled by its ethic of greed, and still be trying to sketch the outlines of a better society" (217).

more Czechs, Poles, and Hungarians we talk to, the more old habits we are
going to have to give up. For example, we shall have to stop regretting the
Cold War, stop excusing the Stalinism of people like Sartre, and start realizing that to a Czech the phrase "the romance of U.S. Communism" sounds
as odd as "the romance of the German-American Bund" sounds to a Jew.

Part of the reason the next century looks so blank and formless to us is
that we intellectuals have grown accustomed to thinking in world-historical,
eschatological terms. We have become impatient with anything smaller, dis-
contented with patchwork solutions and temporary stopgaps. No sooner do
we think that we have an idea about what might help ghetto children in the
United States than we realize that our idea has no relevance to the children
in Uganda. Then we feel guilty for not having a theory that covers children
everywhere. No sooner do we have a suggestion about how to minimize pol-
lution in Los Angeles than we realize it is irrelevant to Calcutta, and then
we feel ashamed of being ethnocentric. Part of our inheritance from Hegel
and Lenin is that we feel guilty about having no planetary project under
which to subsume our local hopes, no *global* leftist strategy. That, I think, is
one reason why we leftists in the U.S. academy now spend more of our time
on postmodernist philosophy, and on what we like to think of as "transgressive" and "subversive" cultural studies, than on deliberating about what
might reenergize the Democratic Party or about how to refund Head Start
programs.[14]

Lately we have been concentrating on cultural politics and trying to persuade ourselves that cultural, and especially academic, politics are continuous
with real politics. We have been trying to believe that upsetting our students'
parents will sooner or later help upset unjust institutions. As long as we can
believe that, we can still feel that the gifts that got us our cushy jobs in universities are being used on behalf of human solidarity. We can escape, at least

---

14 Much of what goes on under the heading "cultural studies" in U.S. universities seems to me
   well described by the words Kenneth Burke (whom I shall discuss later) used to describe
   Marinetti and futurism: "To any who might say 'This modern world is disease,' it could answer 'But what a *perfect* example of disease!' Its affinity with the antics of our recent 'hard-
   boiled' school is apparent. We may also note (unruly thought!) the *sentimental* aspect of
   both. Futurism, so cast, could provide the most rudimentary kind of solace. Were the streets
   noisy? It could counter by advocating an uncritical cult of noise. Might there be stench? It
   would discuss the 'beauties' of stench. *Apparently* active, it was in essence the most passive
   of frames, an elaborate method for feeling *assertive* by a resolve to drift with the current"
   (Burke, *Attitudes Toward History*, reprint ed. [Los Altos, Calif.: Hermes, 1959], 33). This description of futurism and of the 'hard-boiled' school seems to me to apply quite well to, for
   example, Frederic Jameson's *Postmodernism: Or the Cultural Logic of Late Capitalism* (Durham,
   N.C.: Duke University Press, 1991).

for a while, the suspicion that we are just using those gifts for our private pleasures, in aid of private projects of self-creation.

But these maneuvers are, I suspect, only ways of postponing the questions
we shall be asked by students whose collective imaginary has been irradiated
by Havel rather than by Lenin. These are questions about what exactly we
would *do* if we suddenly achieved *real* political power: what sort of utopia
would we try to create, and how we would set about it? I hope that we can
learn to reply to such questions by saying that, at the moment, we have no
clear idea *what* a redeemed social order would look like, that we can sketch
no ground plan for the egalitarian cooperative commonwealth whose spires
we glimpse in our dreams. Still, we *can* offer a long list of laws, international
agreements, border rectifications, judicial decisions, and the like that we
would try to have promulgated.

To be satisfied with making such a reply, we shall have to get over our fear
of being called "bourgeois reformers" or "opportunistic pragmatists" or
"technocratic social engineers" – our fear of becoming mere "liberals" as opposed to "radicals."[15] We shall have to get over the hope for a successor to
Marxist theory, a general theory of oppression which will provide a fulcrum
that lets us topple racial, economic, and gender injustice simultaneously. We
shall have to drop the "ideology" idea, the idea Havel mocks when he says
that a mark of the good communist is that he "subscribes to an ideology and

15 Two friends who have criticized my claim to be a faithful follower of John Dewey – Richard
Bernstein and Thomas McCarthy – have quoted against me the passage in *Liberalism and Social Action* (*The Later Works of John Dewey* [Carbondale: Southern Illinois University Press,
1987], 11: 45) at which Dewey says that "liberalism must become radical, meaning by 'radical' perception of the necessity of thoroughgoing changes in the set-up of institutions and
corresponding activity to bring the changes to pass . . . 'reforms' that deal now with this
abuse and now with that without having a social goal based upon an inclusive plan, differ
entirely from effort at re-forming, in its literal sense, the institutional scheme of things. . . .
If radicalism be defined as perception of the need for radical change, then today any liberalism which is not also radicalism is irrelevant and doomed."

I interpret this passage as presupposing Dewey's claim, a few pages earlier, that "[t]he
system that goes by the name of capitalism is a systematic manifestation of desires and purposes built up in an age of ever-threatening want and now carried over into a time of ever
increasing potential plenty." This claim seems to me wrong – both in its suggestion that we
know how to replace capitalism with something better and about ever-increasing plenty. I
think that Dewey was occasionally tempted, especially in the 1930s, to assume that we already knew about a satisfactory alternative to market economies and private property. I wish
that assumption had been true, but I do not think it was. After 1989, I see even less reason
to think that the left has anything remotely like "an inclusive plan" for "thoroughgoing
changes in the set-up of institutions." I devoutly wish we did, but until I can peruse such a
plan, I shall continue to view Bernstein's and McCarthy's descriptions of themselves as "radicals" as amiable exercises in nostalgia.

believes that anyone who doesn't subscribe to it must therefore subscribe to another ideology, because he can't imagine anyone's not subscribing to an ideology."[16] This will mean giving up the claim that philosophical or literary sophistication is important because it prepares us for the crucial, socially indispensable role that history has allotted to us – the role of "critic of ideology."

Finally, to come back to the topic with which I began, it will mean dropping History as a temporalized substitute for God or Nature, as a large blurry object around which to weave our concrete local fantasies. Instead, we might come to see the record of the past as Kenneth Burke suggested we see it: as a collection of anecdotes that help us construct what he called "a comic frame."[17] Instead of looking for a world-historical trend that would help us prognosticate, we could echo Burke's remark that "the future is really disclosed by finding out what people can sing about."[18] We can supplement this remark by adding, with Havel, that in any given year you will probably not be able to guess which songs will be on people's lips in twelve months' time.

In his 1936 book, *Attitudes Toward History*, Burke says, under the entry "Opportunism":

> Every situation in history is unique, requires its own particular gauging or sizing-up of the factors that shall be considered pivotal in the situation. The "scientists" of history have brought us unintentionally to the realization that the gauging of the "right historical moment" is a matter of *taste*.[19]

In a section called "Comic Correctives" he says:

> The comic frame, in making a man the student of himself, makes it possible for him to "transcend" occasions when he has been tricked or cheated, since he can readily put such discouragements into his "assets" column, under the heading of "experience." . . . In sum, the comic frame should enable people to be observers of themselves, while acting.[20]

---

16 Havel, *Disturbing the Peace*, 80.
17 Burke, characteristically, never quite defines this phrase. In *Attitudes Toward History* he says, "In this book . . . we have said much about the 'comic frame.' We have advocated, under the name of 'comedy,' a procedure that might just as well have been advocated under the name of 'humanism.' Presumably we selected 'comedy' because, for one reason or another, the word 'sounded better' to us. And when the author selects one word rather than another because it 'sounds better' to him, his choice is guided by 'overtones' that may not apply to his auditor at all" (237). I take it that Burke's use of "comic" has overtones of "rueful" rather than of "amusing."
18 Ibid., 335.   19 Ibid., 308.   20 Ibid., 171.

Burke says that he prefers comic to tragic frames, even though what he calls "contemporary exasperations" (by which I take him to mean the world of the 1930s) "make us prefer the tragic (sometimes melodramatic) names of 'villain' and 'hero' to the comic names of 'tricked' and 'intelligent.'"[21] I take his point to be that we should view history's slaughter-bench through the eyes of the prudent calculator of the consequences of future actions rather than with those of the moralist. We should see the horrors of our century not as clues to something deep in ourselves or as hints of our ultimate destiny, but as instructive lessons.

One application of Burke's suggestion to our more recent exasperations would be to see what Laclau calls "the cycle of events which opened with the Russian Revolution" as one in which we leftists, often with the best intentions, tricked ourselves, fooled ourselves, outsmarted ourselves, yet gained a lot of useful experience. That attitude would help us avoid either congratulating ourselves on our heroism or accepting the Reagan–Thatcher view that we were cruel villains or idiotic dupes. Accepting Burke's suggestion that we view recent history as within a "comic" frame rather than an epic or a tragic one would mean making the best we could out of the deaths of millions by viewing the circumstances of those deaths as instructive in the avoidance of future deaths. It would mean using our acquaintance with the various butchers who have presided over the slaughter-benches of history – people like Hadrian and Attila, Napoleon and Stalin, Hitler and Mao – to avoid imitating them.

Burke develops his rather idiosyncratic, and probably misleading, sense of the term "comedy" – a sense that does not have much to do with laughter – in the following passage:

> Comedy requires the maximum of forensic complexity. In the tragic plot the *deus ex machina* is always lurking. . . . Comedy deals with *man in society,* tragedy with the *cosmic man.* . . . Comedy is essentially *humane,* leading in periods of comparative stability to the comedy of manners, the dramatization of quirks and foibles. But it is not necessarily confined to drama. The best of Bentham, Marx and Veblen is high comedy.[22]

Seen from a Burkean angle, Hegel-style philosophy of history is a device for getting by with a bare *minimum* of forensic complexity. It is a continuation of metaphysics by other means – a continuing attempt to put humanity in a *cosmic* context even after the cosmos was found to be largely irrelevant to our hopes. It is a way of short-circuiting political argument by labeling any new

---

21 Ibid., 4–5. 22 Ibid., 42.

work of art or philosophical movement or political suggestion "progressive" or "reactionary." The people whom Burke calls "the 'scientists' of history" suggested that all one had to do was enter the new item as the value of a variable in a set of equations, calculate the result, and thereby discover whether the new suggestion would accelerate or retard the movement of the big blurry object on which their theory had given us a firm conceptual grasp.

If we could drop the pursuit of this pseudo-science and stop using "History" as the name of a large blurry object about which large theories are required, we could read Bentham, Marx, Veblen – and, nowadays, Foucault – as people who help us understand how we tricked ourselves in the past rather than as people who tell us the right thing to do in the future. They could be read as exhibiting the unexpected and painful consequences of our ancestors' attempts to do the right thing rather than as explaining the inadequacy of our ancestors' concepts to the great big object they and we are trying to grasp. Reading them in that way might help us stop attempting to find a successor to "capitalism" or "bourgeois ideology" as the name of the Great Bad Thing. We might then stop trying to find a successor to "the working class" – for example, "Difference" or "Otherness" – as a name for the latest incarnation of the Logos. Reading this historical record in Burke's way might help us avoid what Stanley Fish calls "anti-foundationalist theory hope" – the idea that a materialism and a sense of historicity more radical even than Marx's will somehow provide a brand-new, still bigger, albeit still blurrier, object – an object called, perhaps, "Language" or "Discourse" – around which to weave our fantasies.[23]

Burke strikes me, in short, as having the sort of attitude toward history that Havel might like. I see him as a sort of anti-Marx, a counterpart to Havel's anti-Lenin. For Burke thinks of history as a collection of cautionary tales rather than a coherent dramatic narrative. If we adopt Burke's conception of history, we might become less fond of apocalyptic talk of "crisis" and "endings," less inclined toward eschatology. For we would no longer imagine a great big Incarnate Logos called "Humanity" whose career is to

---

23 Frank Lentricchia, in his *Criticism and Social Change* (Chicago: University of Chicago Press, 1983), has set Burke over against Paul de Man and criticized de Man's attempt to make "Language" the name of a new object of the sort I describe. I agree with the gist of what Lentricchia says about the relative value of Burke's and de Man's work, and have made some similar points in my "Deconstruction" (in volume 8 of *The Cambridge History of Literary Criticism*) (Cambridge University Press, 1995). In particular, I agree with Lentricchia that "one of the great things about Burke is that he knew the truths of de Man early" (*Criticism*, 51), a claim confirmed by Burke's Nietzschean remarks about concepts as dead metaphors in *Attitudes*, 12, 229.

be interpreted either as heroic struggle or as tragic decline. Instead, we should think of many different past human communities, each of which has willed us one or more cautionary anecdotes. Some of these anecdotes may serve the turn of one or more of the different human communities of the present day, depending upon their different needs and options.

To think of history in this way would be to stop trying to pick out world-historical turning points or figures, stop trying to find historical events that somehow encapsulate and reveal the whole sweep of History by laying out the whole range of possibilities open to Humanity. It would be to apply to social criticism what Burke said of literary criticism:

> Works vary in their range and comprehensiveness. One man's character is but another man's mood. We are simply suggesting that, when you lump the lot, discounting each poetic category according to its nature, they seem to add up nearest to comedy. Which might be a roundabout way of saying: whatever poetry may be, criticism had best be comic.[24]

A few years ago, Havel and the other signers of Charta 77 supplied us with a new example of social poetry, of the poetry of social hope. That example makes clear that such hope can exist, and can sometimes even be fulfilled, without backup from a philosophy of history and without being placed in the context of an epic or tragedy whose hero is Humanity. Burke's way of thinking about social criticism – as comparison and contrast between such social poems, comparison and contrast that eschews the attempt to be long-range and cosmic and is content to be short-range and prudential – can be recommended to students whose imaginations have been irradiated by that example.

---

24 Burke, *Attitudes*, 107. This passage chimes with Dewey's claim that there is no such thing as radical evil. Evil, Dewey said, is always a rejected good – the good of some previous situation. I suspect that adopting this Deweyan attitude toward evil will be necessary if we are to throw away the ladder of world-historical romance. My view contrasts with Cornel West's, who sees Josiah Royce's insistence on the radicality of evil as essential to what West calls "left romanticism."

III

THE ROLE OF PHILOSOPHY
IN HUMAN PROGRESS

13

THE HISTORIOGRAPHY OF PHILOSOPHY: FOUR GENRES

Rational and Historical Reconstructions

Analytic philosophers who have attempted "rational reconstructions" of the arguments of great dead philosophers have done so in the hope of treating these philosophers as contemporaries, as colleagues with whom they can exchange views. They have argued that unless one does this one might as well turn over the history of philosophy to historians – whom they picture as mere doxographers, rather than seekers after philosophical truth. Such reconstructions, however, have led to charges of anachronism. Analytic historians of philosophy are frequently accused of beating texts into the shape of propositions currently being debated in the philosophical journals. It is urged that we should not force Aristotle or Kant to take sides in current debates within philosophy of language or metaethics. There seems to be a dilemma: either we anachronistically impose enough of our problems and vocabulary on the dead to make them conversational partners, or we confine our interpretive activity to making their falsehoods look less silly by placing them in the context of the benighted times in which they were written.

Those alternatives, however, do not constitute a dilemma. We should do both of these things, but do them separately. We should treat the history of philosophy as we treat the history of science. In the latter field, we have no reluctance in saying that we know better than our ancestors what they were talking about. We do not think it anachronistic to say that Aristotle had a

I am grateful to David Hollinger for helpful remarks on an earlier version of this essay and to the Center for Advanced Study in the Behavioral Sciences for providing ideal circumstances for its composition.

false model of the heavens or that Galen did not understand how the circulatory system worked. We take the pardonable ignorance of great dead scientists for granted. We should be equally willing to say that Aristotle was unfortunately ignorant that there are no such things as real essences, or Leibniz that God does not exist, or Descartes that the mind is just the central nervous system under an alternative description. We hesitate merely because we have colleagues who are themselves ignorant of such facts and whom we courteously describe not as "ignorant," but as "holding different philosophical views." Historians of science have no colleagues who believe in crystalline spheres or who doubt Harvey's account of circulation, and they are thus free from such constraints.

There is nothing wrong with self-consciously letting our own philosophical views dictate terms in which to describe the dead. But there are reasons for *also* describing them in other terms, their own terms. It is useful to recreate the intellectual scene in which the dead lived their lives – in particular, the real and imagined conversations they might have had with their contemporaries (or near contemporaries). There are purposes for which it is useful to know how people talked who did not know as much as we do – to know this in enough detail so that we can imagine ourselves talking the same outdated language. The anthropologist wants to know how primitives talk to fellow primitives as well as how they react to instruction from missionaries. For this purpose he tries to get inside their heads and to think in terms he would never dream of employing at home. Similarly, the historian of science, who can imagine what Aristotle might have said in a dialogue in heaven with Aristarchus and Ptolemy, knows something interesting that remains unknown to the Whiggish astrophysicist who sees only how Aristotle would have been crushed by Galileo's arguments. There is knowledge – historical knowledge – to be gained that one can get only by bracketing one's own better knowledge about, for example, the movements of the heavens or the existence of God.

The pursuit of such historical knowledge must obey a constraint formulated by Quentin Skinner:[1]

> No agent can eventually be said to have meant or done something which he could never be brought to accept as a correct description of what he had meant or done.

Skinner says that this maxim excludes "the possibility that an acceptable account of an agent's behavior could ever survive the demonstration that it

---

1 Quentin Skinner, "Meaning and Understanding in the History of Ideas," *History and Theory* 8 (1969): 28.

was itself dependent on the use of criteria of description and classification not available to the agent himself." There is an important sense of "what the agent meant or did," as of "account of the agent's behavior," for which this is an ineluctable constraint. If we want an account of Aristotle's or Locke's behavior that obeys this constraint, however, we shall have to confine ourselves to one that, at its ideal limit, tells us what they might have said in response to all the criticisms or questions that would have been aimed at them by their contemporaries (or, more precisely, by that selection of their contemporaries or near contemporaries whose criticisms and questions they could have understood right off the bat – all the people who, roughly speaking, "spoke the same language," not least because they were just as ignorant of what we now know as the great dead philosopher himself). We may want to go on to ask questions like "What would Aristotle have said about the moons of Jupiter (or about Quine's antiessentialism)?" or "What would Locke have said about labor unions (or about Rawls)?" or "What would Berkeley have said about Ayer's or Bennett's attempt to "linguistify" his views on sense perception and matter?" But we will not describe the answers we envisage them giving to such questions as descriptions of what they "meant or did," in Skinner's sense of these terms.

The main reason we want historical knowledge of what unreeducated primitives, or dead philosophers and scientists, would have said to each other is that it helps us to recognize that there have been different forms of intellectual life than ours. As Skinner rightly says, "The indispensable value of studying the history of ideas" is to learn "the distinction between what is necessary and what is the product merely of our own contingent arrangements."[2] The latter is indeed, as he goes on to say, "the key to self-awareness itself." But we also want to imagine conversations between ourselves (whose contingent arrangements include general agreement that, e.g., there are no real essences, no God, etc.) and the mighty dead. We want this not simply because it is nice to feel one up on one's betters, but because we would like to be able to see the history of our race as a long conversational interchange. We want to be able to see it that way in order to assure ourselves that there has been rational progress in the course of recorded history – that we differ from our ancestors on grounds our ancestors could be led to accept. The need for reassurance on this point is as great as the need for self-awareness. We need to imagine Aristotle studying Galileo or Quine and changing his mind, Aquinas reading Newton or Hume and changing his, and so on. We need to think that, in philosophy as in science, the mighty mistaken dead

2 Ibid., 52–3.

look down from heaven at our recent successes and are happy to find that their mistakes have been corrected.

This means that we are interested not only in what the Aristotle who walked the streets of Athens "could . . . be brought to accept as a correct description of what he had meant or done" but in what an ideally reasonable and educable Aristotle could be brought to accept as such a description. The ideal aborigine can eventually be brought to accept a description of himself as having cooperated in the continuation of a kinship system designed to facilitate the unjust economic arrangements of his tribe. An ideal Gulag guard can eventually be brought to regard himself as having betrayed his loyalty to his fellow Russians. An ideal Aristotle can be brought to describe himself as having mistaken the preparatory taxonomic stages of biological research for the essence of all scientific inquiry. Each of these imaginary people, by the time he has been brought to accept such a new description of what he meant or did, has become "one of us." He is our contemporary, or our fellow citizen, or a fellow member of the same disciplinary matrix.

To give an example of such conversation with the reeducated dead, consider Strawson on Kant.[3] *The Bounds of Sense* is inspired by the same motives as *Individuals* – the conviction that Humean psychological atomism is deeply misguided and artificial and that attempts to replace the commonsense "Aristotelian" framework of things with "events" or "stimuli" (in the manner common to Whitehead and Quine) are deeply misguided. Since Kant agreed with this line of thought, and since much of the "Transcendental Analytic" is devoted to making similar points, it is natural for someone with Strawson's concerns to want to show Kant how he can make those points without saying some other, less plausible things that he said. These are things that the progress of philosophy since Kant's day has freed us from the temptation to say. Strawson can, for example, show Kant how to get along without notions like "in the mind" or "created by the mind," notions from which Wittgenstein and Ryle liberated us. Strawson's conversation with Kant is the sort one has with somebody who is brilliantly and originally right about something dear to one's heart, but who exasperatingly mixes up this topic with a lot of outdated foolishness. Other examples of such conversations are Ayer's and Bennett's conversations with the British empiricists about phenomenalism – conversations that try to filter out the pure essence of phenomenalism from questions about the physiology of perception and about the existence of God (subjects about which we are now better informed, and

3 P. F. Strawson, *The Bounds of Sense: An Essay on Kant's "Critique of Pure Reason"* (London: Methuen, 1966).

thus able to perceive the irrelevance).[4] Here again we have a fulfillment of the natural desire to talk to people some of whose ideas are quite like our own, in the hope of getting them to admit that we have gotten those ideas clearer or in the hope of getting them clearer still in the course of the conversation.[5]

Such enterprises in commensuration are, of course, anachronistic. But if they are conducted in full knowledge of their anachronism, they are unobjectionable. The only problems they raise are the verbal one of whether

4 A. J. Ayer, *Language, Truth and Logic* (London: Gollancz, 1936); Jonathan Bennett, *Locke, Berkeley, Hume: Central Themes* (Oxford: Oxford University Press, 1971).

5 Thus, I cannot agree with Michael Ayers's strictures on such attempts, or with his claim that it is an "illusion" that ideas in metaphysics, logic, and epistemology share with Euclid's mathematical ideas "an independence of the accidents of history" ("Analytic Philosophy and the History of Philosophy," in *Philosophy and Its Past*, ed. Jonathan Rée, Michael Ayers, and Adam Westoby [Brighton: Harvester Press, 1978], 46). I agree with Jonathan Bennett's claim, quoted by Ayers, that "we understand Kant only in proportion as we can say, clearly and in contemporary terms, what his problems were, which of them are still problems and what contribution Kant makes to their solution" (54). Ayers's reply is "On its natural interpretation, this statement [of Bennett's] implies that there can be no such thing as understanding a philosopher in his own terms as something distinct from, and prior to, the difficult achievement of relating his thought to what we ourselves might want to say" (54). I would rejoin, on Bennett's behalf, that there is indeed a sense in which we can understand what a philosopher says in his own terms before relating his thought to ours, but that this minimal sort of understanding is like being able to exchange courtesies in a foreign tongue without being able to translate what one is saying into our native language. Similarly, one might learn to prove Euclid's mathematical theorems in Greek before learning how to translate them into contemporary mathematical jargon. Translation is necessary if "understanding" is to mean something more than engaging in rituals of which we do not see the point, and translating an utterance means fitting it into *our* practices. (See note 7 below.) Successful historical reconstructions can be performed only by people who have some idea of what they themselves think about the issues under discussion, even if only that they are pseudo-issues. Attempts at historical reconstruction that are selfless in this respect (e.g., Wolfson's book on Spinoza) are not so much reconstructions as assemblages of raw material for such reconstructions. So when Ayers says, "Instead of holding Locke's terminology up against that of our own theories, we should try to understand his purposes in relating thought and sensation as he does" (61), I would urge that we cannot do much of the latter until we have done quite a bit of the former. If you do not believe that there are such mental faculties as "thought" and "sensation" (as many of us Post-Wittgensteinian philosophers of mind do not), you are going to have to spend some time figuring out acceptable equivalents to Locke's terms before reading on to see how he uses them – the same sort of thing we atheists have to do when reading works of moral theology. In general, I think that Ayers overdoes the opposition between "our terms" and "his terms" when he suggests that one can do historical reconstruction first and leave rational reconstruction for later. The two genres can never be *that* independent, because you will not know much about what the dead meant before figuring out how much truth they knew. These two topics should be seen as moments in a continuing movement around the hermeneutic circle, a circle one has to have gone round a good many times before one can begin to do *either* sort of reconstruction.

rational reconstructions are to be viewed as "making clear what the dead really said" and the equally verbal one of whether rational reconstructors are "really" doing *history*. Nothing turns on the answer to either question. It is natural to describe Columbus as discovering America rather than Cathay and not knowing that he had done so. It is almost equally natural to describe Aristotle as unwittingly describing the effects of gravity rather than of natural downward motion. It is slightly more strained, but just a further step along the same line, to describe Plato as having unconsciously believed that all words were names (or whatever other premise modern semantically minded commentators find handy in reconstructing his arguments). It is fairly clear that in Skinner's sense of "mean" Plato meant nothing like this. When we anachronistically say that he "really" held such doctrines we mean that, in an imagined argument with present-day philosophers about whether he should have held certain other views, he would have been driven back on a premise he never formulated, dealing with a topic he never considered – a premise that may have to be suggested to him by a friendly rational reconstructor.

Historical reconstructions of what unreeducated dead thinkers would have said to their contemporaries – reconstructions that abide by Skinner's maxim – are, ideally, reconstructions on which all historians can agree. If the question is what Locke would be likely to have said to a Hobbes who had lived and retained his faculties for a few more decades, there is no reason why historians should not arrive at a consensus, a consensus that might be confirmed by the discovery of a manuscript of Locke's in which he imagines a conversation between himself and Hobbes. Rational reconstructions, on the other hand, are not likely to converge, and there is no reason why they should. Somebody who thinks that the question of whether all words are names, or some other semantical thesis, is the sort of question that is decisive for one's views about a lot of other topics will have a quite different imaginary conversation with Plato than somebody who thinks that philosophy of language is a passing fad, irrelevant to the real issues that divide Plato from his great modern antagonists (Whitehead, Heidegger, or Popper, for example). The Fregean, the Kripkean, the Popperian, the Whiteheadian, and the Heideggerian will each reeducate Plato in a different way before starting to argue with him.

If we picture discussion of great dead philosophers as alternating between historical reconstruction, which depends on obeying Skinner's maxim, and rational reconstruction, which depends on ignoring it, there need be no conflict between the two. When we respect Skinner's maxim we shall give an account of the dead thinker "in his own terms," ignoring the fact that we should think ill of anyone who still used those terms today. When we ignore Skinner's maxim, we give an account "in our terms," ignoring the fact that the dead thinker, in his linguistic habits as he lived, would have repudiated these terms as foreign to his interests and intentions. The contrast between these two tasks, however, should not be phrased as that between finding out what the dead thinker meant and finding out whether what he said was true. Finding out what someone meant is a matter of finding out how his utterance fits into his general pattern of linguistic and other behavior – roughly, finding out what he would have said in reply to questions about what he said previously. So "what he meant" is different depending upon who is asking such questions. More generally, "what is meant" is different depending upon how large a range of actual and possible behavior one envisages. People often say, quite reasonably, that they found out what they meant only by listening to what they said later on – when they heard themselves reacting to the consequences of their original utterance. It is perfectly reasonable to describe Locke as finding out what he really meant, what he was really getting at, in the *Second Treatise* only after conversations in heaven with, successively, Jefferson, Marx, and Rawls. It is also perfectly reasonable to set aside the question of what an ideal and immortal Locke would have decided that he meant. We do the latter if we are interested in the differences between what it was like to be a political thinker in Locke's England and in our twentieth-century transatlantic culture.

We can, of course, restrict the term "meaning" to what we are after in the latter, Skinnerian enterprise rather than using it in a way that permits there to be as many meanings of a text as there are dialectical contexts in which it can be placed. If we wish to so restrict it, we can adopt E. D. Hirsch's distinction between "meaning" and "significance" and confine the former term to what accords with the author's intentions around the time of composition, using "significance" for the place of the text in some other context.[6] But nothing hangs on this, unless we choose to insist that it is the task of the "historian" to discover "meaning" and (in the case of philosophical texts) of "the philosopher" to inquire into "significance" and eventually into truth. What does matter is making clear that grasping the meaning of an assertion is a matter of placing that assertion in a context – not of digging a little nugget of sense out of the mind of the asserter. Whether we privilege the

---

6 For this distinction, see E. D. Hirsch, Jr., *The Aims of Interpretation* (Chicago: University of Chicago Press, 1976), 2–10. I would disagree with Hirsch's Ayers-like claim that we cannot start discovering significance unless we first discover meaning, for the same Davidsonian reasons as I disagreed with Ayers in the preceding note.

context that consists of what the asserter was thinking about around the time she made the assertion depends upon what we want to get out of thinking about the assertion. If we want, as Skinner says, "self-awareness," then we need to avoid anachronism as much as possible. If we want self-justification through conversation with the dead thinkers about our current problems, then we are free to indulge in as much of it as we like, as long as we realize that we are doing so.

What, then, of finding out whether what the dead thinker said was true? Just as determining meaning is a matter of placing an assertion in a context of actual and possible behavior, so determining truth is a matter of placing it in the context of assertions that we ourselves should be willing to make. Since what counts for us as an intelligible pattern of behavior is a function of what we believe to be true, truth and meaning are not to be ascertained independently of one another. There will be as many rational reconstructions that purport to find significant truths, or pregnant and important false-hoods, in the work of a great dead philosopher as there are importantly different contexts in which his works can be placed. To repeat my initial point, the appearance of difference between the history of science and the history of philosophy is little more than a reflection of the uninteresting fact that some of these differing contexts represent the differing opinions of members of the same profession. That is why we find more disagreement about how many truths are to be found in the writings of Aristotle among historians of philosophy than among historians of biology. The resolution of these debates is a "philosophical" rather than a "historical" question. If similar discord obtained among historians of biology, then its resolution would be a "biological" rather than a "historical" matter.

Geistesgeschichte as Canon Formation

So far I have been suggesting that the history of philosophy differs only incidentally from the history of one of the natural sciences. In both we have a

7 See Donald Davidson's articles in his *Inquiries into Truth and Interpretation* (Oxford: Clarendon Press, 1984) for a defense of my claim in the preceding notes that we cannot find out what somebody means before finding out how his linguistic and other practices resemble and differ from ours, or independently of the charitable assumption that *most* of his beliefs are true. Ayers's assumption that historical reconstruction is naturally prior to rational reconstruction, and Hirsch's that discovery of meaning is naturally prior to discovery of significance, both seem to me to rest on an insufficiently holistic account of interpretation – an account I have defended elsewhere (e.g., in "Pragmatism, Davidson and Truth," in *Truth and Interpretation: Perspectives on the Philosophy of Donald Davidson*, ed. Ernest LePore [Oxford: Blackwell, 1986], 333–68).

contrast between contextualist accounts that block off later developments from sight and "Whiggish" accounts that draw on our own better knowledge. The only difference I have mentioned is that, because philosophy is more controversial than biology, anachronistic reconstructions of great dead philosophers are more various than those of great dead biologists. But my discussion so far has ignored the problem of how one picks out who counts as a great dead *philosopher*, as opposed to a great dead something else. So it has ignored the problem of how one picks out the history of *philosophy* from the history of "thought" or "culture." The latter sort of problem does not arise for the history of biology, because it is coextensive with the history of writing about plants and animals. The problem arises only in a relatively trivial form for the history of chemistry, because nobody much cares whether we call Paracelsus a chemist, an alchemist, or both. Questions about whether Pliny was a biologist in the same sense as Mendel, or about whether Aristotle's *De Generatione et Corruptione* counts as chemistry, do not inspire profound passions. This is because we have, in these areas, clear stories of progress to tell. It does not make much difference at what point we start telling the story – at what point we see a "discipline" emerging out of a chaos of speculation.

It does however, make a difference when we come to the history of philosophy. This is because the "history of philosophy" covers a third genre, in addition to the two I have discussed so far. Besides such Skinnerian historical reconstructions as John Dunn's of Locke or J. B. Schneewind's of Sidgwick, and the sort of rational reconstructions offered by Bennett of the British Empiricists or Strawson of Kant, there are the big sweeping *geistesgeschichtlich* stories – the genre of which Hegel is paradigmatic. This genre is represented in our time by, for example, Heidegger, Reichenbach, Foucault, Blumenberg, and MacIntyre.[8] It aims at self-justification in the same

8 I am thinking of Heidegger's "Sketches for a History of Being," in *The End of Philosophy*, trans. Joan Stambaugh (New York: Harper & Row, 1973), and of the way in which his later works fill out these sketches. I have discussed Reichenbach's *The Rise of Scientific Philosophy* (the most comprehensive version of the positivist story of how philosophy gradually emerged from prejudice and confusion) in my *Consequences of Pragmatism* (Minneapolis: University of Minnesota Press, 1982), 211–14. Foucault's *The Order of Things* is discussed as an example of *Geistesgeschichte* in the section of this essay titled "Intellectual History." My references to Blumenberg and to MacIntyre are to *The Legitimacy of the Modern Age* and *After Virtue*, respectively. When I say that these are works of self-justification, I of course do not mean that they justify the present state of things, but rather that they justify the author's attitude toward the present state of things. Heidegger's, Foucault's, and MacIntyre's downbeat stories condemn present practices but justify the adoption of their authors' views toward those practices, thereby justifying their selection of what counts as a pressing philosophical issue – the same function as is performed by Hegel's, Reichenbach's, and Blumenberg's upbeat stories.

way as does rational reconstruction, but on a different scale. Rational reconstructions typically aim at saying that the great dead philosopher had some excellent ideas, but unfortunately couldn't get them straight because of "the limitations of his time." They usually confine themselves to a relatively small portion of the philosopher's work – for example, Kant on the relation between appearance and reality, or Leibniz on modality, or Aristotle on the notions of essence, existence, and prediction. They are written in the light of some recent work in philosophy that can reasonably be said to be "about the same questions" as the great dead philosopher was discussing. They are designed to show that the answers he gave to these questions, though plausible and exciting, need restatement or purification – or, perhaps, the kind of precise refutation that further work in the field has recently made possible. In contrast, *Geistesgeschichte* works at the level of problematics rather than of solutions to problems. It spends more of its time asking, "Why should anyone have made the question of ____ central to his thought?" or "Why did anyone take the problem of ____ seriously?" than on asking in what respect the great dead philosopher's answer or solution accords with that of contemporary philosophers. It typically describes the philosopher in terms of his entire work rather than in terms of his most celebrated arguments (e.g., Kant as the author of all three *Critiques,* the enthusiast for the French Revolution, the forerunner of Schleiermacher's theology, etc., rather than Kant as the author of the "Transcendental Analytic"). It wants to justify the historian and his friends in having the sort of philosophical concerns they have – in taking philosophy to be what they take it to be – rather than in giving the particular solutions to philosophical problems they give. It wants to give plausibility to a certain image of philosophy rather than to give plausibility to a particular solution of a given philosophical problem by pointing out how a great dead philosopher anticipated, or interestingly failed to anticipate, this solution.

The existence of this third, *geistesgeschichtlich* sort of history of philosophy is an additional reason for the prima facie difference between history of science and history of philosophy. Historians of science feel no need to justify our physicists' concern with elementary particles or our biologists' with DNA. If you can synthesize steroids, you do not require historical legitimation. But philosophers do need to justify their concern with semantics or perception or the unity of subject and object or the enlargement of human freedom or whatever the philosopher who is telling the big sweeping story is in fact concerned with. The question of which problems are "the problems of philosophy," which questions are *philosophical* questions, are the questions to which *geistesgeschichtlich* histories of philosophy are principally devoted. By contrast, histories of biology or chemistry can dismiss such questions as verbal. They can simply take the currently uncontroversial portions of the discipline in question as that to which history leads up. The *terminus ad quem* of history-of-science-as-story-of-progress is not in dispute.

I said earlier that one reason for the apparent difference between the history of philosophy and the history of science stemmed from the fact that philosophers who differ about, say, the existence of God are nevertheless professional colleagues. The second reason for the apparent difference is that those who differ about whether the existence of God is an important or interesting or "real" question are also professional colleagues. The academic discipline called "philosophy" encompasses not only different answers to philosophical questions but total disagreement on what questions are *philosophical.* Rational reconstructions and *geistesgeschichtlich* reinterpretations are, from this point of view, different only in degree – degree of disagreement with the great dead philosopher who is being reconstructed or reinterpreted. If one disagrees with him mainly about solutions to problems rather than about which problems need discussion, one will think of oneself as reconstructing him (as, e.g., Ayer reconstructed Berkeley). If one thinks of oneself as showing that one need not think about what he tried to think about (as in, e.g., Ayer's dismissive interpretation of Heidegger, or Heidegger's dismissive description of Kierkegaard as a "religious writer" rather than a "thinker"), then one will think of oneself as explaining why he should not count as a fellow-philosopher. One will redefine "philosophy" so as to read him out of the canon.

Canon formation is not an issue for the history of science. There is no need to affiliate one's own scientific activity to that of a great dead scientist in order to make it look more respectable or to disparage some purportedly distinguished predecessor as a pseudo-scientist in order to justify one's own concerns. Canon formation is important in the history of philosophy because "philosophy" has an important honorific use in addition to its descriptive uses. Used descriptively, the term "philosophical question" can mean a question that is currently being debated by some contemporary "school," or it can mean a question debated by all or many of those historical figures customarily catalogued as "philosophers." Used honorifically, however, it means questions that *ought* to be debated – that are so general and so important that they *should* have been on the minds of thinkers of all places and times, whether these thinkers managed to formulate these questions explicitly or not.[9]

<hr/>

9 The need for an honorific use of "philosophy," for a canon, and for self-justification seems to me to explain what John Dunn calls "the weird tendency of much writing, in the history

This honorific use of "philosophical question" is, in theory, irrelevant to rational reconstructions. A contemporary philosopher who wants to argue with Descartes about mind–body dualism or with Kant about the appearance–reality distinction or with Aristotle about meaning and reference need not, and usually does not, claim that these topics are inescapable whenever human beings reflect upon their condition and their fate. The rational reconstructor typically confines himself to saying that these are topics that have had an interesting career and on which interesting work is still being done – as an historian of science might say the same about the taxonomy of birds or the varieties of insanity. For purposes of rational reconstruction and ensuing argument, there is no need to worry about whether a topic is "inescapable." For *Geistesgeschichte*, the sort of intellectual history that has a moral, there is such a need. For the moral to be drawn is that we have, or have not, been on the right track in raising the philosophical questions we have recently been raising and that the *Geisteshistoriker* is justified in adopting a certain problematic. The rational reconstructor, by contrast, feels no more need to ask whether philosophy is on the right track than the historian of science needs to ask whether contemporary biochemistry is in good shape.

The honorific use of "philosophy" is also irrelevant, in theory, to historical reconstruction. If the *Geistesgeschichte* of the day reads Locke or Kierkegaard out of the philosophical canon, contextualist historians can continue imperturbably describing what it was like to be Locke or Kierkegaard. From the point of view of contextualist history, there is no need for great big stories, sweeping over many centuries, in which to embed an account of what it was like to be concerned with politics in seventeenth-century England or with religion in nineteenth-century Denmark. For such historians, the question of whether their chosen figure was "really" a major philosopher, a minor philosopher, a politician, a theologian, or a belletrist, is as irrelevant as the taxonomic activities of the American Ornithological Union are to the field naturalist taking notes on the mating behavior of a flicker, one that the AOU

---

of political thought especially, to be made up of what propositions in what great books remind the author of what propositions in what other great books" (*Political Obligation in Its Historical Context* [Cambridge University Press, 1980], 15). This tendency is the mark of most *Geistesgeschichte* and does not seem to me weird. It is the tendency both historians and philosophers indulge in when they doff their robes and converse about what they have found useful in their favorite great books The nice thing about *Geistesgeschichte*, in my view – the thing that makes it indispensable – is that it meets needs that neither unphilosophical history nor unhistorical philosophy is likely to fulfill. (See the section titled "Intellectual History" below for discussion of the suggestion that we repress these needs.)

has just reclassified behind his back. One might, in one's philosophical capacity, share the Anglo-Saxon belief that no philosophical progress occurred between Kant and Frege and still, as a historian, delight in recapturing the concerns of Schiller and Schelling.

But this theoretical independence of both historical and rational reconstructions from canon formation is rarely lived up to in practice. Rational reconstructors do not really want to bother reconstructing, and arguing with, minor philosophers. Historical reconstructors would like to reconstruct people who were "significant" in the development of something – if not philosophy, then perhaps "European thought" or "the modern." Work in both reconstructive genres is always done with one eye out for the most recent work in canon formation, and that is the prerogative of the *Geisteshistoriker*. For he is the person who wields terms like "philosophy" and "philosophical question" in their honorific senses. He is thus the person who decides what is worth thinking about – which questions are matters of the "contingent arrangements" of our day and which are the ones that tie us together with our ancestors. As the person who decides who was "getting at" what was really important and who was merely distracted by the epiphenomena of his times, he plays the role that, in the ancient world, was played by the sage. One difference between that world and ours is that the high culture of modern times has become aware, as the ancient world was not, that we may not know which questions are the really important ones. We fear that we may still be working with philosophical vocabularies that are to "the real" problems as, say, Aristotle's vocabulary was to "the real" subject matter of astrophysics. This sense that one's choice of vocabulary matters at least as much as one's answers to the questions posed within a given vocabulary has caused the *Geisteshistoriker* to displace the philosopher (or, as with Hegel, Nietzsche, and Heidegger, has caused "philosophy" to be used as the name of a certain particularly abstract and freewheeling kind of intellectual history).

This last point can be put more simply by saying that nowadays nobody is sure that the descriptive sense of "philosophical question" has anything much to do with the honorific sense of this term. Nobody is quite sure whether the issues discussed by contemporary philosophy professors (of any school) are issues that are "necessary" or merely part of our "contingent arrangements." Furthermore, nobody is sure whether the issues discussed by all or most of the canon of great dead philosophers offered by books called *The History of Western Philosophy* – for example, universals, mind and body, free will, appearance and reality, fact and value – are *important* issues. Occasionally, both inside and outside of philosophy, the suspicion is voiced that some or all of these are "merely philosophical" – a term used in the same pejorative way as a chemist uses "alchemical," or a Marxist "superstructural," or an aristocrat "middle class." The self-awareness that historical reconstructions have given us is the awareness that some people who were our intellectual and moral equals were not interested in questions that seem to us inescapable and profound. Because such historical reconstructions are a source of doubt about whether philosophy (in either of its descriptive senses) is important, the *Geisteshistoriker* now puts the philosopher in his place, rather than the converse. He does this by assembling a cast of historical characters and a dramatic narrative that show how we have come to ask the questions we now think inescapable and profound. Where these characters left writings behind, those writings then form a canon, a reading list that one must have gone through in order to justify being what one is.

I can sum up what I have been saying about the third genre of historiography of philosophy by saying that it is the genre that takes responsibility for identifying which writers are "the great dead philosophers." In this role, it is parasitic upon, and synthesizes, the first two genres – historical reconstructions and reconstructions. Unlike rational reconstructions, and unlike the history of science, it has to worry about anachronism, for it cannot regard the question of who counts as a philosopher as settled by the practices of those presently so described. Unlike historical reconstructions, however, it cannot stay within the vocabulary used by a past figure. It has to "place" that vocabulary in a series of vocabularies and estimate its importance by placing it in a narrative that traces changes in vocabulary. It is self-justificatory in the way that rational reconstruction is, but it is moved by the same hope for greater self-awareness that leads people to engage in historical reconstructions. For *Geistesgeschichte* wants to keep us aware of the fact that we are still en route – that the dramatic narrative it offers us is to be continued by our descendants. When it is fully self-conscious it wonders whether *all* the issues discussed so far may not have been part of the "contingent arrangements" of earlier times. It insists on the point that even if some of them really *were* necessary and inescapable, we have no certainty about which these were.

Doxography

The three genres I have described so far bear little relation to the genre that comes first to mind when the term "history of philosophy" is used. This genre, my fourth, is the most familiar and most dubious. I shall call it "doxography." This is exemplified by books that start from Thales or Descartes and wind up with some figure roughly contemporary with the author, ticking off what various figures traditionally called "philosophers" had to say about problems traditionally called "philosophical." It is this genre that inspires boredom and despair. It is the one to which Gilbert Ryle referred when he offhandedly said, as an excuse for his own risky rational reconstructions of Plato and others, that the existence of "our standard histories of philosophy" was "calamity itself, and not the mere risk of it."[10] I suspect that most of his readers heartily agreed. Even the most honest and conscientious and exhaustive books called *A History of Philosophy* – especially these, indeed – seem to decorticate the thinkers they discuss. It is this calamity to which proponents of historical reconstruction respond by insisting on the need for spelling out the contexts in which the texts were written, and to which proponents of rational reconstruction respond by insisting that we look at the great dead philosophers in the light of "the best work now being done on the problems they discussed." Both are attempts to revitalize figures who have unintentionally been mummified.

The explanation of the calamity, I think, is that most historians of philosophy who try to tell "the story of philosophy from the pre-Socratics to our own day" know in advance what most of their chapter headings are going to be. Indeed, they know their publishers would not accept their manuscripts if a substantial number of the expected headings were missing. They work, typically, with a canon that made sense in terms of nineteenth-century neo-Kantian notions of "the central problems of philosophy," notions few modern readers take seriously. This has resulted in desperate attempts to make Leibniz and Hegel, Mill and Nietzsche, Descartes and Carnap talk about some common topics, whether the historian or his readers have any interest in those topics or not.

In the sense in which I shall use the term, doxography is the attempt to impose a problematic on a canon drawn up without reference to that problematic or, conversely, to impose a canon on a problematic constructed without reference to that canon. Diogenes Laertius gave doxography a bad name by insisting on answering the question "What did X think the good was?" for every X in an antecedently formulated canon. Nineteenth-century historians gave it a worse one by insisting on answering the question "What did X think the nature of knowledge was?" for every X in another such canon. Analytic philosophers are in a fair way to worsening the situation by insisting on an answer to the question "What was X's theory of meaning?" as are Heideggerians by insisting on an answer to "What did X think Being was?" Such awkward attempts to make a new question fit an old canon remind us,

10 Gilbert Ryle, *Collected Papers,* vol. 1 (London: Hutchison, 1971), x.

however, that new doxographies usually started off as fresh, brave, revisionist attempts to dispel the dullness of the previous doxographic tradition, attempts inspired by the conviction that the true problematic of philosophy had finally been discovered. So the real trouble with doxography is that it is a *halfhearted* attempt to tell a new story of intellectual progress by describing all texts in the light of recent discoveries. It is halfhearted because it lacks the courage to readjust the canon to suit the new discoveries.

The main reason for this recurrent halfheartedness is the idea that "philosophy" is the name of a natural kind – the name of a discipline that, in all ages and places, has managed to dig down to the same deep, fundamental questions. So once somebody has somehow been identified as a "great philosopher" (as opposed to a great poet, scientist, theologian, political theorist, or whatever), he has to be described as studying those questions.[11] Since each new generation of philosophers claims to have discovered what those deep fundamental questions really are, each has to figure out how the great philosopher can be viewed as having been concerned with them. So we get brave new doxographies that look, a few generations further on, just as calamitous as their predecessors.

To get rid of this idea that philosophy is a natural kind, we need more and better contextualist historical reconstructions on the one hand and more self-confident *Geistesgeschichte* on the other. We need to realize that the questions which the "contingent arrangements" of the present time lead us to regard as *the* questions are questions which may be *better* than those our ancestors asked, but need not be the *same*. They are not questions that any reflective human being must necessarily have encountered. We need to see ourselves not as responding to the same stimuli to which our ancestors responded, but as having created new and more interesting stimuli for ourselves. We should justify ourselves by claiming to be asking better questions, not by claiming to give better answers to the permanent "deep, fundamental questions" our ancestors answered badly. We can think of the fundamental questions of philosophy as the ones everybody really ought to have asked, or as the ones everybody would have asked if they could, but not as the ones everybody *did* ask whether they knew it or not. It is one thing to say

---

11 Jonathan Rée is very informative on the development of the idea that there is a common a-historical set of questions for philosophers to answer. In his excellent essay "Philosophy and the History of Philosophy" (in *Philosophy and Its Past*, ed. Rée, Ayers, and Westoby), Rée speaks of Renouvier's conviction that "the so-called history of philosophy was really only the story of individuals opting for different philosophical positions; the positions themselves were always there, eternally available and unchanging" (17). This is the guiding assumption of what I call doxography.

that a great dead philosopher would have been driven to have a view on a certain topic if we had had a chance to talk to him, thus enabling him to see what the fundamental questions of philosophy really were. It is another thing to say that he had an "implicit" view on that topic which we can dig out of what he wrote. What is interesting about him often is that it never crossed his mind that he had to have a view on the topic. This is just the sort of interesting information we get from contextualist historical reconstructions.

My claim that philosophy is not a natural kind can be restated with reference to the popular notion that philosophy deals with "methodological" or "conceptual" metaissues thrown off by the special disciplines or more generally by other areas of culture. Such a claim is plausible if it means that, in every period, there have been questions that arose from the clash between old ideas and new ideas (in the sciences, in art, in politics, etc.) and that these questions are the concern of the more original, dilettantish, and imaginative intellectuals of the day. But it becomes implausible if it means that these questions are always about the same topics – for example the nature of knowledge or reality or truth or meaning or the good or some other abstraction sufficiently fuzzy to blur the differences between historical epochs. One can parody this notion of philosophy by imagining that at the dawn of the study of animals, a distinction became established between "primary biology" and "secondary biology," analogous to Aristotle's distinction between "first philosophy" and "physics." On this conception, the larger, more salient, more impressive and paradigmatic animals were the concern of a special discipline. So theories were developed about the common features of the python, the bear, the lion, the eagle, the ostrich, and the whale. Such theories, formulated with the help of some suitably fuzzy abstractions, were rather clever and interesting. But people kept coming along with other things to be fit into the canon of "primary animals." The giant rat of Sumatra, the giant butterflies of Brazil, and (more controversially) the unicorn had to be taken into account. Criteria for the adequacy of theories in primary biology became less clear as the canon was enlarged. Then came the bones of the moa and the mammoth. Things got still more complicated. Eventually the secondary biologists got so good at producing new forms of life in test tubes that they amused themselves by bringing their gargantuan new creations upstairs and challenging the bewildered primary biologists to make a place for them. Watching the contortions of the primary biologists as they tried to devise theories to accommodate these new canonical items engendered a certain contempt for primary biology as an autonomous discipline.

The analogies I wish to draw are between "primary biology" and "history of philosophy" and between "secondary biology" and "intellectual history." History of philosophy, disconnected from the wider history of the intellectuals, makes some sense if it covers only a century or two – if it is, for example, a story of the steps that led from Descartes to Kant. Hegel's story of the unfolding of Cartesian subjectivity into transcendental philosophy and Gilson's story of the reductio ad absurdum of representationalist theories of knowledge are examples of interesting narratives that can be constructed by ignoring wider contexts. These are just two among many plausible and interesting ways of noting similarities and differences among a dozen salient and impressive figures who span about 175 years (Descartes, Hobbes, Malebranche, Locke, Condillac, Leibniz, Wolff, Berkeley, Hume, and Kant – plus or minus a few names at the historian of philosophy's discretion). But when one tries to tack on Hegel himself at one end of such a story, or Bacon and Ramus at the other, things get rather tendentious. When one tries to tie in Plato and Aristotle, there seem so many ways to do so – depending upon which Platonic dialogue or Aristotelian treatise one takes as "fundamental" – that alternative stories proliferate wildly. Further, Plato and Aristotle are *so* big and impressive that describing them in terms originally developed for use on people like Hobbes and Berkeley begins to seem a little odd. Then there is the problem of whether to treat Augustine, Aquinas, and Ockham as philosophers or as theologians – not to mention the problems raised by Lao-tsu, Shankara, and similar exotic specimens. To make everything worse, all the time that historians of philosophy are wondering how to get all these people in under the old rubrics, mischievous intellectuals keep concocting new intellectual compounds and daring historians of philosophy to refuse to call them "philosophies." Once it becomes necessary to contrive a story that connects all or most of the people previously mentioned with G. E. Moore, Saul Kripke, and Gilles Deleuze, historians of philosophy are about ready to give up.

They *should* give up. We should just stop trying to write books called *A History of Philosophy* that begin with Thales and end with, say, Wittgenstein. Such books are interspersed with desperately factitious excuses for not discussing, for example, Plotinus, Comte, or Kierkegaard. They gallantly attempt to find a few "continuing concerns" that run through all the great philosophers who do get included. But they are continually embarrassed by the failure of even the most silent and unskippable figures to discuss some of those concerns, and by those vast arid stretches in which one or other concern seems to have slipped everybody's mind. (They have to worry, for example, about the absence or the skimpiness of chapters headed "Epistemology in the Sixteenth Century" or "Moral Philosophy in the Twelfth Century" or "Logic in the Eighteenth Century.") It is no wonder that *geistesgeschichtlich* intellectual historians – those who write the great sweeping self-justifying stories – are often contemptuous of the sort of doxography common to Windelband and Russell. Nor is it any wonder that analytic philosophers and Heideggerians should try – each in their separate ways – to find something new for the history of philosophy to be. The attempt to skim the cream off intellectual history by writing a history "of philosophy" is as foredoomed as the attempt of my imaginary "primary biologists" to skim the cream off the animal kingdom. Both attempts assume that certain elementary components of the miscellaneous stuff churning around at the bottom naturally float up to the top.

This cream-skimming picture assumes a contrast between the higher and purer history of something called "philosophy" – the quest for knowledge about permanent and enduring topics by people who specialized in that sort of thing – and "intellectual history" as the chronicle of quaint tergiversations of opinion among people who were, at best, litterateurs or political activists or clergymen. When this picture, and this implicit contrast, are challenged, offense is often taken at the suggestion that philosophy is not the pursuit of knowledge, that it is (as freshmen like to say) "all a matter of opinion." Alternatively, this same offense is expressed by saying that if we discard the traditional contrast we shall have reduced philosophy to "rhetoric" (as opposed to "logic") or "persuasion" (as opposed to "argument") or something else low and literary rather than high and scientific. Since the self-image of philosophy as a professional discipline still depends upon its quasi-scientific character, criticism of the assumption behind the cream-skimming picture is taken as a challenge to philosophy itself as a professional activity, not merely to one branch of it called "history of philosophy."

One can mitigate the offense while still avoiding the cream-skimming picture by adopting a sociological view of the distinction between knowledge and opinion. On this view, to say that something is a matter of opinion is just to say that deviance from the current consensus on that topic is compatible with membership in some relevant community. To say that it is knowledge is to say that deviance is incompatible. For example, in the United States the choice of whom to vote for is "a matter of opinion," but we *know* that the press should be free from government censorship. Good-thinking Russians know that such censorship is necessary, but they regard the question of whether to send dissidents to labor camps or asylums as a matter of opinion. These two communities do not accept as members those who fail to claim as knowledge what is generally so claimed. Analogously, to say that the existence of real essences, or of God, is a "matter of opinion" within philosophy departments is to say that people who differ on this point can still get grants from, or be employed by, the same institutions, can award degrees to the same students, and so on. By contrast, those who share Ptolemy's opinions on the planets or William Jennings Bryan's on the origin of species are excluded from respectable astronomy and biology departments, for membership there requires that one know that these opinions are false. So anybody can legitimize his use of the term "philosophical knowledge" simply by pointing to a self-conscious community of philosophers, admission to which requires agreement on certain points (e.g., that there are, or are not, real essences or inalienable human rights or God). Within that community, we shall have agreement on known premises, and the pursuit of further knowledge, in just the sense in which we find such premises and such a pursuit in biology and astronomy departments.

The existence of such a community is, however, entirely irrelevant to the question of whether anything interesting links that community to Aristotle, Plotinus, Descartes, Kant, Moore, Kripke, or Deleuze. Such communities should be at liberty to seek out their own intellectual ancestors, without reference to a previously established canon of great dead philosophers. They should also be free to claim to have no ancestors at all. They should feel free to pick out whatever bits of the past they like and call those the "history of philosophy," without reference to anything anybody has previously called "philosophy," or to ignore the past entirely. Anybody who is willing to give up the attempt to find common interests that unite her with all the other members of, say, the American Philosophical Association or the Mind Association or the Deutsche Philosophische Gesellschaft (and one would have to be a bit mad to be unwilling to give up *that* attempt) is thus free to give up the attempt to write *A History of Philosophy* with the usual chapter headings. She is free to create a new canon, as long as she respects the right of others to create alternative canons. We should welcome people who, like Reichenbach, wave Hegel aside. We should encourage people who are tempted to dismiss Aristotle as a biologist who got out of his depth, or Berkeley as an eccentric bishop, or Frege as an original logician with unjustified epistemological pretensions, or Moore as a charming amateur who never quite understood what the professionals were doing. They should be urged to try it, and to see what sort of historical story they can tell when these people are left out and some unfamiliar people are brought in. It is only with the aid of such experimental alterations of the canon that doxography can be avoided. It is just such alterations that *Geistesgeschichte* makes possible and that doxography discourages.

Intellectual History

So far I have distinguished four genres and suggested that one of them be treated with a certain contempt. The remaining three are indispensable and do not compete with one another. Rational reconstructions are necessary to help us present-day philosophers think through our problems. Historical reconstructions are needed to remind us that these problems are historical products, by demonstrating that they were invisible to our ancestors. *Geistesgeschichte* is needed to justify our belief that we are better off than those ancestors by virtue of having become aware of those problems. Any given book in the history of philosophy will, of course, be a mixture of these three genres. But usually one or another motive dominates, since there are three distinct tasks to be performed. The distinctness of these tasks is important and not to be broken down. It is precisely the tension between the brisk Whiggery of the rational reconstructors and the mediated and ironic empathy of the contextualists – between the need to get on with the task at hand and the need to see everything, including that task, as one more contingent arrangement – that produces the need for *Geistesgeschichte,* for the self-justification this third genre provides. Each such justification, however, ensures the eventual appearance of a new set of complacent doxographies, disgust with which will inspire new rational reconstructions, under the aegis of new philosophical problematics that will have arisen in the meantime. These three genres thus form a nice example of the standard Hegelian dialectical triad.

I should like to use the term "intellectual history" for a much richer and more diffuse genre – one that falls outside this triad. In my sense, intellectual history consists of descriptions of what the intellectuals were up to at a given time and of their interaction with the rest of society – descriptions that, for the most part, bracket the question of what activities which intellectuals were conducting. Intellectual history can ignore certain problems that must be settled in order to write the history of a discipline – questions about which people count as scientists, which as poets, which as philosophers, and so on. Descriptions of the sort I have in mind may occur in treatises called something like *Intellectual Life in Fifteenth-Century Bologna,* but they may also occur in the odd chapter or paragraph of political or social or economic or diplomatic histories, or indeed in the odd chapter or paragraph of histories of philosophy (of any of the four genres distinguished in this essay). Such treatises, chapters, and paragraphs produce, when read and pondered by someone interested in a certain spatiotemporal region, a sense of what it was like to be an intellectual in that region – what sort of books one read, what sorts of things one had to worry about, what choices one had of vocabularies, hopes, friends, enemies, and careers.

To have a sense of what it was to be a young and intellectually curious person in such a region one has to know a lot of social, political, and economic history as well as a lot of disciplinary history. A book like E. P. Thompson's *Making of the English Working Class* tells one a lot about the chances and audiences open to Paine and Cobbett as well as about wages, the living conditions of miners and weavers, and the tactics of politicians.[12] A book like Norman Fiering's *Moral Philosophy at Seventeenth-Century Harvard* tells one a lot about what kind of intellectual it was possible to be at Harvard in that period.[13] Fiering's book flows together with passages in biographies of Harvard presidents and Massachusetts governors to produce a sense of how these possibilities changed. Passages in Thompson's flow together with passages in biographies of Bentham and Melbourne to show how other possibilities changed. The totality of such books and passages comes together in the minds of those who read them in such a way as to produce a sense of the differences among the options open to an intellectual at different times and places.

I should want to include under "intellectual history" books about all those enormously influential people who do not get into the canon of great dead philosophers, but who are often called philosophers either because they held a chair so described or for lack of any better idea – people like Erigena, Bruno, Ramus, Mersenne, Wolff, Diderot, Cousin, Schopenhauer, Hamilton, McCosh, Bergson, and Austin. Discussion of these "minor figures" often coalesces with thick descriptions of institutional arrangements and disciplinary matrices, since part of the historical problem they pose is to explain why these non-great philosophers or quasi-philosophers should have been taken so much more seriously than the certifiably great philosophers of their day. Then there are the books about the thought and influence of people who are not usually called philosophers but are at least borderline cases of the species. These are people who in fact did the jobs that philosophers are popularly supposed to do – impelling social reform, supplying new vocabularies for moral deliberation, deflecting the course of scientific and literary disciplines into new channels. They include, for example, Paracelsus, Montaigne, Grotius, Bayle, Lessing, Paine, Coleridge,

---

12 E. P. Thompson, *The Making of the English Working Class* (Harmondsworth: Penguin Books, 1963).

13 Norman Fiering, *Moral Philosophy at Seventeenth-Century Harvard: A Discipline in Transition* (Chapel Hill: University of North Carolina Press, 1981).

Alexander von Humboldt, Emerson, T. H. Huxley, Matthew Arnold, Weber, Freud, Franz Boas, Walter Lippmann, D. H. Lawrence, and T. S. Kuhn – not to mention all those unfamiliar people (e.g., the authors of influential treatises on the philosophical foundations of *Polizeiwissenschaft*) who turn up in the footnotes to Foucault's books. If one wants to understand what it was to be a scholar in sixteenth-century Germany or a political thinker in the United States in the eighteenth century or a scientist in late-nineteenth-century France or a journalist in early-twentieth-century Britain – if one wants to know what sort of issues and temptations and dilemmas confronted a young person who wanted to become part of the high culture of those times and places – these are the sort of people one has to know about. If one knows enough about enough of them, one can tell a detailed and convincing story of the conversation of Europe, a story that may mention Descartes, Hume, Kant, and Hegel only in passing.

Once we drop below the skipping-from-peak-to-peak level of *Geistesgeschichte* to the nitty-gritty of intellectual history, the distinctions between great and non-great dead philosophers, between clear and borderline cases of "philosophy," and between philosophy, literature, politics, religion, and social science are of less and less importance. The question of whether Weber was a sociologist or a philosopher, Arnold a literary critic or a philosopher, Freud a psychologist or a philosopher, Lippmann a philosopher or a journalist, like the question of whether we can include Francis Bacon as a philosopher if we exclude Robert Fludd, are obviously matters to be settled after we have written our intellectual history rather than before. Interesting filiations that connect these borderline cases with clearer cases of "philosophy" will or will not appear, and on the basis of such filiations we shall adjust our taxonomies. Furthermore, new paradigm cases of philosophy produce new termini for such filiations. New accounts of intellectual history interact with contemporary developments to readjust continually the list of "philosophers," and eventually these readjustments produce new canons of great dead philosophers. Like the history of anything else, history of philosophy is written by the victors. Victors get to choose their ancestors, in the sense that they decide which among their all too various ancestors to mention, write biographies of, and commend to their descendants.

As long as "philosophy" has an honorific use, it will matter which figures count as "philosophers." So if things go well, we can expect continual revisions of the philosophical canon in order to bring it into line with the present needs of high culture. If they go badly, we can expect the stubborn perpetuation of a canon – one that will look quainter and more factitious as the decades pass. On the picture I wish to present, intellectual history is the raw material for the historiography of philosophy – or, to vary the metaphor, the ground out of which histories of philosophy grow. The Hegelian triad I have sketched becomes possible only once we have, with an eye both to contemporary needs and to the recent writings of revisionist intellectual historians, formulated a philosophical canon. Doxography, on the other hand, as the genre that pretends to find a continuous streak of philosophical ore running through all the space-time chunks that the intellectual historians describe, is relatively independent of current developments in intellectual history. Its roots are in the past – in the forgotten combination of transcended cultural needs and outdated intellectual history that produced the canon it enshrines.

This role as inspiration for the reformulation of the (philosophical and other) canons is, however, not the only use for intellectual history. Another is to play the same dialectical role with respect to *Geistesgeschichte* as historical reconstruction plays with respect to rational reconstruction. I have said that historical reconstructions remind us of all those quaint little controversies the big-name philosophers worried about, the ones that distracted them from the "real" and "enduring" problems we moderns have managed to get in clearer focus. By so reminding us, they induce a healthy skepticism about whether we are all that clear and whether our problems are all that real. Analogously, Ong on Ramus, Yates on Lull, Fiering on Mather, Wartofsky on Feuerbach, and so on remind us that the great dead philosophers whom we spend our time reconstructing were less influential – less central to the conversation of their own and several intervening generations – than a lot of people we have never thought about. They also make us see the people in our current canon as less original, less distinctive than they had seemed before. They come to look like specimens reiterating an extinct type rather than mountain peaks. So intellectual history works to keep *Geistesgeschichte* honest, just as historical reconstruction operates to keep rational reconstructions honest.

Honesty here consists in keeping in mind the possibility that our self-justifying conversation is with creatures of our own fantasy rather than with historical personages, even ideally reeducated historical personages. Such a possibility needs to be acknowledged by those setting out to write *Geistesgeschichte*, because they need to worry about whether their own chapter headings may have been too much influenced by those of the doxographies. In particular, when a professor of philosophy sets out on such a self-justificatory project, he usually does so only after decades of giving courses on various great dead philosophers – those whose names appear in the syllabus for examinations to be taken by his students, a syllabus he is likely to have inherited rather than composed. It is natural for him to write *Geistes-geschichte* by stringing a lot of those notes together, thus skipping between the same old peaks, passing over in silence the philosophical flatlands of, for example, the third and fifteenth centuries. This sort of thing leads to such extreme cases as Heidegger's attempt to write "the history of Being" by commenting upon texts mentioned in Ph.D. examinations in philosophy in German universities early in this century. In the aftermath of being enthralled by the drama Heidegger stages, one may begin to find it suspicious that Being stuck so closely to the syllabus.

Heidegger's followers changed the syllabus in order to make everything lead up to Nietzsche and Heidegger, just as Russell's changed the syllabus to make it lead up to Frege and Russell. *Geistesgeschichte* can change canons in a way that doxography does not. But such partial canon revision highlights the fact that Nietzsche may seem that important only to people overly impressed by Kantian ethics, just as Frege may seem that important only to people overly impressed by Kantian epistemology. It still leaves us bemused by the question of how Kant ever got to be that important in the first place. We tend to explain to our students that their own philosophical thinking must go through Kant rather than around him, but it is not clear that we mean more than that they will not understand our own books if they have not read Kant's. When we draw back from the philosophical canon in the way made possible by reading the detailed and thickly interwoven stories found in intellectual history, we can ask whether it is all that important for students to understand what we contemporary philosophers are doing. That is the sort of honest self-doubt that gives people the motive and the courage to write *radically* innovative *Geistesgeschichte* – the kind exemplified by Foucault's *The Order of Things*, with its famous reference to "the figure we call Hume."

Foucauldians may object to my description of that book as *Geistes-geschichte*, but it is important for my argument to group it together with, for example, Hegel's and Blumenberg's histories. For all of Foucault's insistence on materiality and contingency, his conscious opposition to the *geistlich* and dialectical character of Hegel's story, there are a lot of resemblances between that story and his own. Both help to answer the question doxography eschews: in what ways are we better and in what ways worse off than this or that set of predecessors? Both assign us a place in an epic, the epic of modern Europe, though in Foucault's case it is an epic over which no *Geschick* presides. Foucault's, like Hegel's, is a story with a moral; it is true that both Foucault and his readers have trouble formulating that moral, but we should remember that the same was true for Hegel and his readers. Foucault ties in "the figure we call Hume" with what the doctors and the police were up to at the time, just as Hegel tied in various philosophers with what the priests and the tyrants of their times were doing. Hegel's subsumption of the material under the spiritual attempts the same task as Foucault's account of truth in terms of power. Both try to convince us intellectuals of something we badly need to believe – that the high culture of a given period is not just froth, but rather an expression of something that goes all the way down.

I insist on this point because the example of Foucault, taken together with the suspicion I have voiced about philosophy as a natural kind, and about the cream-skimming model of the relation between intellectual history and the history of philosophy, might lead one to suggest that if doxography goes it should take *Geistesgeschichte* with it. Many admirers of Foucault are inclined to think that we do not need any more accounts of how *die Gipfel sehen einander*. Indeed, one might be tempted to go further and suggest that "the historiography of philosophy" is itself a notion which has outlived its usefulness – because, roughly, the honorific use of "philosophy" has outlived its. If we have the sort of complicated, thick intellectual history that is wary of canons (philosophical, literary, scientific, or other) do not we have enough? Is there any need for a history of something special called "philosophy" any more than there is a need to carry on a discipline that goes by that name? If we really believe that there is no God, no real essences, or any surrogate for either, if we follow Foucault in being consistently materialistic and nominalist, will we not want to stir things up so that there is no way at all to distinguish the cream from the milk, the conceptual and philosophical from the empirical and historical?[14]

As a good materialist and nominalist, I am obviously sympathetic to this line of thought. But as an amateur of *Geistesgeschichte* I want to resist it. I am all for getting rid of canons that have become merely quaint, but I do not think that we can get along without canons. This is because we cannot get along without heroes. We need mountain peaks to look up toward. We need to tell ourselves detailed stories about the mighty dead in order to make our hopes of surpassing them concrete. We also need the idea that there is such a thing as "philosophy" in the honorific sense – the idea that there are, had

---

14 One expression of this skeptical line of thought is Jonathan Rée's polemic against the role of "the idea of the History of Philosophy" in presenting "philosophy as a self-contained, eternal sector of intellectual production" and as having "a history of its own going back like a tunnel through the centuries" ("Philosophy and the History of Philosophy," 32). I entirely agree with Rée, but think that one can avoid this myth, while continuing the three genres I have commended, simply by *self-consciously* using "philosophy" as an honorific rather than a descriptive term.

we but the wit to pose them, certain questions that everybody should always have been asking. We cannot give up this idea without giving up the notion that the intellectuals of the previous epochs of European history form a community, a community of which it is good to be a member. If we are to persist in this image of ourselves, then we have to have both imaginary conversations with the dead and the conviction that we have seen further than they. That means that we need *Geistesgeschichte*, self-justificatory conversations. The alternative is the attempt that Foucault once adumbrated but that he has, I hope, given up – the attempt to have no face, to transcend the community of European intellectuals by affecting a contextless anonymity, like those characters in Beckett who have given up self-justification, conversational interchange, and hope. If one does wish to make such an attempt, of course, then *Geistesgeschichte* – even the sort of materialistic, nominalistic, *entzauberte Geistesgeschichte* I am attributing to Foucault – is one of the first things one has to get rid of. I have been writing on the assumption that we do not want to make this attempt, but rather want to make our conversation with the dead richer and fuller.

On this assumption, what we need is to see the history of philosophy as the story of the people who made splendid but largely unsuccessful attempts to ask the questions we ought to be asking. These will be the people who are candidates for a canon – a list of authors whom one would be well advised to read before trying to figure out what questions are the philosophical ones, in the honorific sense of "philosophy." Obviously, any given candidate may or may not share the concerns of this or that group of contemporary philosophers. One will not be in a position to know whether this is his fault or the fault of the group in question until one has read all the other candidates and settled on one's own canon – told one's own *Geistesgeschichte*. The more intellectual history we can get, of the kind that does not worry about what questions are philosophical and who counts as a philosopher, the better are our chances of having a suitably large list of candidates for a canon. The more various the canons we adopt – the more competing *Geistesgeschichten* we have at hand – the more likely we are to reconstruct, first rationally and then historically, interesting thinkers. As this competition grows more intense, the tendency to write doxographies will be less strong, and this will be all to the good. The competition is not likely ever to be resolved, but as long as it continues we will not lose that sense of community that only impassioned conversation makes possible.

14

THE CONTINGENCY OF PHILOSOPHICAL
PROBLEMS: MICHAEL AYERS ON LOCKE

In an interesting article called "History of Philosophy Today; and the Case of Sensible Qualities," Margaret Wilson agrees with Jonathan Rée in finding unconvincing "the case . . . for the categorical importance of historical consciousness to philosophers."[1] Like Wilson, I agree with Rée that "the actual opinions [of great dead philosophers] might well be philosophically impoverished compared with the imagined ones."[2] I also agree with Wilson that certain views which Jonathan Bennett incorrectly ascribes to Locke provide a nice illustration of Rée's point.[3] More generally, I agree with both Rée and Wilson that much philosophical work is best done with only the sort of cavalier attention to historical context found in what Richard Watson has called "shadow histories of philosophy"[4] – dramatic narratives of how egregious past errors were overcome.

The kind of philosophy best done in this way is what I call, echoing Kuhn, "normal" philosophy. Watson is right, I think, in suggesting that the practice of this sort of philosophy usually requires general acceptance of a particular "shadow history" (the sort offered in, for example, the second book of Aristotle's *Metaphysics* and in Ayer's *Language, Truth and Logic*). As he goes on to say, the claim of such history to "display the important logical or conceptual guts of history" is a "strong self-fulfilling assumption." The normal philosopher, the one who has no doubt that many problems currently under

1 Margaret Wilson, "History of Philosophy Today; and the Case of Sensible Qualities," *Philosophy in Review*, centennial issue of *Philosophical Review* 101, no. 1 (1992), 207.
2 Cited in ibid., 201.
3 Ibid., 219.
4 Richard Watson, "Shadow History in Philosophy," *Journal of the History of Philosophy* 31 (January 1993), 95–109.

discussion are real problems, uses such a shadow history to assure herself that she need not question the terms in which these problems are posed. This provides her with the same sort of assurance that her colleague in physics gets from a triumph-of-reason-over-prejudice-and-superstition narrative of the history of cosmological inquiry, the sort of narrative that focuses on Galileo's struggle with the Inquisition. In shadow histories of philosophy, a role analogous to Galileo's – the role of first putting the discipline on the secure path along which it now purposefully strides – is played by such figures as Locke, Kant, Frege, and Nietzsche.

But in addition to normal philosophy there is revolutionary philosophy: philosophy that stands to current philosophy as Galileo stood to the Aristotelian tradition. That sort of philosophy often starts off from a challenge to the currently prevalent shadow history and to its concomitant self-fulfilling assumption. A typical revolutionary move in philosophy, as in science, consists in saying that all or most work being done in a certain area has been based on a mistake. But whereas revolutionary scientists typically claim to be in a position to replace a mistaken answer to a good question with the right answer, revolutionary philosophers typically claim that their predecessors' mistake consisted in asking a bad question. That therapeutic move typically requires historical backup.

One cannot go so far as to say that historical consciousness is "categorically" important for therapeutic philosophers; Wittgenstein managed nicely without it. But for less gifted philosophical therapists, it is important to be able to say the sort of thing Habermas says about Hegel, and Ryle and Toulmin about Descartes: here is the point in history at which a great thinker should have done such and such rather than what he actually did; had they done the right thing, contemporary philosophers would not still be asking certain bad questions.

The distinction between bad answers and bad questions is, to be sure, fuzzy. One can describe any scientific revolution in terms of a bad question rather than a bad answer by making the question in question sufficiently small. For example, one can criticize Aristotle for answering the good large question "What is the moon made of?" with the bad answer "the fifth element." Or one can criticize him for asking the bad smaller question "Why doesn't the moon keep rising upward from the earth like all other fiery things?" – a question that presupposes the bad distinction between natural and violent motion. Similarly, one can redescribe any philosophical revolution in terms of a bad answer by making it sufficiently large. Thus one can criticize Kant for asking the bad small question "How are synthetic a priori propositions possible?" – a question that presupposes two bad distinctions, as well as the dubious claim that we know how to detect noncausal conditions of possibility as opposed to causal conditions of actuality. But one could also criticize him for giving a bad answer – "only phenomenal reality" – to the good large question "What can I know?"[5]

Despite this fuzziness, scientists can always phrase their revolutionary discovery as a better answer to some good question – if only one as broad as "How can we cure sick people?" or "How can we predict the motions of heavenly bodies?" – a question that all their predecessors and successors will agree deserves an answer. The persistence of such uncontroversial questions gives us reason to say that science makes progress. Doubt that philosophy makes progress is of a piece with doubt that there is a continuing discipline called "philosophy." Mechanics is still mechanics and astronomy still astronomy, even after Galileo and Copernicus displace Aristotle and Ptolemy. This is because historians of science agree to use terms like "mechanics" and "astronomy" in senses that emerged only retrospectively, taking into account our present notions of what these terms signify. But this retrospective technique is more controversial among historians of philosophy. One of the things such historians argue about is whether, for example, epistemology and metaphysics have a continuing history from Aristotle through Locke to Heidegger.

Those of us who have doubts about the continuity of such philosophical subdisciplines try to discern a sequence of largely discontinuous problematics of the sort called "philosophical," each created by different cultural crises – crises so different that there is little point in seeing Locke as a successor of Aristotle or as a predecessor of Heidegger. In particular, therapeutic philosophers like myself are inclined to accept the metaphilosophy offered in the first chapter of Dewey's *Reconstruction in Philosophy*, and in particular Dewey's conclusion:

> When it is acknowledged that under disguise of dealing with ultimate reality, philosophy has been occupied with the precious values embedded in social traditions, that it has sprung from a clash of social ends and from a conflict of inherited institutions with incompatible contemporary tendencies, it will be seen that the task of future philosophy is to clarify men's ideas as to the social and moral strifes of their own day.[6]

---

5 Actually, I do not think that "What can I know?" has turned out to be a very good question. But it is at least more attractive and plausible than questions that presuppose such distinctions as analytic–synthetic and a priori–a posteriori.

6 John Dewey, *Reconstruction in Philosophy*, in *The Middle Works of John Dewey* (Carbondale: Southern Illinois University Press, 1982), 12: 94.

If one shares Dewey's sense of what philosophy is good for, one will ask whether we should ask metaphysical or epistemological questions, before asking what the right answers to the questions might be. So when one finds Michael Ayers, in the introduction to his book on Locke, saying that it is "absurd" to think of "a particular moral, political or religious orientation's motivating a theory of knowledge or being,"[7] one will reply: maybe, but surely it is not absurd to have such a motive for questioning whether we need a theory of knowledge or a theory of being.

Within the framework of the Christian religion, it was absurd (though not uncommon) to let one's attachment to a particular political faction within the Roman Curia dictate one's views about the Immaculate Conception. But one might well have nonabsurd moral or political motives (such as Tom Paine's or Nietzsche's) for questioning the need for the Christian religion. Within the framework of epistemology it makes sense to ask whether all knowledge is based on the senses, but Dewey was making a moral and political point when he complained about the vested interests who hoped to perpetuate what he called "the epistemology industry." He saw this industry as Descartes and Hobbes saw scholastic philosophy: as consuming resources that, though appropriately used in a previous cultural epoch, should now be devoted to more worthwhile ends.[8]

One of the many things Wilson dislikes about the collection (which I helped edit) called *Philosophy in History* is that many of the contributors to this volume emphasize "a sense of the 'contingency' of one's philosophical concerns as an advantage deriving from historical consciousness." This seems to her "a quite suspect idea, given the strongly absolutist stances of many of the greatest philosophers."[9] What Wilson calls "the absolutist stance" is, I take it, the conviction that the problems one addresses are inescapable once one begins to reflect – where "philosophical reflection" denotes the activity of reconciling those persistent intuitions that survive

---

7 Michael Ayers, *Locke* (London: Routledge, 1991), 1: 8. This claim seems to me hard to reconcile with Ayers's claim that "[v]irtually every paragraph of the *Essay* was directed towards a common end, that of forging an account of human knowledge . . . which would serve as a weapon against dogmatism in religion, morals and the study of nature" (Ayers, *Locke*, 2: 1). To reconcile these two passages, Ayers would have to argue that the urge to resist dogmatism was a purely epistemic one, unsullied by moral or political convictions.

8 Apologists for scholastic philosophy (such as Étienne Gilson, in his *Being and Some Philosophers*) typically see what we now call "early modern philosophy" as bad, confused, third-rate scholastic philosophy. Analogously, apologists for British empiricism, like Michael Ayers, typically see antiepistemology as just bad epistemology. For both writers, what is advertised as revolution is merely degeneration.

9 Wilson, "History of Philosophy," 208n38.

changes in sociocultural circumstance. That conviction is shared by Ayers, who says that philosophy differs from science in that in the former "there are no such [i.e., experimental] checks, for philosophical explanations are a priori." Ayers enlarges on this point by saying, "In epistemology and metaphysics we have in the end only our judgement and 'intuitions' to guide us in distinguishing good explanations from bad."[10]

The contributor to *Philosophy in History* who put most emphasis on the contingency of philosophical problems and the historicity of philosophy was Lorenz Krüger. Krüger criticized "the assumption that philosophy is characterized by a specific set of tasks which remain constant through history."[11] He argued for what he called "the global historicity" of both philosophy and science: the claim that in both areas "the discovery as well as the justification of an advanced theory requires the predecessor theory, or rather the chain or net of predecessor theories."[12] This historicity gives one reason to doubt that the history of philosophy can be written independently of cultural history and to wonder whether such history can (or should) be uncontaminated by what Ayers calls "a moral or political or religious orientation." It gives reason to doubt the utility of what Krüger calls "problem history," the sort of history which assumes, for example, that there is a continuing problem about the nature of "sensible qualities."

Krüger thinks, and I agree, that problem history is "often useful, and sometimes excellent, philosophy" but that it "fails to confront a central part of the historical task," because it replaces genuine temporal development by a spurious present."[13] This spurious present is produced by taking "the current problem situation" in philosophy (or, more exactly, one's own view of that situation) for granted.[14] As Krüger says, "[T]he problem-history view by its very nature leaves no room for a philosophical account of the origin and the (relative) weights of these problems."[15]

This last point seems to me well illustrated by the case of what Thomas Reid called "the theory of ideas" and by the cluster of problems to which this theory gives rise. For global historicists like myself, who insist on the contingency of philosophical problems, Locke provides a good illustration of the proliferation of bad problems, problems engendered by bad terminology and question-begging assumptions. So Reid's, T. H. Green's, and Wilfrid

10 Ayers, *Locke*, 1: 8.
11 Lorenz Krüger, "Why Do We Study the History of Philosophy?" in *Philosophy in History*, ed. Richard Rorty, J. B. Schneewind, and Quentin Skinner (Cambridge University Press, 1984), 79.
12 Ibid., 93.   13 Krüger, "Why Do We Study?" 81.   14 Ibid., 85.   15 Ibid., 82.

Sellars's accounts of where Locke went wrong strike us as doing the sort of job on Locke that needs to be done – namely, tracing the origin of the problems he discusses to certain assumptions, assumptions to which we are now able to provide plausible alternatives.[16]

But philosophers inclined to assume that the normal philosophy of the present day is dealing with real, significant problems are more likely to think of Locke's writings as (in Ayers's words) "an invaluable repository of unfashionable truth for those with the sympathy, judgement and patience to discern and make use of it."[17] Ayers's approach exemplifies the assumption that, in Krüger's words, "the problems and the possible approaches to their solution are themselves ahistorical."[18] It relies, to quote Krüger again, "on an evaluation of the current problem situation"[19] – a positive evaluation of such problems as "the nature of colors" and "the mind–body problem."

Ayers suggests that the "crucial difference" between philosophy and science is illustrated by the fact that, as he says,

> Aristotle's account of the names of natural kinds, implicated as it was with a now untenable conception of the relationship between species and individual, can nevertheless influence a present-day philosopher's thought about the same topics; whereas the astrological reasonings of John Dee have no significance for Roger Penrose.[20]

Ayers says that in philosophy, but presumably not in science, "suspended in what is now alien or even absurd may be something that can still count as insight or truth."[21] I should think this would happen occasionally in the sciences too – that a Penrose might sometimes get a good idea from reading a Paracelsus – but I will not pursue this point. Rather, I want to focus on the question: is the history of philosophy an efficient way to get at such insights, or are they equally available without going back to the past?

Ayers's own answer to this question is clear. He says that getting truth out of a philosopher such as Locke is like "identifying the truth in a largely misleading caricature, unfair at every point: a truth, as it is important to stress, of which we might not previously have been aware."[22] My problem with this answer is that one is likely to see the truth in a caricature only if one *was* previously aware of it. Caricatures of hitherto unknown politicians fall flat. One

yes – See my treatment of Locke

---

16 Ayers's 600-odd pages on Locke contain (if the somewhat unreliable index can be trusted) no references to Green or Sellars and only four (rather incidental) references to Reid. Ayers is as little impressed by these predecessors' therapeutic approaches to Locke as by Jonathan Bennett's.

17 Ayers, *Locke*, 1: 9.   18 Krüger, "Why Do We Study?" 84.   19 Ibid., 85.

20 Ayers, *Locke*, 1: 6.   21 Ibid., 7.   22 Ibid., 7.

will not know what to look for if one has not seen the original of which the caricature is a distortion.[23] So my doubts on this point harmonize with Krüger's remark that, for the problem historian, "the reasons for doing historical work remain *ad hoc* and merely pragmatic."[24] Ayers's book on Locke seems to me "merely pragmatic" in the sense that it uses Locke as an occasion to protest against all the holistic, contextualistic, Wittgensteinian strains in contemporary philosophy, and in particular against the idea that "it is language that imposes form or articulation both on experience and on reality."[25] Ayers's two volumes are a sustained criticism of what he calls "linguistic idealism" or "linguistic conceptualism."[26]

There is nothing wrong with this pragmatic use of commentary on Locke to fend off Sellars, Wittgenstein, et al., any more than there was anything wrong with Green's and Sellars's use of commentary on Locke to fend off, respectively, Alexander Bain and A. J. Ayer. But if one makes use of Locke in this way one should not, as Ayers does, sneer at the idea that it may be "a necessary task for each generation to rewrite the history of philosophy according to its own philosophical lights." Ayers condemns this suggestion in the name of the "duty here as elsewhere in historiography to try to cut through the barriers set up by the immediate context of our own thinking and to reconstruct and judge the past as it was."[27]

The suggestion that we have such a duty, and that Ayers himself may manage to be faithful to it in a way in which "linguistic idealists" like Sellars were not, begs all the questions against those who argue (as I and the other editors of *Philosophy in History* argued in our introduction to that volume) that you can no more cut through those barriers than you can step out of your own skin. On this contextualist view, the historian of philosophy *must* use her sense of which contemporary philosophical problems are real and

23 Consider the predicament of a historian of cartography trying to get along without a knowledge of present-day maps and trying to resist the thought that it may be necessary to rewrite the history of cartography in each generation in order to bring this history into line with new geographic knowledge.

24 Krüger, "Why Do We Study?" 84.   25 Ayers, *Locke*, 1: 76.

26 Ibid., 77. Ayers says that he wishes both to "recover the meaning and original significance of the main philosophical argument of . . . [Locke's *Essay*], by reading it in the context of some of the ideas which were current or available at the time it was written" and to assess "the theory . . . which emerges from this interpretive enterprise . . . in comparison both with its antecedent and contemporary rivals, and with . . . theories current today" (ibid., 2: 1). In fact, about 90 percent of Ayers's space and energy is devoted to the latter goal. Compared with, for example, James Tully's work on Locke's political philosophy, Ayers's book pays very little attention to Locke's contemporaries.

27 Ayers, *Locke*, 1: 2.

which pseudo in exactly the way in which the historian of science must use her sense of which of Aristotle's or Paracelsus's questions were good and which bad. Sellars uses his sense, Ayers his. Both are equally dutiful, equally pragmatic historians.

It seems to me no accident that the contemporary historians of philosophy who are most dubious about the historicity of philosophy – about the contingent and transitory character of philosophical problems – are also those who, in their role of philosophers rather than historians, are most insistent upon the need to recognize the existence of the ineffable. Consider, for example, Robert Adams's essay "Flavors, Colors and God," which argues that only God's existence can explain the correlation of qualia with brain processes.

Adams's argument turns on the unanalyzability of qualia and the consequent impossibility of integrating them into a corpuscularian and atheistic account of how everything hangs together. Against people like Sellars, David Armstrong, Donald Davidson, Daniel Dennett, and myself – people who are, as he puts it, "prepared to deny what I take to be obvious facts about phenomenal qualia" – Adams urges that "eliminationism or reductionism" about phenomenal qualia "can be refuted by seeing red and yellow or tasting onions."[28] This mode of refutation is an example of what I am calling an appeal to the ineffable. It is an appeal to a kind of knowledge that cannot be rendered dubious by a process of redescription. For this knowledge is knowledge not by description but rather by acquaintance. Only if we in fact possess such knowledge will it be plausible to claim that the materials of philosophy are provided by intuitions that are not themselves the product of historically conditioned choices of description.

I suspect that only philosophers who are willing to appeal to the ineffable in this way will be last-ditch opponents of Krüger's contextualist arguments for the global historicity of philosophy. For those who make such an appeal, the two Gadamerian slogans approvingly quoted by Krüger – "being that can be understood is language" and "In the end, all understanding is understanding of oneself"[29] – are equally repellent. The first slogan is refuted by tasting onions. The second is refuted by contrasting the solipsistic and nihilistic tendencies of "linguistic idealism" with openness to Otherness – an openness prized by those philosophers who think it important to

28 Robert Merrihew Adams, "Flavors, Colors and God," in *The Virtue of Faith and Other Essays in Philosophical Theology* (New York: Oxford University Press, 1987), 243–62.
29 See Krüger, "Why Do We Study?" 90.

delimit the areas of inquiry in which there is what they call "a fact of the matter," areas in which it would be intellectually irresponsible not to be a philosophical "realist." Philosophers who think issues about realism versus antirealism important typically hold that the views common to Gadamer and Davidson lack what Thomas Nagel calls "robustness."[30] They amount to a refusal to acknowledge human finitude. But for their opponents, such as Krüger and myself, the appeal to either example of ineffability is the latest form of an appeal to *parousia*, to the sort of nonrelational, noncontextual presence for which, according to Heidegger, Gadamer, and Derrida, Western metaphysics has always yearned. So we antimetaphysicians try to turn the accusation of a refusal to acknowledge human finitude around and use it against such appeals. We argue that acknowledgment of our finitude requires what Sellars calls "psychological nominalism" – the doctrine "that all awareness is a linguistic affair" and so, like language, is up for sociocultural grabs.

We psychological nominalists are the people whom Ayers describes as linguistic idealists. We try to take the sting out of the latter epithet by saying, with Davidson, that it is "futile to reject or accept the slogan that the real and the true are 'independent of our beliefs.'"[31] We thereby attempt to toss the topic of realism versus idealism into the dustbin of history (a move our ahistoricist opponents prefer to describe as sweeping it under the carpet). We back up our refusal to be impressed by the taste of onions by interpreting the Gadamerian claim that "[b]eing that can be understood is language" in a Sellarsian way – redescribing knowledge by acquaintance as the ability to make noninferential linguistic responses to features of the passing scene (including states of our brains) – thereby claiming that (in Ayers's words) "there is no 'raw material of sensations.'"[32]

30 For the overlap between Gadamer and Davidson, see Bjorn T. Ramberg, *Donald Davidson's Philosophy of Language* (Oxford: Blackwell, 1989), chap. 10. See also J. E. Malpas, *Donald Davidson and the Mirror of Meaning* (Cambridge University Press, 1992), 96–9, 176–7, 260–77. For Nagel's views on the insufficient robustness of verificationists and pragmatists, see the introduction to his *The View from Nowhere* (New York: Oxford University Press, 1986). For a rejoinder to Nagel, see my "Daniel Dennett on Intrinsicality," in this volume.

31 Donald Davidson, "The Structure and Content of Truth," *Journal of Philosophy* 87 (June 1990), 305.

32 See Ayers, *Locke*, 1: 174. Ayers here quotes a passage from my *Philosophy and the Mirror of Nature* (Princeton, N.J.: Princeton University Press, 1980), a passage summarizing one of the points made in Sellars's *Empiricism and the Philosophy of Mind* (Cambridge, Mass.: Harvard University Press, 1997). Ayers generously says that I succeed in "explaining the position with impressive brutality" and correctly notes that Sellarsians like myself try "to explain perceptual belief in purely causal terms." Ayers would agree with Roderick Chisholm's objections to Sellars (in the Sellars–Chisholm correspondence, printed in *Minnesota Studies in the Philosophy of Science* [Minneapolis: University of Minnesota Press, 1958], vol. 1). He says that

I hope that this example of the differences between Krüger and myself on the one hand and Ayers and Adams on the other is enough to show that one cannot hope to disentangle metaphilosophical views about the nature and function of philosophy, and about the relevance of the history of philosophy to philosophy, from "substantive" philosophical views about, for example, knowledge by acquaintance. One would do better to be as explicit as possible about how these two sorts of views interact.

As a suggestion about this interaction, consider the following ten theses. Though one probably cannot find strict entailments linking each of these theses to every other, it is no surprise to find that they tend to be held by the same people:

(1) There is a real issue about whether there is a fact of the matter about certain topics (e.g., physical reality, moral values). Questions of "realism" and "antirealism" should be taken seriously. Davidson is wrong to try to dissolve these issues by saying that the slogan that the real is "independent of our beliefs" and the associated idea of the possible correspondence of beliefs to the real are "without content."

(2) Michael Dummett is right in thinking that the crucial episodes in the history of philosophy are struggles between realist and antirealist views.

(3) Wilson is right to be dubious about the contingency of philosophical problems.

(4) Ayers is right in saying that one must take pains not to let one's moral or political views influence one's metaphysical and epistemological views.

(5) The problem of "the nature of colors," and thus the mind–body problem, are indissoluble; attempts to dissolve these problems are instances of what Nagel thinks of as a childish rebellion against "the philosophical impulse itself" – an impulse inseparable from "the ambition of transcendence" and from the conviction that, as Nagel says, "the content of some thoughts transcend every form they can take in the human mind."[33]

(6) Skepticism of the sort illustrated by Descartes's *Meditations* is a permanent, ahistorical issue, not one created at a certain historical moment

---

it is a point in Locke's favor that "it is a blatant paradox to cut consciousness out of our account of meaningful speech altogether" (*Locke*, 1: 70). For Sellarsians and Davidsonians, of course, this paradox is no worse than cutting the Divine Will out of our account of moral obligation or natural motion out of our account of the movements of the heavens. We hope that our blatant paradox will seem increasingly inoffensive to successive future generations, just as these earlier blatant paradoxes did.

33 Nagel, *The View from Nowhere*, 102.

by a dubious theory. What holds Descartes and Barry Stroud captive is not an optional picture but a problem permanently built into the human situation.

(7) Sellars and Davidson are wrong to think of the senses as playing a merely causal role in the genesis of beliefs rather than as quasi-informants possessing intrinsic intentionality. There is much to be said for John McDowell's attempt to reverify empiricism.

(8) The self-identity of an object is not relative to alternative descriptions of the object, but is a matter of intrinsic, nonrelational features of that object. Some terms designate rigidly.

(9) Acknowledgment of ineffability is, *pace* Peirce, commendable intellectual humility rather than an attempt to block the road of inquiry.

(10) Locke's *Essay* is a great work of philosophy, to be plumbed for as yet unarticulated truth rather than a monument marking the spot at which we turned onto a side path leading to a quagmire. Locke more closely resembles Isaac Newton than he does John Dee.[34]

This list could be extended indefinitely, and I claim no special virtue for it. I should not even claim that my list includes the most basic issues in the area. For we global historicists cannot make much use of the notion of "basic issue." This is because we are trying to get away from the idea (common to Aristotle's *Analytics* and Descartes's *Rules*) of a "natural order of reasons" – from the idea that clear thinking consists in spotting the presuppositions of what we say. We insist that the process of reweaving our web of beliefs and desires is too complex and unpredictable to be interpreted in terms of any such order. That process is closer to restructuring a neural network via parallel distributed processing than to working our way back up a nice neat flowchart.

So some people will be far more certain of thesis (10) or its contradictory than they are of either (1) or its contradictory. Others will cling passionately to (5), while remaining relatively indifferent about, say, (4) or (8). The justification for a philosophical position, like that for a political decision, will vary depending on the audience addressed. We will never find a knockdown,

---

34 Ayers thinks that "Locke's rambling, chatty, repetitive, rhetorical masterpiece deserves the seat once generally accorded it beside Newton's *Principia Mathematica* as the culmination of the process by which 'the new philosophy' replaced the old" (*Locke*, 1: 13). I see Locke's book as deserving much of the blame for having kept the idea of a distinct quasi-scientific discipline called "philosophy" alive at a moment when this discipline might have been replaced by a historicist conception of philosophy, the conception suggested by the metaphilosophical passage from Dewey quoted earlier.

audience-invariant argument for or against any of the ten theses I have listed – an argument that is purely "logical" and not at all "rhetorical." In particular, every attempt to do what Watson calls "presenting the logical or conceptual guts of history" will be an attempt to explain to a particular audience – an audience united by an overlapping consensus about current "substantive" philosophical issues – what is living and what is dead in a given historical text or figure or period. To return to Ayers's metaphor, one's sense of what is the truth hidden within the caricature, as opposed to what is *mere* caricature, will be a function of one's own "substantive" convictions.[35]

Let me now return to the topic of what Ayers calls my "linguistic idealism." We psychological nominalists think that it took quite a lot of what Wittgenstein called "stage-setting in the language" to make plausible appeals to the taste of onions. We see the ideas of the Cartesian Theater and of "consciousness" as part of that stage-setting. On our view, nobody was conscious of being conscious before we started talking about "consciousness," just as nobody had redness or hummingbirds present to their senses (as opposed to interacting with their bodies) before we started talking about colors and birds. Whereas Adams and Nagel see consciousness and sensible qualities as data, we global historicists see them as dubious seventeenth-century inventions.

We also see essences – the intelligible natures of natural kinds of substances – as dubious inventions of the fourth century B.C. So we see the "scientific realism" shared by early modern and contemporary philosophers as an awkward and hopeless attempt to reconcile Aristotelian essentialism with a worldview – atomistic materialism – which Aristotle rightly thought destructive of that notion. We wish that early modern philosophers had appreciated the possibilities offered by Hobbes's antiessentialism and nominalism. Had they done so, they might have discarded the appearance–reality

---

35 This audience relativity might tempt one to say, as Watson (in "Shadow History") takes me to have said, that there is no such thing as getting Locke right – no "purely historical" inquiry to be fruitfully pursued. I would not say this, because it sounds like a denial that there are questions that can be univocally construed, by all interested readers of Locke. I think that there are such questions – for example, the one raised by John Yolton and discussed by Ayers in *Locke*, 1: chaps. 6–7: was Reid right in attributing to Locke a representative theory of perception?

I have never satisfactorily replied to Yolton's extended and powerful criticism of my own agreement with Reid, but I still cannot bring myself to agree with Yolton's "act" reading of Locke's doctrine of ideas. For a recent discussion of the issues that Yolton raises, sympathetic to my side of the argument, see Peter J. Dlugos, "Yolton and Rorty on the Veil of Ideas in Locke," *History of Philosophy Quarterly* 13 (July 1996), 317–29.

distinction as well as the accident–essence distinction. This would have made it unnecessary for them to invent the notion of "idea," thereby opening up the pathway that led to the Kantian quagmire.

The seventeenth century could have forestalled Kant if it had done what Dewey later did: used the widening gap between Aristotle-influenced common sense and the New Science as an occasion to remark that we might substitute the notion of "useful way of describing things for a certain purpose" for that of "getting at the real essences of things."[36] Instead, most seventeenth-century thinkers held on to the Aristotelian idea that some descriptions really got at the way things are in themselves and others did not, and so got stuck with the idea that the vocabulary of physical science picked out "reality" as opposed to "appearance." This, in turn, saddled them with the bad question "So what *are* the appearances? and with the bad answer to that question: "ideas that do not correspond to the real essences of things." Then they wanted to know more about these "ideas" – entities that had now begun to seem inescapable – and eventually became convinced that there were serious problems about, for example, "the nature of colors" and the relation between mind and body (for colors had become, by this time, things that exist "only in the mind"). This road led straight to the familiar quagmire.

From my psychological nominalist and global historicist point of view, Ayers's book is a precious find. For Ayers shows us the full horror of what happens to people who take Locke's problems with full seriousness. He shows us what one has to believe if one still wants to solve, rather than dissolve,

---

36 Ayers says, dismissively, that some commentators have viewed Locke's attempt to state "the truth that now seems axiomatic to most of us, that fundamental explanations in science cannot start from the natures and essences of complicated physical objects such as are large enough to be perceived" (Ayers, *Locke*, 2: 25) in terms of Aristotelian notions like "substance" and "essence" as "an uncritical inheritance, a signal failure to shake off the conceptual shackles forged by the very philosophy under attack" (16).

    I think that the commentators whom Ayers criticizes are right on target. Dewey was right in saying that philosophy still has not yet come to terms with the substitution of a law–event framework of fundamental explanation for a substance–nature framework. In particular, he was right in saying, "Only when the older theory of knowledge and metaphysics is retained, is science thought to inform us that nature in its true reality is but an interplay of masses in motion, without sound, color, or any quality of enjoyment and use" (*The Quest for Certainty*, in *The Later Works of John Dewey* [Carbondale: Southern Illinois University Press, 1984], 4: 84). Ayers and I could, I think, agree that the distinction between primary and secondary qualities, and the consequent "problem of the nature of colors," would not have occurred to anyone innocent of the essence–accident distinction. The difference between us is that Ayers thinks this is a good, natural, commonsensical distinction, and I think it is a makeshift and unprofitable one.

these problems. Ayers gives us excellent reasons to think that one cannot separate Locke's concern with skepticism and foundationalism from his scientific realism – reasons to think that these, together with the problems of the nature of colors and of the relation between mind and body, are parts of a package deal that also includes full-strength Aristotelian essentialism. For Ayers is concerned to revive "a form of realism which has been out of fashion for centuries," one that refuses to see "the system of categories or conceptual scheme we employ as in principle subject to change."[37] He thinks it essential both to a proper appreciation of Locke and to the pursuit of philosophical truth to recognize that "consciousness is the source of meaning, the intermediary between language and reality."[38] On his view, any instance of conscious experience, including prelinguistic sense experience, possesses intrinsic intentionality. He believes that nobody would doubt all this who had not been corrupted by linguistic idealists: people like Wittgenstein, Quine, and Davidson.

Ayers's *Locke* and my *Philosophy and the Mirror of Nature* are admirable foils for one another. We offer, so to speak, equal and opposite package deals. Whereas I scorn the analogy between knowing and seeing, and the proliferation of visual metaphors among epistemologists, as a historical mischance, Ayers says that "the linguistic theory [of a priori knowledge] fails to do justice to the natural inescapable analogy with sight."[39] Whereas I see the linguistic turn in philosophy as leading us away from epistemology and metaphysics, Ayers sees this turn as bad epistemology reinforced by degenerate metaphysics. On *all* the issues touched upon by theses (1) through (10), Ayers and I hold diametrically opposite views. So the reader who wants a sense of the connections between these disparate issues can, by looking on this picture and on that, get a good sense of the choice she will sooner or later have to make.

I can happily agree with Ayers both that we linguistic idealists coalesce real distinctions with distinctions of reason and that "[n]othing but an intensive training in modern philosophy could make the traditional contrast between real distinctions and distinctions of reason actually difficult to apprehend."[40] The difference is that I think that an intensive training in modern philosophy – a course of Wittgensteinian therapy – is just what we need. For if we linguistic idealists could once get people to give up on the question common to Aristotle and Locke – "Which of my distinctions are real distinctions?" – we might persuade them to substitute "Which of my distinctions are useful for which purposes?" That done, it would be fairly easy

37 Ayers, *Locke*, 2: 4–5.　　38 Ibid., 1: 301.　　39 Ibid., 1: 303.　　40 Ibid., 2: 9.

to persuade them not only to stop contributing to the profits of the episte-mology industry but also to adopt Dewey's metaphilosophical views. We might get them to become both psychological nominalists and global his-toricists. One way to expedite this double conversion might be to convince them that Ayers is right about Locke: that, as he says, "to achieve an under-standing of Locke's motives and presuppositions it is necessary to take ab-solute ontology seriously, and to step right outside the framework of mod-ern linguistic conceptualism."[41]

I shall end by trying to tie up a few dangling threads. I want to return to Krüger's description of global historicism and to comment on the sugges-tion, with which he concludes his essay, that a properly historicist philoso-phy might function as "something like the professionalized consciousness of the scientific-technological world – and, we may hope, as its conscience."[42]

I see what Krüger means, but I am dubious about the phrase "the scien-tific-technological world." This phrase seems to me tainted by an assump-tion that, as Krüger says, was shared by Husserl, Heidegger, and Gadamer – the assumption that "viewing science and technology as something like our historical fate or our historical task requires, first of all, some distance from science – some science-free space, as it were, for intellectual maneuver-ing."[43] These philosophers' search for such a science-free space has helped people as diverse as Popper, C. P. Snow, and Habermas to think of Heideg-ger and Gadamer, and of the "literary" culture associated with them, as on the wrong political side: as enemies of human freedom.

I agree with Krüger that the quest for such a space is vain and with the drift of his remark that "the starting point of philosophical analysis can only be a 'scientific *Lebenswelt.*'"[44] To be a historicist is to give up the nostalgia that Hei-degger and Gadamer share. But I think that this nostalgia may persist as long as we view "science and technology as something like our historical fate."[45] This Heideggerian use of *Schicksal* – with its overtones of *Seinsgeschick* – seems to me likely to prolong Heidegger's nostalgia-ridden sense of the West as the land of metaphysics rather than as the land of freedom.

It seems to me better to follow Dewey in thinking of the role of science and technology not in terms of our relation to Being but rather in explicitly political terms. The world of which Kruger hopes that philosophy may be the professionalized consciousness or conscience is better described as "the democratic world" or "the world in which democracy has, thanks in some

41 Ibid.   42 Krüger, "Why Do We Study?" 99.   43 Ibid., 97.   44 Ibid., 98.
45 Krüger seems to accept this description (ibid., 96).

measure to scientific and technological developments, become a possibility" than as "the scientific-technological world."

Dewey once described "democracy" as "neither a form of government nor a social expediency, but a metaphysic of the relation of man and his experience in nature."[46] I think Dewey was on to something important here, something that Habermas has helped us to grasp. We can avoid Dewey's ill-chosen term "metaphysic" by rephrasing his point as follows: our experience of democratic politics has made it possible for us philosophers to change our notion of "reason" from what Habermas calls "subject-centered reason" to what he calls "communicative reason." This seems to me a change whose significance is on a par with the shift from a Christian and Aristotelian outlook to an atheist and Galilean outlook. For it is a change that lets us stop asking "Which of my concepts, distinctions, and practices are related to the *real?*" and ask instead "To what extent do I, or can I, share them with which other people?" It lets us turn from the love of truth, conceived of as a correct relation to reality, to the need for justification, conceived of as a relation to other human beings. It helps remove not only the impulse that leads us to want what Ayers calls "an absolute ontology" but also the impulse that makes us think that the point of politics is to get people to recognize the True and the Right, as opposed to making them free to make up their own minds about what is true and what is right.

Science and technology have, for reasons Dewey spelled out in *Reconstruction in Philosophy* and *The Quest for Certainty,* done a lot for democracy. But it would be a mistake to put them first and democracy second. Having said that, however, I can still heartily agree with Krüger that only by keeping our consciousness determinately historical can we philosophers be useful to the hopes of the contemporary world.

As I see it, our main job these days is to help convince the citizens of democratic communities that they will get no more political guidance from scientists and technologists than they got in the past from priests and philosophers. We should try to convince them that the goals of their communities can be set neither by "reality" nor by putative experts on reality (and, in particular, that the latter experts are no more to be trusted than experts on God or experts on Being). We should say, in the spirit of Habermas's "communicative reason," that they need respect no authority save that of their own freely obtained agreements.

46 John Dewey, "Maeterlinck's Philosophy of Life," in *The Middle Works,* 6: 125–35.

15

DEWEY BETWEEN HEGEL AND DARWIN

James Kloppenberg sees Dewey as one of the philosophers of "the via media," the via media between idealism and empiricism. The second chapter of his admirable *Uncertain Victory* is titled "The Radical Theory of Knowledge." The heart of that theory, as Kloppenberg tells the story, consists in a new, nonatomistic conception of experience – a conception that is the least common denominator of Dilthey's notion of *Erlebnisse* and James's notion of "a world of pure experience." On Kloppenberg's account, this new conception of experience has a pragmatist account of truth as a corollary.[1]

Like Kloppenberg's discussion of Dewey, David Hollinger's treatment of James emphasizes the connections between pragmatism and radical empiricism in James's work.[2] Both Kloppenberg and Hollinger see James's and Dilthey's talk about the flux of experience – talk that is continuous with Bergson's and Whitehead's talk of misplaced concreteness – as an important part of what Hollinger calls "a cluster of assertions and hopes about the basis for culture in an age of science."[3] They both see what Hollinger calls James's "shift toward the panpsychism of the idealists" as an important part of the contribution of German idealism to American pragmatism. Kloppenberg rightly says that Dewey's claim that experience "carries principles

---

1 James Kloppenberg, *Uncertain Victory: Social Democracy and Progressivism in European and American Thought, 1870–1920* (New York: Oxford University Press, 1985), 90.
2 David Hollinger, *In the American Province* (Bloomington: Indiana University Press, 1985), 16–17.
3 Ibid., 42. Hollinger distinguishes this cluster as one of "three interpenetrating layers" that make up "pragmatism as a presence in the discourse of American intellectuals." The other two are "a theory of meaning and truth" and "a range of general ideas stereotypical of American life."

of connection and organization within itself" is an "echo" of Green and Hegel.

I have no wish to challenge the claim that this sort of panpsychism and this rejection of Humean atomism loomed large in James's and Dewey's minds. A survey of the most interesting and original philosophers of the year 1900 would indeed show, as Kloppenberg suggests, that most of them wanted to close the epistemological gap between subject and object by some form of the panpsychist claim that the two were somehow continuous. For panpsychism seemed an obvious way to perform what Kloppenberg calls "the marriage of Hegel and Darwin." Bracketing these two men under the rubric "evolutionary thought" – something Dewey did constantly – is easiest if one can answer the question "*What* evolves?" with "experience" and if one can manage to treat that term and the term "nature" as quasi-synonymous. Insofar as there was an emerging consensus in philosophy in 1900, it was that we could get beyond the sterile arguments of the philosophical tradition only if we could see nature and experience as two descriptions of the same thing. Peirce spoke for the best philosophical thought of his time when he said, "All the creations of our mind are but patchworks from experience. So that all our ideas are but ideas of real or transposed experience."[4]

Nevertheless, if one looks at the end of the twentieth century rather than at its beginning, one finds something of a renaissance of pragmatism, but no similar renaissance of panpsychism.[5] The philosophers of today who speak well of James and Dewey tend to speak ill of Bergson. They tend to talk about *sentences* a lot, but to say very little about ideas or experiences, as opposed to such sentential attitudes as beliefs and desires. They would reject the question "Are relations given immediately in experience?" as presupposing a notion of "givenness" that is just one more "dogma of empiricism." Following up on Sellars's criticism of the Myth of the Given, they do not think *anything* is "given immediately in experience." They are enthusiastic about Peirce's claim that "my language is the sum total of myself"[6] and about the passages in which Peirce distinguishes sharply between cognitions and sensations – between sentential attitudes and mental states that can be described without reference to sentences. But they regret that these are

---

4 Charles Peirce, *Collected Papers* (Cambridge, Mass.: Harvard University Press, 1936), 6: 492.
5 One of the few contemporary philosophers to say a good word for panpsychism (at least one of the few who do not belong to the neo-Whiteheadian school centering around Charles Hartshorne) is Thomas Nagel. But Nagel has no use whatever for pragmatism and thinks it the root of much philosophical evil.
6 Peirce, *Collected Papers*, 5: 314.

passages to which neither James nor Dewey, nor even Peirce himself, paid much attention.[7]

In short, contemporary philosophers who profess sympathy with pragmatism show little sympathy with empiricism – they would rather forget empiricism than radicalize it. Donald Davidson speaks for many when he rejects – as one more hangover of Hume's attempt to be the Newton of the mind – Quine's notion of "stimulus meaning" (stated in terms of such nerve endings as the retina). Davidson substitutes a "distal" theory of meaning formulated in terms of public external objects; he allows no intermediate terrain of philosophical inquiry between linguistically formulated beliefs and physiology.[8]

As an alternative to Dewey's own self-understanding of his relation to Hegel and Darwin – a self-understanding accurately presented by Kloppenberg – I want to suggest an account of this relation that emphasizes Hegel's historicism rather than his idealism, and Darwin's affinities with positivism rather than with vitalism. So I shall describe what Dewey might have said, and in my view should have said, rather than what he did say. I shall construct a hypothetical Dewey who was a pragmatist without being a radical empiricist, and a naturalist without being a panpsychist. The point of constructing such a Dewey is to separate out what I think is living and what I think is dead in Dewey's thought, and thereby to clarify the difference between the state of philosophical play around 1900 and at the present time.[9]

---

7 The locus classicus for this distinction is Peirce's two papers "Questions Concerning Certain Faculties Claimed for Man" and "Some Consequences of Four Incapacities" (*Collected Papers*, 5: 213–317). See the discussion of these papers in John Murphy, *Pragmatism: From Peirce to Davidson* (Boulder, Colo.: Westview, 1990). Murphy's presentation helps one see the connection between such contemporary holist philosophies of knowledge as Davidson's and Peirce's claim that "at no one instant in my state of mind is there cognition or representation, but in the relation of my states of mind at different instants there is" (Peirce, *Collected Papers*, 5: 289).

8 What Davidson calls "the crucial step from the nonpropositional to the propositional" is not taken by looking where Locke and James looked – at the way in which experience (supposedly) sorts itself out, gradually changing from a buzzing confusion to a coherent inner discourse. Rather, it views the propositional as occurring only in language-using organisms. The question of "the origin of intentionality" is, from a Davidsonian point of view, no more mysterious than the question of how organisms began tossing around certain marks and noises in particular sequences. For a detailed account of how intentional discourse comes into being, see Robert Brandom, *Making It Explicit* (Cambridge, Mass.: Harvard University Press, 1994) discussed in my "Robert Brandom on Social Practices and Representations," in this volume.

9 I defend this sort of anachronistic reading of Dewey in my contributions to *Rorty and Pragmatism*, ed. Herman Saatkamp (Nashville, Tenn.: Vanderbilt University Press, 1995), especially in my responses to the comments of Richard Bernstein, Thelma Lavine, and James

When thinking about Dewey, it pays to begin by thinking about Hegel. Charles Taylor has helped us see Hegel as having brought Kant together with Herder and Humboldt – as having combined transcendental idealism with a sense of historical relativity – the same sense of relativity that C. I. Lewis urged in his *Mind and the World-Order.* Manfred Frank, in his important book, *What Is Neostructuralism?*, has helped us see "the fundamental insight of all post-Hegelian philosophy" as the abandonment of a "claim to a transhistorical frame of orientation beyond linguistic differentiality."[10] Frank speaks of this insight as "perhaps the fundamental insight of postclassical philosophy in its entirety, insofar as it participates in the *linguistic turn.*"[11] On Frank's account, the sense of historical relativity, the sense of relativity to available linguistic resources, the sense of human finitude, and the sense that "it is not possible to interpret our world from an Archimedean point"[12] are at bottom the same. Frank thinks that the linguistic turn was first taken by Herder and Humboldt, thinkers who made it possible, as Frank puts it, to think of "transnational and transhistorical 'reason'" as itself just one more "'image of the world' inscribed in a linguistic order."[13]

Frank's account suggests a different way of viewing Dewey as a "philosopher of the via media." From this angle, the extremes between which Dewey hopes to navigate are not idealism and empiricism, but rather historicism and scientism. By "historicism" I mean the doctrine that there is no relation of "closeness of fit" between language and the world: no image of the world

Gouinlock. See also my reviews of recent contributions to the Dewey literature: "Just One More Species Doing Its Best" (a review of Robert Westbrook's *John Dewey and American Democracy*) in *London Review of Books* 13 (1991) and "Something to Steer By" (a review of Alan Ryan's *John Dewey and the High Tide of Americal Liberalism*) in *London Review of Books* 18 (1996). Kloppenberg's "Pragmatism: An Old Name for Some New Ways of Thinking?" (*Journal of American History* 83, no. 1 [1996], 100–38) is, for the most part, a judicious account of the similarities and differences between classical and "neo"-pragmatism. Further reflection on these similarities and differences can be found in many of the essays collected in *The New Pragmatism*, ed. Morris Dickstein (Durham, N.C.: Duke University Press, 1997).

10 Manfred Frank, *What Is Neostructuralism?* trans. Sabine Wilke and Richard Gray (Minneapolis: University of Minnesota Press, 1989), 87.

11 Ibid., 93. Frank says, "The linguistic turn consists in the transferral of the philosophical paradigm of consciousness onto that of the sign" (217). I myself would have said "the sentence" rather than "the sign," in order to exclude the sorts of iconical and indexical signs Peirce included in his semiotic. This would accord with what Frank, following Tugendhat, says about propositional attitudes being "the basic form of all intentional consciousness" (219). He there quotes Tugendhat as saying that "the question of consciousness dissolves into the question of propositional understanding"; I take that dissolution to be the crucial difference between philosophers' talk of "experience" circa 1900 and their talk of "language" circa 1990.

12 Ibid., 87.   13 Ibid., 7.

projected by language is more or less representative of the way the world really is than any other. By "scientism" I mean the doctrine that natural science is privileged over other areas of culture, that something about natural science puts it in closer – or at least more reliable – touch with reality than any other human activity.

If one wishes to wed historicism and scientism, then one will marry Hegel and Darwin not by finding a holistic, panpsychist way of describing the relations between experience and nature, but rather by finding a historicist, relativist way of describing Darwin's claim upon our attention. By a historicist and relativist way, I mean a way of seeing natural science in general, and Darwin in particular, as simply one more image of the world to be placed alongside others, rather than as offering the *one* image that corresponds to reality. Whereas Kant, Fichte, and Hegel had to condemn natural science's image of the world to the realm of "appearance" in order to avoid conflict with our common moral consciousness – had to say that natural science did not, appearances to the contrary, *really* coincide with reality as it was in itself – a historicist way of avoiding this conflict cannot invoke an appearance–reality distinction. Nor can it resort to notions of misleading abstraction and misplaced concreteness, for "concrete" implies a special relation of closeness to reality for which historicism has no room. On a historicist account, there is no description of nature that is more or less accurate or concrete than some rival (unless "more accurate" and "more concrete" are construed pragmatically, as meaning something like "more useful for the following purposes . . . ").

On the interpretation of Dewey that I want to suggest, the point of the pragmatist theory of truth is to provide such a nonidealistic, historicist way of avoiding the conflict between science and religious or moral consciousness. That theory substitutes "expediency" for "accuracy" or "concreteness" as a term of epistemic approbation. But the pragmatist theory of truth, notoriously, comes in two distinct forms, only one of which will do for my interpretation of Dewey. This is the form embodied in James's claim that "the true . . . is only the expedient in the way of our thinking, just as the right is only the expedient in our way of behaving."[14]

This statement of the theory of truth is quite distinct from James's unfortunate claim that "ideas (which are themselves but parts of our experience) become true just insofar as they help us get into satisfactory relation with other parts of our experience."[15] That claim is unfortunate for two rea-

14 William James, *Pragmatism* (Cambridge, Mass.: Harvard University Press, 1976), 106.
15 Ibid., 35.

sons. First, it runs together the truth of a sentence (which, unless it contains a referent to a time, is eternally true or eternally false and cannot "become" true) with the expediency of believing a sentence to be true. Second, it runs together sentences with experiences – linguistic entities with psychical ones.

James and Dewey usually spoke as if these two formulations came to much the same thing – that anyone who accepted the first would be inclined to accept the second. But whereas the former statement of the pragmatist theory points in the direction of Herder, Humboldt, and a historicist sense of truth as a property of linguistic entities, the latter does not. The first formulation can easily be made compatible with the linguistic turn, but not the second. The second, but not the first, contains the germ of panpsychism and radical empiricism. "Getting into satisfactory relation with other parts of our experience" will be acceptable as an account of true beliefs only if both the distinction between the propositional and the nonpropositional and that between properties of the agent and properties of her environment are blurred in the way Dewey blurs both in *Experience and Nature*.[16]

One way of highlighting the difference between the first and the second formulation can be put in terms of pragmatism's relation to Darwin. Darwinism requires that we think of what we do and are as continuous with what amoebas, spiders, and squirrels do and are. One way to expound this continuity is suggested by the second formula: we may think of these members of other species and of ourselves as sharing something called "experience" – something not the same as consciousness or thought, but something of which consciousness or thought is a more complex and developed form. This way of obtaining continuity is illustrated by Locke's attempt to tell a story about how we get from the baby's mind to the adult's – by adding in more simple ideas and then joining them to produce complex ideas. This way of procuring continuity blurs the distinction Peirce draws between cognitive and noncognitive mental states – between, for example, sensations and beliefs. As I have argued in my *Philosophy and the Mirror of Nature*, it also blurs the distinction between the question "What causes our beliefs?" and

---

16 I have criticized this blurring in "Dewey's Metaphysics," in my *Consequences of Pragmatism* (Minneapolis: Minnesota University Press, 1982), 72–89. Robert Westbrook (*John Dewey and American Democracy* [Ithaca, N.Y.: Cornell University Press, 1991], 540) criticizes me for saying, in effect, "Thumbs up for *Reconstruction in Philosophy*, thumbs down for *Experience and Nature*," and for ignoring the fact that Dewey "believed effective cultural criticism still might profit from the general 'ground-maps' that philosophers could provide." I think that the most profitable ground maps Dewey provided were those to the history of Western philosophy. His attempts to provide ground-maps to the range of human experience still seem to me hopeless.

the question "What justifies our beliefs?" – a blurring that is essential for any representationalist theory of knowledge.

This blurring is characteristic both of British empiricism and of British idealism. All that the "radical empiricism" side of pragmatism did was to qualify this blurring by denying that relations among ideas are "contributed by the mind" rather than "given" in the way in which qualia are purportedly "given" – denying that, as Green put it, "only thought relates." As Dewey said, "Unless there is breach of historic and natural continuity, cognitive experience must originate within that of a noncognitive sort."[17] Because Dewey was committed to such blurring, he refused to separate intentionality and intelligence from consciousness in the manner of contemporary philosophers who (like Daniel Dennett) have gotten on intimate terms with intelligent but insensate machines. Even as late as *Experience and Nature,* a book in which language gets considerable play, we find Dewey saying, "Sentiency in itself is anoetic . . . but nevertheless it is an indispensable means to any noetic function."[18]

The problem with this way of obtaining continuity between us and brutes is that it seems to shove the philosophically embarrassing discontinuity back down to the gap between, say, viruses and amoebas. But why stop there? Only giving something like experience to protein molecules, and perhaps eventually to quarks – only a full-fledged panpsychism – will eliminate such embarrassments. But when we invoke panpsychism in order to bridge the gap between experience and nature, we begin to feel that something has gone wrong. For notions like "experience," "consciousness," and "thought" were originally invoked to *contrast* something that varied independently of nature with nature itself. The philosophically interesting sense – the only sense relevant to epistemology – of "experience" is one that goes back to *ta phainomena* rather than to *empeiria,* to a realm that might well be "out of touch" with nature because it could vary while nature remained the same, and remain the same when nature varied. Much of Dewey's work was a desperate, futile attempt to get rid of the *phainomena* versus *ontōs onta,* appearance versus true reality, distinction and to replace it with a distinction of degree between less organized and directed and more organized and directed *empeiria.* This attempt was futile because his fellow philosophers insisted on language in which they could discuss the possibility of our being "out of touch with reality" or "lost in a realm of mere appearance." Dewey often rejoined by insist-

---

17 John Dewey, *Experience and Nature,* in *The Later Works of John Dewey* (Carbondale: Southern Illinois University Press, 1988), 1: 29–30.
18 Ibid., 199.

ing that we replace the appearance–reality distinction by a distinction between beliefs useful for some purposes and beliefs useful for others. If he
had stayed with *that* rejoinder, he would have been on firm ground. But unfortunately he also rejoined that his opponents had "misdescribed experience" and this rejoinder was utterly ineffectual.

In his "Empirical Survey of Empiricisms," Dewey said that we needed "a
new concept of experience and a new type of empiricism" – one that invoked
neither the Greek contrast of experience and reason nor the atomistic sen-
sationalism of Hume, Mill, and Russell. But he admitted that "this third view
of experience . . . is still more or less inchoate."[19] Most of Dewey's critics felt
that it was not only inchoate but confused and disingenuous. For it seemed
to them that any sense of "experience" that did not acknowledge a possible
divergence between experience and nature merely blurred the issues that a
theory of knowledge ought to discuss.[20] So they saw Dewey not as presenting what Kloppenberg calls a "radical theory of knowledge" but as dodging
hard epistemological questions by redefining the terms in which they had
been raised.[21]

I think that these critics were justified and that the force of the pragmatist
theory of truth was blunted by Dewey's unpersuasive redefinitions. James and
Dewey never, alas, made up their minds whether they wanted to just forget
about epistemology or whether they wanted to devise a new improved epistemology of their own. On my view, they should have opted for forgetting.
Dewey should have dropped the term "experience," not redefined it. He
should have looked elsewhere for continuity between us and the brutes. He
should have agreed with Peirce that a great gulf divides sensation and cog- *good*
nition, decided that cognition was possible only for language users, and then
said that the only relevant break in continuity was between non–language
users (amoebas, squirrels, babies) and language users.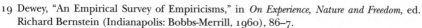

He could then have gone on to note that the development of linguistic

19 Dewey, "An Empirical Survey of Empiricisms," in *On Experience, Nature and Freedom*, ed.
Richard Bernstein (Indianapolis: Bobbs-Merrill, 1960), 86–7.
20 I have mounted criticisms of Dewey's *Experience and Nature* along these lines myself in
"Dewey's Metaphysics."
21 See E. B. McGilvary, "The 'Chicago Idea' and Idealism," reprinted in John Dewey, *The Early
Works of John Dewey* (Carbondale: Southern Illinois University Press, 1971), 4: 317–27, esp.
322, where McGilvary says of the scheme produced by Dewey's redefinitions that "it is beautifully simple, and if you adhere to it, you get rid of some very disagreeable questions [i.e.,
the traditional epistemological problems about the relation of thought to reality] which
force themselves on you if you refuse to adopt it. But if the questions referred to are asked
with a view to determining whether the new way of ideas comports with facts, then we have
a different matter on our hands."

behavior – of social practices that use increasingly flexible vocal cords and thumbs to produce longer and more complex strings of noises and marks – is readily explicable in naturalistic, Darwinian terms. We can tell as good stories about the success of species that gradually developed such practices as we can about the success of species that developed practices of migrating or hibernating. How meaning became a property of certain strings of marks and noises is as unmysterious as how tableness became a property of batches of molecules.[22] It differs in this respect from experience or consciousness. So, my alternative Dewey would have said, we can construe "thinking" as simply the use of sentences – both for purposes of arranging cooperative enterprises and for attributing inner states (beliefs, desires) to our fellow humans. If we have thinking in this sense – the ability to have and ascribe sentential attitudes – we can see it as something that has nothing in particular to do with "experiences of a noncognitive sort." To be sure, there is a *causal* continuity between experience as what Dewey called "a matter of functions and habits, of active adjustments and readjustments, of co-ordinations and activities"[23] and thinking, but for that matter there is a causal continuity between nutrition and thinking too. Such continuity does not require us to find a sort of protolanguage in amoebas.

The point of these last paragraphs may be summed up as follows: Dewey's and James's attempts to give a "more concrete," more holistic, and less dualism-ridden account of experience would have been unnecessary if they had not tried to make "true" a predicate of experiences and had instead let it be a predicate of sentences. For then they would not have thought of "ideas (which are themselves but parts of our experience)" *becoming* true or being *made* true. They would not have set themselves the bad question "Granted that truth is *in some sense* the agreement or correspondence of experiences with reality, what must experience and reality be such that they can stand in such relations?"

Asking this question made James and Dewey think that the cause of the endless disputes about subject and object, mind and body was a misunderstanding of the nature of experience or reality or both. But this was not the cause. The cause was the idea that truth is a matter of a certain relation between subject and object, mind and the physical world – a relation of "agreement" or "correspondence." James and Dewey agreed that this relation could not be a matter of "copying" – of features shared by the experience

22 See, once again, Brandom's *Making It Explicit*.
23 John Dewey, "A Short Catechism Concerning Truth," in *The Middle Works of John Dewey* (Carbondale: Southern Illinois University Press, 1985), 6: 5.

and the reality. But they thought they had to find a substitute for "copying" and asked what "agreement" might mean instead.[24] James said that it must mean "verification" in the sense of "agreeable leading" from one bit of experience to another. "Truth *happens* to an idea," James said, when it succeeds in marrying new experience to old experience.[25] Again:

> To 'agree' in the widest sense with a reality, *can only mean to be guided either straight up to it or into its surroundings, or to be put into such working touch with it as to handle either it or something connected with it better than if we disagreed.*[26]

Dewey's version of this goes as follows:

> ... the pragmatist holds that the relation in question is one of correspondence between existence and thought; but he holds that correspondence instead of being an ultimate and unanalyzable mystery, to be defined by iteration, is precisely a matter of correspondence in its plain, familiar, sense. A condition of dubious and conflicting tendencies calls out thinking as a method of handling it. This condition produces its own appropriate consequences, bearing its own fruits of weal and woe. The thoughts, the estimates, intents, and projects it calls out, just because they are attitudes of response and of attempted adjustment (*not* mere 'states of consciousness') produce their effects also. The kind of interlocking, of interadjustment that then occurs between these two sorts of consequences constitutes the correspondence that makes truth.[27]

These redefinitions of "agreement" and "correspondence" would be harmless enough if they were simply ways of saying "truth is what works" – if they were simply restatements of what I previously called "the first formulation" of the pragmatist theory of truth. But James and Dewey thought of them as more than that, and that is why they were led down the garden path of "radical empiricism." It is why they ran together an insistence on what Kloppenberg calls "the contingent quality of our most basic categories of thought" with the claim that we need what he calls "a new conception of immediate lived experience."[28]

Much of what I have been saying can be summarized as the claim that Dewey and James thought that an appropriate philosophical response to Darwin required a kind of vitalism – an attempt to coalesce the vocabulary of epistemology with that of evolutionary biology. This was the attempt whose most

---

24 James, *Pragmatism*, 96: "Where our ideas cannot copy definitely their object, what does agreement with that object mean?"
25 See ibid., 97, 103.   26 Ibid., 102.   27 Dewey, "A Short Catechism," 5–6.
28 See Kloppenberg, *Uncertain Victory*, 65.

notorious products were the jargons of *A Pluralistic Universe, Creative Evolution, Process and Reality, Experience and Nature,* and *Knowing and the Known.* But in his "Influence of Darwin on Philosophy" Dewey suggests a better alternative.[29] This is that we see Darwin as showing us how to naturalize Hegel – how to have Herderian historicism without Kantian idealism, how to hold on to a Hegelian narrative of progress while dispensing with the claim that the real is the rational.

The problem with wedding Hegel and Darwin has always been that Hegel seems to say that human civilization just *couldn't* casually be wiped out by a plague or a comet and that language-using beings just *had* to emerge from the evolutionary process so that the Idea could finish off Nature and get started on Spirit. He seems to say that there really is a power, not ourselves, that is more like us than it is like amoebas or squirrels – or, more precisely, a power of which we are better manifestations than they are. So the purely mechanical account of biological evolution offered by a synthesis of Darwin with Mendel, though commending itself to atheists, seems antithetical to a philosophy built, as Hegel's was, around the idea of the Incarnate Logos.[30]

The nice thing about purely mechanical accounts of nature, from an atheist's point of view, is that they tell us that there are no purposes to be

---

29 John Dewey, "The Influence of Darwin on Philosophy," in *The Middle Works,* 4: 3–14.

30 See *Hegel's Philosophy of Mind,* trans. William Wallace (Oxford: Oxford University Press, 1971), 17 (sec. 383, *Zusatz*): "God has revealed that his nature consists in having a Son, i.e., in making a distinction within himself, making himself finite, but in his difference remaining in communion with himself . . . so that the Son is not the mere organ of the revelation but is himself the content of the revelation." Compare the polemic against the "idea of knowledge as an instrument and as a medium" in the introduction to *The Phenomenology of Spirit.* Hegel thought that whenever you had a picture of knowledge as a matter of relating (via an organ or a medium) two independently existing entities (the Subject and the Object), you automatically brought about the sort of skepticism that culminates in the Kantian claim that things-in-themselves are unknowable. This is why Absolute Idealism is the only alternative to skepticism. For a sample of the early Dewey's version of this Hegelian line of thought, see chapter 9, "Stages of Knowledge: Intuition," in *Psychology (The Early Works,* vol. 2), especially 212: "The true self-related must be the organic unity of the self and the world, of the idea and the real, and this is what we know as God. It must be remembered that this intuition is one like in kind to the other intuitions, and involves the process of mediation as much as they. . . . Every concrete act of knowledge involves an intuition of God." Dewey's *Psychology* insouciantly mingles Absolute Idealism with Wundtian empirical psychology – mingling metaphysics with psychophysical correlation in just the way that James, at the outset of his own *The Principles of Psychology,* said he was going to avoid. Dewey gave up on God *qua* Absolute Idea not long after writing that book. But the themes of the need to insist on continuity to avoid skepticism, and of cognitive development as continuous with animal and infantile feeling and as consisting in ever-expanding relationality, continue to be sounded throughout Dewey's later work.

served save our own and that we serve no purposes except those we dream up as we go along. As Dewey said in his Darwin essay,

> [T]he classic [Greek] notion of species carried with it the idea of purpose. . . . Purposefulness accounted for the intelligibilty of nature and the possibility of science, while the absolute or cosmic character of this purposefulness gave sanction and worth to the moral and religious endeavours of man.[31]

Dewey argued that Darwin had finished the job Galileo began – the job of eliminating from nature any purpose that transcends a particular organism's needs in a particular situation.[32] But once purpose leaves nature, there is no longer a philosophical problem about the "possibility of science" (or, more generally, of knowledge). For there is no longer a problem of reconciling the subject's purposes with the object's – of getting the two on the same wavelength. The object becomes an object of manipulation rather than the embodiment of either a *telos* or a *logos,* and truth becomes "the expedient in the way of thinking." The contrast between the pursuit of truth and the pursuit of expediency goes when the notion of truth as "agreement" or "correspondence" with something that has purposes of its own goes.

In other words, if one *wholeheartedly* adopts the first formulation of the pragmatist theory of truth, one will feel no need to follow it up with the second formulation. So one will feel no need to ask about what experience is *really* like, as opposed to the way in which the Greeks or the British empiricists described it, or to ask whether nature is better described in vitalistic or mechanistic terms. For all descriptions of experience, nature, and their relation to one another will be evaluated *simply* in terms of expediency – of suitability for accomplishing the purpose at hand. That is how Dewey wanted the pragmatic theory of truth evaluated. He says:

> Naturally, the pragmatist claims his theory to be true in the pragmatic sense of truth; it works, it clears up difficulties, removes obscurities, puts individuals into more experimental, less dogmatic, and less arbitrarily sceptical relations to life; aligns philosophy with scientific method; does away with self-made problems of epistemology; clarifies and reorganizes logical theory, etc.[33]

Consider the claim that the pragmatist theory of truth "aligns philosophy with scientific method" in the light of Dewey's impish remark that Hegel is the "quintessence of the scientific spirit."[34] His point is that whereas Kant's transcendental idealism "starts from the accepted scholastic conception of

31 Dewey, "The Influence of Darwin," 8–9.   32 See ibid., 7.
33 Dewey, "A Short Catechism," 9.
34 John Dewey, "The Present Position of Logical Theory," in *The Early Works,* 3: 134.

thought,"[35] Hegel's Absolute Idealism broke free of the notion of "a special faculty of thought with its own peculiar and fixed forms."[36] Hegel, Dewey says, "denies the existence of any faculty of thought which is other than the expression of fact itself."[37] He holds that "the only possible thought is the reflection of the significance of fact."[38]

The terms "expression of fact" and "significance of fact" are not very perspicuous, but it seems fair to interpret them as meaning "the significance of what is going on for the purposes of the community of inquirers doing the thinking." More generally, it seems fair to interpret the invidious contrast Dewey draws between Kant and Hegel in terms of the contrast between a pre-Darwinian attachment to the idea of purposes not our own and a post-Darwinian ability to see inquiry as continuous with practical deliberation.[39] It seems fair, in short, to interpret Dewey as seeing the opposition between Kant and Hegel as an opposition between a nonpragmatic and a proto-pragmatic view of inquiry.

Once one starts to look for pragmatism in Hegel, one finds quite a bit to go on. In particular, one can capitalize on Hegel's remark that "philosophy is its time apprehended in thought" – a remark that might serve as a motto for Dewey's attempts to see the changing problematics of philosophers as reflections of sociocultural developments. The more one pursues the theme of *embodiment* in Hegel – explores what Taylor calls the "anti-dualist" implications of the "expressivist" line of thought that Hegel took over from Herder[40] – the more one wants to brush aside the ontology of Absolute Idealism and the insistence that the real is the rational. One finds oneself trying to wean Hegel away from the Idea, just as Hegel (and later Peirce) tried to wean Kant from the thing-in-itself. To succeed in doing so would be to get Hegel to stop talking about human communities as expressions of something greater than themselves – stages in the realization of some purpose

35 Ibid., 134–5.
36 Ibid., 135.
37 Ibid., 138–9.
38 Ibid., 140.
39 See Dewey's "The Intellectualist Criterion of Thinking," in *The Early Works*, 4: 58, for a polemic against F. H. Bradley's "intellectualist" claim that "[t]hinking is the attempt to satisfy as *special* impulse." The same claim appears in contemporary critics of pragmatism like Bernard Williams, whose notion of "the absolute conception of reality" incorporates almost all the features Dewey thought undesirably "intellectualist." See J. E. Tiles, *John Dewey* (London: Routledge, 1988), chap. 5, for a very useful account of Williams as Dewey's antithesis. For a similiar comparison, see my "Is Natural Science a Natural Kind?" my *Objectivity, Relativism, and Truth* (Cambridge University Press, 1991), 46–62.
40 See Charles Taylor, *Hegel* (Cambridge University Press, 1975), 24, 539–40.

greater than they themselves could envisage. Then one could just see such communities "expressivistically," in terms of their own local needs. But this shift would lead Hegel, and us, to describe our own community and our own philosophical views in terms of parochial, temporary, contingent needs.

It would lead one, for example, to put forward an account of truth not as something that clears up all difficulties or removes all obscurities connected with the topic, but as something useful in clearing up *our* difficulties and removing *our* obscurities. If one claims that a theory of truth is what works better than any competing theory, one is saying that it works better by reference to *our* purposes, *our* particular situation in intellectual history. One is not claiming that that was how it would have paid, always and everywhere, to have thought of truth. It is simply what it would be best for *us* to believe about truth. Taken as part of an overall philosophical outlook, such a theory would be part of an attempt to hold *our* age in thought.

I can describe this area of overlap between Hegel and Dewey in another way by considering a standard objection to pragmatist theories of truth: pragmatism tells you that truth is what works but doesn't answer the question "works for what?" It doesn't tell you what purposes to have; its ethics is situational at best. So, of course, was Hegel's ethics, and that was another reason Dewey consistently preferred Hegel to Kant. The dualism of "ought" and "is," of categorical and hypothetical imperatives, was for Dewey one more symptom of Kant's "scholastic" presuppositions.[41]

Dewey's fundamental contribution to moral philosophy has always been taken as his insistence on a "means–end continuum" – that is, as the claim that we change our notions of the Right and of the Good on the basis of the particular mixture of success and failure produced by our previous efforts to act rightly and do what is good. This insistence can be seen as one more consequence of his historicism. The historicism that Taylor and Frank find in Herder and Humboldt is one which insists that the language of moral deliberation, and of moral praise or blame, is a function of the needs a society hopes to fulfill. Societies evolve into other societies by finding that the moral language they have been using brings with it consequences they do

---

41 See John Dewey, "Moral Theory and Practice," in *The Early Works*, 3: 104, on "the movement of German ethics from Kant to Hegel." See also "Poetry and Philosophy," *The Early Works*, 3: 118, for a criticism of "the Stoics, Kant and Matthew Arnold" as holding a "conception of the individual as shut off from real communion with nature and with fellow-man, and yet as bearing within himself a universal principle" – a conception to which Robert Browning stands as the antithesis. Although the "Poetry and Philosophy" essay does not mention Hegel, it seems reasonable to suppose that Dewey saw Hegel standing to Browning as Kant to Arnold.

not like – just as species evolve into other species by finding that some of the habits their ancestors developed for coping with one environment have become liabilities in coping with a changed environment. To say that moral progress occurs is to say that later societies are more complex, more developed, more articulate, and above all more flexible than their predecessors. It is to say that later societies have more varied and interesting needs than earlier ones, just as squirrels have more varied and interesting needs than amoebas.

If one asks why flexibility, articulation, variety, and interestingness are worthy ends to pursue – why they are morally relevant ends for individuals or societies – Dewey has nothing more to tell you than "so act as to increase the meaning of present experience."[42] "We do not," he says, "require a revelation of some supreme perfection to inform us whether or not we are making headway in present rectification."[43] It is as futile for human communities to ask, "Is our recent political history, the one we summarize in a narrative of gradual progress, taking us in the right direction?" as it would have been for squirrels to ask whether their evolution from shrews had been going in the right direction. Squirrels do what is best by their lights, and so do we. Both of us have been moving in the direction of what seems, by our respective lights, more flexibility, more freedom, and more variety.

In this attitude toward morality, it seems to me, we get a genuine marriage of Darwin with a de-absolutized Hegel. Just as, in the case of truth and knowledge, we had to introduce a seemingly un-Darwinian discontinuity between language and sentience in order to get an unparadoxical account of truth and to capture the point of Hegel's distinction between Nature and Spirit, so here we have to introduce a seemingly un-Hegelian sense of irrationality and contingency in order to get a suitably Darwinian account of morality. But just as in the preceding case we can give a naturalistic account of the difference of kind between the intentional and the nonintentional (by viewing the social practices that make language and intentionality possible as continuous with those that made cooperative hunts for woolly mammoths possible), so here we can give a more or less teleological account of seemingly irrational accident. We can say that a given irrational and accidental event (e.g., the decline of dinosaurs, the desire for gold among bigoted and fanatical sixteenth-century monarchs) in fact contributed to an admirable result (anthropoids, the United States of America), not because world-historical Reason was cunning, but just by good luck.

---

42 John Dewey, *Human Nature and Conduct*, in *The Middle Works*, 14: 196.
43 Ibid., 195.

Teleological thinking is inevitable, but Dewey offers us a relativist and materialist version of teleology rather than an absolute and idealist one. Whereas Hegel held that the study of history brings over from philosophy the thought that the real is the rational, the Hegel–Darwin synthesis Dewey proposes must de-ontologize this claim and make it simply a regulative, heuristic principle. Narratives of historical progress are legitimized not by the philosopher's explanation that the slaughter-bench of history is where the Incarnate Logos is redemptively tortured, but because we want historians to be able to discern what Hegel called "the rose in the cross of the present." A historian should be able to tell her community how it is now in a position to be, intellectually and morally, better than predecessor communities thanks to its knowledge of the struggles of those predecessors. As the saying goes, we know more than our ancestors because they are what we know; what we most want to know about them is how to avoid their mistakes.[44]

I said earlier that the most Dewey can claim is that truth as what works is the theory of truth it now pays us to have. It pays us to believe this because we have seen the unfortunate results of believing otherwise – of trying to find some ahistorical and absolute relation to reality for truth to name – and we must now try to do better. Similarly, the theory that, as Dewey said, "growth itself is the only moral end" is the moral theory it now pays us to have, for we have seen the unfortunate results of trying to divinize and eternalize a given social practice or form of individual life.[45] In both epistemology and moral philosophy, in short, we have seen the unfortunate results of trying to think of normative terms like "true" or "good" or "right" as signifying relations of "agreement" or "correspondence" between something human and something nonhuman.

From this perspective, the question "Does Dewey give us a satisfactory theory of the true, the good, and the right?" presupposes an answer to the

---

44 Note that this is true not only for onward-and-upward stories like Hegel's but for stories of decline from greatness like Heidegger's. Only because we have reached our present nadir can a Heidegger draw the redemptive moral of this decline. "Wo aber Gefahr ist, wächst das Rettende auch."

45 The doctrine that evil is just out-of-date good is as central to Dewey as it was to Hegel. See, e.g., "Outlines of a Critical Theory of Ethics," in *The Early Works,* 3: 379: "Goodness is not remoteness from badness. In one sense, goodness is based upon badness; that is, good action is always based upon action good once, but bad if persisted in under changing circumstances." See also *Human Nature and Conduct,* 193: "The worse or evil is a rejected good. In deliberation and before choice no evil presents itself as evil. Until it is rejected, it is a competing good. After rejection, it figures not as a lesser good, but as the bad of that situation."

question "What, at the present moment in history, is the function of such theories?" Dewey thought that the function of all philosophical theories was the same: not to "deal with ultimate reality" but to "clarify men's ideas as to the social and moral strifes of their own day."[46] This function is, however, that of high culture in general, rather than of philosophy in particular. So I think it would have been a bit more precise to say that the particular charge of philosophy is to make sure that old *philosophical* ideas do not block the road of inquiry – that continued use of the normative language employed in the social and moral strifes of an earlier day does not make it harder to cope with contemporary problems.

Dewey thought that the reductionist use of Darwin and the rationalist use of Hegel had produced some normative language that was, in fact, blocking our road. Darwin's scientistic followers (those who emphasized what he had in common with Hobbes rather than what he had in common with St. Francis) suggested that there was an underlying reality – the struggle for survival – that high culture is a conspiracy to conceal. Hegel's rationalist followers (those who read him as a historicized Spinoza rather than a metaphysicized Herder) had suggested that there was an underlying reality called "the Absolute" – a reality that somehow validated our religious and moral aspirations. The nineteenth century spent a lot of time dithering between these alternative conceptions of what "ultimate reality" or "human nature" was really like, and thus between traditional and scientistic ways of describing the moral and political choices it faced.

Dewey would have been pleased by the fact that the twentieth century has spent increasingly little time talking about the nature of ultimate reality. In part this has been because the increasing prominence of Language as a topic, accompanied by an increasing recognition that one can describe the same thing in different ways for different purposes, has helped to make pragmatism, as a doctrine of the relativity of normative judgments to purposes served, more palatable. More important, perhaps, is that many different developments in our century – Freudian accounts of inner moral conflicts, ethnographic descriptions of alternative forms of social life, experimentalism in literature and the arts – have made it steadily easier for us to substitute Deweyan questions like "Which communities' purposes shall I share?" and "What sort of person should I try to become?" for the Kantian questions "What should I do?" "What may I hope?" and "What is man?" ?

46 Dewey, *Reconstruction in Philosophy*, in *The Middle Works*, 12: 94.

16

HABERMAS, DERRIDA, AND THE
FUNCTIONS OF PHILOSOPHY

I think of Jacques Derrida as the most intriguing and ingenious of contemporary philosophers, and of Jürgen Habermas as the most socially useful – the one who does the most for social democratic politics. Admiring both men as I do, I should like to iron out some of the differences between them. In this essay, I want to examine Habermas's criticisms of Derrida in his *Philosophical Discourse of Modernity*[1] and then go on to a discussion of Habermas's attempt to put philosophy in the service of human emancipation. My strategy will be to urge that Derrida and Habermas complement rather than oppose each other.

I argued in my *Contingency, Irony, and Solidarity* that Derrida's books are just what you need if you have been impressed and burdened by Heidegger – if you feel the power of Heideggerian language but want to avoid describing yourself in terms of it.[2] A text like "Envois" (the initial section of Derrida's

---

1 Jürgen Habermas, *The Philosophical Discourse of Modernity*, trans. Frederick G. Lawrence (Cambridge, Mass.: MIT Press, 1987).

2 This essay is a reworking of material I had intended to include in *Contingency, Irony, and Solidarity* (Cambridge University Press, 1989) but left out of the final version for organizational reasons. So it sometimes contains bits of the jargon I developed in that book – e.g., a contrast between the "ironist" and the "metaphysician." I defined those terms on pages 73–5. Roughly, the ironist is a nominalist and historicist who strives to retain a sense that the vocabulary of moral deliberation she uses is a product of history and chance – of her having been born at a certain time in a certain place. The metaphysician, by contrast, believes that there is one right vocabulary of moral deliberation, one in touch with reality (and, in particular, with our essential humanity). The heroine of my book is the "liberal ironist" – someone devoted to social justice who nevertheless takes her own devotion to this cause as merely contingent. I discuss Habermas on pages 61–9 as a "liberal who is unwilling to be an ironist." I discuss Derrida's "Envois" in chapter 6. The core of my book is a distinction between private concerns, in the sense of idiosyncratic projects of self-overcoming, and public concerns,

The Postcard) is an edifying account of how one reader of Heidegger wrestled with an overweening grandfather, and won. On the other hand, Habermas's *Philosophical Discourse* is just what you need if you find Heidegger and Derrida equally pointless. Habermas helps you feel justified in circumventing the Nietzsche–Heidegger–Derrida genre of ironist theorizing, in going around it rather than through it. If you remain unimpressed by Heidegger's litanies and Derrida's fantasies, Habermas gives you good reasons for saying that, at least for purposes of doing some public good, you can just *ignore* both.

Habermas sees Heidegger and Derrida as belonging to the tradition he calls "the philosophy of subjectivity," which he traces back to Kant and Hegel. Using my own jargon, I should describe this tradition as one more misguided metaphysical attempt to combine the public and the private. It is an attempt to synthesize activities that it would be better to keep distinct – the effort of an individual thinker to free himself from his predecessors on the one hand, and the collective political enterprise of increasing freedom and equality on the other. The "egoism" that Santayana remarked in German philosophy from Fichte onward was typically combined, until Nietzsche, with an attempt at greater social justice.

But, as Habermas rightly says, "With Nietzsche the criticism of modernity dispenses for the first time with its retention of an emancipatory content."[3] Since Nietzsche's time, the philosophy of subjectivity has been taken over by the ironists – by people who are interested in their own autonomy and individuality rather than in their social usefulness and whose excursions into politics are incidental to their principal motives. What I call "ironist theorizing" – theorizing that emphasizes its own contingency – remained a subtext in Hegel (emerging only at odd moments, such as the end of the introduction to *The Philosophy of Right,* and then thrust back out of sight). But after Nietzsche, this sort of theorizing began to crowd out other genres.

Habermas thinks that the philosophy of subjectivity was a false start and that its political uselessness became increasingly obvious in our century, as we watched philosophers concentrating more and more on the "game of mutually outdoing" each other. As ironist theorizing shoved a concern for human solidarity aside, concern for the emancipation of the individual philosopher from his predecessors replaced concern for the emancipation

---

those having to do with the suffering of other human beings. This distinction is emphatically *not* the one with which some readers (notably feminist critics, such as Nancy Fraser) have identified it: the distinction between the domestic hearth and the public forum, between *oikos* and *polis*.

3 Habermas, *Philosophical Discourse,* 94.

of the oppressed. So Habermas wants to replace this tradition with something of greater social utility: what he calls a "philosophy of intersubjectivity." This sort of philosophy will keep what is still usable in Enlightenment rationalism while jettisoning both metaphysical attempts to "ground" this rationalism in "the nature of the subject" and ironist attempts to "subvert" it.

This philosophy of intersubjectivity centers around a practice characteristic of liberal societies – treating as true whatever can be agreed upon in the course of free discussion and waving aside the question of whether there is some metaphysical object to which the result of such discussion might or might not correspond. Such a philosophy politicizes epistemology, in the sense that it takes what matters to the search for truth to be the social (and in particular the political) conditions under which that search is conducted, rather than the deep inner nature of the subjects doing the searching. Habermas says that he

> conceives of intersubjective understanding as the telos inscribed into communication in ordinary language, and of the logocentrism of Western thought, heightened by the philosophy of consciousness, as a systematic *foreshortening* and *distortion* of a potential always already operative in the communicative practice of everyday life but only selectively exploited.[4]

In other words, what is wrong with what Heidegger calls "metaphysics" and Derrida "logocentrism" is that it has hoped to do by reflection – by looking inward – what can be done only by expanding the scope and membership of a conversation. It has delved into the privacy of "the subject" instead of going public. If we do go public, we shall identify the rational with the procedures, and the true with the results, of "undistorted communication" – the sort of communication characteristic of an ideally democratic society. What stands in the way of such communication has nothing much to do with "logocentrism" and everything to do with practical politics. All that the philosopher, in her professional capacity, can do for social justice is to point out present obstacles to "undistorted communication." These obstacles do not include the esoteric matters discussed by Heidegger and Derrida (e.g., the confusion of Being with the most general features of beings, the presupposed primacy of speech over writing). Rather, they include such things as the control of mass-circulation magazines by people who want to safeguard their own wealth and power at the expense of the poor and weak.

Habermas is certainly right that if we look to the texts commonly identified as "philosophical" for help in realizing the ideals of liberal democracies,

4 Ibid., 311.

we can just *skip* Nietzsche, Heidegger, Derrida, and (most of) Foucault.[5] But I think that he goes one step too far when he says:

> A more viable solution suggests itself if we drop the somewhat sentimental pre-supposition of metaphysical homelessness, and if we understand the hectic to and fro between transcendental and empirical modes of dealing with issues, between radical self-reflection and an incomprehensible element prior to all production – that is to say, when we understand the puzzle of all these dou-blings for what it is: a symptom of exhaustion. The paradigm of the philoso-phy of consciousness is exhausted. If this is so, the symptoms of exhaustion should dissolve with the transition to the paradigm of mutual understanding.[6]

Habermas is right in saying that the ironists' quest for ever deeper irony and ever more ineffable sublimity has little direct public utility. But I do not think this shows that "the paradigm of the philosophy of consciousness is a symp-tom of exhaustion." What he sees as symptoms of exhaustion I see as symp-toms of vitality. This is because I read people like Heidegger and Nietzsche as good *private* philosophers, and he reads them as bad *public* philosophers.

I argue in *Contingency, Irony, and Solidarity* that Heidegger's and Derrida's only relevance to the quest for social justice is that, like the Romantic poets before them, they make more vivid and concrete our sense of what human life might be like in a democratic utopia – a utopia in which the quest for autonomy is impeded as little as possible by social institutions. They do little to justify the choice of such a utopia or to hasten its arrival. But they do show how the creation of new discourses can enlarge the realm of possibility. They thereby help free us from the picture that gave rise to the philosophy of sub-jectivity in the first place – the metaphysician's picture of something deep within us, at the center of every human self, uncaused by and unreachable

---

5 Foucault is the one person on this list who might be thought to have reversed Nietzsche's in-clination to disengage philosophy from projects of human emancipation. Foucault certainly said a lot of useful things about contemporary institutions, but I agree with Habermas's crit-icism of Foucault in chapters 9 and 10 of *The Philosophical Discourse of Modernity*, and in par-ticular with his claim that Foucault's notion of emancipation turns on a contrast between "power" and "the implicit knowledge of the people" upon whom power is exercised – a con-trast to which Foucault is not, given his view of the interconnection of truth and power, en-titled. Some readers of Derrida, such as Richard Bernstein, have attempted to attribute ethicopolitical, egalitarian motives to his work; Derrida himself obviously believes that de-construction has some sort of political relevance. I am dubious about such claims, but I will not try to argue the issue here. Derrida's own attempt to make deconstruction relevant to politics is ably criticized by Thomas McCarthy in "On the Margins of Politics," *Journal of Phi-losophy* 86 (1989), 645–8.

6 Habermas, *Philosophical Discourse*, 296.

by historically conditioned processes of acculturation, something that privileges one vocabulary of moral deliberation over all the others.

Because Habermas reads these writers as unsuccessful public philosophers – philosophers who still aim at the "self-reassurance of modernity," at giving the modern age something that will replace religion – he makes a move I do not want to make. He demands that writers like Heidegger and Derrida provide a public justification of their own practice – an intersubjectively arguable account of what they are doing. He wants to treat them as claiming what he calls "universal validity," whereas I regard the question of universal validity as irrelevant to their practices.[7] Whereas I want to see the line of thought that runs from Nietzsche to Heidegger to Derrida as (even if this was not the intent of these writers themselves) opening up new private possibilities, possibilities only incidentally and contingently relevant to liberal social hope, Habermas sees this line of thought as a public danger, as a threat to democratic society. When discussing Heidegger, he puts Heidegger's diagnosis of the state of the modern world – his crusade against technology, giantism, and Americanism – in the foreground. I would treat this crusade as epiphenomenal. When discussing Derrida, he insists that Derrida not just *exhibit* a new kind of writing, but justify writing that way by argument. Derrida, he says,

> can only attain Heidegger's goal of bursting metaphysical thought-forms from the inside by means of his essentially rhetorical procedure if the philosophical text is *in truth* a literary one – if one can *demonstrate* that the genre distinction between philosophy and literature dissolves upon closer examination.[8]

---

7 Habermas says that "the transcendent moment of *universal* validity bursts every provinciality asunder; the obligatory moment of accepted validity claims renders them carriers of a *context-bound* everyday practice" (ibid., 322). But no provincial context is going to burst before somebody has recontextualized current everyday practice by dreaming up new words in which to express alternative possibilities. Revolutionary recontextualization is the sort of thing both poets and ironist theorists (like Heidegger and Derrida) are good at. Sometimes Habermas talks as if he had adopted the metaphysician's assumption that all the alternative candidates for belief and desire are already available and as if the only problem were making sure they got thrashed out freely. That sort of assumption is suggested, e.g., in his discussion of Schiller's *Aesthetic Education of Man;* he takes Schiller to be treating "art as primarily a form of communication" (ibid., 48) and to be sowing the germ of the Weberian idea of "the independent logics of the value spheres of science, morality and art" (50). Romanticism seems to make Habermas nervous. He does not discuss Schiller's exaltation of "play," nor is he inclined to follow Shelley (as Dewey did) in thinking of poets as unacknowledged legislators. Still, I take it he might agree with me that all social institutions can do is give you freedom of discussion; you still need the poetic imagination, still need revolutionary recontextualizers to give you new alternatives to discuss. For he remarks that "the specialized languages of science and technology, law and morality, economics, political science, etc. . . . live off the illuminating power of metaphorical tropes" (205).

8 Ibid., 189.

In what follows, I shall confine myself to this last claim.[9] Examining it will, I hope, let me clarify my own sense of the distinct functions fufilled by Habermas's public sort of philosophy and by Derrida's privatized sort of philosophy.

Habermas says that "Derrida does not belong to those philosophers who like to argue."[10] He therefore looks to Derrida's admirers in the United States for the arguments he thinks Derrida needs. He finds what he wants in Jonathan Culler's claim:

> If serious language is a special case of non-serious, if truths are fictions whose fictionality has been forgotten, then literature is not a deviant, parasitical instance of language. On the contrary, other discourses can be seen as cases of a generalized literature, or archi-literature.[11]

Putting aside for a moment the question of whether one needs to put forward any such large, metaphysical-sounding theses in order to defend Derrida's practice,[12] let us see what Habermas says in reply to Culler's claim.

In the course of an intricate argument, which I will not try to summarize, he makes two principal points. The first is that one can distinguish between "ordinary" and "parasitical" uses of language by distinguishing between language that operates under the constraint of being "open to criticism on the basis of making validity claims" and language that is free from this constraint.[13] The second point, which undergirds and clarifies the first, is that

9 This means that I will not go into the interesting, but large and tangled question, much discussed ever since the days of *Knowledge and Human Interests,* of the respective roles of ahistoricist universalist "transcendentalism" and of pragmatic kibitzing in Habermas's thought. To discuss this topic adequately would involve getting into the further question of whether Habermas wants a theory of rationality that "grounds" democratic institutions in an ahistorical foundation or simply one that summarizes the tendencies of those institutions – whether Habermas's metaphilosophy is or is not, like Rawls's, explicitly historicist. I have mooted this question briefly in "Habermas and Lyotard on Post-Modernity" (in my *Essays on Heidegger and Others* [Cambridge University Press, 1991], 11–12) and in a review of *Philosophical Discourse* (*London Review of Books,* September 3, 1987).

10 Habermas, *Philosophical Discourse,* 193.

11 Jonathan Culler, *On Deconstruction* (Ithaca, N.Y.: Cornell University Press, 1982), 181, quoted by Habermas, *Philosophical Discourse,* 193.

12 I argue, in various essays included in Part II of my *Essays on Heidegger and Others,* that no such need exists.

13 Habermas, *Philosophical Discourse,* 199. Habermas backs up this distinction by saying "Language games only work because they presuppose idealizations that transcend any particular language game; as a necessary condition of possibly reaching understanding, these idealizations give rise to the perspective of an agreement that is open to criticism on the basis of validity claims. A language operating under these kinds of constraints is subject to an ongoing test. Everyday communicative practise, in which agents have to reach an understanding about something in the world, stands under the need to prove its worth, and it is the idealizing suppositions that make such testing possible in the first place." I agree with

there is a distinction between the "world-disclosing" and the "problem-solving" functions of language. Habermas thinks that Derrida denies the existence both of an "independently structured domain of everyday communicative practise" and of an "autonomous realm of fiction." He says:

> Because Derrida denies both, he can analyze any given discourse in accord with the model of poetic language, and do so as if language generally were determined by the poetic use of language specialized in world-disclosure. From this viewpoint, language as such converges with literature or indeed with "writing." This *aestheticizing of language, which is purchased with the twofold denial of the proper senses of normal and poetic discourse,* also explains Derrida's insensitivity toward the tension-filled polarity between the poetic-world-disclosive function of language and its prosaic, innerworldly functions. . . . An aesthetic contextualism blinds him to the fact that everyday communicative practice makes learning processes possible (thanks to built-in idealizations) in relation to which the world-disclosive force of interpreting language has in turn to prove its worth. . . . He permits the capacity to solve problems to disappear behind the world-creating capacity of language.[14]

On my reading of Derrida, he does not "deny" the existence of any of the things to which Habermas accuses him of being blind. He knows perfectly well that there are communicative practices to which argumentation by reference to standard rules is essential, and that these are indispensable for public purposes. He does not need to say, with Culler, that "the serious is a special case of the non-serious," though he and Habermas should be able to agree that "other discourses *can* be seen as cases of a generalized literature" if some useful purpose is served by so seeing them. Derrida has developed a way of writing that helps us so to see them. But, *pace* Culler (and Rodolphe Gasché),[15] this way of writing neither presupposes nor demonstrates any view about "the nature of language," nor, *pace* Habermas, can it be criticized by reference to any such view.

It is one thing to "analyze any given discourse in accord with the model of poetic language" – that is, to play around with it in the way Derrida plays around with texts from Heidegger, Freud, Hegel, and others – and another thing to claim that "language generally is determined by the poetic use of language specialized in world-disclosure." Derrida need not, and I take it

the gist of this, though I should argue, against Habermas and Apel, that the relevant idealizations need not involve the notion of "universal validity."

14 Ibid., 205.

15 See my criticisms of Gasché's interpretation of Derrida in "Is Derrida a Transcendental Philosopher?" in my *Essays on Heidegger and Others,* 119–28.

would not, think in terms of "language generally" being "determined" by anything. But he might say, as I would, that many of the expressions used in everyday public problem solving were, once upon a time, startling metaphors – bits of world-disclosing discourse that nobody, at first, knew how to argue about, or with. Derrida could, I think, wholeheartedly agree with Habermas that "the world-disclosing force of interpreting language has . . . to prove its worth" before such metaphors get literalized and made into socially useful tools. A lot of poetic achievements remain "just" poetic achievements; they never get used by anybody but their creators. A lot of attempts at private autonomy – notably, I should argue, Nietzsche's and Heidegger's – remain "merely" such attempts. Others turn out to have socially useful spinoffs. But there is no reason why recognizing the source of such useful products should cause "the capacity to solve problems to disappear behind the world-creating capacity of language."[16]

Habermas seems to me to beg all the important questions against Derrida when he assumes that treating X as Y requires an argument to show that X is "a special case" of Y or that there "really" is no difference between X and Y – that one cannot simply treat X as Y in order to see what happens. But admirers of Derrida (e.g., Culler, Gasché, and Paul de Man) set Derrida up for this question-begging treatment when they commit him to having "demonstrated" something original and startling about the nature of language. His defenders make him into a quasi-metaphysician and refuse to let him remain an ironist. Habermas takes them at their word and points out, correctly enough, that if language were what U.S. "deconstructive literary theory" says it is, it would be hard to use marks and noises as tools in solving our public problems. If "philosophy" could indeed show that "language" was something more than people manipulating marks and noises for various private and public purposes – if "language" could be "demonstrated" to be something that could (as deconstructive critics suggest) act on its own, go out of control, stab itself in the back, tear its own head off, and so on, then we really *would* be in trouble. But nothing except the urge to make Derrida into a man with a great big theory about a great big subject suggests that "language" can do anything of the sort.

Derrida's friends in the United States, the ones who want to make him into a theorist and are not content to let him remain an ironist about theory, exhibit just the sort of reverence for "philosophy" that is satirized in "Envois." De Man, for example, thinks that "the necessary immanence of read-

16 Habermas, *Philosophical Discourse*, 205.

ing in relation to the text" stands out as "the irreducible philosophical problem raised by all forms of literary criticism" and that "[i]n France it took the rigor and intellectual integrity of a philosopher whose main concern is not with literary texts to restore the complexities of reading to the dignity of a philosophical question."[17] Many of Derrida's fans can imagine nothing nicer than having a big bouncy child by Socrates.[18] Habermas is not this reverential about philosophy, but he still thinks that before anybody "levels" the philosophy–literature distinction he is honor-bound to demonstrate some philosophical theses – and in particular to agree with Culler that

> [f]ar from there being a genre distinction between philosophy and literature, philosophical texts can be rendered accessible in their essential contents by literary criticism and literary texts can be rendered accessible in their essential contents by a critique of metaphysics.[19]

But surely if there is one idea that Derrida has no use for, it is that of "essential contents." Like Quine, Goodman, Wittgenstein, Bergson, Whitehead, and many other twentieth-century philosophers, Derrida dissolves substances, essences and all, into webs of relations. The result of his reading is not to get at essences but to place texts in contexts – placing books next to other books (as in *Glas*) and weaving bits of books together with bits of other books. One result of this activity is to blur genres, but that is not because genres are not "real." It is because one way to create a new genre is to stitch together bits and pieces of old genres – an activity that would not produce interesting new effects if the old genres were not just as distinct as we had always thought they were. It is one thing to weave differently colored

17 Paul de Man, *Blindness and Insight*, 2d ed. (Minneapolis: University of Minnesota Press, 1987), 110. De Man's respect for the power of philosophy is so great that he thinks "Derrida's work is one of the places where the future possibility of literary criticism is being decided." He takes the Kantian idea of "conditions of possibility" with full seriousness and thinks that philosophers might discover that critics cannot continue to do what they have apparently been doing. But when Kant showed that metaphysics was "impossible," his argument was that it was always possible to "demonstrate" antithetical propositions once one trespassed across the bounds of sense. It is hard to see what the analogue for literary criticism might be; nobody would be surprised, or disturbed, to hear that critics are unable to resolve disputes over antithetical interpretations of a text. De Man could not really have supposed that literary criticism must meet Northrop Frye's demands for "scientific status," yet only some such presupposition could make sense of his tributes to Derrida.

18 "The attempt to have a child by Socrates" is one of Derrida's figures, in *The Postcard*, for doing the sort of thing the metaphysical tradition has always tried to do – produce one more candidate for the role of all-powerful, all-encompassing vocabulary. It is an attempt Derrida explicitly repudiates.

19 I here conflate Habermas's "Proposition 2" on page 190 of *Philosophical Discourse* with "Proposition 2'" on page 193.

strands together in the hope of making something new and another to think that "philosophy" has "demonstrated" that colors are *really* "indeterminate" and "ambivalent."

Habermas wonders why Heidegger and Derrida are "still battling against the 'strong' concepts of theory, truth and system that have actually belonged to the past for over a century and a half," why they still think that "they have to tear philosophy away from the madness of expounding a theory that has the last word."[20] I am suggesting that they are not interested in tearing "philosophy" away from this madness, but simply in tearing themselves away from their own past – from the particular words that threatened to be, for them, the last ones (namely, the words of Nietzsche in the case of Heidegger, the words of Heidegger in the case of Derrida). They are not as public-spirited as Habermas assumes every philosopher must be, nor are they (any more than Nietzsche) easily understood as stages in the attempt of "modernity" to achieve "self-reassurance" – the drama within which Habermas tries to situate them.

Habermas does not feel he has done justice to a philosopher unless he places him within a religiopolitical context and has connected his work up with the need to "regenerate the unifying power of religion in the medium of reason."[21] So when he says that in Derrida and Foucault the "philosophy of subjectivity" has exhausted its possibilities, it is possibilities of public usefulness that he has in mind. Where Habermas sees a contrast between a socially useless, exhausted philosophy of subjectivity and a socially unifying philosophy of rationality-as-intersubjectivity, I see a contrast between the private need for autonomy and the public need for a synoptic view of the goals of a democratic society, a society held together by an agreement, in Rawls's words, to give "the right priority over the good," to make justice "the first virtue."

I have argued elsewhere[22] that part of the force of these Rawlsian slogans is that democratic societies need not concern themselves with "the subject" or "human nature" – that such a society privatizes questions concerning such topics. This claim chimes with Habermas's view that the only "univer-

20 Habermas, *Philosophical Discourse*, 210n28.
21 Ibid., 20. Also: "Since the close of the eighteenth century, the discourse of modernity has had a single theme under ever new titles: the weakening of the forces of social bonding, privatization and diremption – in short, the deformations of a one-sidedly rationalized everyday praxis which evoke the need for something equivalent to the unifying power of religion."
22 See "The Priority of Democracy to Philosophy," in my *Objectivity, Relativism, and Truth* (Cambridge University Press, 1991), 175–96.

sals" that a philosophy of intersubjectivity will come up with will be procedural ones, not decisions on such matters of "substance" as the point of human life. So perhaps Habermas would not have to modify anything very fundamental to his view in order to make room for Heidegger and Derrida, viewed as people engaged in enterprises irrelevant (at least as far as we can presently see) to the public life of our society. Such enterprises are useful only to that quite small group of people for whom "the tradition of Western metaphysics" still looms large – the people whose self-image is stated in terms of the quarrel between the ironists and the metaphysicians. The extent to which these ways of articulating that self-image – Heidegger's litanies or Derrida's puns – eventually spill over into the public realm is unpredictable, and usually irrelevant to their private aims.

One obstacle to my treatment of Habermas and Derrida as complementary is that the two men appear to disagree over the nature and function of philosophy. Such a disagreement, it is easy to think, must be profound. On my view, however, "the nature and function of philosophy" is a pseudo-topic, as much so as "the nature and task of the novel." Talk of "the end of philosophy" is as easy, but as empty, as talk of "the end of the novel." The term "the novel" by now covers so many different kinds of things (from *Tristram Shandy* to *Gone with the Wind,* from *Lolita* to *Malone Dies,* from *Oliver Twist* to *The Executioner's Song*) that everyone knows that "the death of the novel" means no more than "the death of a certain kind of novel." The same cynicism should be felt about announcements of "the end of philosophy," which typically mean something like "the end of metaphysical system building" or "the end of empiricism" or "the end of Cartesianism." No definition of "philosophy" can cover Carnap and Rawls, early Hegel and late Wittgenstein, Derrida and Habermas, and still isolate something coherent enough to have an "end."

Yet there is something that Derrida and Habermas disagree about and that makes it hard to view them as complementary – something that, unlike the question about "the nature of philosophy," is not merely verbal. The disagreement is hard to pin down, but it comes out when we find Habermas treating the Nietzsche–Heidegger–Derrida tradition as a "critique of reason" and identifying his own view with a recovery of Enlightenment rationalism. Although Habermas says that his "communications-theoretic concept of the lifeworld has been freed from the mortgages of transcendental philosophy,"[23] and that "the purism of pure reason is not resurrected again

23 Habermas, *Philosophical Discourse,* 358.

in communicative reason,"[24] he has no intention of freeing "communicative reason" from the ideal of "universal validity." He still wants an Archimedean point from which, for example, to criticize Foucault for "relativism" and for being unable to give an account of "the normative foundations of [his theory's] own rhetoric."[25] He still wants to say that "the validity claimed for propositions and norms transcends spaces and times, 'blots out' space and time."[26]

This urge toward *universal* validity makes Habermas distrust what he calls "linguistic historicism" – the line of thought that, I have argued, unites Dewey and Heidegger, James and Nietzsche, Derrida and Davidson. He thinks that this view results in "hypostasizing the world-disclosing force of language."[27] He thinks that such hypostatization confines discourse to the limits of that particular time and space in which a given language game is played, excluding "any interaction between world-disclosing language and learning processes in the world."[28] But I can see no basis for Habermas's insistence that people like Castoriadis and Derrida must *exclude* such interaction or for the claim that they are "criticizing reason." If reason is interpreted not as a universal human faculty that somehow transcends the invention of new vocabularies, but as what Habermas calls "communicative reason," none of us linguistic historicists has any interest whatever in "criticizing" it.

Habermas sees an antidemocratic bogeyman – "the subject" – hiding behind the "linguistic" masks that Foucault, Derrida, and Castoriadis assume. Yet all three men would be happy to grant Habermas's point that "reason is by its very nature incarnated in contexts of communicative action and in structures of the life world,"[29] nor are any of them interested in undertaking "an explanation of the intersubjectivity of social praxis" that "begins from the premise of isolated consciousness."[30] It is one thing to say that the individual's unconscious is a "unique and private world which runs up against the socially institutionalized world" – that there is a "blind impress" on each of us that has nothing in particular to do with socializing "learning processes" – and quite another to say that the "psyche and society stand in a kind of metaphysical opposition to each other."[31] There is no reason to think we have to choose between Dewey and Derrida, between public problem solving and private struggles for autonomy. The two activities can coexist peacefully. There is no reason why philosophy should have to choose between them, nor is there any need to assign one some sort of epistemic

24 Ibid., 301.   25 Ibid., 294; cf. 284.   26 Ibid., 323.   27 Ibid., 320.
28 Ibid., 319.   29 Ibid., 322.   30 Ibid., 333.   31 Ibid., 333, 334.

priority over the other. The choice between the two activities, in any given concrete case, is no more susceptible to the application of general criteria than is any other painful conflict between duties to others and duties to self. Habermas is disgusted by every sign of the reemergence of *Lebensphilosophie*, something he despises almost as much as Heidegger did.[32] This is because he overdramatizes the contrast between the "subject-centered reason" and "communicative reason," and looks for signs of "subject-centeredness" in everything that claims the status of "philosophy" without being socially useful. He thinks that in both Castoriadis and Heidegger, "the 'truth' of semantic world-disclosure also founds the propositional truth of statements; it prejudices the validity of linguistic utterances generally."[33] But this criticism confuses the source of new ideas with the "ground of their validity." It confuses causes with reasons. It also confuses an initial stage, in which new metaphors are produced to satisfy private needs, with a later stage, in which, after these metaphors are literalized, we are able to argue about the truth of sentences formulated in terms of them. Derrida and Castoriadis can happily agree with Davidson that *nothing* "founds the propositional truth of statements" except social practice, argument, and intersubjective conversational exchange. But they would be right to insist that nothing *could* "prejudice the validity of linguistic utterances generally," except the absence of freedom and leisure to engage in such free exchanges (thanks to, for example, illiteracy, hunger, or the secret police). The only other thing that might prejudice this validity would be the failure of new "semantic world-disclosures" to provide fresh grist for the argumentative mill – the sort of novelties of which totalitarian regimes are rightly fearful.

Habermas's suspicions of *Lebensphilosophie*, of Romanticism, and of "world-disclosure" can be traced back to his continuing commitment to the claim that there is something called "critical reason" that can detect the difference between "invariant regularities of social action as such" and "ideologically frozen relations of dependence that can in principle be transformed."[34] This claim contrasts with the view of us linguistic historicists: that "ideologically frozen relations of dependence" become detectable only

---

32 See ibid.: "Castoriadis ends where Simmel began: with *Lebensphilosophie*" (318). Cf. 206, where, commenting on my view that "science and morality, economics and politics, are delivered up to a process of language-creating protuberances *in just the same way* as art and philosophy," Habermas says, "One sees how the Nietzschean pathos of a *Lebensphilosophie* that has made the linguistic turn beclouds the sober insights of pragmatism."
33 Ibid., 331.
34 Appendix to Jürgen Habermas, *Knowledge and Human Interests*, trans. Jeremy Shapiro (Boston: Beacon Press, 1986), 310.

when somebody suggests concrete alternatives to them. Our main argument for this view is that there is no way to tell in advance whether any given regularity is "invariant," since the conditions of the possibility of social action are forever being enlarged by "semantic world-disclosure." We linguistic historicists think that there is no such thing as "humanity" to be emancipated by being ushered from an age of "distorted" to one of "undistorted" communication – no common core to men and women of all ages and climes distinct from their shared susceptibility to pain and humiliation.[35]

On the view of a naturalistic historicist like Dewey – a philosopher who was as remote from the philosophy of subjectivity as Mead, and as remote from ironism as Habermas – *every* form of social life is likely, sooner or later, to freeze over into something the more imaginative and restless spirits of the time will see as "repressive" and "distorting." What is wrong with these forms of life is not that they are "ideological," but just that they have been used to justify the systematic administration of pain and humiliation. Typically, they once played a role in liberation – in freeing people from some still-worse alternative.[36] So to say that pain and humiliation are *now* unnecessary is to say that *now* an alternative form of social life has become available – one that we could not have envisaged had not a brave new possible world been disclosed by a linguistic innovation, an innovation that may have been caused by some merely private turbulence. From this point of view "distorted communication" is a relative term – one given sense by contrast with a proposed alternative communication situation, the disclosure of an alternative social world. As Marx and Foucault helped us see, today's chains are often forged from the hammers that struck off yesterday's. As Foucault was more inclined to admit than Marx, this sequence of hammers into chains is unlikely to end with the invention of hammers that *cannot* be forged into chains – hammers that are *purely* rational, with no ideological alloy. Still, the chains might, with luck, get a little lighter and easier to break each time.

If Habermas were content with this sort of historicism and contextualism,

---

35 For some attempts to defend this claim about the nonexistence of "humanity," see "Cosmopolitanism Without Emancipation: A Reply to Jean-François Lyotard," in my *Objectivity, Relativism, and Truth*, 211–22. See also my "Feminism and Pragmatism," in this volume.

36 We linguistic historicists tend to agree with Dewey that "[t]he worse or evil is a rejected good. In deliberation and before choice no evil presents itself as evil. Until it is rejected, it is a competing good. After rejection, it figures not as a lesser good, but as the bad of that situation" (*Human Nature and Conduct*, in *The Middle Works of John Dewey* [Carbondale: Southern Illinois University Press, 1983] 14: 193). See also Dewey's "Outlines of a Critical Theory of Ethics," *The Early Works of John Dewey* 3: 379: "Goodness is not remoteness from badness. In one sense, goodness is based upon badness; that is, good action is always based upon action good once, but bad if persisted in under changing circumstances."

he would have little motive for his suspicions of "subject-centered thinking." But his attachment to the idea of "universal validity" makes it impossible for him to accept it. I see this attachment as a species of the same temptation that made Plato, Augustine, Kant, Nietzsche, and Heidegger try for affiliation or incarnation – for a relation to something larger than themselves and the contingent circumstances in which they find themselves (e.g., the Good, God, the Moral Law, the Will to Power, Being). As soon as the notion of "emancipation" is separated from suggestions about how to break a particular set of manicles (e.g., chattel slavery, priestcraft, wage slavery, racial or gender discrimination, mindless bureaucracy) and made the aim of an ahistorical "human interest," it gets connected with the idea that there is something called "human nature" or "humanity itself" that needs to be emancipated. On my view, Humanity and Critical Reason are (like God, the Good, the Subject, Language, *Ereignis,* and *différance*) just more dubious candidates for this position of Something Larger.

The best account of this use of "humanity" with which I am familiar is given in Bernard Yack's *The Longing for Total Revolution.* In this book, Yack identifies the least common denominator of the sort of social theory that aims at "enabling human beings to realize their humanity" as a Kant-style contrast between "nature" and "freedom," with its accompanying demand that "our autonomy be realized in our institutions."[37] He shows that, although this antinaturalist, idealist contrast is officially repudiated by both Marx and Nietzsche, both desert their official naturalism when they start to talk about a "transformation of mankind." Yack sees Hegel as having accepted contingency in a way in which neither Marx nor Nietzsche was able to accept it – as having been willing to admit that there would never be a political realization of the ideal that, Hegel thought, could be realized in the private activity of the philosopher who attains Absolute Knowledge.[38] By contrast, he sees Marx and Nietzsche as officially willing to accept the brute materiality of contingent conditions while remaining committed, unofficially, to a future state of humanity in which this materiality has been evaded. Yack concludes his book by saying that

> the premiss that suggests the identification of dehumanization . . . as the obstacle to a world without social sources of dissatisfaction – a definition of the individual's humanity in terms of the individual's ability to resist external

37 See Bernard Yack, *The Longing for Total Revolution: Philosophical Sources of Social Discontent from Rousseau to Marx and Nietzsche* (Princeton, N.J.: Princeton University Press, 1985), 365.

38 See chapter 5 of ibid., 209–10, in the course of which Yack cites Dieter Henrich's claim that Hegel's "is the only philosophic theory which recognizes absolute contingency."

conditioning – rules out the realization of our humanity in the external world. Any institution that conditions our behavior will be dehumanizing, as long as we hold this understanding of man's humanity.[39]

This idea of people having an "inside" – a central core – which "resists external conditioning" is one of those that we linguistic historicists reject. If we drop this idea, then we shall need the sort of private–public distinction upon which I have been insisting. For then we shall view autonomy not as the actualization of a common human potentiality but as self-creation: the process of fighting free of very particular inheritances in order to work out the consequences of idiosyncratic "blind impresses." The ideal liberal community will be one in which respect for such particularity and idiosyncrasy is widespread, one in which the only sort of human liberty that is hoped for is Isaiah Berlin's "negative liberty" – being left alone.

For such a community, "universal validity," freedom from a limited spatiotemporal context, is not to the point. That ideal community would see the task of social theory as what Rawls calls "attaining reflective equilibrium" between our old moral principles (the generalities we invoke to justify old institutions) and our reactions to new developments, our sense of the desirability or undesirability of various recently disclosed possibilities. Out of this attempt there will come initiatives to reform old institutions, or to replace them with new ones. The question of the intrinsic validity of the principles would not arise. In particular, the question of whether they were "universally valid" or "merely ours" would not. So there would be continual social *criticism*, but no *radical* social *theory*, if "radical" means appealing to something beyond inherited principles and reactions to new developments.

What would guard such a society from feeling comfortable with the institutionalized infliction of pain and humiliation on the powerless? From taking such pain for granted? Only detailed descriptions of that pain and humiliation – descriptions that brought home to the powerless the contrast between their lives and the lives of others (thus inciting revolution) and brought the same contrast home to the privileged (thus inciting reform). Instead of a general theoretical test for the presence of "ideology" and "distortion of communication" of the sort Habermas envisages, there would be only particular descriptions of injury and concrete suggestions about ways of avoiding injury.

Who provides such descriptions? In contemporary liberal society, a vast range of people: journalists, anthropologists, sociologists, novelists, drama-

---

39 Yack, *The Longing for Total Revolution*, 366.

tists, moviemakers, painters. Providing a continual supply of such descriptions is one of the things liberal societies do best. Think of books like *Uncle Tom's Cabin* and *Les Misérables,* of stretches of Dickens and Zola, of *The Story of an African Farm, All Quiet on the Western Front, The Well of Loneliness, The People of the Abyss, Black Boy,* and *Animal Farm.* These novels are continuous with nonfiction like *The Drapier Letters, The Children of Sanchez, The Road to Wigan Pier,* and *The Gulag Archipelago,* and also with articles and columns written by muckraking reporters or social scientists and with reports written by committees of do-gooders or bureaucrats. Such books both mobilize those who are being injured and unsettle those who are doing, or countenancing, injury. They provide the intuitions – the strong reactions to novel stimuli – that theoretical attempts at reflective equilibrium take into account.

The expectation of getting something *more* than this constant provision of new stimuli – the desire for a theory that supersedes the search for reflective equilibrium by offering "*radical* criticism of society" – has been the most exciting feature of intellectual life since the French Revolution. It is exciting for the same reasons that the promise of affiliation with or incarnation of Something Larger has always been exciting: it suggests that we may get taken behind the scenes, behind the appearances to a hidden place where we may, for the first time, become what we really are. Such a theory, if it existed, would do *wholesale,* for everybody, what one might have thought could be done only by each person for himself, one at a time – it would give us autonomy.

The dangers of the search for such autonomy have been exhibited in detail by analysts of fascism, by historians of Marxism like Kolakowski, and by many others who have written on the sociology of radical movements and on the psychological roots of what Yack calls "the longing for total revolution." The question of whether this longing has, so far, done more harm than good – a question that divides, for example, Kolakowski from E. P. Thompson, as it divided Orwell from Isaac Deutscher – is not one about which I feel any certainty, though I incline toward Kolakowski's and Orwell's side. All I feel able to do is to try to spell out what the intellectual world might look like if the desire for "radical" social theory were absent. In that world, the switch from an ideal of universal validity to linguistic historicism would encourage irony at the expense of metaphysics – encourage a sense of the contingency of final vocabularies rather than attempts to escape this contingency. For such a switch would make it difficult to invoke the reality–appearance distinction in the contexts in which metaphysicians have sought to deploy it. More specifically, it would make it impossible to think of autonomy as "release from repressive external forces" or "as the distortion by social institutions of the essentially human." It would make it impossible to run together the diminution of pain and humiliation with the idea of "transforming the nature of man." To be bluntly chauvinist about it: this switch would emphasize the Anglo-Saxon utilitarian-reformist brand of social thought and deemphasize the German *Ideologiekritik* brand. It would set aside the "ideology–nonideology" distinction for the same reason that it sets aside the "humanizing–dehumanizing" distinction.[40]

In such an intellectual world, there would be an ever-recurring need to restore reflective equilibrium between old platitudes and reactions to new stimuli. But it would be evident that the impetus to social change came from those stimuli, not from theoretical discoveries. So neither the analogy between social theory and natural science nor the metaphor of penetrating to ever-deeper levels in order to expose ever-deeper roots would any longer seem attractive. Social theory would be analogized rather to literary criticism and to jurisprudence – areas of culture in which metaphors of depth and radicality are not of much use.

In *Contingency, Irony, and Solidarity* I drew a contrast between an intellectual world dominated by the "German" longing for some destiny higher than that of Nietzsche's "last men" and one dominated merely by the "Anglo-Saxon" desire to avoid the infliction of unnecessary pain and humiliation in terms of the distinction between the sublime and the beautiful.[41] Radicals want sublimity, but liberals just want beauty. Liberals in the Mill–Dewey tradition dream of a utopia in which everybody has a chance at the things only the richer citizens of the rich North Atlantic democracies have been able to get – the freedom, wealth, and leisure to pursue private perfection in idiosyncratic ways. This utopia is just a lot more of the same kind of thing we have had a little of already – not a transfiguration but a redistribution. Radicals, by contrast, want a world in which all things have been made new and in which the rearrangement of little private things, the pursuit of idiosyncratic autonomy, is subsumed under some higher, larger, more thrilling communal goal. They want a public version of a sublimity that is, I think, necessarily private – the sublimity one attains by breaking out of some particular inheritance (a vocabulary, a tradition, a style) that one had feared might bound one's entire life.

Because they despise the prospect of a world of "last men," radicals treat

---

40 See Raymond Geuss, *The Idea of Social Theory* (Cambridge University Press, 1981), on "ideology-critique."
41 Nietzsche had another way of putting it: "Man does not live for pleasure; only Englishmen do that" (*The Twilight of the Idols*, "Maxims and Arrows," no. 12).

"bourgeois society" and "bourgeois ideology" in the way in which ironist theorists treat metaphysics – as an insidious temptation that it is our duty to sur-
mount. This has often produced the illusion that to criticize metaphysics *is*
to criticize bourgeois ideology, and conversely. This casual assimilation produces, among radicals, the illusion that there is an important connection
between ironist theory and radical politics. Among liberals, it produces the
conviction that the ironists' sense of contingency rots the moral fabric of democratic societies. Both illusions are encouraged by memories of Nietzsche's occasional antidemocratic frothings, Heidegger's attempt to climb on
Hitler's bandwagon, Sartre's period of mindless allegiance to Stalin, and
Foucault's quasi-anarchism.

The wide variety of political views with which the first of these illusions is
compatible – fascism, Stalinism, anarchism – confirms Yack's view that the
common element of radical politics is the craving for a sublime Otherness,
something to which the everyday predicates in terms of which we describe
the difference between the beautiful and the ugly, the pleasant and the
painful, do not apply. It seems strange to associate Habermas – the most sensible, temperate, and effective spokesperson for social democracy among
contemporary philosophers – with such a craving. Yet from the perspective
of my linguistic historicism, Habermas's distrust of contextualism, his search
for "universal validity," is one more symptom of that craving. His conviction
that there is an "emancipatory interest" distinct from the merely "technical
interest" in how to rearrange things so as to produce less pain and more happiness is another. Further, there is his conviction that mere Anglo-Saxon
"positivism" and "scientism" are insufficient for an understanding of contemporary society, and his suspicion that they are somehow "complicit" in
what is worst in that society.[42] As I see it, this conviction represents a residual

---

42 See Habermas, *Knowledge and Human Interests:* "Positivism . . . has regressed behind the level
    of reflection represented by Kant's philosophy" (5). For the Habermas of that early book,
    Kant's nature–freedom distinction remains an essential propaedeutic to Hegel's discovery
    of what Habermas called "the emancipatory power of reflection, which the subject experi-
    ences in itself to the extent that it becomes transparent to its own genesis" and to a denial
    of the "positivist" doctrine that "knowledge is a mere instrument of an organism's adapta-
    tion to its environment" (97) – a doctrine Dewey thought entirely compatible with the crit-
    icism of contemporary institutions. Although Habermas has changed his views a great deal
    in the ensuing twenty years, I think he remains faithful to the conviction that social theory
    can do something for contemporary societies analogous to what individuals can do privately
    (in, e.g., psychoanalysis): namely, become "transparent to their own genesis." For a good
    critical discussion of Habermas's theory of "the emancipatory interest" see Thomas Mc-
    Carthy, *The Critical Theory of Jürgen Habermas* (Cambridge, Mass.: MIT Press, 1978), sec.
    2.5, esp. 99–101. McCarthy is very helpful on Habermas's attempt to bring Kant together with
    Marx.

acceptance of Kant's nature–freedom distinction and of Marx's contrast between "ideology" and a mode of thought that, because it represents "human
freedom" rather than any "external constraints," succeeds in being nonide-
ological. To this extent, at least, I view Habermas himself as still enmeshed
in what he calls "the philosophy of subjectivity."

If one starts off from the view that freedom is the recognition of contingency rather than of the existence of a specifically human realm exempt
from natural necessity, one will be more dubious about the social utility of
philosophy than Habermas is. One will hope for less from philosophy, at
least from the sort of philosophy characterized by what Habermas calls "universalist problematics and strong theoretical strategies."[43] Instead, one will
put most of one's hopes for the relief of unnecessary, socially countenanced
pain and humiliation in two things. First, the sorts of writing I listed earlier:
novels, articles, and reports by those who are able to make specific kinds of
pain and humiliation visible. Second, proposals for specific changes in social arrangements – in laws, company regulations, administrative procedures, educational practices, and so on. This means that terms like "late capitalism," "modern industrial society," and "conditions of the production of
knowledge" will be employed less frequently and terms like "worker representation," "laws against unproductive financial manipulation," and "journalists' union" more.

A preference for this level of concreteness rather than that characteristic
of large-scale German-style "social theory" is, of course, not simply a deduc-
tion from large philosophical premises. It is justified, if at all, not simply by
a desire for the recognition of contingency but by a political judgment:
namely, that the rich democracies of the present day already contain the
sorts of institutions necessary for their own reform and that communication
among the citizens of those democracies is not "distorted" by anything more
esoteric than greed, fear, ignorance, and resentment. This amounts to saying that the instruments of perfectibility are already, in the rich North Atlantic constitutional democracies, in place – that the principal institutions
of contemporary democratic societies do not require "unmasking" but
rather strenuous utilization, supplemented by luck. Such a judgment is risky,
and perhaps mistaken. But if it is mistaken, it will not be shown to be so by
"universalist problematics and strong theoretical strategies," but by continued trial and error.

43 Habermas, *Philosophical Discourse*, 208. On this topic see my "The Ambiguity of 'Rationality,'" *Constellations* 3, no. 1 (1996), 73–82.

17

DERRIDA AND THE
PHILOSOPHICAL TRADITION

In the actual world Nietzsche was a twitchy, irresolute, nomadic nerd who never got a life outside literature. But consider the possible world in which Nietzsche got lucky early on, and wound up a happy, affectionate, suburban paterfamilias. In this more satisfactory world, the ridicule of Wilamowitz-Möllendorf (the John Searle of his day) failed to sink *The Birth of Tragedy*. On the contrary, that book enjoyed, simultaneously with Moriarty's treatise on the binomial theorem, a European vogue. Outrageously successful, Nietzsche's U.S. lecture tours eclipsed those of Dickens. The many books about him by American fans and imitators in the United States (the old Mark Twain, the young H. L. Mencken), as well as the equally many books that excitedly warned against his dangerous influence, kept his name constantly before the public. Instead of breaking down at forty-five, he kept right on writing, joyously and prolifically, "having a great time."[1]

Would success, sanity, and suburbia have spoiled Friedrich Nietzsche? Would perfection of the life have wrecked the work? Could he have written so well against resentment if he had experienced it less often? Could he have written *The Will to Power* if he had gotten some? Maybe not. But the example of Derrida, like that of Dickens, should make us suspicious of the idea that loneliness and neglect are good for genius and that fame and money always

---

1 In *Jacques Derrida* (Paris: Editions du Seuil, 1991), by Geoffrey Bennington and Jacques Derrida, Derrida refers to himself as "s'amusant beaucoup." This essay is a revised version of a review article about this book, and I refer frequently to the English translation: *Jacques Derrida* (Chicago: University of Chicago Press, 1991). All page numbers in the text are to this book, unless otherwise noted. The book consists of two parts – "Derridabase" by Bennington, which runs along the tops of the pages, and "Circumfession" ("Circonfession" in the original) by Derrida, which runs along the bottoms.

corrupt. Derrida remains as fresh, as moving, and as funny as ever, despite all the puffing and all the bashing he has endured. He has somehow managed to take both in his stride. He has kept himself as open to the books he reads and rereads, and as responsive to the power of fantasy, as he was when he started out.

Geoffrey Bennington is quite right when he says that "we are still far from having taken the measure of a thought whose richness and complexity is [*sic*] equal to that of the great names of the philosophical tradition" (1). Imaginations as candescent as Nietzsche's, Heidegger's, and Derrida's do not blaze very often. We should not let the constant brouhaha around Derrida – created, for the most part, by people who have not read his books – either rush us into premature judgments or hinder us from being glad to be his contemporaries. We should be grateful that there is somebody around who can still, even after we have read quite a lot of him, blow us away with something we could never have expected – something like "Circumfession."

Nor should we be distracted by the question "What *sort* of richness and complexity? Literary or philosophical? Intellectual or imaginative?" That question has never been satisfactorily answered when asked about much of Hegel, or about most of Nietzsche, or about the late Heidegger. The recurrent failure of attempts to answer it about Derrida should make us impatient with the question rather than with him. If somebody suggests new answers to questions posed in old terms, especially terms used by Plato or Kant, we often call the result "philosophy." If somebody suggests new questions, posed in new terms, we typically call the result "literature." Sometimes, as in the case of Nietzsche, we call their books "literature" at first and then, after a sufficient number of philosophy professors have borrowed from them or refuted them, librarians quietly reshelve them. But neither the initial nor the later classification tells us much.

In what follows, I shall raise some critical questions about Derrida as presented by Bennington. But I should say first that Bennington's account of what Derrida is up to is better in almost all respects – more intelligent, more plausible, more readable, and less pretentious – than any other I have read. Bennington succeeds in making himself largely transparent to the writer he is glossing. He does not trot out his own hobbyhorses, and he never overlays Derrida's neologisms with his own.[2]

---

2 Such overlaying is characteristic of the many (tiresome and unprofitable, to my mind) books that offer what Bennington calls "Derridean" readings of Derrida. On the last page of "Derridabase," Bennington says that he has been "forbidden" to give such a reading because "we have said everything about deconstruction *except* the supplementary remark whereby it is

Bennington's "Derridabase" is not, however, the book that analytic philosophers keep hoping somebody will write about Derrida, the book that will meet them halfway.[3] That book would heed Searle's advice that a fuzzy distinction may still be a very useful one, and so would not claim that Derrida has "placed a distinction in doubt" by fuzzing it up (93). It would not say that one of the consequences of Derrida's arguments is "a refutation of humanism" (48) while saying nothing at all about what "humanism" might mean in this context.[4] It would not confine its criticism of Davidson's treatment of metaphor to the cryptic and seemingly question-begging claim that Davidson "singularly restricts the terrain of meaning, and thereby of philosophical concern, to simply propositional meaning" (131). It would not claim that "all ethical and political choices are made a priori in the milieu of this complicity [with metaphysics]" (39), without spelling out what such complicity amounts to and how it affects those choices.[5]

---

named in texts signed by Jacques Derrida." I am not sure I understand what this means, but I guess I am grateful that the fatal supplementary remark was omitted. For Derrida seems inimitable: I have yet to read a Derridean reading of anything, written by somebody other than Derrida himself, that was not contrived, wooden, and humorless.

3 I wish somebody would write this book, not because I think that books written to the taste of analytic philosophers have an intrinsic clarity that Derrida's own books lack, but simply because such a book would have considerable pedagogical and ecumenical utility. It might break down a few of the barriers to international communication among philosophy professors, barriers erected by the very different courses of reading that different countries demand of their philosophy students. While waiting for this book, the best places for analytic philosophers to go for light on Derrida are Samuel Wheeler's admirable articles on Derrida and Davidson: "The Extension of Deconstruction," *Monist* 69, no. 1 (1986), 3–21; "Indeterminacy of French Interpetation," in *Truth and Interpretation: Perspectives on the Philosophy of Donald Davidson*, ed. Ernest LePore (Oxford: Blackwell, 1986), 477–94; "Metaphor in Davidson and de Man," in *Donald Davidson and Literary Theory*, ed. Reed Way Dasenbrock (University Park: Pennsylvania State University Press, 1993), 144–59.

4 My hunch is that "humanism" here means something like what I call "nominalism" below. But I am not sure.

5 There is not much about politics or about the possible relevance of deconstruction to politics in "Derridabase." At one point, however, Bennington speaks of "this classical question (you criticize the existing order of things; what do you propose to put in its place?) which tends to reinforce the political order as order of an order, precisely, and which regulates many 'political' reactions to deconstruction in the Anglo-Saxon countries" (264). Bennington goes on to say that this practical question is "exceeded" by deconstruction and that "if deconstruction had a goal or a regulating idea, it would be: that something happen, that there be some event."

As a pragmatist, I am not about to admit that anything can exceed questions of the form "What is to be done?" Such questions seem to me to trump all others. Bennington's claim that "the classical question" reinforces the political order reminds me of my least favorite sentence in Foucault: "I think to imagine another system is to extend our participation in the present system."

Most important, this unwritten book would not say that the concept of "autonomy" (or any other concept) exhibits "naïveté" (253) or that "our deductions have demonstrated a sort of incoherence in the construction of the concept 'sign'" (37). It would not treat concepts as quasi-persons. Instead, it would say that some people who use the word "autonomy" do not ask themselves certain questions they should ask themselves, and that certain ways of using the word "sign" have suggested insoluble transcendental pseudo-problems (e.g., how is intentionality *possible* in a world of atoms and voids?) that we may safely neglect. It would treat the claim that "the signified is just a signifier put in a certain position by other signifiers" (31) as a way of making the Wittgensteinian point that to possess a concept is to know how to use a word. So charges of naïveté or incoherence against concepts would be replaced by suggestions for changes in the linguistic behavior of particular people (mostly philosophers).

This unwritten book would not cast doubt on whether one "has a very clear idea of what a mother is" (207) or claim that "we do not yet know what the social and the political are." It would consider the question "What is the political?" to be as bad as Socrates' question to Euthyphro: what is piety? For both questions presuppose that concepts like "pious" and "political" are names for natures, essences, self-contained signifieds – the kinds of things that, one would have thought, only phallogocentrists believe in. In a book addressed to people who think that nothing lies behind the use of words except the causal conditions of those uses – people who agree with Davidson that we should break down the distinction between knowing a language and knowing how to get around in the world – one would ask, instead, whether a given bunch of people are using the word "political" in a way that avoids specific unfortunate consequences (e.g., the tacit legitimation of dubious social practices or the generation of insoluble philosophical pseudo-problems).

Such a book might ask whether the word ought to be used – in some contexts, for some purposes – differently. But it would not suggest that there was a mystery about what the word means or about what it refers to. For it would be consistently nominalist: it would not follow the adventures of concepts, but rather those of human beings, people using marks and noises as tools to accomplish specific purposes. It would not say that widely used words stand for *incoherent* concepts, for there can be no better proof of a concept's coherence than the fact that (in Wittgenstein's words) "this language-game is *played*." Such a book would say that certain concepts were awkward, of limited utility, and replaceable, but not that they were incoherent or unintelligible or complicit with the forces of darkness. "The concept" would not be used as the name of an (often incompetent) agent or of a hapless subject (as in the epigraph to *Jacques Derrida:* "Dès qu'il est saisi par l'écriture, le concept est cuit").

Bennington would, I imagine, say that the alternative book I have described – a book that tries to get Derrida, Wittgenstein, and Davidson on the same wavelength – would be thoroughly misleading about Derrida. Whether he would be right to say this depends on the answers to some questions that have puzzled me ever since I started reading Derrida (twenty-odd years ago): Can he get along *without* treating concepts as agents or subjects? If not, can this seemingly Platonist way of speaking be reconciled with his criticism of the metaphysics of presence? Can his occasional big swooshy transcendental claims be reconciled with his debunking of all earlier swooshes? These are the questions I shall pursue in the remainder of this essay.

People like me, who esteem Davidson and Wittgenstein equally and for the same reasons, typically read both men as nominalists, and thus as people who will have no truck with transcendental philosophy – with the discovery of conditions of possibility (of consciousness or language or *Dasein* or whatever). We see both philosophers as helping to convince people that, in Bennington's words, "any philosophy which gives itself world and language as two separate realms separated by an abyss that has to be crossed remains caught, at the very point of the supposed crossing, in the circle of dogmatism and relativism that it is unable to break" (103). As we read Davidson and Wittgenstein, and as we should like to be able to read Derrida, only that notion of two separate realms – only what Davidson has called "the third dogma of empiricism: the distinction between scheme and content" – permits the idea that we can engage in two distinct sorts of activity: empirical inquiry into causal conditions of actuality and philosophical inquiry into transcendental conditions of possibility.

If you are a nominalist, any exploration of presuppositional relations between concepts in which you may engage will take the form of an argument that you could not use some words in certain ways if you did not use some other words in certain other ways.[6] So we nominalists have no use for a refurbished version of Kant's "transcendental logic." We are grateful to Wittgenstein for having mocked the Kantian–Fregean idea that, as he put it, "logic is something sublime." We read Wittgenstein as a therapeutic

---

6 I have argued elsewhere for this claim that the only good transcendental argument is a parasitism argument. I defend it in "Transcendental Argument, Self-reference, and Pragmatism," in *Transcendental Arguments and Science*, ed. Peter Bieri et al. (Dordrecht: Reidel, 1979), 77–103, and develop the same line of thought in "Strawson's Objectivity Argument," *Review of Metaphysics* 24 (December 1970), 207–44, and in "Verificationism and Transcendental Arguments," *Nous* 5 (Fall 1971), 3–14.

philosopher, whose importance lies in helping us escape from ways of using words that generate pseudo-problems.[7] But for all of the jokey and raunchy desublimizing that goes on in Derrida's books, it is not clear that such escape, escape from a dusty fly bottle, is what he wants.

Bennington, like many other commentators on Derrida, does not want him to be read as a sort of French Wittgenstein,[8] and he may think that nobody should try to write the book – *Derrida for Davidsonians* – that I have sketched. For such a book would leave out what he calls the "quasi-transcendental" character of Derrida's thought. Although Bennington is quite clear that "deconstruction is not essentially a Kantian type of philosophy, and cannot be content with the idea of conditions of possibility and everything that that idea entails" (88), he insists that escape from the philosophical tradition is not what Derrida has in mind. He warns us against thinking that "philosophical discourse" is "merely forgotten or worn-out metaphors, a particularly gray and sad fable, mystified in proposing itself as the very truth" (122).[9] Quasi-transcendentality is what you go in for if you heed both of these warnings – if you respect philosophy enough to realize that it is inescapable, but not enough to take the idea of conditions of possibility as seriously as Kant did.

Bennington thinks that people like me, who suspect that pragmatic therapy may be all we need from our philosophers, are closer to Kant than they realize. For such philosophers accept Kant's distinction between the empirical and the transcendental, and then opt for the empirical – attempt to make whatever remains of philosophical discourse an empirical discourse. What is distinctive about Derrida's quasi-transcendentalism, on Benning-

---

7 There is an alternative interpretation of Wittgenstein – the one put forward by Stanley Cavell – according to which Wittgenstein regards at least some of the traditional philosophical problems as "deep" and as inextricable from something ahistorical and transcultural called "the human." For examples of this intepretation and for criticism of my own escapist tendencies, see James Conant's introductions to two books by Hilary Putnam: *Realism with a Human Face* and *Words and Life* (Cambridge, Mass.: Harvard University Press, 1990 and 1994, respectively). Cavell and Derrida have a lot in common, especially their suspicion of the kind of pragmatic approach to the philosophical tradition I favor.

8 I suggested that Derrida be viewed in this way in a discussion of Rodolphe Gasché's *The Tain of the Mirror*, titled "Is Derrida a Transcendental Philosopher?" (reprinted from *Yale Journal of Criticism* in my *Essays on Heidegger and Others* [Cambridge University Press, 1991]). The present essay is a sort of sequel to that paper. Bennington's commentary has helped me get the issues I discussed in connection with Gasché's into clearer focus.

9 With some qualifications (such as substituting "metaphysical" for "philosophical"), this is exactly how I *do* think of the discourse of the philosophical tradition, and how I think Dewey thought of it. Bennington follows up by saying that "one can see how tempting such a reading can be for a critique of philosophy from the human sciences or from literature." Quite so. Dewey can be thought of as formulating just such a critique from the side of the human sciences. I have tried to formulate one from the side of literature.

ton's view, is that Derrida neither opts for one side of the distinction over the other nor tosses the distinction itself out the window, but instead insists it is both forever inescapable and forever unusable. When people like me protest on behalf of Wittgenstein and Davidson that they can do their stuff without even mentioning this dubious distinction, much less choosing a side, Bennington will rejoin that we only think this is what these two men are doing. What they are *really* doing, he claims, is letting the empirical play the role once played by the transcendental. That, at any rate, is how I interpret the following passage from "Derridabase":

> If one says that finitude is in some sense the condition of transcendence, one makes it into the condition of possibility of transcendence, and one thus puts it into a transcendental position with respect to transcendence. But the ultra-transcendental thus produced puts into question the very structure of transcendence, which it pulls back down onto a feature that transcendence would like to consider as empirical. . . . This deconstruction moves toward a comprehension of any discourse ruled by the empirical/transcendental opposition and everything that goes along with it: but this movement, which would traditionally be represented as a movement upward, even beyond what has up until now been recognized as transcendental, is in fact, or at the same time, a movement "downward," for it is the empirical and the contingent, themselves necessarily displaced, in this movement, toward the singular event and the case of chance, which are found higher than the high, higher than height, in height's falling. *L'érection tombe.* "Quasi-transcendental" names what results from this displacement, by maintaining as legible the trace of a passage through the traditional opposition, and by giving this opposition a radical uncertainty which we shall call "undecidability" on condition that we take a few supplementary precautions. (279)

Bennington's argument depends upon the premise formulated in the first sentence of this passage. Is it really the case that anybody who says "finitude is in some sense the condition of transcendence" thereby puts the finite "in a transcendental position with respect to transcendence"? I am inclined to protest that the only reason anybody would want to say the former is to urge that the word "transcendence," like all other words, is a human invention designed to serve various human, finite purposes. This is just to repeat what Feuerbach said about God. Or, perhaps more to the point, it repeats what Kierkegaard said about Hegel: that he was a "poor existing individual" who invented the System in the vain hope of losing his finitude by absorption into it. Analogously, I should urge, Kant was just a poor existing individual who invented a gimmick called "transcendental philosophy" in order to wiggle out of the bind he found himself in (between, roughly speaking, Newton on corpuscles and Rousseau on freedom).

Does being nominalist and historicist in this way put the finite in a "transcendental position with respect to transcendence"? Are Feuerbach and Kierkegaard, or Dewey and Davidson, conducting transcendental inquiries or making assumptions about conditions of possibility, whether they like it or not? Dewey, at least, would reply that he is conducting empirical inquiries into the causal conditions of certain actual events – namely, the uses of certain words in certain ways, the origins of certain terms around which certain social practices crystallized. So it is tempting to protest against Bennington that all any of these philosophers are doing is putting the finite in a causal position *with respect to the invention and use of the word "transcendence,"* not putting it in a transcendental position with respect to *transcendence.* They cannot be doing the latter, they would protest, because there is no such thing as transcendence.

But Bennington would reply, I suspect, that this protest ignores what he calls

> a law that any attempt to explain transcendental effects by invoking history must presuppose the historicity of that same history as the very transcendental which this system of explanation will never be able to comprehend. This is what we earlier called transcendental contraband, and it cannot resolve the paradox (*plus de . . .*) according to which it is the very concept to which appeal is made to explain everything that will never be understood in the explanation. This is basically the stumbling block of any empiricism whatsoever. No doubt the worst naïvetés in this respect affect sociological "explanations" of philosophy. From this point of view, discourses like those of Foucault and Habermas – which recognize that one cannot do without transcendental analysis but which still want to limit that analysis by invoking a certain historical periodization of the transcendental itself – no doubt avoid the worst contradictions, but deprive themselves at the same stroke of the means to understand the historicity of those periods, and appeal rather feebly to diverse motors of history as a way out. (281–2)

The opening chapters of Dewey's *The Quest for Certainty* are a good example of the sort of "sociological 'explanations' of philosophy" which take for granted that one can "do without transcendental analysis." So Bennington would presumably regard that book both as naive and as afflicted with "the worst contradictions." But one can contradict oneself only if one says things that cannot be rendered consistent. Dewey does not, as far as I can see, contradict himself. He just tells his historicosociological tale and then suggests that we might now be in a position to escape from the philosophical tradition, to put a rather gray and sad episode behind us. But Bennington would rejoin, I take it, that Dewey contradicts his own tacit, and perhaps unconscious, *presuppositions* – specifically, presuppositions about the historicity of the history he describes.[10]

How can one tell whether this charge is accurate? More generally, how can one tell what a philosopher is presupposing, especially if he denies that he is presupposing what his critic says he is? Bennington's answer can be inferred from his claim that

> any attempt to unseat philosophy from a classically defined region can only replace in the final instance something which will play the part of philosophy without having the means to do so. Thinking one can do without philosophy, one will in fact be doing bad philosophy: this entirely classical philosophical argument . . . cannot be refuted without the deconstruction of the general structure, and such a deconstruction is therefore no longer philosophy, without for all that falling into the empiricism that philosophy can always see in it. (283)

If that claim is true, then Dewey, Wittgenstein, and anybody else who tries to explain why this might be a good time to walk away from philosophy – to crawl out of the gray, sad fly bottle – will be inventing something that "will play the part of philosophy." They will be doing "bad," because unconsciously self-contradictory, philosophy – philosophy that is blind to its contradiction of its own presuppositions. This kind of philosophy will not grasp "the impossibility in principle of cutting oneself cleanly from the metaphysical *logos*" (309).

The "entirely classical philosophical argument" that any criticism of philosophy is just bad philosophy ("Philosophy always buries its undertakers," "You can't end philosophy prolonging philosophy," etc.) has always struck me as pretty weak.[11] Its only empirical basis seems to be the fact that librarians automatically put criticisms of philosophy on the philosophy shelf. So they do, but then they automatically put criticisms of Hitler on the Hitler shelf and criticisms of astrology on the astrology shelf, without thereby suggesting that critics of Hitler (or astrology) are confused or inadequate or bad Hitlerians (or astrologers) who have failed to grasp their own presuppositions.

---

10 I am not sure what these presuppositions are. *What,* exactly, do you presuppose when you presuppose the historicity of a history? That people talk as they do because of the historical situation in which they are brought up? That seems a platitude rather than a tacit presupposition.

11 Marx was surely right to be exasperated by people saying to atheists, "Well, then, atheism is your religion."

The analogy between philosophy and Hitler would fail, of course, if philosophy, unlike Hitler but like pitch, were the sort of thing you can't touch without its sticking to you. But is it? Why shouldn't the word "philosophy," rather than naming an exceptionally adhesive substance, just pick out a sequence of texts? Why should it matter whether we extend the term to cover present and future texts criticizing previous members of the sequence, or instead confine the extension of the term to the past? Why should the choice between these alternatives have any particular importance or interest? How, without turning back into phallogocentists, can we know as much about the inescapability of philosophy – and about the presuppositions that people have whether they admit to them or not – as Bennington claims to know? Isn't the condition of possibility of knowing that sort of thing precisely the metaphysics of presence and essence that deconstruction was supposed to help us wiggle free from? Couldn't the different species of antimetaphysician – deconstructionists, Deweyans, and Davidsonians – at least agree on the need to be nominalists? Might not such nominalism rescue us from the "classical" idea that abstract entities have a sort of supernatural ability to adhere to people who try to toss them away? Shouldn't we stop rummaging through texts in a hunt for "transcendental contraband"? Granted that you cannot cut yourself off *cleanly* (*se couper nettement*) from the metaphysical *logos*, surely you could do it raggedly, piecemeal, a little bit at a time, just as the child (or, belatedly, the analysand) cuts herself off raggedly, by fits and starts, from her parents. Cannot we gradually change the subject, until the metaphysical *logos* begins to look like a pathetic, lonely, sad, gray, distant relative?

Toward the end of the last passage I quoted, we find Bennington suggesting that Derrida has taught us to succeed where so many distinguished predecessors have failed: he has taught us to "deconstruct the general structure" and, best of all, how to do it without doing philosophy. He has, apparently, exceeded philosophy, just the trick we were beginning to think nobody could perform. But where did all of Derrida's predecessors go wrong? Were they wrong in thinking they had done their bit toward getting rid of "the general structure" by explaining the sociological origins of the theory–practice distinction (Dewey), or viewing Platonism as a power play (Heidegger), or explaining the need to replace a subject-centered notion of reason as faculty with a social notion of reason as the activity of communication (Habermas), or recognizing that candidates for truth-value are nominated by people who hold power (Foucault, Hacking, Latour),[12] or set-

---

12 I group these three men together because I think that Hacking's notion of "truth-value candidates" offers the best way of epitomizing the results of Foucault's discussions of truth and

ting aside the scheme–content distinction (Davidson), or realizing that presuppositional relationships are, at most, habits of expectations on the part of participants in a social practice (Wittgenstein)? How does Bennington tell a genuine deconstruction of "the general structure" from an abortive, self-contradictory attempt to circumvent that structure – an attempt that is blind to its own presuppositions? These flurries of rhetorical questions indicate that I have reached the end of my tether. I do not know how to use the notion of "quasi-transcendentality," except as a name for the advantage that Bennington claims for Derrida over all the other philosophers whom I have just listed. But I am not clear what that advantage is supposed to be, or that it exists.

Maybe, instead of thinking of Derrida as Bennington does – as somehow transcending the competition, seeing farther than they have seen, avoiding their mistakes – we should see him as a collaborator, rather than as a competitor, with the various philosophers I have just mentioned. Consider the analogy of what the English Romantic poets did to a cluster of assumptions about literature, and its relation to life, which were common in the eighteenth century. We do not view Wordsworth as in competition with Shelley, or Blake in competition with Byron, in a race to discover the *right* way of undermining these assumptions, the right way for the nineteenth century to "exceed" the eighteenth, the only consistent way, the way that no longer shares any presuppositions with what is being exceeded. Instead, we look back on these poets as having done disparate things for various idiosyncratic reasons rather than with an eye to effecting a sweeping cultural change. These poets seem like participants in a movement only when we look back and notice that such a change occurred and that they deserve much of the credit.

I suspect that all the twentieth-century philosophers I have mentioned – Dewey, Heidegger, Habermas, Foucault, Hacking, Latour, Davidson, Wittgenstein, and Derrida – will look like unconscious participants in a single movement to the intellectual historians of the end of the twenty-first century. With the exception of Davidson, perhaps, none of them would mind describing themselves as Bennington describes Derrida – as doing something that "is no longer philosophy," any more than it is "rifling through the dustbins of philosophy to get out of them the meager nourishment that the tradition has not managed to swallow" (285). What Bennington says of deconstruction is true for all of them: what each is doing "only ever takes place, for reasons of

power, and because I think that Latour (in *We Have Never Been Modern*) works out the (Deweyan, to North American eyes) consequences of Foucault's and Hacking's work.

principle, through a more or less relaxed attachment to what has traditionally been called philosophy, which it never simply repudiates" (262). Getting out from under one's parents or one's predecessors – setting aside the
assumptions of the preceding century or the preceding few millennia – is
never a matter of simple repudiation, any more than it is a clean cutoff.

From the syncretic, ecumenical perspective I have just suggested, there is
no more need to isolate a method of "quasi-transcendental philosophy" or
"deconstruction" practiced by Derrida than to isolate a method called "critical theory" exemplified by Habermas, one called "ordinary-language philosophy" utilized by Wittgenstein, or one called "genealogy" practiced by
Foucault. There is no need to worry about how to locate a middle ground
called "quasi-transcendentality," intermediate between taking the transcendental–empirical distinction with full Kantian seriousness and simply forgetting it. More specifically, there is no need to be more precise about the
nature and procedure of deconstruction than to say, "You know – the sort
of thing Derrida does."

Bennington describes this sort of thing nicely when he says that "every
system excludes or expels something which does not let itself be thought
within the terms of the system" and that "the reading work carried out by
Derrida consists in the location of these excluded terms or these remains
that command the excluding discourse: the supplement (masturbation or
writing) in Rousseau; the index in Husserl; the parergon or vomit in Kant,
etc." (283–4). But might it not be enough to say that by seeking out such
excluded terms Derrida has succeeded in placing Rousseau, Kant, and the
others in marvelously illuminating new contexts, contexts that bring out unexpected resemblances among these figures? Is it necessary to claim that this
success is due to the rigorous application of a method called "deconstruction" that "exceeds philosophy"?

Bennington would insist, I take it, that this would not be enough. He
wants to say that Derrida's success is due to just such rigorous work – the
same sort of rigorous work that detects presuppositional relationships which
remain invisible to inquirers who are less methodical and less rigorous. Bennington is big on rigor, and in this respect he resembles Culler, Norris, and
other commentators who deplore descriptions of Derrida's work as free
imaginative play. But Bennington's use of "rigor" calls up an image of the
careful and exacting quasi-transcendental logician teasing out preexistent
relations among concepts – as if concepts were like bits of DNA molecules.
That image is hard to reconcile with the holism and contexualism that are
common to Derrida, Davidson, and Wittgenstein. The notion of rigor also
seems to entail that there is something to be gotten right – that the quasi-

transcendental logician would have made a big mistake if he had identified the excluded something in Rousseau as anything *other* than "supplement (masturbation or writing)," just as Kant would have made a mistake if he had given us a list of two, or twenty, Categories of the Pure Understanding rather than twelve, or if Hegel had said that the synthesis of Being and Nothingness was anything *other* than Becoming (if, for example, he had identified it as Time or Ambivalence or Sex or Fudge Ripple).

It is hard to know what would count as showing that Derrida had *mis*identified the excluded elements in some of the texts he discusses, just as hard as to know what would show that Kant got the Table of Categories wrong. This is because it is hard to separate the notion of rigor from that of a consensus of inquirers, of participants in an ongoing social practice (like the Human Genome Project or attempts by counterexample-mongering analytic philosophers to give necessary and sufficient conditions for the correct application of certain terms). Rigor, it seems to me, is something you can have only after entering into an agreement with some other people to subordinate your imagination to their consensus. At any rate, this is the notion of rigor you will have if, as a good nominalist, you take objectivity to be another name for intersubjectivity.[13] It is hard to be rigorous all by yourself, and equally hard to praise the same accomplishment both for originality and for rigor. When somebody does something for the first time, she may do it brilliantly, but she cannot do it rigorously.[14]

I doubt that there is a middle ground between this nominalist, pragmatist notion of rigor and the (quasi- or fully) transcendental logician's picture of concepts, and presuppositional relations between concepts, waiting to be gotten right. But this latter notion – the notion of the path-breaking

---

13 I think I see what Bennington means when he says that "the readings carried out by Derrida never give the impression of being arbitrary" (98), but I do not regard this as evidence of rigor or accuracy. The reason they never (to fans like Bennington and myself) give that impression the first time around is the same reason the sequence of events in *The Critique of Pure Reason* or *Murder on the Orient Express* does not seem arbitrary the first time around: the authors of these books had, as Derrida has, sufficiently powerful imaginations to sweep most first-time readers up into willing suspension of skeptical questioning.

An impression of arbitrariness becomes possible only when you become detached enough to ask, "But couldn't it have gone like that, instead?" You *can* always ask that, about *any* sequence, but only once the initial spell has been broken or if the spell never took effect in the first place. There are many non-fans who, grimly unwilling to let Derrida's spell bind them, get a strong impression of arbitrariness as soon as they open one of his books.

14 This seems to me one of the morals of Kuhn's work and one of the reasons his work has aroused so much antagonism. Kuhn's suggestion that scientific, like political, revolutions are often led by geniuses who are not so much utilizing a method as enlarging on an ingenious metaphor is repellent to our image of the natural scientist as the paradigmatic man of reason.

philosophical hero seeing what nobody else has seen, questioning presuppositions never questioned before – seems to epitomize the metaphysics of presence from which Derrida, like my favorite nominalists, wants to move away. So I am back with the questions I posed earlier. I am not sure that Derrida can get away from this metaphysics as long as he insists on treating concepts as quasi-agents and quasi-subjects or that he can combine criticism of metaphysics with criticism of competing antimetaphysicians.

The long passages I have quoted from Bennington come mostly from the section titled "The Series: (Quasi-) Transcendental Questions," which occupies the tops of pages 267–84. Together with the tops of the ensuing thirty-two pages, this section makes up the most explicitly metaphilosophical portion and the climactic conclusion of "Derridabase." Presumably somewhere in these final pages are Bennington's answers to the rhetorical questions I have been posing. I found these pages full of good things, but very difficult to relate to one another. They encompass sections titled "The Closure," "The Jew," "Striction," "Being and the Other," "The Machine," and, finally, "Envoi."

From these, I pick out "The Jew," because I can use some of the things Bennington says there to approach the problems I have raised from a different angle. This choice lets me hook up with "Circumfession," down at the bottom of the pages. For in that text Derrida says a lot about being Jewish, more than he has ever said before. More specifically, he says a lot about one of the most brutally undialectizable parts of being Jewish: getting circumcised.[15]

Hegel, as Derrida and Bennington note, thought of Kant as too Jewish: not Greek enough, because not dialectical enough. This was primarily because Kant could not, and did not want to, synthesize knowledge and moral faith, but had to demote the former to make room for the latter. Because he could not bring Newton and Rousseau together into a higher unity, he had to be skeptical about natural science and dogmatic about morality. So when Bennington says that "the point in deconstruction is . . . by rendering explicit the quasi-transcendental conditions even of speculative philosophy, to introduce a radical nondialectizable alterity into the heart of the same"

---

15 As one moves from "Derridabase" to "Circumfession," one is reminded that it is possible to read a lot of Derrida with relish and profit without knowing or caring what deconstruction is, just as one can read a lot of Sartre or Heidegger without worrying about what existentialism or phenomenological ontology might be. All three men are larger than the movements, schools of thought, and slogans associated with them. This is not always the case. One cannot read much Husserl without caring what phenomenology is or much Dummett without caring what analytic philosophy is.

(291), I am tempted, recalling hints to this effect in earlier Derrida (e.g., the quotation of Joyce's "Jewgreek is greekjew" at the end of "Violence and Metaphysics," an essay on Levinas), to say, "Right, that insistence on nondialectizable alterity is what is specifically *Jewish* about Derrida's way of doing things." I am tempted to add that it is just his refusal to play Greek games that makes it pointless to think of Derrida as even a *quasi*-transcendental philosopher, since outdialecticizing your opponent by spotting his unnoticed presuppositions is as Greek as a philosophical strategy can get.

But Bennington warns against just such temptations. In "The Jew" he says that

> one might be tempted to take Kant's part against Hegel here, and assimilate what we have said of the law to this Jewish setup. . . . Derrida would be neither the Kant of the *Aufklaerung*, nor the Hegel who absorbs everything into philosophy, but in some sense Hegel's Kant, the Jew, condemned to the interminable elaboration of a law always in retreat, mysterious, jealous of its truth that one will never know, but whose traces one will follow, traces that will never give rise to a present perception or to an experience. (296)

By succumbing to this temptation, one could assimilate Derrida to Kierkegaard – an honorary Jew who thought that being fully human meant avoiding quasi-Socratic attempts to dialecticize one's way into identity with the Divine. One could then try to answer the question "What is the appropriately relaxed relation to philosophy?" by saying: Keep in touch with it just enough to remind yourself that it would be both inhuman to ignore it and fatal to take it too seriously. Remember that, from a pragmatic point of view, it does not always pay to be a pragmatist.[16] Imitate Kierkegaard, who praised Kant for the honesty of his resistance to dialectic, yet knew that it would never have occurred to him that he was only a poor existing individual unless Hegel had hinted that he might, in a dialectical way, be God.[17]

Why will Bennington not let us succumb to this temptation? It would be

---

16 Dewey quoted G. K. Chesterton's remark: "Pragmatism is a matter of human needs, and one of the first of human needs is to be something more than a pragmatist."

17 Derrida gets a kick out of turning luminous spiritual presences into poor existing individuals. He did this with Plato and Socrates, and with Freud and Heidegger, in *The Post Card*. At one point in "Circumfession," after describing himself as "a sort of *marrane* [converted Jew] of French Catholic culture" and as having "my Christian body, inherited from SA [Saint Augustine] in a more or less twisted line, *condeibar eius sale* [seasoned with his salt]" (170), he says that "I have the vision of SA, too, as a little homosexual Jew (from Algiers or New York, he has repressed everything, basically converts himself quite early on into a Christian Don Juan for fear of Aids, which he could see coming like me . . .)" (172).

nice (I found myself complaining) if he could rest content with a description that seems to catch something very important about Derrida: that he is

> in the position of Moses, proposing an unintelligible liberation in so abstract and forced a rhetoric, a writing so artificial and full of ruses that one would say that it was a foreign language. This writing would be like the Jewish tabernacle, a construction of bands, empty inside, signifier without signified, containing nothing at the center. (297)

But Bennington plows remorsely on, past Athens and Jerusalem, following the coastline into uncharted territory ("Africa, in its predialectical status, figures an undecidability . . . " [298]). He insists that it would be a "simplification" (294, 303) to settle for Derrida as Moses, because then we would miss

> the unavoidable necessity of speaking alterity in the philosophical language of the Greek *logos:* if Jewish thought is other than Greek thought, it cannot be absolutely external to it, but folded, along the nonenveloping figure of invagination, into this nonidentical same which has been one of our most constant themes. (303–4)

Bennington is (I grudgingly had to concede) right about this. Between Moses and Moses, after all, there were Plato and Aristotle. Who knows what it would be to be a Jew nowadays if there had been no Maimonides? Come to think of it, who knows how Hegel would be read, what language games we philhellenes would be playing nowadays, had there been no Jews (no Heine, no Freud, no Kafka)?

Still, one might ask whether the only way not to be a Greek is to be a Jew, and whether the only way out of the metaphysics of presence is to become, as Derrida puts it, jewgreek and greekjew. Maybe these two comic figures, the glib Greek with his all-enveloping dialectic[18] and the sardonic Jew with his reliably undialecticizable alterity, are just barely managing to keep each other going. Maybe they have become partners in an old, tired vaudeville act. Maybe the only way to move still further away from "the philosophical language of the Greek *logos*" is to turn one's back on Levinas and his ubiquitous Other at the same time one turns one's back on Heidegger and his attempt to remember what the Greeks thought about Being.

The problem with walking out on this vaudeville act, however, is that for some people – and in particular for Derrida – to turn one's back on all that would be to turn one's back on oneself. Here is one of the points at which,

---

18 "Graeculus esuriens, in coelum jusseris ibit" (Juvenal; translated by Dr. Johnson as "All sciences a fasting Monsieur knows / And bid him go to hell, to hell he goes").

for Derrida, philosophy and autobiography run together. In "Circumfes-sion" Derrida tells us that

> I pretended to learn Hebrew so as to read it without understanding it, like the
> words of my mother today, at one moment, in 1943, with a Rabbi from the rue
> d'Isly, just before the *bar-mitzvah*, which they also called the "communion," at
> the moment when French Algeria in its Governor-General, without the inter-
> vention of any Nazi, had expelled me from school and withdrawn my French
> citizenship, the undertaking of Decremieux [a government decree that gave
> naturalized citizenship to descendants of Jews who had lived in Algeria before
> 1830 – see page 325] thus being annulled, a decree less old than my grand-
> fathers, it is true, Abraham and Moses, so that thus expelled, I became the out-
> side [si bien qu'ainsi mis dehors, je suis devenu le dehors, moi], try as they
> might to come close to me they'll never touch me again, they masculine or
> feminine, and I did my "communion" by fleeing the prison of all languages,
> the sacred one they tried to lock me up in without opening me to it, the sec-
> ular they made clear would never be mine, but this ignorance remained the
> chance of my faith as of my hope, of my taste even for the "word," the taste for
> letters, *nam si primo sanctis tuis litteris informatus essem et in earum familiaritate
> obdulcisses mihi et post in illa volumina incidissem, fortasse aut abripuissent me a sol-
> idamento pietatis, aut si . . .* [For, if I had been first informed by Thy holy writ-
> ings and if Thou hadst grown dear to me through my familiarity with them,
> and if I had later fallen upon those other books, perhaps they would have torn
> me away from a firm foundation of piety; or, if . . . (Augustine, *Confessions* VII.
> xx. 26)]. (288–90)

If you get tossed out of a school system that is designed to lead up to the phi-losophy course, and thus to the metaphysical *logos,* because you are a Jew – and if this happens in a year when being found to be circumcised meant, in most of Europe, being sent to one's death – you may be less capable than most of forgetting about the Jew–non-Jew distinction. If you nevertheless go on to become a philosopher, you may be less capable than most philoso-phers of turning your back on the Jew–Greek distinction. There is no easy way to untangle oneself from the books upon which one has fallen and from the things that people (quasi-assimilating parents, eager beaver governors-general) have done to one. Nobody gets to be *pure* outside. You have to be outside some particular regions.

Looking at the matter in terms of the autobiographies of philosophers rather than in terms of the nature of philosophy, we can give a different sort of answer to the question of why end-of-philosophy books often look like just more philosophy books. Maybe the point is that some of us (not everybody) cannot circumvent the metaphysical *logos* without mutilating ourselves, with-out curtailing our knowledge of what made us what we are (including the mutilations that made us what we are), and thus our knowledge of what we are. If so, the point is not that there is an exceptionally adhesive substance called "philosophy" (one whose properties are understood by Derrida but not by his nominalistic competitors in the antimetaphysics business), but rather that Derrida and Bennington are, following Heidegger, using "philosophy" as a name for the sequence of "words of Being" – the words that, had they not been uttered, would have resulted in our being different people.[19] Some people may not be able to walk away from the metaphysical *logos* or from the Greek–Jew contrast without losing their sense of where they are. That was why Heidegger insisted that *denken ist andenken,* and it may be why Derrida and Bennington view nominalistic pragmatists like me as light-minded escapists.

If we adopted this way of looking at the matter, we could drop Bennington's notion of "transcendental contraband," as well as his claim that every attempt to set aside transcendental inquiry into conditions of possibility presupposes a view about what those conditions are. Instead, we could say that the reason some people cannot just walk away from philosophy is the same reason some people cannot just walk away from their parents – or, more generally, from their past. This reason is, so to speak, Freudian and empirical rather than Kantian and transcendental. If you were raised on philosophy – raised on the distinctions between soul and body, essence and accident, real and apparent, empirical and transcendental – you may not be able to just walk away from your upbringing without losing touch with yourself. Not every human being has been raised this way (perhaps they order these things better in China), and there is no reason to think that all future human beings will be, but *you* were. *Your* behavior cannot be explained without reference to various unconscious beliefs that your upbringing produced, various pictures that will always, in some measure, hold you captive.

Looking at the matter this way would resolve some of the problems I have raised. For now we no longer have to ask how we can invoke the notion of presuppositional relations among reified, particulate concepts without becoming metaphysicians, or how such relations can exist if there is no invisible and ahistorical scheme that limits the range of variation of empirical and historical content (the sort of scheme that is the traditional topic of

19 This interpretation of Heidegger's notion of "words of Being" and the question about why these words should be found only on philosophy shelves are both spelled out in my "Heidegger, Contingency and Pragmatism," in *Essays on Heidegger and Others* (Cambridge University Press, 1991), 27–49. On the possibility of circumventing the philosophical tradition rather than working through it, see, in the same volume, "Deconstruction and Circumvention: An Essay on Derrida" (85–106). The latter essay, now more than fifteen years old, was my first attempt at figuring out Derrida's relation to previous philosophers.

metaphysics). By substituting "unconscious assumption" for "presupposition" we move from the transcendental to the empirical, from the metaphysically inevitable to the culturally or idiosyncratically contingent.[20] Instead of saying that Derrida is conducting rigorous quasi-transcendental inquiries into presuppositional relations among concepts, we can say that he is sketching psychobiographies of the authors of the books among which he fell (Plato, Augustine, Rousseau, Hegel, Heidegger, et al.) in aid of the overall project of writing his own autobiography, the autobiography of somebody who is "fleeing the prison of all languages," of somebody whose writing is not easily distinguished from his life, from the process of becoming who he is.

This suggestion will be plausible, however, only if we do not try either to reduce psychobiography to philosophy or to reduce philosophy to psychobiography, but rather keep them compresent in the way in which the tops and the bottoms (that is to say, Bennington's part and Derrida's part) of *Jacques Derrida* are compresent. Bennington suggests that in order to be appropriately jewgreek and greekjew you have to rejoice in impurity: "What deconstruction affirms, what it says 'yes, yes' to, is not pure game or expenditure, but the necessity of contamination" (310).[21] You have to see the Apollonian Greek as needing the blood and semen that bespatter his

20 One could, of course, resurrect the transcendental by conflating Kant and Freud. Then one would claim, first, that every human being has the same unconscious assumptions, because history and culture are not powerful enough to change the psychosexual dynamics of the parent–child relationship, and, second, that these psychosexual dynamics are best described in philosophical terminology. I take Lacan to have put forward both claims, but my grasp of Lacan is not firm enough for me to be sure. Whether or not this was Lacan's view, it seems thoroughly implausible – not so much because we know that psychosexual dynamics are a function of culture as because the terminology of philosophy seems an entirely optional way of describing these dynamics. Even if everything somehow goes back to sex and parents, that seems no reason to think the metaphysics of presence ineluctable. Even if everybody will always be stuck with some unobtainable, sublime object of desire, that object does not have to consist in a grasp of transcendental conditions of possibility.

21 Earlier Bennington noted that "in Derrida what makes possible immediately makes impossible the purity of the phenomenon made possible" (276–77). I should prefer not to speak of possibility and impossibility, and just to say that nobody has ever managed to disentangle her philosophy from her autobiography except by accepting professionalization – by subordinating her imagination to a consensus of her chosen peers, throwing herself into *Philosophie als strenge Wissenschaft*, as in the old days she would have immured herself in a nunnery. One reason why professionalized philosophers dislike Derrida so much (and why professional Derridean deconstructors, praising one another for the rigor with which yet another excluded element has been exposed as the presupposition of yet another text, are so hilarious) is that some people would rather be pure than get a life. See "Keeping Philosophy Pure: An Essay on Wittgenstein," in my *Consequences of Pragmatism* (Minneapolis: University of Minnesota Press, 1982), 19–36.

Dionysian alter ego, the patriarchal Talmudist as needing the impure menstrual effusions of his mother, *and vice versa.* You have to go back and forth between Freud's topics and Heidegger's (as Derrida constantly does). You must constantly contaminate sex and psychoanalysis with philosophy, and philosophy with a lot of personal details and fantasies about, for example, your parents and your genitals. The need for contamination of the transcendental by the empirical, of the philosophical by the idiosyncratic, offers a natural and easy transition from the concluding sections of "Derridabase" (Bennington's part of the book) to "Circumfession" (Derrida's part). For the latter is full of images like "the loved woman herself circumcising (me), as the mother did in the biblical narrative, slowly provoking ejaculation in her mouth just as she swallows the crown of bleeding skin with the sperm as a sign of exultant alliance" (218).[22]

"Circumfession" is described on the title page as "Fifty-nine periods and periphrases written in a sort of internal margin, between Geoffrey Bennington's book and work in preparation (January 1989–April 1990)." These fifty-nine run-on sentences follow, to some extent, the course of Derrida's mother's terminal illness, which ended (the "curriculum vitae" in "Acts" tells us) in her death in December 1991. References to this illness are intertwined with long quotations from St. Augustine's *Confessions* (especially passages having to do with the death of St. Augustine's own mother, St. Monica) as well as with reflections on Derrida's circumcision, on his Jewishness, on French anti-Semitism, and on the need to write something that will surprise

---

22 Before turning the reader over to Derrida, Bennington ends "Derridabase" with a few pages on computers and hypertexts. Presumably this is because there is something hypertextual about the relations among the various parts of this book and because part of the difference between "the book" (in Derrida's special, pejorative sense of that term) and the hypertext is the difference between the apparently pure and self-contained and the obviously and self-confessedly contaminated.

Jacques Derrida is even more hypertextual than it first seems. After "Derridabase" and "Circumfession," the reader comes upon a third, subdivided part called "Acts (the Law of Genre)." This includes a very useful bibliography, many intriguing photographs (Derrida as a little boy with his family and as a young soccer player, shots of the school from which Derrida was expelled for being Jewish and of the prison in which the Communist government of pre-1989 Czechoslovakia held him), and a "curriculum vitae" that includes some very illuminating autobiographical remarks made by Derrida in conversation or correspondence with Bennington (for example, "1948–49: The movement toward philosophy takes place. 'Awed' [*impressionée*] reading of Kierkegaard and Heidegger.") Taken as a whole, the book is the closest thing to an autobiography we are likely to get from Derrida. It leaves a lot out – there are no pictures of his wife and children, for example, and no information about them except his wife's maiden name and the fact that there are two uncircumcised sons. But, as the passage I just quoted suggests, "Circumfession" includes much that most autobiographies leave out.

and startle Bennington. As "Circumfession" goes along, Augustine and Derrida – two boys from North Africa who made it big in Europe, two writers whose styles have much in common,[23] two men who suffered through their mothers' last illnesses – begin to blend into one another.

One's dying mother's bedsores and the mutilation of one's own genitals are as idiosyncratic as topics can get, so the shift from quasi-transcendental conditions of the realm of possibility in "Derridabase" to datable and locatable actuality in "Circumfession" is as startling as a textual transition can get. Derrida keeps the tension as high as possible – for example, by saying that his mother's groaned exclamation "I want to kill myself" is "me [Derrida] all over" and by wondering if "those who read me from up there [from above the line that traverses the page, from 'Derridabase']" see his tears (38). The effect of "Circumfession" is to rub one's nose in the fact that all the quasi-transcendental, rigorous philosophizing that Bennington describes is being done by a poor existing individual, somebody who thinks about certain things in certain ways because of certain weird, private contingencies.

Ever since Freud, biographers of great thinkers have gotten their effects, and their kicks, by revealing that Oz, the Great and Powerful, is just a nerd with a gimmick. But these biographers' inability to synthesize the nerd with the world-transforming mind, the idiosyncratic hang-ups of the author with the mind-bending words of power he inscribed, the Freud who wrote to Fliess with the Freud who changed our self-understanding, parallels our inability to reconcile the transcendental and the empirical. If there really is a world in which concepts live and move and have their being independent of the linguistic behavior of users of words – the world that is the transcendental condition of the possibility of transcendental philosophy – how can it also be an empirical fact that a concept is just the use of a word by us poor existing individuals? If the world in which that is what a concept is, is real, how could that other world also be real? If the great imaginations assumed the shapes they did because the organisms that contain them were jerked around in certain particular ways by mothers and mohels, how can the life of the mind be worth living? If Freud's account of us as malleable protoplasm beaten into shape by mothers and other contingencies is *itself* a marvelous, world-shaping, life-enhancing intellectual achievement, how could

---

23 Both delight in repetition and reinflection, as in Augustine's "Nondum amabam, et amare amabam, quaerebam quid amabam, amans amare" (Not while I loved, and I loved to love, did I ask what I loved, loving to love). Derrida tells us that Augustine (here abbreviated "SA," which in *Glas* meant "Savoir absolu" and which has meant many other things in other texts) was one of the people he read a lot of when he was young.

it have been achieved by mere protoplasm? If transcendental philosophy was just a gimmick Kant whomped up to reconcile Newton and Rousseau, and if quasi-transcendental deconstruction is just a gimmick Derrida whomped up to reconcile Heidegger and Freud, where does that leave us? We are, as Sartre pointed out, too great for ourselves.[24]

My best guess as to how to get "Derridabase," "Circumfession," and "Acts (the Law of Genre)"[25] together is to treat the psychoanalytic contrasts between the organic and the sublimated form of the organic (e.g., the Monica–God, or sex–text, contrast) as an allegory of the philosophical contrast between the empirical and the transcendental, then to treat the latter as an allegory of the former, and then to refrain from asking which was *really* the allegory and which the allegorized. If we do that, we can read *Jacques Derrida* as the autobiography of a man constantly and deliberately teetering between the accounts of himself that his psychoanalytic biographers will hasten to give as soon as he is dead and his own accounts of the world as he found it.

On this account, "Derridabase"'s contribution to *Jacques Derrida* is the philosophy as it took shape in the mind of Bennington, one of Derrida's best readers: the philosophy as the adventures of a quasi-person, neither circumcised nor uncircumcised, named "Deconstruction." The life of this quasi-person is what Bradley called "an unearthly ballet of bloodless categories." "Circumfession" contributes some specific reminders of the blood-stained empirical conditions of actuality of this particular quasi-person, conditions that include a real person getting circumcised, getting tossed out of school, getting tossed in jail, hoping that his mother will die before the bedsores get much worse, and so on. "Acts (the Law of Genre)" provides a generic reminder that these two are somehow one. So *Jacques Derrida* as a whole reminds one that the bloodless quasi-person is no less, and no more, Derrida than the mother's son whose infantile penis dripped blood. Deconstruction and that particular circumcised male successfully contaminate each other.

As a longtime puzzled admirer of Derrida, I am grateful to this book, and the difficulties of reviewing it, for helping me overcome my previous inclination to just forget about this tiresome quasi-person called "Deconstruction" (whom I have sometimes thought of as a plastic dummy around whose

---

24 We are all too great for ourselves, but in different ways, which present us with different options. Philosophy is not a live option for many people, and they will get neither kicks nor profit out of the discovery of "excluded elements" and "transcendental contraband" in the texts of the tradition. But some of us will.

25 See note 22 above.

navel one can read the words "Made in USA") and to focus instead on Derrida, that extraordinarily imaginative, poetic, inventive, ingenious, funny, flesh-and-blood writer. This inclination made me wish, earlier in this essay, that Bennington had written *Derrida for Davidsonians* rather than what he actually wrote. But *Jacques Derrida* made me realize that I need to put a leash on my nominalism when I read Derrida – that I should not to be so quick to exclaim, "Oh, come off it! Stop treating concepts as agents!"

Such expostulations are, I have come to think in the course of writing this essay, a little too greek, a little too metaphysical. Bennington has convinced me that I cannot get away with my stance of tough-minded, hypostatization-bashing empiricism without falling a bit too much under the sway of the metaphysical *logos*, the one that tells you that it just isn't logical to treat one thing as if it were something else and that it just isn't rational not to try to figure out which is the allegory and which the allegorized. I still cannot help becoming impatient with the bloodless ballet that Bennington very skillfully choreographs, but I think I now understand better why he thinks it has to be done – why he thinks we can't just let deconstruction go hang if we still want to hang on to Derrida.

Being desirably jewgreek or greekjew now seems to me just the ability to balance the quasi-person, the hypostasized and personalized concept, with the empirical facts about people of flesh and blood. I find this balancing act difficult, but *Jacques Derrida* has convinced me that I had better start practicing. So I guess my answer to the question "Is Bennington right in describing Derrida as a quasi-transcendental philosopher?" has to be "No, if 'transcendental' means that he has rigorously and accurately traced the interconnections that link concepts together in a nonempirical world and that form conditions of possibility" but "Yes, if 'quasi-' means that he couldn't say what he needs to say, be what he needs to be, be as good a jew as he is a greek and vice versa, if he didn't talk as if there were such a world and as if he were tracing such interconnections and discovering such conditions."

You cannot, after all, deny someone his medium. There is no point in wishing that Wagner had written sonatas, or Emily Dickinson epics.[26] Derrida, a Jew born on the rue Saint-Augustin, is also the man who, having read Plato and Kant, could not forget them – could not just walk away from them.

---

26 Nor, as I suggested earlier, is there any point in suggesting that Dickinson somehow succeeded where Wagner failed, or that Habermas or Foucault failed where Derrida somehow succeeds. The increase in my tolerance for deconstruction as a result of reading *Jacques Derrida* does not extend to agreement with Bennington that deconstruction has triumphed where others were vanquished.

Maybe non-Jewish kids who go to school in places where nobody has heard much about Plato and Kant (California? Indonesia?) can forget about the metaphysics of presence, but *he* cannot. Maybe Dewey was right to hope that some day, with luck, there will be neither greekjew nor jewgreek. Maybe what Bennington calls "the impossibility in principle of cutting oneself cleanly from the metaphysical *logos*" is, as we nominalists like to think, at most a local, transitory, and empirical impossibility – one that prevails only over half the planet's surface and will last, even there, only another few centuries. But those words – Plato's and Kant's words – certainly helped make *some* of us (Derrida, Bennington, me, and, probably, any readers of this book who have gotten as far as this essay) what we are.

What can *we* do, then, but work with the medium that is *our* very substance? Even if the metaphysical *logoi*, those who invented them and those who deconstructed them, will all be of merely antiquarian interest a few thousand years down the road, the people who fell among them have to live in the present. Derrida has never lived so much in the present as he does at the bottoms of the pages of *Jacques Derrida*.

INDEX